BEST PRACTICE

New Standards
for Teaching and Learning
in America's Schools

SECOND EDITION

STEVEN ZEMELMAN

HARVEY DANIELS

ARTHUR HYDE

HEINEMANN • Portsmouth, NH

Heinemann
A division of Reed Elsevier, Inc.
361 Hanover Street
Portsmouth, NH 03801–3912
http://www.heinemann.com

Offices and agents throughout the world

The author and publisher wish to thank those who have generously given permission to reprint borrowed material:

Excerpt from *Standards for the English Language Arts,* by the International Reading Association and the National Council of Teachers of English, Copyright 1996 by the International Reading Association and the National Council of Teachers of English. Reprinted with permission.

Excerpts from *New Policy Guidelines for Reading: Connecting Research and Practice* by Jerome C. Harste. Copyright © 1989. Reprinted by permission of the National Council of Teachers of English.

Excerpts from *A Community of Writers: Teaching Writing in the Junior and Senior High School* by Steven Zemelman and Harvey Daniels. Copyright © 1988. Published by Heinemann, a division of Reed Elsevier, Inc., Portsmouth, NH. Reprinted by permission of the authors and publisher.

Library of Congress Cataloging-in-Publication Data
Zemelman, Steven.
   Best practice : new standards for teaching and learning in
America's schools / Steven Zemelman, Harvey Daniels, Arthur Hyde.—
2nd ed.
     p.   cm.
   Includes bibliographical references and index.
   ISBN 0-325-00091-3 (alk. paper)
   1. Teaching—United States—Case studies.   2. Direct instruction—
United States—Case studies.   3. Active learning—United States—
Case studies. 4. Teaching—Standards—United States.
5. Education—Curricula—Standards—United States. 6. Educational
change—United States. I. Daniels, Harvey, 1947–   . II. Hyde,
Arthur A. III. Title.
LB1025.3.Z46   1998
371.102—dc21   92–17027
                                                 CIP

Editor: William Varner
Production: Elizabeth Valway
Cover photo: Bob Tanner
Cover design: Jenny Jensen Greenleaf
Manufacturing: Louise Richardson

Printed in the United States of America on acid-free paper
02 01   EB   09 10

Contents

Preface

Origins of Best Practice

This book is not just about the schools and teachers in our own neighborhood, but it did begin there. It all started around eight years ago, amid the furious, exciting movement for school decentralization and reform here in Chicago. Because the three of us had been active for years in school change projects in the city, it was natural for us to pitch in. One problem in Chicago's reform process was immediately apparent: no one was paying enough attention to actual, day-to-day teaching and learning. Most of the early energy of reform was devoted to issues of governance, power, turf, logistics, authority, and money. Anyone familiar with Chicago politics knows that these topics always generate enthusiastic involvement around here. There was nonstop exhorting, declaiming, wrangling, and logrolling about the arrangements of education, but just as at the national level, hardly anyone was talking about what kids and teachers actually did together.

The three of us, as veteran teachers, staff development leaders, and curriculum specialists in several different fields, were worried about this direction. It seemed that reform might never get through the classroom door. So, as a way of helping to turn the dialogue from governance to curriculum, we decided to create a publication that would aggressively raise the issues of teaching and learning—the ultimate challenges of reform. We got a generous grant from the Joyce Foundation to create an instruction-centered newspaper that would be sent to all teachers, administrators, parent leaders, politicians, community groups, and foundation officers in the city—the whole constellation of people concerned with school renewal in Chicago.

Our inaugural issue was simple. All we did was draw together the current, national consensus recommendations about "best educational practice" in each of the traditional school curriculum areas: reading, writing, math, science, and social studies. We used mainstream sources only, nothing overly partisan or controversial, relying mainly on the key professional associations and research centers. We illustrated these recommendations with stories from Chicago teachers who were bringing them to life, practicing state-of-the-art instruction in their classrooms every day. We optimistically named our sixteen-page tabloid *Best Practice 1,* printed 55,000 copies, and dropped 570 carefully addressed bundles—one for each school building in the city—on the loading dock at the Board of Education.

Why did we adopt the term "Best Practice," first for our newspaper and now for this book? We borrowed the expression, of course, from the professions of medicine and law, where "good practice" and "best practice" are everyday phrases used to describe solid, reputable, state-of-the-art work in a field. If a practitioner is following best practice standards, he or she is aware of current research and consistently offers clients the full benefits of the latest knowledge, technology, and procedures. If a doctor, for example, does not follow contemporary standards and a case turns out badly, peers may criticize his or her decisions and treatments by saying something like, "that was simply not best practice."

In education, we generally haven't had such an everyday standard; on the contrary, some veteran teachers will even *deny* the significance of current research or new standards of instruction. "I just give 'em the basics," such teachers say. "It's worked just fine for thirty years, and I don't hold with any of this new mumbo-jumbo." One wonders how long such self-satisfied teachers would continue to go to a doctor who says, "I practice medicine exactly the same way today that I did thirty years ago. I haven't changed a thing. I don't hold with all that newfangled stuff."

Some people insist that education as a field does not enjoy the clear-cut evolution of medicine, law, or architecture. But still, if educators are people who take ideas seriously, who believe in inquiry, and who subscribe to the possibility of human progress, then our professional language must label and respect practice that is at the leading edge of the field. That's why we have imported (and capitalized) the term "Best Practice"—as a shorthand emblem of serious, thoughtful, informed, responsible, state-of-the-art teaching.

In assembling that first cross-curriculum newspaper, we discovered an unrecognized consensus—a surprisingly high level of agreement among seemingly disparate content fields—about how kids learn best. What is recommended across all subjects can only be called a neo-progressive transformation: virtually all the authoritative voices in each field are calling for schools that are student-centered, active, experiential, democratic, collaborative, and yet rigorous and challenging. As unashamed graduates of 1960s and 1970s school reforms, this renewed consensus sounded familiar and welcome to us. So this book is, in a sense, the full-length version of *Best Practice 1,* elaborated with stories from real schools in and beyond Chicago, and with more detailed treatment of the theoretical, historical, and political aspects of school reform in America. That means we have several goals:

> To concisely explain the current consensus on what constitutes Best Educational Practice in each of six key school curriculum areas, providing documentation from national standards projects, research summaries, and professional association reports. We also want to trace the often ancient historical roots of these "new" ideas.

> To move beyond the subject-bound view of these principles and show the deep underlying commonalities in all these sets of best practices. We also

will show how these connections and commonalities have their own surprisingly long history.

To offer concrete examples of key classroom activities and practices that embody the new paradigm, especially by describing specific learning events in real classrooms.

To suggest ways that teachers, administrators, and parents can work together to enact and extend the new curriculum.

We hope that this book will be a significant contribution to the growing literature on school renewal. We think it fills a gap for people who have read such disparate works as Jonathan Kozol's *Savage Inequalities,* Deborah Meier's *The Power of Their Ideas: Lessons for America from a Small School in Harlem,* Theodore Sizer's *Horace's School*, John Goodlad's *A Place Called School,* George Wood's *Schools That Work: America's Most Innovative Education Programs,* Ernest Boyer's *High School,* and *Rethinking Schools: An Agenda for Change* by David Levine, Robert Lowe, Bob Peterson, and Rita Tenorio. We hope this book will be both complementary and challenging to this emerging canon of school reform.

While we do believe that this book deals mostly in facts, it also has a strong, unabashed, and partisan vision: we believe (and we hope we are about to prove) that progressive educational principles can and should govern classroom practice in American schools. While others belittle the past cycles of progressive reform during the 1930s and 1960s as meaningless fads, this book shows how the current wave of reform connects and culminates those past eras, and offers hope of creating the strongest and most enduring school renewal in this century.

Best Practice and the Standards Movement of the 1990s

When the first edition of this book was published six years ago, the national curriculum standards movement was just peaking, with one eagerly awaited document after another being released to expectant audiences. The consensus around Best Practice instruction already was emerging in the reports completed by that time. Since then, additional standards reports have confirmed the mandate for the kinds of teaching and learning we have just described. However, the national standards movement itself now seems sidetracked. Attacked from the right as a conspiracy to federalize the school system and repudiated by the left as an attack on equity, the standards-setters are on the defensive. Meanwhile, the action has shifted to the state and local level, where many groups are using the new national documents as a baseline for creating their own homemade standards.

It all seemed like such a simple idea back in the late 1980s: why not develop clear-cut descriptions of what to teach and how to teach it in every major subject field? The notion was born in 1987, when educators from the National Council of Teachers of Mathematics (NCTM) outlined a challenging curriculum that stressed math as a way of thinking and required state-of-the-art teaching. The NCTM Standards were welcomed by teachers, school reformers, and politicians alike, and the idea quickly took root that every subject field should develop parallel documents. With funding from the U.S. Department of Education, a dozen other professional organizations were eventually commissioned to develop similar standards for their own fields.

Trickling in over the next several years, the results, while not quite contradictory, have been uneven and asymmetrical. Some standards reports specified the content to be mastered in minute detail; others kept to broad, general guidelines. Some gave careful attention to teaching methodology, others hid it in the background. A few reports frontally addressed issues of access and equity, while most simply assumed that all children would have equal opportunities under new standards. Almost all the commissioned groups used their standards projects to lobby for more money, personnel, and classroom time for their own subjects, at the expense of others. Former Department of Education official Chester Finn was not far wrong when he noted the standards-setters' "gluttonous and imperialistic tendencies."

Individual standards projects ran into their own difficulties. The reading-writing standards, under development by the National Council of Teachers of English (NCTE), the Center for the Study of Reading, and the International Reading Association (IRA), had their grant terminated after one year in a wrangle with federal funders over their draft's alleged lack of specificity and its fixation on "opportunity-to-learn" issues. The NCTE and IRA went on to spend more than a million dollars of their own funds to complete the project, and issued their still-unchallenged standards in 1996. The "shotgun" consortium of arts associations, instead of predictably stressing the humanistic and creative values of music, dance, drama, and visual art, produced a micro-content–based document that mandated, among many other things, that high schoolers memorize the names of ballet dancers from the nineteenth century. The social studies standards were politically polarized from the start: a first draft of the history standards was vilified in the press as being insufficiently patriotic and was promptly condemned by the U.S. Senate in a ninety-nine to one vote.

Meanwhile, state governments, business groups, independent school reform organizations, and many individual school districts were getting into the act. Some confined themselves to a single subject; others, like the New Standards Project, offered recommendations across several disciplines. By 1998, almost every state in the Union, along with many cities and districts, had commenced its own standards projects, most linked to high-stakes student testing and teacher accountability schemes. As the millennium approached, there were about fifteen major national standards projects, plus countless state and local iterations. All told, they totaled millions of pages of text, offered thousands of specific recommendations, and were enforced by scores of standardized tests. The one book that bravely attempted to summarize the main ones ran to six hundred pages (Kendall and Marzano 1996).

Why has there been such a standards boom? Clearly, some standards enthusiasts have just been along for the ride. For someone more interested in lip service than action, promoting educational standards can be a very economical approach to school reform. Except for providing hotel rooms for a few blue-ribbon commissioners and printing up the bubble forms for machine-scored tests, "standards-based reform" can be cost-free. After all, standards aren't necessarily action; they can be just talk—words intoned, words written down, words printed up, words with "A, B, C, or None of the Above" in front of them. Politicians, business leaders, even school district officials can come out bravely in favor of high educational standards without spending many taxpayer dollars or taking any political risk (after all, who could oppose Mom, apple pie, or world-class schools?). Hopping aboard the standards bandwagon allows you to sound tough and rigorous and concerned: you can wring your hands about what's the matter with kids today and you can fret conspicuously about America losing the war of global economic domination, all without actually doing anything.

If you want to *do* something to help schools and students achieve at higher levels, that's a whole other matter, involving at least two major commitments: spending money and doing things differently. As the *New York Times* put it in a 1996 editorial, ". . . simply setting new goals is not enough—improvements require substantial investments of time and money" "It Takes More," (22). Focusing on a group of ten schools that had significantly raised achievement, the *Times* noted: "The schools credited their revival to stronger arts, literature, and music programs that revived flagging student interest. They also spent significant amounts of money on textbooks, tutoring programs, and especially on forming relationships with arts, business, and community groups. Career development and retraining opportunities had a dramatic impact on teacher performance." In New York and elsewhere, achieving higher standards, by any realistic appraisal, requires paying for teacher-training, materials, equipment—and probably outside-of-school costs too, like improved child care and nutrition. But these solutions are so big, so broad, so costly that many people find it more comfortable to talk about "raising the bar." It costs far less to raise the bar than to help someone jump over it.

Of course, the push for standards has never been a single unified effort. All along, it has been a temporary and volatile alliance of the two different school reform movements afoot in the land, which we might label the accountability reformers and the curriculum reformers. Although both share some of the same rhetoric and draw their rationale from some of the same reports, the two forces have quite incompatible visions of teaching and learning, and now seem to be returning to their original camps after a decade of uneasy collaboration. On the one hand are the conservative, accountability reformers: many state legislatures and governors, education agencies, and business panels, as well as some urban school districts and even teacher unions. Their standards movement is preoccupied almost entirely with systems of high-stakes testing and accountability, linked to elaborate rewards and punishments for students, teachers, schools, and districts. Although wary that federal tests might undermine local authority, these standards-seekers claim they can raise student achievement by measuring it more frequently and by encircling everyone in the educational enterprise with more extensive rules and regulations. In its reliance on control and specification, this reform approach recapitulates the failed school efficiency movement of the 1920s and the similarly discredited "behavioral objectives" movement of the 1970s.

On the other hand are the curriculum reformers, composed mostly of subject-area experts, classroom teachers, discipline organizations, professional associations, and research centers. This book, while respectful of the need for organizational improvements, is clearly part of this latter movement for educational renewal through curriculum reform. This vision of school improvement relies not on new rules and controls, but rather on improving instruction. We believe that schools are clinging to inefficient, ineffective teaching practices that urgently need to be replaced. We reject the idea that doing the same things harder, longer, and stronger will materially improve education. We repudiate the assumption that achievement can be elevated by giving students more and more tests, no matter how "rigorous." As one of our agriculturally savvy friends recently commented: "You can weigh the pig as many times as you want; the scale won't fatten him up." We are deeply concerned with issues of equity and opportunity-to-learn, because these have tripped up almost all previous reform movements in America. Reform means nothing unless all students have genuine access to the kind of instruction that makes reaching high standards possible. We can't help commenting that the suburban town we happen to be sitting in today as we work on this book spends more than $15,000 per year on each of its high school students. Cross Howard Street into Chicago and the expenditure drops to $5,700. Like it or not, genuine school reform requires changes in accounting, not just accountability.

The fracture between the accountability reformers and the curriculum reformers has exploded in California, where even the once-sacred NCTM standards have come under attack. California's conservative governor and his appointed school board recently eviscerated the state's NCTM-based curriculum, asserting that even math word problems were too innovative and experimental. Ignoring the guidance of his own state experts, the governor mandated a return to computation-based, skill-and-drill mathematics curriculum, ordering teachers to de-emphasize higher-order reasoning and problem-solving activities. Mathematics curriculum experts around the country were stunned by this abandonment of rigorous standards. Luther Williams of the National Science Foundation (NSF), which had provided $50 million in math and science grants to California schools the previous year, was blunt: "The board action is, charitably, short-sighted and detrimental to the long-term mathematical literacy of children in California. . . . You must surely understand that the foundation cannot support individual school systems that embark upon a course that substitutes computational proficiency for a commitment to deep, balanced mathematical learning" (Lawton 1998, 6).

Undoubtedly, this debate, along with its acrimony and political chicanery, will continue long into the future. But the legacy of the standards movement is nevertheless substantial and valuable. As a nation, we stopped for a moment and asked each school subject field to define itself, to identify its key content, processes, and habits of mind. No matter how imperfect and controversial the results, this has been a rare episode of national reflection.

The standards projects have given us a sense—sometimes an overwhelming and quite diverse sense—of what each school subject entails. They have encouraged us to think of all students as capable and valuable. They have revealed an underlying consensus among subject fields that many of our traditional instructional practices are ineffective and must be revised. They have pointed to some specific, alternative methods that help students to learn more, achieve more, and develop the work habits that can help them succeed in the complex world they will inherit. Above all, the standards projects uplift teaching, bringing honor and respect back to one of the most important jobs in our society: caring for and developing our young people.

Works Cited

"It Takes More Than Standards" (Editorial). 1996. *New York Times* (6, December): 22.

Kendall, John S., and Robert Marzano. 1996. *Content Knowledge: A Compendium of Standards and Benchmarks for K–12 Education.* Aurora, CO: Mid-Continent Regional Educational Laboratory.

Lawton, Millicent. 1998. "California Education Officials Approve Back-to-Basics Standards in Math." *Education Week* (14, January): 6.

Acknowledgments

Like all writers, we have many people to thank—though some of them might wish we hadn't remembered. Above all, this book reflects the brave, intelligent, and loving practice of the elementary and secondary educators we work with, many of whom appear personally in these pages. In the "Exemplary Program" section that follows each curriculum chapter, these teacher-authors invite all of us into the classrooms where they are bringing alive the principles of Best Practice.

During the last twenty years, we've had the privilege of gathering a family of brilliant, committed teacher-consultants who work with schools and teachers in our staff development projects. This team includes nine full-time facilitators: Barbara Morris, Pat Bearden, Pete Leki, Toni Murff, Marianne Flanagan, Lynnette Emmons, Yolanda Simmons, Julie Flinn, and Bobbi Stuart. We have borrowed these amazing people from different branches of the Chicago public schools (classrooms, parent councils, and computer labs) and watched with delight as they entered hundreds of colleagues' classrooms, sharing their expertise with tact, energy, and concern. These full-timers are supported by a much larger corps of talented classroom teachers who, while still bringing the best of Best Practice to their own students every day, somehow find the energy to conduct extended workshops for colleagues after school and on weekends through the Illinois Writing Project. It's when we're working with all these dedicated professionals that we feel most confident—sometimes downright euphoric—about the prospects for reform in America's schools. We've seen schools change in deep and enduring ways when outstanding teachers like these are empowered to lead.

Lately, much of our work has been focused through a new branch of our university, the Center for City Schools. The Center serves as an umbrella for a dozen interrelated, foundation-funded projects that support teachers and parents in restructuring schools around Chicago and the Midwest. In addition to the Joyce Foundation, our work has been supported by the DeWitt Wallace-Reader's Digest Fund, the Chicago Annenberg Challenge, the Polk Bros. Foundation, the Lloyd A. Fry Foundation, the Chicago Tribune Foundation, the J.C. Penney Foundation, the Prince Charitable Trust, the Oppenheimer Family Fund, the Quest Center of the Chicago Teachers Union, the McDougal Family Foundation, and the National Writing Project.

One of our Center's most ambitious and character-building projects has been helping start a new, small Chicago public high school (not private, not charter) on the near west side of the city. Two years ago today, with lead teachers Kathy and Tom Daniels, we were scouring the city for a neighborhood where residents wouldn't oppose the establishment of a new high school. One year ago, we welcomed 132 freshmen to our newly rehabbed building across the street from Michael Jordan's United Center, and were still unpacking boxes and tinkering with the schedule. Today, we have 260 freshmen and sophomores, we just got on the Internet at last, we're still tinkering with the schedule, and we're already running out of space. Threaded throughout this book are stories about the amazing students and dedicated faculty who are pathfinding every day at 2040 West Adams, trying to bring to life the ideals of our ambitious name: Best Practice High School.

No university professors can pursue all these disparate, off-campus projects without a highly supportive dean, and we have the prime example in Linda Tafel. As Dean of the National College of Education, Linda has enthusiastically supported our efforts during the past five years, encouraging us to carry on our college's 112-year commitment to urban education. Linda says that our college's founder, Elizabeth Harrison, who started the nation's first professional training school for kindergarten teachers in 1886, would approve of what we're up to.

We owe a special debt to our cherished colleague Marilyn Bizar, who has been our partner in leading the Best Practice network over the past five years. Her deep knowledge of literacy education, of cross-cultural curriculum, of school change processes—not to mention her dynamism and humor—have knitted our disparate group snugly together in a thousand critical ways.

Arnold Aprill, Executive Director of the Chicago Arts Partnerships in Education (CAPE), has shown us our future, patiently pointing out the deep parallels among reading, writing, and the arts. After working with Arnie and the wonderful CAPE artist corps for three years, our own work has become arts-infused, and so has this book. One of the biggest differences between this and the previous edition of *Best Practice* is the attention to the arts as a lever for whole-school renewal.

Jim Vopat, director of the Milwaukee Writing Project and founder of the Parent Project, is an old friend entangled with us in countless ways. We've worked to create a Chicago-Milwaukee connection for parents and teachers, exchanged models of staff development, and taught together at the Walloon Institute. More importantly, we always draw insight from Jim's fresh and open-hearted ideas about children and childhood. Drawing on his varied experiences as a curator of children's art exhibits, a Senior Fulbright Scholar in Sri Lanka, and a writer of rare gifts, Jim has a readiness to be delighted by kids that never fails to inspire us.

The faculty and students of Washington Irving School in Chicago, led by their amazing principal, Madeleine Maraldi, have been especially important to our growth—and our morale—in the past decade. They have showed how to do school reform right, putting kids first and adhering to the principles and methods of Best Practice, sometimes in the face of fierce pressures to the contrary. They've been rewarded, after years of effort, with accomplished graduates, elevated test scores, and national recognition. They deserve every accolade.

For the past few summers, most of the people mentioned herein and many of this volume's contributors have been gathering at the Walloon Institute in Petoskey, Michigan. There, in an energizing north-woods atmosphere, we spend a week with other teachers, parents, and principals from around the country, all of whom are trying to bring Best Practice teaching and learning to life in their schools. We don't know whether it's the provocative speakers, the respite from back-home pressures, the late-night dormitory debates, or the lumberjack buffets, but we always come back from Walloon smarter, stronger, and more committed than ever to progressive principles. Our thanks go to the forty-member staff who make Walloon possible each summer.

This new edition of *Best Practice* required drafts, artwork, references, and correspondence to be swapped back and forth among more than twenty-five people. Somehow, Clarke Schneider and Allison Van Duyse kept track of all the people and articles just as skillfully as they keep our office running at the Center for City Schools. Our other publications guru is Carol Jones of JonesHouse, who has been our graphic designer, editor, and coconspirator throughout the life of the *Best Practice* newspaper.

We also have some other, smaller networks of people who support us—our families. Steve wants to thank his wife, Susan, for pursuing her own teaching in the corporate world with demanding standards for herself, making her a valuable and sympathetic model to follow and share with. And he has especially admired his sons, Mark and Daniel, for their unremitting struggles to find meaning and joy and achievement as they negotiated the school world and now their own artistic careers. Their search constantly reminded their parents about all that children can do, and about the freedoms and supports they need as they grow up.

One of the best ways to learn about education is to have some children and then watch what happens. Harvey's children, Marny and Nick, have provided quite a demonstration over their twenty and fourteen years. Traveling through schools that embody the best of Best Practice, they have grown into two creative, passionate, independent, and completely different young people. Elaine, in addition to mothering these now-large children, teaches, advises, and supervises student teachers, and always manages to be Harvey's friendliest and most insightful reader.

Art is blessed with a family who provides a continual testing ground for teaching ideas. Pam has wonderful insight into how to stimulate thoughtful connections among ideas in her third graders. With a clear sense of what builds real understanding, she keeps the university professors honest. For many years, Alicia, David, and Adam have offered an ongoing ethnography of schooling, teaching, and learning. Their running commentaries on human emotions, the forces of nature, and the absurdities of contemporary society have been the source of inspiration and delight.

1

Renewing Our Schools
An Emerging Consensus

This is an agitating, painful, and exciting time for America's schools. Since the mid-1980s, we have been enjoying and enduring the most intense period of educational reform in this century. Everyone has gotten into the act: politicians, parents, teachers, taxpayers, teacher educators, social critics, journalists, and researchers—all are passionately involved in school renewal. Education-oriented cover stories, blue-ribbon commissions, government reports, exposés, recommendations, talk shows, documentaries, conferences, jokes, gossip, and legislation abound. Indeed, we are writing this book during the reign of yet another "Education President," in a state with a self-declared "Education Governor," and in a city in the middle of the most visible school decentralization experiment in American history. For the moment, at least, education is the issue of the day.

This universal worry about the health of the public schools was deliciously portrayed in a *New Yorker* cartoon. A horrifying, ten-story-tall reptile, presumably from outer space, rampages through a downtown square as crowds of citizens run for their life in every direction. One man at the head of the fleeing crowd turns to a fellow runner and comments: "Just when citywide reading scores were edging up!"

While all the heartfelt public concern about education is certainly useful, very little of this sudden interest has been admiring, pleasant, or even civil. Our national reappraisal of education began with widespread anger and worry about low test scores and the perceived slippage in American workers' global competitiveness. Indeed, the education crisis of the 1990s may have been fueled as much by the Hondas cruising America's highways as by the downhill ride of Scholastic Aptitude Test (SAT) scores. Much of the contemporary school reform movement's energy has been spent on blaming and finger-pointing: responsibility for our nation's educational disappointments has been

1

enthusiastically and variously apportioned among TV, video games, single-parent families, ill-trained teachers, urban gangs, bad textbooks, sexual permissiveness, drugs, schools of education, and dozens of other causes.

Undeniably, the current debate about schools has included plenty of nonconstructive turmoil and rancor. Still, on balance, those of us who work in schools must welcome the scrutiny and even the fractiousness. After all, it is a rare and overdue moment when education leaps to the top of the national agenda—and it is during unstable periods like this one that true change often begins. So no matter what misgivings we might have about the current era of school reform, one thing is sure: today, millions of Americans are thinking hard and talking urgently about their schools. And that is welcome.

What About Learning and Teaching?

But one topic is too often missing from this loud, ongoing conversation: **what** shall we teach and **how**? At first, it seems unlikely that amid all this furor the substance of education could somehow be overlooked, but the record of the reform era so far sadly bears this out. Except for the standards documents we'll soon be describing, most official discourse has concerned the organizational features of schooling and "accountability" for its outcomes, rather than its content and procedures. From the trend-setting *A Nation at Risk* onward, most major reports, commission papers, books, and state and local reform efforts have focused on the logistics of schooling rather than its content and process: the central concerns have been the length of the school day and year, the credentials and pay of teachers, the roles and duties of principals, the financing of schools and of school reform, forging connections to the worlds of work and higher education, articulating educational policy with national defense, and, above all, the testing and measurement of school "products." Indeed, the federal government's touted "Goals 2000" reform package challenges nothing in the traditional ingredients or processes of schooling, and promises only one direct governmental action in the name of educational renewal: a set of national examinations at fourth and eighth grades.

Writing in *Educational Leadership*, our colleague James Beane addressed the peculiar imbalance in contemporary school reform debates. "It seems that no matter how radical restructuring talk may otherwise be, it almost never touches upon the curriculum itself. Much of what passes for restructuring is, in a sense, new bottles for old wine that has not gotten better with age. How is it that we can claim to speak of school reform without addressing the centerpiece of schools, the curriculum?" (1991). With the exception of a few school leaders like Beane and the commercial purveyors of "cultural literacy" (Bennett 1993; Hirsch 1996), surprisingly few reformers have paid serious attention to the **content** of schooling. What should schools teach? What should be the curriculum? What subject matter should children encounter and when? If our schools indeed have failed as utterly as so many blue-ribbon commissions claim, then immediate changes in the curriculum would seem advisable.

Similarly, the methods of teaching have been thoroughly ignored in the current debate. Except for Theodore Sizer and Deborah Meier, few prominent reformers have focused systematically on teaching **processes**—the nature of the interactions between kids and teachers in school. Again, if our educational system truly has collapsed, then the careful critique and revision of instructional methods would seem an urgent priority. We should be figuring out how to rearrange the basic ingredients of school—time and space and books and ideas and people—to maximize student learning. Instead, the topic of teaching methods is not just ignored, it is often explicitly ridiculed by the accountability reformers as a time-wasting distraction best left to the pea-brained teacher educators in their despised colleges of education.

This neglect of what and how we teach has predictable results: nothing changes. After nearly ten years of zealous "reform," students are still sitting in pretty much the same classrooms with the same teachers, divided into the same instructional groups, doing the same activities, working through the same textbooks and worksheets, and getting pretty much the same scores on the many new standardized tests that are the only tangible legacy of a decade's exhortation. In a backhanded and ironic way, the mainstream school reform movement actually has ended up **endorsing** old modes of schooling. The accountability enthusiasts have never really questioned the basic day-to-day process and content of American education; instead, they simply assume that if the same activities are conducted within an enhanced framework—with more time, more teachers, more tests—then student achievement and outcomes will improve. In this version of reform, you simply do the same things harder, longer, and stronger. Now, this can be a perfectly fine approach to change if what you already are doing works well and merely requires intensification. Unfortunately, we are coming to understand that the basic things we do in American schools—what we teach and how—**don't** work: we don't empower kids, don't nurture literacy, don't produce efficient workers, don't raise responsible citizens, don't create a functional democracy. If we really want to change student achievement in American schools, we must act directly on teaching and learning. More of the same is not the answer.

Real Reform

While legislatures, blue-ribbon panels, and media sages have tinkered with the logistics of education, another quieter school reform movement has been growing. Our national curriculum research centers, a dozen subject-matter professional associations, many capable individual researchers, and thousands of on-the-line classroom teachers have been struggling to determine "what works" in the different school subjects and to clearly define "best edu-cational practice" in each teaching field. These groups and individuals share a curriculum-driven view of education: they assume that if American schools are to be genuinely reformed, we must begin with a solid definition of the content of the curriculum and the classroom activities through which students may most effectively engage that content. Unlike the better publicized (and often more official) reformers, they do not see the failure of American schools as an administrative breakdown, but rather as a failure of what we teach and how.

The decade of tumultuous national debate, although it certainly hasn't concentrated enough on instruction and curriculum, has nevertheless prodded further research in these areas. All the people in this alternate, uncoordinated reform movement—teachers, instructional researchers, professional associa-tions, subject-area leaders—have been rethinking the substance, content, pro-cesses, methods, and dynamics of schooling. As a result, in virtually every school subject, we now have recent summary reports, meta-analyses of instructional research, reports from pilot classrooms, and landmark sets of professional recommendations. Some of these reports were produced with funding from the U.S. Department of Education, while others were indepen-dent and self-financed. Taken together, this family of authoritative docu-ments provides a strong consensus definition of Best Practice, of state-of-the-art teaching in every critical field.

One might expect that when experts and practitioners from such dispar-ate fields as art, science, mathematics, reading, writing, and social science sit down to define their own field's Best Practice, the results would be some very different visions of the ideal classroom, contradictory ways of organiz-ing subject matter, and divergent models of what good teachers do. But, in fact, such polarities do **not** characterize these reports. Whether the recom-mendations come from the National Council of Teachers of Mathematics (NCTM), the Center for the Study of Reading, the National Writing Project, the National Council for the Social Studies, the American Association for the Advancement of Science (AAAS), the National Council of Teachers of English (NCTE), the National Association for the Education of Young Chil-dren, or the International Reading Association (IRA), the fundamental insights into teaching and learning are remarkably congruent. Indeed, on many key issues, the recommendations from these diverse organizations are unanimous. Following is a list of these common conclusions, features that begin to define a coherent paradigm of learning and teaching across the whole curriculum.

Common Recommendations of National Curriculum Reports

- LESS whole-class, teacher-directed instruction (e.g., lecturing)
- LESS student passivity: sitting, listening, receiving, and absorbing information

- LESS presentational, one-way transmission of information from teacher to student
- LESS prizing and rewarding of silence in the classroom
- LESS classroom time devoted to fill-in-the-blank worksheets, dittos, workbooks, and other "seatwork"
- LESS student time spent reading textbooks and basal readers
- LESS attempt by teachers to thinly "cover" large amounts of material in every subject area
- LESS rote memorization of facts and details
- LESS emphasis on the competition and grades in school
- LESS tracking or leveling students into "ability groups"
- LESS use of pull-out special programs
- LESS use of and reliance on standardized tests

- MORE experiential, inductive, hands-on learning
- MORE active learning in the classroom, with all the attendant noise and movement of students doing, talking, and collaborating
- MORE diverse roles for teachers, including coaching, demonstrating, and modeling
- MORE emphasis on higher-order thinking; learning a field's key concepts and principles
- MORE deep study of a smaller number of topics, so that students internalize the field's way of inquiry
- MORE reading of real texts: whole books, primary sources, and nonfiction materials
- MORE responsibility transferred to students for their work: goal setting, record keeping, monitoring, sharing, exhibiting, and evaluating
- MORE choice for students (e.g., choosing their own books, writing topics, team partners, and research projects)
- MORE enacting and modeling of the principles of democracy in school
- MORE attention to affective needs and the varying cognitive styles of individual students
- MORE cooperative, collaborative activity; developing the classroom as an interdependent community
- MORE heterogeneously grouped classrooms where individual needs are met through inherently individualized activities, not segregation of bodies

- MORE delivery of special help to students in regular classrooms
- MORE varied and cooperative roles for teachers, parents, and administrators
- MORE reliance on teachers' descriptive evaluations of student growth, including observational/anecdotal records, conference notes, and performance assessment rubrics[*]

The latent agreement on these principles is so strong in the different subject fields that it seems fair to call it an **unrecognized consensus**. Although school people are often portrayed as lost and fragmented, the fact is that a remarkably consistent, harmonious vision of "best educational practice" already exists. But this emergent consensus hasn't yet been widely recognized across subject boundaries. The coherence of this vision, the remarkable overlap across fields, may be quite striking, but so far most people in government, the media, and even the educational system haven't quite grasped its significance and potential transforming power.

Admittedly, this emerging consensus is not perfectly symmetrical across the different school subjects; some fields are ahead of others. Reading and writing are probably the most advanced fields in implementing Best Practice instruction, although they were among the slowest to prepare and publish official standards. The Writing-Across-the-Curriculum and Whole Language movements, which have been solidly in place for decades, have been leading the way for practitioners and researchers alike. Although no comparably broad instructional movements yet exist in mathematics, math leaders have made a tremendous contribution with the series of NCTM standards documents published since 1987. These frameworks and guidelines have shown other fields how learning goals for children can be described in Best Practice terms—progressive, developmentally appropriate, research-based, and eminently teachable. Science educators, on the other hand, have a decades-long tradition of supporting progressive, hands-on, student-centered instruction, but less success with implementation in schools. This relative lack of impact undoubtedly reflects the low priority given to science at all levels of American education: science often gets pushed to the bottom of the curricular agenda, while worries about reading, writing, and math gobble up time, attention, funding, and the energy for staff development and curriculum reform.

---

[*] AAAS 1989 and 1993; Anderson et al. 1985; Bybee et al. 1989 and 1991; Center for Civic Education 1994; Consortium of National Arts Organizations 1994; Crafton 1996; Geography Education Standards Project 1994; Harste 1989; Hillocks 1986; IRA and NCTE 1996; Joint Committee on National Health Education Standards 1995; National Center for History in the Schools 1994; National Research Council 1996; NCTM 1989, 1991, and 1995; National Council for the Social Studies 1994; Saunders and Gilliard 1995; Sierra-Perry 1996; Smagorinsky 1996; Wilhelm 1996

The social sciences have been especially uneven in embracing progressive practices and disseminating them throughout the profession. At first, this seems surprising, because subjects like history, civics, and geography appear to cry out for collaborative, experiential, student-centered, cognitive approaches—key structures in the emerging Best Practice paradigm. But, as we discuss further in Chapter 6, social studies education has been dragged down by its political baggage. Because this is the one school subject with the explicit duty to inculcate patriotic values and transmit "necessary" cultural information, it becomes a battleground on which partisans take non-negotiable stands. The first draft of the national history standards, by some accounts a balanced but warts-and-all version of U.S. and world history, was voted down by the U.S. Senate after a furious media campaign waged by right-wing commentators.

For several years, the vociferous and virulent attacks of high-profile critics like E.D. Hirsch and William Bennett intimidated social studies teachers and silenced discussion. For some reason, educators rarely pointed out the obvious conflict of interest: Bennett and Hirsch, far from being judicious observers of the educational scene, are both tireless commercial vendors, marketing millions of dollars worth of "cultural literacy" products (i.e., *What Every Second-grader Should Know, The Book of Virtues*) to American schools and parents. Finally, after years on the defensive, the National Council for the Social Studies in 1994 issued a set of documents that, along with the revised history and geography standards, staked out a solid progressive position for social science education, despite the continuing fulminations of royalty-rich pundits.

Principles of Best Practice Learning

As the More/Less chart suggests, there is more afoot here than the congruence of certain teaching recommendations from the traditionally separate fields of the American school curriculum. A more general, progressive educational paradigm is emerging across content boundaries and grade levels. This coherent philosophy and spirit is reaching across the curriculum and up through the grades. Whether it is called Best Practice, or Whole Language, or integrated learning, or interdisciplinary studies, by some other name, or by no name at all, this movement is broad and deep and enduring. It is strongly backed by educational research, draws on sound learning theory, and, under other names, has been tested and refined over many years.

What is the nature of this new/old curriculum? What assumptions and theories about learning inform this approach? What is the underlying educational philosophy of this reemergent paradigm? If we study the More/Less chart more systematically, we can identify thirteen interlocking principles, assumptions, or theories that characterize this model of education.

STUDENT-CENTERED. The best starting point for schooling is young people's real interests; all across the curriculum, investigating students' own questions should always take precedence over studying arbitrarily and distantly selected "content."

EXPERIENTIAL. Active, hands-on, concrete experience is the most powerful and natural form of learning. Students should be immersed in the most direct possible experience of the content of every subject.

HOLISTIC. Children learn best when they encounter whole ideas, events, and materials in purposeful contexts, not by studying subparts isolated from actual use.

AUTHENTIC. Real, rich, complex ideas and materials are at the heart of the curriculum. Lessons or textbooks that water-down, control, or oversimplify content ultimately disempower students.

EXPRESSIVE. To fully engage ideas, construct meaning, and remember information, students must regularly employ the whole range of communicative media—speech, writing, drawing, poetry, dance, drama, music, movement, and visual arts.

REFLECTIVE. Balancing the immersion in experience and expression must be opportunities for learners to reflect, debrief, abstract from their experiences what they have felt and thought and learned.

SOCIAL. Learning is always socially constructed and often interactional; teachers need to create classroom interactions that "scaffold" learning.

COLLABORATIVE. Cooperative learning activities tap the social power of learning better than competitive and individualistic approaches.

DEMOCRATIC. The classroom is a model community; students learn what they live as citizens of the school.

COGNITIVE. The most powerful learning comes when children develop true understanding of concepts through higher-order thinking associated with various fields of inquiry and through self-monitoring of their thinking.

DEVELOPMENTAL. Children grow through a series of definable but not rigid stages, and schooling should fit its activities to the developmental level of students.

CONSTRUCTIVIST. Children do not just receive content; in a very real sense, they re-create and reinvent every cognitive system they encounter, including language, literacy, and mathematics.

CHALLENGING. Students learn best when faced with genuine challenges, choices, and responsibility in their own learning.

The remainder of this book, as it discusses each subject in the school curriculum, spells out what these key principles really mean in practice. However, to explain why these ideas are so important, we'll elaborate briefly on them now.

Schooling should be STUDENT-CENTERED, taking its cues from young people's interests, concerns, and questions.   Making school student-centered involves building on the natural curiosity children bring to school and asking kids what they want to learn. Teachers help students list their own questions, puzzles, and goals, and then structure for them widening circles of experience and investigation of those topics. Teachers infuse into such kid-driven curriculum all the skills, knowledge, and concepts that society mandates, though always in original sequences and combinations. But student-centered schooling does not mean passive teachers who respond only to students' explicit cues. Teachers also draw on their deep understanding of children's developmentally characteristic needs and enthusiasms to design experiences that lead students into areas they might not choose, but that they will enjoy and engage in deeply. Teachers also bring their own interests and enthusiasms into the classroom to share, at an age-appropriate level, demonstrating how a learner gets involved with ideas. Thus, student-centered education begins by cordially inviting children's whole, real lives into the classroom; it solicits and listens to their questions; and it provides a balance between activities that follow children's lead and ones that lead the children.

As often as possible, school should stress learning that is EXPERIEN-TIAL.   Children learn most powerfully from doing, not just hearing about, any subject. This simple psychological fact has different implications in different subjects. In writing and reading, it means that students grow more by composing and reading whole, real texts, rather than doing work-sheets and exercises. With mathematics, it means working with objects—sorting, counting, and building patterns of number and shape; and carrying out real-world projects that involve collecting data, estimating, calculating, drawing conclusions, and making decisions. In science, it means conducting experiments and taking field trips to investigate natural settings, pollution problems, and labs at nearby factories, universities, or hospitals. For social studies, students can conduct opinion surveys, prepare group reports that teach the rest of the class, and role-play famous events, conflicts, and political debates. In all school subjects, the key is to help students think more deeply, to discover the detailed implications of ideas through direct or simulated immersion in them.

Learning in all subjects needs to be HOLISTIC.   In the traditional American curriculum, information and ideas are presented to children in small "building blocks." While the teacher may find these subparts meaningful and may know they add up to an eventual understanding of a subject, their purpose and significance aren't always apparent to the children. This part-to-whole approach undercuts motivation for learning because children don't perceive why they are doing the work. It also deprives children of an essential condition for learning—encountering material in its full, lifelike context. When the "big picture" is put off until later, later often never comes. We know that children do, in fact, need to acquire skills and abilities that are parts of a larger whole—skills such as spelling and multiplying and evaluating good evidence for written arguments. But holistic learning means that children gain these abilities most effectively by going from whole-to-part, when kids read whole books, write whole stories, and carry out whole investigations of natural phenomena. Brief lessons on the use of quotation marks are learned fastest and remembered longest when the class writes scripts for plays they've decided to stage. And, meanwhile, the focus on a rich whole text or inquiry ensures that children are simultaneously making far more mental connections—albeit often unconscious ones—than the teacher ever has time to directly teach within the one or two or three "skills" that she covers.

Learning activities need to be AUTHENTIC.   There is a natural tendency in schools to offer children simplified materials and activities so they are not overwhelmed with complexity. But too often we underestimate children and oversimplify things, creating materials or situations that are so synthetic as to be unlifelike—and, ironically, educationally worthless. The most notorious examples of this, of course, are the linguistically deprived stories appearing in many basal reading texts. We now understand that children routinely handle phenomenal complexity in their own daily lives—indeed, kids' learning of the thousands of abstract rules underlying spoken language is proof of their ability to sort out the complex tangle of data the real world inevitably presents. What does authenticity mean in the curriculum? In reading, it means that the rich, artful, and complex vocabulary of Grimm's fairy tales is far more educational than dumbed-down "decodable" versions in trendy commercial reading programs. In math, it means that children might investigate ways of dividing a pizza or a cake, rather than working the odd-numbered fractions problems at the end of the chapter. Authenticity also means that children are reading and writing and calculating and investigating for purposes that they have chosen, not just because the teacher gave an assignment or because a task appears in a textbook. Yes, teachers can and should sometimes give assignments that a whole class can work on, to share and compare the resulting ideas they've generated. But if teachers don't also take steps to turn schoolwork into something the children truly own, then the results will be mechanical, more an exercise in dutifully following directions than in real valuing of thought and knowledge.

Students need to learn and practice many forms of EXPRESSION to deeply engage ideas.   Traditional school has been reception-based; that is, students are supposed to sit quietly and listen while the teacher talks, presents, tells, shows, and explains—supposedly "filling them up" with the curriculum.

We now understand that learning doesn't work this way and we recognize the sad irony of schools in which teachers are the ones doing all the expressing. To understand, own, and remember ideas, students need not just to receive, but also to express them. Expressing ideas can mean something as simple as talking in pairs and informal peer groups, all the way to preparing and presenting a formal, public report or artifact that embodies the concepts under study. When a learner can successfully translate an idea from one medium to another—for example, expressing the sixth amendment to the U.S. Constitution in a dramatic skit or a sonnet—we realize that she possesses the information in a solid and flexible way. And, aside from the cognitive benefits of an expression-rich instruction, we acknowledge that expression is energizing and that many children love to perform. Indeed, it is a natural human tendency to find a friendly audience and exercise your strongest medium of expression. For all these reasons, a progressive curriculum stresses exhibitions and performances, inviting students to express ideas through the widest possible array of media.

Effective learning is balanced with opportunities for REFLECTION. Too often, school is a process of stimulus-response. The work cycle is: "Do it, turn it in, get your grade, forget it, and move on." But learning is greatly strengthened when children have time to look back on what they've learned, to digest and debrief, to recognize broader principles, to appreciate their accomplishments and understand how they overcame obstacles. Of course, it is hard to think reflectively in the middle of doing an experiment or revising a draft, but afterwards students can review what happened and apply what they learned to future efforts. Do children need to be introduced to this reflective process? No—we can find evidence of it in their play and family interactions all the time. But kids need **time** set aside for reflection, and they need to become consciously aware of its power and their ability to use it. Adding reflective thinking to school learning is one of the simplest of all instructional innovations. Although there are other more elegant approaches, many teachers have found that the simple addition of a student learning log for each subject, with time set aside each day for responding to well-structured teacher "prompts," builds reflection into the day and moves students to a new level of thinking.

Teachers should tap into the primal power of SOCIAL relations to promote learning. Much research has shown how social interactions in the family and community support early language learning. This occurs unconsciously and naturally in families and in groups of children playing together. Such spontaneous social helping is often called "scaffolding" because, just as a temporary scaffold allows bricklayers to construct a wall that finally stands on its own, these interactions support young language-builders along the way, but ultimately leave the child independent. Children are far from passive in this scaffolding process. They learn not only by imitating grownup behavior, but by taking an active part, constructing and testing hypotheses, and initiating action themselves. Babies learn language swiftly and effectively without being directly "taught" because they are learning words and structures that help them get their needs met in their families. Following this model, schools can reverse their old counterproductive patterns of isolation and silence, tapping the power of social interaction to promote learning.

Some of the most efficient social learning activities are COLLABORA-TIVE.   When we think of the social side of learning, we most readily envision group discussions, kids listening to one another's work, carrying out projects and writing letters and stories **for** one another. Collaborative learning goes on to promote children's learning **with** one another. Even in the workplace, we're recognizing how much collaboration actually goes on in American life and how valuable group problem solving is, compared to perpetual competitiveness and isolation. Collaborative small-group activity has been shown to be an especially effective mode for school learning—and solid achievement gains have been documented across the curriculum by Johnson et al. (1991), Slavin et al. (1985), Sharan and Sharan (1992), and others.

Collaborative work allows learners to receive much more extensive feedback from fellow students than they can ever get from a single teacher who must spread his time among all students. Of course, group work requires training students and carefully designing meaningful, authentic activities—otherwise, the effort of the group can be inefficient and shallow. But cooperation does work very well when teachers employ the student training techniques that have been refined in recent years. It's worth the effort because habitual cooperation pays off both in time better used in the classroom and, later on, as a valuable skill in life.

Classrooms can become more effective and productive when procedures are DEMOCRATIC.   It is a classic bit of American hypocrisy that we claim to be a democracy and yet send our children off to profoundly authoritarian schools. But even if we don't choose to democratize schools as a matter of principle, there are instructional reasons for doing so. Certain essential democratic processes make learning more efficient, more widely spread throughout the classroom, and more likely to have lifelong effects. First and most important, children need to exercise **choice**—choice in books they read, topics they write about, and activities they focus on during some parts of the day. This means that teachers must help children learn how to make intelligent choices, not just arbitrary ones, or choices of avoidance. When children learn to make good choices, they are not only more committed to the work they do, they also acquire habits that make them lifelong readers, writers, and continuing learners of math, science, and social issues—and, not inconsequentially, active, critical, involved citizens.

But democracy is not just freedom to choose. In a genuinely democratic classroom, children learn to negotiate conflicts so they can work together more effectively and respect and appreciate one another's differences. They learn that they are part of a larger community, that they can gain from it, and that they must also sometimes give to it. They hear about differences in one another's cultures, religions, regional backgrounds, and personal beliefs. Too often, this valuing of community within difference is missing in both rich and poor neighborhoods, and its absence undercuts education in countless ways, leaving us with discipline problems, vandalism, hostility toward school, and low self-esteem among students. Democracy in the classroom is not just a frill or an isolated social studies unit, but an educational necessity.

Powerful learning comes from COGNITIVE experiences. Many teachers have moved well beyond believing that memorized definitions constitute real understanding and are reorganizing their classrooms to facilitate higher-order, conceptual learning. Concepts are the abstract ideas that give special meaning to human experiences. Full comprehension and appreciation for concepts such as **tangent, democracy, metaphor,** and **photosynthesis** come from complex, varied experiences that gradually build deep understanding that is increasingly abstract, general, and powerful.

At the same time, **how** children think is intimately related to **what** they think. Teachers must help students develop the specific types of thinking that our civilization values, such as analytical reasoning, interpretation, metaphorical thinking, creative design, categorization, hypothesizing, drawing inferences, and synthesis. Students need to experience these kinds of thinking for themselves with appropriate modeling and facilitation from their teachers and others. When they do, language, thinking, and conceptual understanding are intertwined as students **construct** ideas, systems, and processes for themselves.

Along with thinking and concepts is **metacognition**, the notion that children can become increasingly aware of their own thinking and concepts. When teachers end an activity with reflective debriefing and questions such as "What happened?" "What did you do?" and "How did you come to that conclusion?" students become conscious of their own cognitive processes and can better monitor their work and thinking. This mental self-awareness helps students develop more effective cognitive strategies for accomplishing tasks, making decisions, and reviewing their own work.

It's no accident that in discussing many of these principles, we've used **psycholinguistic** examples of child language acquisition. Indeed, this magical and universal phenomenon has provided educators with one of our most important bodies of knowledge—and most generative of metaphors—about learning. Childhood language development is the most powerful, speedy, and complex learning any of us will ever do in our life. We learn to speak without being directly "taught" and without conscious intention to learn. It happens in the social settings of families and it becomes internalized through play and crib-talk. Once learned, oral language becomes the main tool for future learning and provides the base for reading and writing. Outer speech gradually becomes storable as inner thought.

Teachers now recognize that the cognitive lessons of language acquisition aren't restricted to preschool children at home. The concept of scaffolding—the special kind of help provided by parents and siblings in a family—can be explicitly built into the structure of work in school. The ideas of hypothesis testing and temporary linguistic forms help us to respect and learn from rather than punish children's errors in school. The natural instincts of parents to engage, support, enjoy, and extend their children's utterances encourage us to rethink teacher feedback and evaluation practices. The fact that language is learned tacitly, during socializing and play, suggests that we make the classroom more playful and interactive. Perhaps above all, the fact that you learn to talk by talking implies that children should simply be allowed to talk far more than they currently do in school. The school norm of silent classrooms must be abolished; ironically, when teachers enforce the standard of silence, they are in a very real sense making learning illegal.

Children's learning must be approached as DEVELOPMENTAL.   This is one of the most carelessly used words in current educational parlance, enlisted in the support of all sorts of contradictory ideas. To us, *developmental* does not mean labeling or teaching students according to their purported level on a fixed hierarchy of cognitive stages. Nor does it mean lockstep instruction according to some textbook company's scope and sequence chart. Instead, *developmental* simply means age-appropriate; developmentally oriented teachers approach classroom groups and individual students with a respect for their emerging capabilities. Developmentalists recognize that kids grow in common patterns but at different rates that usually cannot be accelerated up by adult pressure or input. Developmentally oriented teachers know that variance in the school performance of different children often results from differences in their general growth. Such variations in the speed but not the direction or the ultimate degree of development should not be grounds for splitting up groups, but rather are diversities to be welcomed and melded into the richness of a group.

In developmental schooling, we help children by recognizing and encouraging beginning steps when they occur—whether on schedule or not. We study the research on how children actually advance in math or spelling and build our programs around this knowledge, rather than marching through arbitrary word lists or problems each week. In complex areas like writing, we chart children's progress in many ingredients of composing and understand how some abilities will appear to regress as children challenge themselves with other, more difficult rhetorical tasks. In math, along with review and exploration of this week's topic, we include challenging, enjoyable activities that go beyond the textbook unit so that we find out what various kids are really ready for.

Children's learning always involves CONSTRUCTING ideas and systems.
Studies of early language acquisition, science learning in school, reading
processes, mathematical cognition, and many other areas show that human
beings never just take in and memorize material. Even when staring at clouds
or smoke or trash in an empty lot, we are constantly trying to find and organize meaning in what we see. In a very real sense, people always **reinvent**
whatever they encounter, by constantly making and revising mental models
of the world. Inventing and constructing are exactly how we learn complex
systems like mathematics, language, anthropology, or anything else. For
example, when two-year-olds invent and use words like *feets* or *goed,* words
that they have never heard from anyone, they are demonstrating constructivism. Children don't just imitate the language around them; they use it as a
corpus of raw material from which to generate hypotheses, to reinvent the
language itself. Along the way, they create original, temporary forms that
serve until new hypotheses generate new structures. Kids don't merely learn
to speak; every one of them, in a profound sense, rebuilds his or her native
language.

Constructivist teachers trust that all children can reinvent math, reading,
and writing no matter how "disadvantaged" their backgrounds, and they are
eager to tap into the thinking abilities children bring to school. They know
that the keys are experience, immersion, and engagement in a safe, interactive community. Kids need much time to practice reading, writing, mathing,
experimenting. They need encouragement to reflect, to share their emerging
ideas and hypotheses with others, to have their errors and temporary understandings respected—and they need plenty of time. Constructivist teachers
cheerfully accept that their most helpful role isn't one of direct telling and
teaching. Indeed, given the fundamentally internal nature of this deep learning, teachers can't help by presenting rules, skills, or facts. Instead, they create a rich environment in which the children can gradually construct their
own understandings. When teachers do create an appropriate, stimulating,
healthy setting, children's urge to make sense of their world propels their
own learning.

Following all these principles means that school is CHALLENGING.
While some people think that experiential, collaborative, or self-chosen tasks
are "easier" for students, teachers using state-of-the-art practices know that
the opposite is true. "Letting" students choose their own topics for writing,
for example, makes their task harder, not easier. If the teacher commands:
"Imagine you are a butterfly. Write one paragraph with lots of adjectives
telling how it feels to land on a flower," the author's job is basically fill-in-
the-blank. The really hard job for young writers is to find their own topics
every day—pursuing the promising ones as far as they will go, discarding the
clunkers promptly and starting over. When teachers steadily assign writing
topics without ever asking students to develop their own subjects, as real

writers do, they are establishing a pedagogical welfare system and lowering the standard of instruction.

Even with young children, Best Practice teachers are careful not to inculcate day long dependency on teacher instructions, directions, and decisions. They see their overriding long-term goal as nurturing children's capacity to run their own brain, set up and conduct their own inquiries, keep track of and evaluate their own efforts. So they expect students to take considerable responsibility, establish learning goals, monitor their own learning, make sure they apply the abilities they've acquired, keep their own records, and elect new projects when they're finished with something, rather than just fill in an extra ditto sheet. As the students in a classroom gradually assume more responsibilities, the teacher attends to the needs of individual children, provides a safe space for experimenting with newer and more difficult tasks, and adds challenges as kids are developmentally ready for them. In the rigorous classes where these approaches abound, kids love the challenge.

So What's New?

This set of ideas will be entirely familiar to anyone who worked in American schools during the late 1960s and early 1970s, someone raised on the ideas of Carl Rogers, John Holt, Herbert Kohl, A.S. Neill, Neil Postman, and Charles Weingartner. But then this list doesn't exactly hold any surprises for people who lived through the progressive era of the 1930s or who have studied the work of John Dewey. Yes, today's "new" integrated and holistic educational paradigm can fairly be called a progressive resurgence. **Another** progressive resurgence.

While it is harmonious with and descended from past progressive eras, this new movement is not identical to the open classrooms of the 1960s or the Deweyian schools of the 1930s. Though still rooted in the characteristic view of children as fundamentally good, self-regulating, and trustworthy, today's movement is driven by more than an optimistic conception of children's nature. This time around, the philosophical orientation is better balanced with pedagogical pragmatism and insight about cognition. We are blending a positive view of children with our commitment to certain curriculum content and our improved understanding of how learning works. In the 1960s, many progressive innovations failed because they were backed with more passion than practical, well-thought-out procedures for implementing them. Now, a generation later, we return to the same basic ideas, with the same fundamental understanding of kids' capabilities, but equipped with much better ideas about how adult helpers can make it work.

Yes, many of these ideas are old and familiar. And while this neo-progressive movement does indeed promise a revolution in education, it is the farthest thing from a fad. Although it has reemerged now partly as a result of contemporary forces, it also represents a much older, ongoing, and long-coming shift in the educational philosophy of this nation. This closely related set of ideas has been struggling for acceptance in American culture for many generations, appearing and reappearing in forms that too many educators and citizens have mistakenly taken for meaningless cyclical trends.

Now, near the turn of the century—indeed, the millennium—these ideas appear again, this time in a stronger, more coherent form. Perhaps the current cycle of progressive reform will have a more lasting influence on education in this culture than the innovations of the 1960s and 1970s, or even the era of John Dewey. While the authors of this book have no doubt that this cyclical tendency will continue on into future generations, we also believe in progress. With each cycle, some things change that never change back, and some cycles leave a stronger heritage than others. We believe that today's is potentially the most important, powerful, and enduring phase of progressive educational reform ever to occur in American schools.

How to Read This Book—and Why

Today we enjoy a rich base of research and exemplary practice that points the way to school renewal through curriculum reform. As teachers are showing in schools around the country, this progressive paradigm is not just a dream anymore, but a real, practical, manageable, available choice. But this new/old model enacts learning and teaching in very different ways from those that most contemporary parents, principals, and teachers themselves experienced in school—and, in some ways, it directly contradicts teachers' professional training. So when teachers, schools, or districts want to move toward this new model, everyone involved in the change needs lots of information and reassurance: they need a chance to construct their own understanding of what the new curriculum means, what research and theory supports it, how it can be implemented, and why it holds so much promise for our children.

That's what this book is for: to help all the parties to school reform recognize, understand, appreciate, and start exploiting the remarkably coherent models for across-the-curriculum school reform that already have been built. Toward this end, we take several steps in the next few chapters. First, we want to provide a compact and accurate summary of current Best Practice research in each of six main school teaching fields, drawing on the consensus documents from each subject area. After each field's research base, we tell the story of at least one exemplary program, showing how some real teachers are implementing key content and processes in their classrooms.

This pattern of organization, of course, restricts us for several chapters to the traditional subject-area boundaries. While we certainly don't wish to reify the compartmentalization of the curriculum, the fact remains that knowledge about schooling currently is generated and reported mostly within these customary divisions. The key research centers, professional societies, and even most individual researchers are identified with only one subject field each. In Chapter 8, we discuss ways to move beyond the traditional school subject areas; after all, the new educational paradigm doesn't reach its full potential until better practices are used beyond the same old boundaries.

For all of us, the ultimate goal is more coherent, organic, and integrated schooling for American young people. However, creating that kind of experience does not necessarily **begin** with rescheduling the school day, abolishing separate subjects, or instituting thematic interdisciplinary units. Vast changes and improvements in teaching can be made within the old subject boundaries. Indeed, we would warn that schools that reorganize their schedule and curriculum into interdisciplinary units without fully understanding the current research on reading, writing, mathematics, science, social studies, and art may merely devise an elaborate new delivery system for the same old superficial kind of education. This problem leads us to the question of change, which is the final topic of the book. In later chapters, we talk frankly and realistically—and we hope, practically—about the tough but definitely not insurmountable problems of change in American schools.

There are different ways that different readers may approach this book, depending on their needs and interests. After all, according to the research on reading comprehension that we're about to summarize, meaning in any text is profoundly dependent on the knowledge of the reader. We'd be remiss if we didn't learn from our own inquiry, and we've designed the book to take this variability into account.

So if you are an experienced teacher trying to invigorate your science instruction, you may turn directly to the science chapter for guidelines and possibilities, browse several exemplary classroom segments to see how they actually work, study Chapter 8 for the classroom structures that enable new teaching strategies, and then consult Chapter 9, "Making the Transition," to consider which teacher-development activities to seek for your district. On the other hand, if you are a school administrator searching for policies to improve children's learning throughout your district, you might scan all the subject-area chapters, and then once you see the pattern they reveal, focus most strongly on Chapter 9 to think about the direction of staff development in the district. If you are a school-board member trying to imagine how changes in the curriculum might affect your own and your neighbors' children, you may appreciate most the nine "Exemplary Program" stories that illustrate how new-and-yet-old ideas already are making many schools the exciting and enriching places they ought to be.

Whatever your purpose as a reader, we urge that you view the recommendations and classroom stories in this book as elements of a process and not as examples of perfection. School districts or individual teachers rarely advance in one single, straight-line jump. None of the teachers whose classrooms are described here consider themselves finished or a paragon; all of them talk about being somewhere in the middle of a long, complex journey. Indeed, it is a defining characteristic of good teachers that they are learners themselves, constantly observing to see what enriches children's experience— and what makes teaching more invigorating and rewarding for them. Thoughtful readers will find many ways to improve upon and extend the activities described here. In fact, as we've talked with these teachers about their efforts, we've usually ended up brainstorming additional options and variations that bring even more principles of Best Practice into play. We certainly invite our readers to join in this process of extending and fine-tuning.

And we need to add a warning. It is tempting, as one reads any book about school reform, to be excessively impressed by innovative, highly wrought, teacher-designed activities, implicitly assuming that increased student learning comes mainly from increased teacher doing. But it's not that simple. There always needs to be a balance in the classroom, a balance between teacher-organized activity and children's own initiative and self-directed work. It is during kids' self-sponsored activities that much of the most powerful learning occurs and the effects of good teaching get a chance to bloom. During the buzz and talk that goes on while small groups work, during the jotting and quiet considering of journal time, during the children's play with math manipulatives or puzzles, while kids sketch out a cluster of ideas on a piece of butcher paper—so much is happening that is valuable, even when there's a bit of digressing and fooling around, that an observer gets dizzy watching it.

Two Final Stories

One thing that deeply troubles us about the accountability version of the national standards movement is its heartless and authoritarian way of talking about—and to—children. The prevailing tone is get-tough, no-nonsense, nose-to-the-grindstone, sit-down-and-shut-up. Standards-setters are always issuing demands, exhortations, warnings, and "consequences," as if these were the way to a child's heart and mind, and the keys to motivation. No one cares whether school is a safe place, a comfortable place, or, God forbid, a place that's *fun*. Indeed, the knuckle-knocking invocations of the test-and-punish reformers make you wonder whether any of these people have any children of their own—or ever were children themselves.

Meanwhile, in New York City, there's a wonderfully rigorous small school that has redefined standards in an especially constructive way. When setting forth their curriculum goals for each grade level, the teachers at the Manhattan New School don't issue standards for learning; instead, they share their *hopes for children*. Accordingly, teacher Joanne Hindley and the third-grade team have developed these "hopes" for one part of the curriculum— reading—expressing them as questions for parents to consider (1996).

Our Hopes for Third Graders
Manhattan New School

Does Your Child:

1. Show an interest in reading?

   • Does he/she choose to read other than when it is required?

2. Read for a sustained period of time?

   • Is there an increase in the amount of time your child reads independently as the year goes on?

3. Respond emotionally to text?

   • Does he/she laugh, sigh, smile, allow himself to be "touched" by what is being read?

4. Choose literature at appropriate and challenging levels?

   • Can your child read the books he/she chooses with minimal difficulty?

   • Does he/she challenge him/herself to read new genres (nonfiction, poetry, mystery, etc.)?

5. Make reasonable predictions about what might happen next in the story?

6. Connect personally to the characters and plot of the story?

   • Does he/she talk about his/her own experiences in life because he/she is reminded of them from the story?

7. Use a variety of word recognition strategies to figure out unknown words? Does he/she:

   • Skip a difficult word and come back to it later?

   • Use picture clues?

   • Attempt to "sound out" the word?

   • Ask someone what a challenging word is?

8. Talk about how a story is written? Does he/she comment on choices the author made in creating leads, endings, language in a story?

9. Make connections between books?

   • "This book reminds me of another one I've read . . . "

   • "This is like another book by this author . . . "

10. Use reading for real-life purposes?

11. Is he/she curious about bus signs, advertisements, menus in restaurants, grocery store flyers, signs in store windows, etc.?

How different these standards sound from the benchmarks, cutoffs, multiple-choice tests, and consequences of the accountability reformers!

These *hopes* speak the same language that parents use when they talk about their children, unashamedly framing educational goals within the human context of love, empathy, flexibility, patience, and perspective.

———————————

When ten-year-old Kate, who has really struggled with reading and writing, finally composed her very first coherent story, it wasn't part of an assigned, teacher-planned activity. Kate is an African American fifth grader at Washington Irving School, from a poor neighborhood on the West Side of Chicago. She's belligerent much of the time, a nonparticipant in most lessons, and her teacher agonizes over Kate's seemingly bleak future. For several weeks the class had been working on inferential reasoning, imagining "the story behind" various objects and events, through reading books, brainstorming, and taking a walk in the neighborhood—all activities structured by the teacher. Now the class was generating a list of questions to ask a fascinating visitor who is coming after lunch—an investigator from the city morgue, which is located nearby and thus part of the neighborhood study.

Just now, the teacher discovers that Kate has been doodling in her journal, next to a drawing she's made of a trash-littered lot the class had encountered on its neighborhood walk. The one ability Kate recognizes in herself is that she can draw quite well. Next to the drawing, Kate has begun writing a story titled "The Funky Boot," based on a mysterious object she noticed in the vacant lot. She asks in a whisper if she can work on her story right now, using the computer at the back of the room. Kate works there until lunch time, pauses impatiently for only part of the morgue investigator's talk, returns to the computer, and later asks to skip gym so she can continue writing—the longest continuous attention that she's ever given to any school task except drawing. The piece is barely coherent, but it is Kate's first attempt at authorship. While the classroom climate and activities made this breakthrough possible, the timing and commitment came from Kate.

As much as we value well-structured teaching and creative classroom activities, in this book we hope to show why schools must also make time for kids—creating not just elegant teacher-orchestrated events, but also simple, regular, predictable space for all of our Kates to achieve their own wonderful discoveries.

Works Cited

American Association for the Advancement of Science. 1989. *Science for All Americans.* Washington, DC: American Association for the Advancement of Science.

———. 1993. *Benchmarks for Science Literacy.* New York: Oxford University Press.

Anderson, Richard C., Elfrieda H. Hiebert, Judith A. Scott, and Ian A.G. Wilkinson. 1985. *Becoming a Nation of Readers: The Report of the Commission on Reading*. Washington, DC: National Institute of Education.

Beane, James. 1991. "Middle School: The Natural Home of Integrated Curriculum." *Educational Leadership*. (October).

Bennett, William. 1993. *The Book of Virtues: A Treasury of Great Moral Stories*. New York: Simon & Schuster.

Bybee, Roger, et al. 1989. *Science and Technology Education for the Elementary Years: Frameworks for Curriculum and Instruction*. Washington, DC: National Center for Improving Science Education.

————. 1991. *Science and Technology Education for the Middle Years: Frameworks for Curriculum and Instruction*. Washington, DC: National Center for Improving Science Education.

Center for Civic Education. 1994. *National Standards for Civics and Government*. Calabasas, CA: Center for Civic Education.

Consortium of National Arts Organizations. 1994. *National Standards for Arts Education: What Every Young American Should Know and Be Able to Do*. Reston, VA: Music Educators National Conference.

Crafton, Linda. 1996. *Standards in Practice: Grades K–2*. Urbana, IL: National Council of Teachers of English.

Geography Education Standards Project. 1994. *Geography for Life: National Geography Standards*. Washington, DC: National Geographic Research and Exploration.

Harste, Jerome C. 1989. *New Policy Guidelines for Reading: Connecting Research and Practice*. Urbana, IL: National Council of Teachers of English.

Hillocks, George. 1986. *Research on Written Composition*. Urbana, IL: National Council of Teachers of English.

Hindley, Joanne. 1996. *In the Company of Children*. York, ME: Stenhouse Publishers.

Hirsch, E. D. 1996. *The Schools We Need and Why We Don't Have Them*. New York: Doubleday.

International Reading Association and National Council of Teachers of English. 1996. *Standards for the English Language Arts*. Urbana, IL, and Newark, DE: International Reading Association and National Council of Teachers of English.

Johnson, David W., Roger T. Johnson, Edythe Holubec, and Patricia Roy. 1991. *Cooperation in the Classroom*. Edina, MN: Interaction Book Company.

Joint Committee on National Health Education Standards. 1995. *National Health Education Standards: Achieving Health Literacy*. Reston, VA: Association for the Advancement of Health Education.

National Center for History in the Schools. 1994. *National Standards for United States History: Exploring the American Experience*. Los Angeles: National Center for History in the Schools.

————. 1994. *National Standards for World History: Exploring Paths to the Present.* Los Angeles: National Center for History in the Schools.

National Commission on Excellence in Education. 1985. *A Nation at Risk: The Imperative for Educational Reform.* Washington, DC: National Commission on Excellence in Education.

National Council for the Social Studies. 1994. *Expectations of Excellence: Curriculum Standards for the Social Studies.* Washington, DC: National Council for the Social Studies.

National Council of Teachers of Mathematics. 1989. *Curriculum and Evaluation Standards for School Mathematics.* Reston, VA: Commission on Standards for School Mathematics.

————. 1991. *Professional Standards for Teaching Mathematics.* Reston, VA: National Council of Teachers of Mathematics.

————. 1995. *Assessment Standards for School Mathematics.* Reston, VA: National Council of Teachers of Mathematics.

National Research Council. 1996. *National Science Education Standards.* Washington, DC: National Academy Press.

Saunders, P., and J. Gilliard. 1995. *A Framework for Teaching Basic Economic Concepts with Scope and Sequence Guidelines, K–12.* New York: National Council on Economic Education.

Sharan, Yael, and Shlomo Sharan. 1992. *Expanding Cooperative Learning Through Group Investigation.* New York: Teachers College Press.

Sierra-Perry, Martha, 1996. *Standards in Practice: Grades 3–5.* Urbana, IL: National Council of Teachers of English.

Slavin, Robert, Schlomo Sharan, Karen Spencer, Clark Webb, and Robert Schmuck. 1985. *Learning to Cooperate, Cooperating to Learn.* New York: Plenum Press.

Smagorinsky, Peter. 1996. *Standards in Practice: Grades 9–12.* Urbana, IL: National Council of Teachers of English.

Wilhelm, Jeffrey D. 1996. *Standards in Practice: Grades 6–8.* Urbana, IL: National Council of Teachers of English.

2

Best Practice in Reading

How Reading Was

Ask any group of middle-aged Americans to think back on learning to read, and vibrant and complex memories flood in immediately. Some people start retelling stories about Dick and Jane and Spot and Puff, while others joke nervously about which reading level they were assigned to at the age of six. Most can recall lugging a thick basal text to their reading group each day, where the main activity was round-robin oral reading—children took turns reading aloud while the teacher listened for mistakes. Many of us remember feeling dread as we waited for our turn; others recollect the embarrassment of being corrected in front of everyone. Many of today's adults recall being separated from their friends by reading levels: some of us were shamed by being assigned to the low group, while others were pleased (and maybe just a little pressured) to find ourselves among the "top" readers. Many of us can even recall the sometimes transparent nicknames given to the three levels of reading groups: maybe no teacher **really** called our groups "Bluebirds," "Sparrows," and "Buzzards," but even as first graders, we could always crack the code that camouflaged the winners and losers groups.

Most children of the 1950s and 1960s will also remember plenty of phonics, an important and time-consuming subject with its own curriculum, chunk of the school day, and slot on the report card. In Harvey Daniels' elementary school in semirural Minnesota, for example, phonics was taught right after lunch every day, using special books and worksheets, and never coordinated with reading, which was done in the morning. He remembers the kids' groans when the teacher commanded them to take out their phonics materials: it always signalled a long bout of silent seatwork, in which kids circled countless "same" or "different" sounding words.

What books did kids read in those days? In many classrooms, the basal textbook was the only source of stories, while the *Weekly Reader* and the science and social studies textbooks filled in the nonfiction side. Few classic tales or stories were contained in the basals because these texts were expressly designed to provide synthetically controlled vocabulary and complexity. Children's books were read at home, if at all.

Was this kind of reading instruction effective? Test scores, many of which measured the presumed "subskills" of reading, when looked at over the long term, were remarkably stable. (See Roger Farr's [1986] and Gerald Bracey's [1977] works on the historically flat pattern of U.S. reading achievement.) Most children learned how to decode simple print, but we did not create a nation of mature, effective, voluntary, self-motivated, lifelong readers; on the contrary, most Americans gladly stopped reading the moment they escaped from school. For those graduates forced to read on the job, their employers complained often and publicly about the inability of young employees to comprehend even the simplest texts that work put in front of them.

Yet, some of us ex-students from this dull era, a sizeable fraction of us in fact, **did** somehow learn to read beyond the mere functional level, and we became fluent, skillful, lifelong readers. How did this happen? We share a vague sense that much of our learning, our positive connecting with literacy, happened outside of school—in families and communities where literacy was honored and practiced. When we think back on our warmest, most personally powerful formative experiences with reading and writing, those events are predominantly out of school. So does this mean that schools really can't teach reading? Or that the cultural situation of students constitutes an impenetrable ceiling over their reading achievement? Teachers and researchers today are finding encouraging answers to these tough questions.

Reading the New Way

Marianne Flanagan teaches fifth grade on the South Side of Chicago, in a school and in a district where the basal reading program still holds sway over most teachers and administrators. Indeed, for part of each day, Marianne teaches reading the old way, leading her thirty-two African American and Hispanic students through stories in the basal text, sometimes even marching them through the exact questions prescribed by the thick, glossy teacher's manual. One thing Marianne won't capitulate to, however, is leveled groups; her whole class reads and discusses the basal stories together.

At other times in the day, however, Marianne is experimenting with some very different reading activities. Today, for example, her kids' "Literature Circles" are meeting. You can hear the noise long before you reach the door to Room 213: the buzz of Literature Circles reverberates halfway down the stairwell. When you enter the room, you may not believe that **any** reliable communication could happen amid this din; indeed, that's exactly what a few of Marianne's colleagues, long bred to equate silence with effective teaching, seem to think as they walk past her doorway, shaking their heads. Yet, as a visitor gets acclimated to the noise level, joins a few student groups, and tunes in to the ongoing conversations, the sophisticated quality of these literary discussions becomes apparent. Children are tucked up close to each other, talking with animation, seriousness, and sometimes passion about the novels they have chosen to read. Among the titles being discussed today are Katherine Patterson's *Bridge to Terabithia*, H.G. Wells' *War of the Worlds*, Beverly Cleary's *Dear Mr. Henshaw*, and Sid Fleischmann's *The Whipping Boy*. Using a set of rotating, formalized roles (Discussion Director, Literary Luminary, Vocabulary Enricher, Illustrator, and Connector), the children purposefully and independently discuss questions they have brought to the groups themselves. Even the all-boys group in the corner by the window is completely engrossed and on-task with *Lord of the Rings*. "Man, don't you understand that this book is supposed to be a fantasy?" Robert somewhat impatiently queries his circle-mate, Tyrone. "It's not real, it's a fantasy!"

Marianne skirts around the edges, dipping briefly into the groups. Sometimes she gets drawn into the conversation if the book is one she has read herself; but she hasn't read all the books kids are discussing and she doesn't worry about it. Her job is not to translate or interpret the books; it is to facilitate the work of the groups.

Marianne's Literature Circles turn traditional reading instruction upside down in almost every dimension. The children, not the teacher, pick the books. Everyone doesn't read the same book at the same time. In Marianne's room, with thirty-two kids, there are usually eight different four-member groups meeting at once, each reading a different novel. The groups are temporary and are formed on the basis of student interest in a particular book. The readings are not short, linguistically controlled basal stories, but real, whole, unabridged books, drawn from the worlds of children's, young adult, and classic literature. Kids are pursuing their own discussion questions, not following the cues of the teacher or textbook study questions. The reading teacher's role has shifted from being a presenter/questioner at the center of attention to that of an unobtrusive, quiet facilitator. In this activity, the students are the ones making the assignments, raising the questions, doing the talking and working. Perhaps most distinctively, the kids love **this** reading class. They lobby Mrs. Flanagan for extra meeting time and complain noisily whenever school events rearrange the schedule and shortchange their Literature Circles.

Marianne has worked hard over three years to get the kinks out of the Literature Circles: to refine the roles kids play in their groups, to help the children internalize the importance of coming prepared to circle meetings, and to build a growing classroom library of multiple copies. Nothing has been easy; she's had to solve plenty of problems along the way. During the same time, she's also been experimenting with other Best Practice activities: reading literature aloud more often, introducing regular journal writing, starting a writing workshop, publishing more student work, making more class time for literature discussion. Indeed, one of the things that makes Marianne such an effective reading teacher, especially in a setting where one could think of many

excuses, is that she loves to experiment. Marianne is willing to try any promising idea, and she doesn't worry about preplanning an innovation to the last
detail. She's secure in herself and doesn't obsess about what might go wrong.
She just tries things first and then fixes the weak spots later. She doesn't expect
perfection of herself or her kids. She knows that for kids and teachers alike,
growth comes through risk taking and mistake making.

As she looks back on her efforts with Literature Circles, Marianne says
that the work has been worth it: "My students are more eager and enthusiastic to meet in their discussion groups. They like the idea that they may
choose the books and be in charge of their own discussions. I frequently hear
conversations about what book the group plans to read next. The power of
the Literature Circles has instilled in the students an incredible thirst for
reading. Book-club orders have increased. There are more trade books visible in my classroom than ever before. On library days, children return
eagerly displaying their selection for the week. The librarian has indicated
that the children request works by many authors and various genres. Also, I
have noticed more of my children using their time wisely by reading in
between assignments."

A Look at the Standards Documents

Reading invariably comes first on everyone's list of basic academic skills,
and we certainly endorse that ranking. After all, much of the information that
school (and life) has to offer is coded in print, and students' ability to unlock
and use all this knowledge depends on fluent, skillful, critical, and independent reading.

This means that any credible model for the genuine refreshment of
American schools had better start with a solid plan for teaching reading.
Although the field of reading certainly has been subject to its own passionate internal controversies over the years (which we review later on), the basic
professional consensus about state-of-the-art reading instruction is stronger
and clearer than ever today. Reading is no longer such a mystery: the experts
now understand quite well how it works and agree, at least 95 percent, about
how to teach it to the vast majority of children.

In a moment, we will list the basic qualities and characteristics of Best
Practice in reading instruction, the approach validated by our most reliable
research—the model toward which Marianne Flanagan and thousands of other
teachers are moving. After we detail the ingredients of good reading instruction for students of all ages, from kindergarten through high school, we will
give special consideration to the most critical and controversial phase of
reading instruction: beginning reading with primary-grade children.

Several landmark documents have defined Best Practice in reading. An
early base for national standards was established by the influential *Becoming*

a Nation of Readers, published by the National Institute of Education (Anderson et al. 1985), and *New Policy Guidelines for Reading,* issued by the National Council of Teachers of English (Harste 1989). In 1992, the NCTE and the International Reading Association (IRA) were selected by the U.S. Department of Education to develop a set of unified national reading and writing standards. However, in 1994 a dispute arose over the direction of the project and federal funding was withdrawn. The NCTE and IRA elected to continue the standards work on their own, and the Department of Education, for its own part, decided not to fund any other competing group.

Meanwhile, several other national groups—most prominently the New Standards Project (NSP) and the National Board for Professional Teaching Standards—were developing their own literacy guidelines. The NSP, a joint venture of The National Commission on Education and the Economy and the University of Pittsburgh Assessment Development Laboratory, issued guidelines for reading instruction in 1995. Its standards, while philosophically harmonious with the previous NCTE and IRA documents, also raised the ante: among other things, the NSP called for all students to read twenty-five books per year, effectively mandating far more beyond-the-textbook and across-the-curriculum reading than the majority of U.S. students currently receive. The NSP also developed a variety of new assessments that tried, with varying success, to move beyond simplistic multiple-choice format into performance assessment, measuring students' higher-order thinking.

Meanwhile, the National Board for Professional Teaching Standards (NBPTS), as a first step toward developing a certification process for all teachers, developed a framework for literacy education that was highly congruent with the NCTE/IRA documents, as well as with the NSP. Unfortunately, the certification process that was later harnessed to the NBPTS' admirable standards was highly controversial. Because the NBPTS is essentially a contest in which individual teachers compete against colleagues to win professional recognition, complaints have been raised about its divisive effects on faculty collegiality, as well as its failure to offer equal access to teachers of minority students, its announced commitment to flunk the majority of teachers who apply, and its drain on scarce staff development funds that might otherwise benefit whole faculties. In spite of these regressive side effects, the NBPTS language arts standards themselves were a valuable contribution to the deepening picture of what good literacy instruction looks like.

At last, in 1996, the IRA and NCTE issued their long-awaited *Standards for the English Language Arts,* and shortly thereafter began issuing a series of books that illustrated the standards in classroom practice. In spite of the delays and funding disputes, the resulting document became the definitive national description of good teaching and learning of literacy. While the material that elaborates and applies the IRA/NCTE standards fills more than a dozen volumes, the standards themselves are simple and direct.

IRA/NCTE Standards for the English Language Arts

1. Students read a wide range of print and nonprint texts to build an understanding of texts, of themselves, and of the cultures of the United States and the world; to acquire new information; to respond to the needs and demands of society and the workplace; and for personal fulfillment. Among these texts are fiction and nonfiction, classic and contemporary works.

2. Students read a wide range of literature from many periods in many genres to build an understanding of the many dimensions (e.g., philosophical, ethical, aesthetic) of human experience.

3. Students apply a wide range of strategies to comprehend, interpret, evaluate, and appreciate texts. They draw upon their prior experience, their interactions with other readers and writers, their knowledge of word meaning and of other texts, their word identification strategies, and their understanding of textual features (e.g., sound-letter correspondence, sentence structure, context, graphics).

4. Students adjust their use of spoken, written, and visual language (e.g., conventions, style, vocabulary) to communicate effectively with a variety of audiences and for different purposes.

5. Students employ a wide range of strategies as they write and use different writing process elements appropriately to communicate with different audiences for a variety of purposes.

6. Students apply knowledge of language structure, language conventions (e.g., spelling and punctuation), media techniques, figurative language, and genre to create, critique, and discuss print and non-print texts.

7. Students conduct research on issues and interests by generating ideas and questions, and by posing problems. They gather, evaluate, and synthesize data from a variety of sources (e.g., print and non-print texts, artifacts, people) to communicate their discoveries in ways that suit their purpose and audience.

8. Students use a variety of technological and informational resources (e.g., libraries, databases, computer networks, video) to gather and synthesize information and to create and communicate knowledge.

9. Students develop an understanding of and respect for diversity in language use, patterns, and dialects across cultures, ethnic groups, geographic regions, and social roles.

10. Students whose first language is not English make use of their first language to develop competency in the English language arts and to develop understanding of content across the curriculum.

11. Students participate as knowledgeable, reflective, creative, and critical members of a variety of literacy communities.

12. Students use spoken, written, and visual language to accomplish their own purposes (e.g., for learning, enjoyment, persuasion, and the exchange of information).

Obviously, these literacy guidelines are quite broad and general. They address much more than reading: incorporating writing, speaking, and listening; reaching out to nonprint media and technology; and pointing toward a wide range of higher-order thinking skills. Now we need to focus more narrowly on reading and its teaching. To the extent that reading can be looked at as a separate school subject and set of skills, what are the consensus standards about teaching it well? In describing Best Practice in reading, we draw on all the standards projects mentioned previously. It's worth noting, though, that among these thousands of pages of reading standards issued over the past decade, some of the clearest and most concise explanations appeared in the original 1989 NCTE Policy Guidelines report, which we draw on freely here, with special thanks to its author, Jerome Harste.

Qualities of Best Practice in Teaching Reading

Reading means getting meaning from print. Reading is not phonics, vocabulary, syllabification, or other "skills," as useful as these activities may be. The essence of reading is a transaction between the words of an author and the mind of a reader, during which meaning is constructed. This means that the main goal of reading instruction must be comprehension: above all, we want students to understand what is on a page.

Reading is a process. Reading is a meaning-making process: an active, constructive, creative, higher-order thinking activity that involves distinctive cognitive strategies before, during, and after reading. Students need to learn how skillful, experienced readers actually manage these processes.

Hearing books read aloud is the beginning of learning to read. This practice should extend from the home into school and up through the grades. Teachers should set aside time each day for reading aloud, selecting good literature of high interest to the children.

Beginning reading instruction should provide children with many opportunities to interact with print. These include listening to stories, participating in shared book experiences, making language-experience stories and books, composing stories through play, enacting dialogue, and reading and writing predictable books. From the first day of school, books and paper and pens should be in the hands of children. If children do not have extensive book experiences before coming to school, teachers must begin by providing the reading experiences they have missed. Children should never be treated as though they have not had meaningful encounters with print; in fact, even those from the most deprived families have experienced much more interaction with written symbols than most teachers acknowledge. Instead, teachers should build from and extend what children already know about language, whether that knowledge begins with fairy tales in parents' laps or from the rich (but educationally underestimated) print appearing on TV screens.

Reading is the best practice for learning to read.   Independent reading, both in school and out, is strongly associated with gains in reading achievement. Effective teachers of reading provide time for silent reading every day, encourage reading for varying purposes, and develop creative ways for students to respond to literature.

An effective reading program exposes students to a wide and rich array of print and goes beyond the use of the basal.   Access to interesting and informative books is one of the keys to a successful reading program. An effective reading program goes well beyond the basal reader to include a variety of materials both narrative and expository, provides experiences with children's literature, and encourages students' self-selection of books. The classroom is stocked with a rich array of print of all kinds, including poetry, newspapers, and trade books, as well as content-area books and magazines. Fiction and nonfiction materials should be selected on the basis of quality and student interest and should represent a wide range of difficulty, not only so kids can experience successful independent reading regardless of their level, but also so they can challenge themselves by moving up in difficulty. Content-area teachers should use multiple textbooks and trade books, and set up environments in which students work on self-selected topics within the required units of study. Children in all classrooms should have free and unlimited access to print materials.

Choice is an integral part of literate behavior.   Children should be permitted to choose reading materials, activities, and ways of demonstrating their understanding of the texts they have read. Reading skills and strategies should be presented as options rather than as rules to be universally applied under all reading conditions. Teachers should issue invitations to read and write rather than make reading and writing assignments. Teacher-directed instruction in which all children in a classroom or reading group are required to make the same response may indicate that this guideline is not being met.

Yes, but . . . how can the teacher manage when kids are all selecting and reading different books? Won't many kids waste time or choose unchallenging books?

Providing choice doesn't mean having a "lax" classroom in which little work is done or expectations are low; it simply recognizes the limits of whole-class or group instruction. The teacher can entice kids to try good literature through brief "book talks." She can use quick one-on-one conferences to help them make good choices. Short conferences later on help the teacher to learn how the child is progressing in work habits, engagement, and understanding. When a student is found not to be reading or improving, the teacher's response is to observe, identify the problem or blockage, and design an activity or find a piece of reading that will address the student's need. All along the way, just as with whole-class instruction, the teacher must make behavior norms clear.

Teachers who use strategies like Marianne Flanagan's Literature Circles, described previously, find that the children inspire one another to read and think more. They become involved in heated discussions and debates. One group overhears the excitement in another group and decides to read their book next. Kids share their ideas with one another and with the teacher in frequent journal entries. Motivation to work hard is probably the most powerful when it comes from your peers.

Teachers should model reading.   Teachers should read widely along with their students, explaining their own meaning making and book choosing, telling how they select books, authors, or genres. It is vital that children get to observe a "joyfully literate adult" using print in a variety of ways every day. This modeling not only encourages children, but it also demonstrates for them the complex mental processes involved in skillful reading, especially when the teacher "thinks aloud" about her own meaning-making processes. Children need to see this kind of literate adult behavior over and over to internalize it. Teachers who are good models help ensure that schools don't just graduate students who can read, but people who **do** read.

Effective teachers of reading help children actively use reading and writing as tools for learning.   Research shows that children tend to use learning strategies in the manner in which the strategies have been taught. Teachers can demonstrate the usefulness of reading and writing by offering opportunities for children to engage in meaningful reading and writing during content-area instruction. Brainstorming questions before a subject is explored, pursuing library research projects, integrating reading and writing in content-area learning logs, and classroom activities that engage students in reading and writing in the ways they are used outside of school—all these strategies meet this guideline.

Children learn reading best in a low-risk environment.   Children should be permitted and encouraged to test hypotheses of interest to them. Experiences should be planned that allow children to take risks, make inferences, check their conclusions against the evidence at hand, and be wrong. Reading teachers should help children understand that predicting what will happen next in stories, jumping to conclusions, and confirming or disconfirming their hypotheses are effective and powerful reading strategies rather than errors. For the most part, teachers should avoid questions that require right answers and instead ask questions that encourage a diversity of well-supported responses. Constant penalties for being wrong, as well as an overemphasis on correctness, grades, and being right undermine the climate of safety that young readers need to take risks and grow.

While teachers are becoming sensitized to their own overdomination of reading instruction, and now are rightly concerned with structuring more student-directed reading activities such as sustained silent reading (SSR) and reading workshop, they still need and want to do direct teaching. When they take the floor for a structured reading lesson, **teachers should provide pre-reading, during-reading, and after-reading activities**. Before reading, teachers help students activate prior knowledge, set purposes for reading, and make predictions. During reading, teachers help students monitor their comprehension and construct meaning. After reading, teachers help students savor, share, and reconstruct meaning, and build connections to further reading and writing.

Young children should have well-structured instruction in phonics.   For children just beginning to read—typically in kindergarten and first grade—it is vital to learn the sound-symbol relationships of written language. Indeed, if children do not crack the alphabetic code, reading (i.e., getting meaning from print) is effectively blocked to them. Therefore, skillful teachers provide young children with a variety of high-involvement activities that help them understand, manipulate, and use sound-symbol correspondences. (See the following section for more details.) But even as teachers offer this important experience, they also keep in mind that phonics is not a subject in itself, but rather a tool, and that the goal of teaching word analysis is comprehension. They carefully balance the time given to phonics in the early grades with other key beginning reading activities, and group their students carefully, though temporarily, so that those who have already mastered phonics can go on and read, rather than sitting through whole-class phonics lessons they do not need. In any case, such brief, well-designed lessons in phonics normally should be concluded by the end of second grade.

Teachers should provide daily opportunities for children to share and discuss what they have been reading and writing.   As part of this sharing time, the teacher should help children to value the reading strategies they already have, and also continually introduce and invite children to try new ones. Author-sharing times, peer-tutoring activities, and collaborative research projects can help students reach this goal. Observing this work will provide teachers with much information for gauging students' progress.

In an effective reading program, students **spend less time completing workbooks and skill sheets**. There is little evidence that time spent in these activities is related to reading achievement, and they often consume precious chunks of classroom time. Effective teachers critically evaluate so-called "skill activities" before giving them to students and replace them, where appropriate, with whole, original activities. Once students have internalized the behavioral norms of reading and writing workshops, these structures provide far more valuable and individualized "seatwork" than any pre-packaged ditto sheet.

Writing experiences are provided at all grade levels.   As well as being valuable in its own right, writing powerfully promotes ability in reading. Effective teachers provide a balance of different kinds of writing activities, including both individual, self-sponsored writings like those in journals or writing workshops and teacher-guided writing activities that help students try new genres, topics, and forms for writing.

Reading assessment should match classroom practice.   Many of the current standardized reading achievement and basal series tests focus on atomized subskills of reading, and do not stress what we really value in reading, which is comprehension. The best possible assessment would occur when teachers observe and interact with students as they read authentic texts for genuine purposes, and then keep anecdotal records of students' developing skills, problems, changes, and goals in reading.

Yes, but . . . when does the teacher find the *time* to do all this?

Many of the more traditional approaches to reading eat up loads of class time without moving kids ahead very efficiently. During traditional round-robin reading, when kids take turns reading aloud, only one child is actually reading at any given time, while twenty-nine others often barely pay attention. When kids are completing boring worksheets, the teacher often needs to focus on maintaining discipline. When every activity focuses on teacher direction and information giving, the teacher cannot give children much individual attention—or much sense of their own motivation for reading.

However, when every child is reading a book of her own choosing, the teacher can easily stop by the desks of three or four or five kids who need special attention or who are scheduled for a conference. It's not difficult to jot down a couple of phrases on the outcome during or after each conference. When children are discussing books in small groups, the teacher can circulate, observe the comments of individuals, and take note of children's level of understanding. Indeed, as teachers grow into the habit of "kid-watching," they begin to notice all sorts of behaviors that indicate the level of individual children's literacy. This kind of observation is clearly a major part of the teaching described by Lynn Cherkasky-Davis at the end of this chapter.

Schools that are effective in teaching reading have an ethos that supports reading.   These schools are characterized by vigorous leadership and high expectations for student learning. These schools maintain well-stocked and well-managed libraries with librarians who encourage wide reading and help match books to children.

We think that the foregoing list of ideas and practices is amazingly simple. These recommendations certainly don't require any complex, futuristic innovations; instead, they invite a thoughtful return to certain fundamental instructional strategies that amply predate the basal era: reading good literature aloud; having kids read lots of whole, real books; providing much writing practice; encouraging the patient and varied discussion of the ideas in books; making the teacher a model of literacy.

Beginning Reading: The Special Case of Primary Grades

The so-called "Great Debate," a forty-year war of words that pits phonics-centered instruction against more holistic approaches to reading, has reached a furious new intensity in recent years. The opposing sides constantly launch research studies, invective, and accusations at each other, making primary-grade teachers feel even more nervous about whether they are doing the right thing for the beginning readers in their care. The most recent version of this battle has erupted around the official repudiation of Whole Language in California and the ascendancy of the idea of "decodable text," which arises from research on disabled readers in Texas. We've written elsewhere about the California debate and the dubious kinds of "scientific proof" used to support various partisan and extreme reading programs (Daniels 1996); here we want to offer some perspective on phonics for educators and parents who are just trying to do the right thing for children.

The current phonics fuss is so severe that we should probably remind ourselves that phonics is only one ingredient in a balanced K–12 reading program. To begin with, phonics has nothing whatsoever to do with reading instruction much above second-grade level (for most kids, first-grade level), except for students with specific learning disabilities or other special needs. Once the sound-symbol code is learned, it is learned. We would no more teach phonics as part of, say, a fifth-grade "reading" program than we would teach the alphabet to high schoolers in the name of "writing."

Even during the first couple years of school, phonics is still only one part of an effective reading program. Lessons in word analysis must share time with other key activities that help young readers grow, including hearing good literature read aloud, experimenting with writing, and talking about the ideas found in books. Most reading experts agree that phonics, as one of four or five necessary daily activities, should occupy no more than 20 or 25 percent of total reading time. Furthermore, even given this limited role in a narrow span of grades, we must remember that the majority of children, 60 to 80 percent, by most estimates, can learn all the sound-symbol strategies they'll ever need from naturalistic, fluent, ample real reading and (especially) from practicing spelling in their own writing. Indeed, many children crack the alphabetic code at home before ever coming to school. All this puts the role of phonics in perspective: in a responsible and balanced K–12 reading program, phonics amounts to less than 5 percent of the instructional efforts teachers make.

Phonics may be a proportionally small element of an overall reading program, but it is truly a key part. Phonics is a gateway skill; if you don't crack the alphabetic code, you can't read. Happily, most kids do break the code and do so early. However, a fraction of children, which disproportionately includes poor and minority kids, does not acquire their sound-symbol ideas in this embedded, automatic way, but they can learn and use these strategies when they are taught directly. To be certain that we give all children what they need without overteaching phonics for some and underserving others, we must carefully balance time and activities. Here is a suggested schedule for first-grade reading based upon consensus, mainstream research (Flippo 1998; Braunger and Lewis 1997), and providing proportionate time allocations.

Time Allocations for First-grade Reading

twenty minutes—the teacher reads good literature aloud

twenty minutes—phonics and word study (word sorts, word walls, word families, spelling patterns)

twenty minutes—shared reading (teacher-guided discussions of reading, including language-experience stories, big books, other literature)

twenty minutes—independent reading at child's fluency level (wordless books, picture books, chapter books)

twenty minutes—writing (journal keeping, stories, responding to literature; using age-appropriate developmental spelling and drawing)

In this model, explicit, separate instruction in sounds and words constitutes about one-fifth of the reading and language arts time—a fractional but important component. Nor are the recommended phonics activities dull, mechanistic drills, but rather lively strategies like *word sorts* (when kids arrange words on cards into different kinds of sets), *word walls* (where students cover the classroom walls with huge inventories of words, grouped and regrouped by the way they sound or what they mean), and *personal dictionaries* (in which students record words as they learn how to say, spell, and read them), along with a variety of whole-group choral, singing, and chanting games. Furthermore, sound-symbol relationships get explicit and embedded attention any time that children are spelling words in their own writing, as well as when the teacher draws their attention to sounds, letters, or syllables as part of a guided reading lesson.

Once young children are reading fluently (i.e., consistently applying their phonetic knowledge in making meaning from print), phonics instruction should be over. Children will continue to practice their newly acquired phonetic understandings by reading age-appropriate texts and writing using developmental spelling. The portion of the day previously devoted to word analysis in the form of phonics can now be used on vocabulary study. Further phonics instruction may well be needed for a small fraction of children who still need help, and should certainly be offered to them individually or in small groups, but not as whole-class phonics lessons that would waste most classmates' time.

None of this seems so very radical or controversial. Indeed, we sometimes think that "The Great Debate" should be renamed "The Fake Debate" because no responsible educators—including the most partisan Whole Language leaders—have ever advocated withholding phonics instruction from children. The genuine questions are the same as they always have been: how should we teach phonics, for how long, and to which students? And how does phonics fit into the larger picture of a complete, well-balanced literacy education?

The latest phonics fad to sweep the nation, the subject of hyperbolic claims as this book goes to press, is the idea of "decodable text"—the notion that young children should be exposed only to print that has been created synthetically to include specific, limited sets of sounds that children previously have been taught systematically (Foorman 1997; Texas Reading Initiative 1997). This theory, of course, makes all real children's literature illegal: forget the millions of children who thought otherwise—neither *Mother Goose* nor *Charlotte's Web* is even vaguely "decodable." The doctrine does grudgingly permit classic literature to be read aloud, but only if parents and teachers *hide the book* from their children. You see, looking at real print, according to the decodable doctrine, confuses the kids. Taken to its logical conclusion, decodable dogma means parents must shield their children's eyes from virtually all environmental print—including such dangerous texts as "McDonald's," "Sesame Street," or "Disney World."

Well, the theory of decodable text obviously leaves its advocates with some serious explaining to do. Ever since written language was first invented around 3000 B.C., children have been learning to read just fine by sitting in their parents' laps, looking at real books. And so far, archeologists have unearthed no clay tablets of "decodable text" from the ruined schoolhouses of ancient Sumeria. Are we to believe that some noneducators in modern-day Texas suddenly have discovered that no one in human history learned to read "the right way"? And is it even slightly plausible that if a "right way" were suddenly discovered in 1996, it would involve dumbing-down stories to present children with the textual equivalent of baby talk? It makes one quake to think what would happen if the decodable text theorists took over *oral* language acquisition. They'd probably make parents stop using real language in front of their children and require them to babble instead. Decodable talk, you know.

The "evidence" supporting decodable text has been used to attack Whole Language, a grassroots, teacher-driven movement that has been slowly spreading through the country for twenty years. The term *Whole Language* is essentially a new label for a quite enduring approach to literacy education that traces back through *literature-based reading* all the way to Deweyian progressive education in the 1920s and 1930s. Just for the record, the body of research—the "scientific proof"—supporting Whole Language is vast and deep. The key strategies of Whole Language teachers—using real classic children's literature, developing thematic teaching units, reading aloud daily, structuring regular independent reading, teaching multiple cueing systems for decoding unknown words, creating student-led literature discussions, stressing early writing with developmental spelling, holding regular teacher-student conferences, teaching writing as a staged process, involving parents in the classroom, stressing collaborative versus competitive activities, involving students in goal setting and self-assessment, using the teacher as a model of adult literacy—all have been validated by decades of research.

So where do ideas like decodable text come from and why are people so quick to believe them? In this particular case, decodable text came from overgeneralizing the results from some limited research on seriously disabled readers in Texas. The objectivity of the researchers and the validity of their research methodology were highly questionable. The investigators, completely inexperienced in Whole Language teaching, purported to test its validity by having their own assistants implement it, after being trained by them. Much more problematically, the studies focused on a very small and atypical population—significantly disabled and disadvantaged readers—rather than "normal" beginning readers. Some but not all of the study's phonics-intensive interventions seemed to work better than the researchers' deviant version of Whole Language, as measured by the standardized tests chosen by the researchers. While it is entirely plausible that delayed or disadvantaged readers really would benefit from extra attention to sound-symbol relationships, this research had no implications whatsoever about instructional practices for the great majority of children without these very unusual handicaps.

However, these severe limitations on generalizability did nothing to stop the researchers or their political patrons from promoting the studies as the answer to reading for *all* children. Within months, their "scientific proof" formed the basis for legislation in the California assembly and the race for national misapplication was on. In less than a year, it arrived in Illinois, where our state department of education dutifully issued a "Little Red Reading Book," which lionized the Houston research while omitting almost all the mainstream, validated, responsible reading research of the past century.

Why do the public and their representatives in government get so exercised about phonics and reading instruction when most pedagogical debates leave the citizenry cold? It is amazing that phonics, an activity that occupies only one-twentieth of the reading curriculum, can generate so much controversy, acrimony, and misunderstanding, so far beyond the workaday world of the primary classrooms where it belongs. Why do ordinary civilians even attend phonics coffees, paint pro-phonics placards, and petition their local school board for more phonemes?

The late educational writer James Moffet (1988) had an explanation: he theorized that some parents are unconsciously terrified of their children's dawning intelligence and independence, symbolized by learning to read. Phonics appeals to these fearful parents because it is the only approach to reading instruction that takes meaning out of the bargain. If a child spends most of her reading time enunciating *t*s and *d*s, and never reads any actual text, then she can never encounter any dangerous ideas, or learn to think and read for herself. This links up with some parents' tendency to prefer grammar instruction over writing practice, because if their children only do drills and never write original texts, they can never *utter* any dangerous ideas. Although Moffet never would have said it so inelegantly, people who want to replace whole, balanced, beginning reading programs with phonics-only curricula may be unconsciously trying to keep children ignorant.

When looked at through Moffet's lens, "The Great Debate" isn't a clash over phonics at all, but rather a symbolic skirmish in the broader culture wars between two opposing paradigms of teaching and learning, of child development, and of human nature. In a sense, research studies and journal articles are beside the point; this is a religious controversy. After all, if one believes that children are intrinsically sinful beings who will tend toward evil unless tightly controlled and amply punished, it leads to a very different kind of classroom than the one you design for people who are seen as basically good, worthy of love and respect, and capable of self-actualization. If you believe that books—especially religious scriptures—have only one correct meaning, which is inherent in the text, you are not going to be very friendly to schools that teach children to explore a wide range of books and ideas, to make critical evaluations of what they read, to write and discuss their own responses, and to develop strong and independent voices as authors.

So, finally, we realize that this simple, innocent segment of the public school curriculum called *reading* is perennially afflicted with crazy ideas, crackpot fads, instant cures, political vendettas, professional posturing, and even religious disputes. Nor, unfortunately, does this tangled state of affairs seem likely to change in the immediate future. This leaves all of us raising or educating children to find our own way through the adamant claims and counterclaims. In the end, wise teachers and responsible school districts will ground their reading instruction in a deep understanding of children and in the recommendations of reputable, enduring professional organizations that are guided by the preponderance of responsible research and have shown that they have children's best interests at heart.

How Parents Can Help

The crucial role of home experience in the development of effective readers is well documented and has been widely publicized in the professional and popular press. By and large, when children grow up in print-rich homes, where parents model reading and writing, where literacy is a tool of day-to-day family life, where stories and words are treasured, where reading aloud is a bedtime ritual, good readers usually emerge. But the research doesn't single out only perfect, academic middle-class homes: many effective young readers also watch a lot of TV, and even poor families who don't own many books can create rich print experience with newspapers and library books.

Teachers still worry about the children who come from homes where none of these foundational experiences are known about or practiced. Some parents are so stressed, distracted, or exhausted by their own lives that there's no energy left for reading at home; obviously, this set of problems especially afflicts poor, single-parent families, and it is their kids who disproportionately fail at reading. What can or should the school do to support at-home literacy?

Without becoming intrusive missionaries, teachers can begin to help parents teach, showing them how simple and natural literacy-building experiences can be integrated into the family routine. In Lynn Cherkasky-Davis' kindergarten class in Chicago, each week begins with all the children reporting about the stories their parents read to them most recently. In many inner-city schools like this, teachers assume that parents cannot or will not read to their children regularly. Lynn simply requires that some adult—a grandparent or sibling or neighbor if parents aren't available—does the job. The project begins at the start of the year, when Lynn meets parents for the first time and tells them about the importance of reading to their children. She's sensitive to the parents' own limitations as readers, and makes it clear that strict "school" reading isn't the goal. "Just look at the book together, read it, enjoy it, talk about it," she says. She's pretty direct, though. She tells the parents that their kids must come prepared each week having been read to. In the face of Lynn's energetic commitment to the bedtime stories, saying "no" just isn't a viable option. Once each week, when Lynn's five-year-olds go home to the housing projects where most of them live, each child has identified a book to read that evening with someone. Those who don't have books at home leave the classroom carrying a plastic-handled bag with a book inside, withdrawn overnight from Lynn's large classroom library. These books are always treated with care and respect, and returned on time.

In Milwaukee, Jim Vopat runs a Parents' Literacy Project where inner-city parents meet one night a week to build confidence in their own reading and writing, as well as their ability to help their children. In a safe, trusting atmosphere of fellow parents, they hear stories read aloud, they write or draw in response to these stories, they keep journals, they interview each other, they learn how to use their public library, and they learn exactly what's happening in their children's schoolrooms from their kids' teachers. During each weekly meeting, parents try one new literacy experience within the deepening familiarity of the workshop; then, every week, they return to their own families to try out a variation of this experience with their own children: reading aloud, talking, making lists, interviewing, keeping journals. Everything the parents do in the workshop underscores and supports what teachers are doing with their children every day.

But what about those kids whose parents and families, for whatever reason, currently fail to nurture literacy? What do we do for these children? If we are convinced of the power of parent-child reading (and we certainly are), and if this experience has been missed, then it must be substituted, provided in some analogous form, by the people at school. Every child needs to go through the "lap stage" of reading development, ideally at the ages of two, three, and four with a parent. But if this doesn't happen, then the school must help the child recapitulate this critical experience with someone else, later on. Echoing the intimate, one-to-one reading relationship is exactly what special tutoring programs like Reading Recovery are all about. School must be ready, not to **be** the parent, but to fill in analogous adult-child literacy experiences if they are missed at home. If some children aren't connecting with reading because they were never drawn into it the way most kids are, through intimate personal modeling, then they must be offered some lap learning, too. Ditto sheets and phonics drills can never fill this elemental gap.

How Principals Can Support Best Practice in Reading

In Chicago, our group of about one hundred teacher-leaders from the Illinois Writing Project and the Best Practice network have been giving reading workshops for teachers for several years. Recently, these teacher-consultants created a list of advice for aspiring Best Practice principals:

1. **Be a reader and a writer.** Visit classrooms and read aloud or discuss books with children. Write and share your writing in the school community.

2. **Be an audience for students.** Read kids' work on the walls and in classrooms. Let the authors know you've read and appreciate their

words. Have a principal's mailbox, and enter into active correspondence with kids.

3. **Make sure classrooms have all the supplies and materials needed** to create a true workshop atmosphere; above all, this means **books**. Help teachers tap the right budget lines to buy books, encourage parents to raise money for more books, hold bake sales if necessary to get more books into classrooms. For their writing workshops, teachers and kids need plenty of paper, pens, folders, notepads, scissors, blank books, Post-it notes, computers, and typewriters. You can purchase a hot-glue book-binding machine for less than $300—a superb way to honor the importance of kid-made books.

4. **Celebrate literacy in your school.** Incorporate reading and writing into special school events and programs. Create space and occasions for displaying and sharing written work noncompetitively. Everyone needs an audience, not a contest with few winners and many losers. Contests that stress only quantity of reading or writing degrade literacy and invite cheating.

5. **Help teachers communicate with parents** *proactively,* to let them know how reading and writing are being taught, and why the school has embraced this model of literacy education; and *reactively,* to step in and support the teachers when uninformed or skeptical parents question or attack their instructional choices.

6. **Use your role as instructional leader, supervisor, and evaluator.** Let teachers know it's good to use language arts/reading time to read aloud, do storytelling, conduct a daily reading or writing workshop, share dialogue journals, or adopt other promising practices. In your classroom visitations, evaluate congruently: if teachers are using a process approach, you'll see nonpresentational, highly individualized, student-centered workshop activities in which the teacher mostly takes a facilitator/coach role.

7. **Work at the district level to align the curriculum guide and the standardized testing program with the holistic approach** (e.g., help the school get off atomized subskills and onto real reading and writing). It may be necessary to work for the *dis*adoption of basals, skill-and-drill workbooks, certain standardized tests, or other materials that undermine the new curriculum. Talk to fellow administrators and help them understand and buy into the new paradigm.

8. **Bring in teacher-consultants, the local writing project, or other genuinely facilitative people to help your teachers** explore the philosophy and classroom practices of progressive instruction. After the workshop phase, provide the necessary follow-up and support to help teachers "install" new practices in their classrooms.

9. **Nurture continuing growth and emerging peer leadership among your staff** by sending volunteer teachers to workshops, courses, summer institutes, or teachers-training-teachers events. Support your outstanding and committed teachers by giving them a chance to lead, to share with colleagues.

10. **Even though you don't have time, read the research, scan the journals, and pass along ideas and articles to your teachers.** Order books that teachers request for their own growth—from Heinemann, Stenhouse, Richard Owen, the NCTE, IRA, Teachers College Press, Boynton/Cook, and others.

11. **Help teachers get TIME to talk about teaching together,** exchange ideas, work on joint projects, think and grow as a faculty.

Connecting with Progressive Principles

It is important to recognize how the many recommendations in this chapter reflect our thirteen principles of Best Practice outlined in Chapter 1. While we leave it to the reader to recognize these connections in later chapters, we want to offer here at least one "guided tour"—showing that, in the field of reading, those thirteen principles are not just *pro forma* abstractions, but rather powerful guides to both general policy making and practical teaching. Later, in Chapter 8, we return to the principles to reflect on ways they are commonly applied in all of the major school subjects.

Perhaps the most fundamental theoretical construct in Best Practice reading instruction is its **cognitive,** psycholinguistic orientation, which simply says: children learn to read the way they learn to talk and school ought to operate accordingly. When young children are learning to speak, adults do not try to teach them the subskills of talking or put them through speaking drills. Mostly, what they do is surround kids with real, natural language, talking to them and around them all day long. Young children listen and vocalize, playing and pretending with sounds and words, creating successively better approximations of talking. Parents treat all of the child's utterances, no matter how fragmentary or idiosyncratic, as meaningful. If a nine-month-old infant murmurs "ta," nearby parents are likely to rush to the cribside exclaiming: "She said 'Daddy'!" Parents intuitively offer heaps of immediate feedback and indiscriminate encouragement for any communicative effort. By the time children are five, they have mastered more than 90 percent of the structures of adult language, not through direct teaching or correction but through immersion and experimentation.

In the same way, children learn to read **experientially**, by being immersed in real texts and real literacy events from an early age. No one needs to break down written language into segments or sequences for kids; they learn best **holistically**, when they are exposed to complete, real texts that exist in their world, including books, menus, signs, and packages. They learn to read by playing at reading, by making closer and closer approximations of reading behavior. A familiar example of this is when young children memorize a book that has been read to them repeatedly, until they can recite it while the pages turn. Parents sometimes worry that this is not "real reading" because the child has "only" memorized the words—but teachers recognize that this is the essence of becoming a reader.

Children who are learning to read are not just receiving and absorbing a system that exists outside of them, but rather they are **constructing** that system anew, for themselves. In oral language, we recognize this phenomenon in kids' use of unheard forms like *goed* or *foots*. The existence of these invented but entirely logical word forms shows that the kids are not merely absorbing an adult system, but are creating new intermediate language systems, using rules that they originate. In literacy, we see this constructivism clearly in the phenomenon of invented spelling, where children who are first trying to spell the short vowel sounds will substitute from their existing inventory of long vowel sounds the one with the most similar manner of articulation in the mouth. And, of course, all this literacy learning is individually developmental—that is, it proceeds through a number of predictable and well-defined stages. Although the sequence is roughly the same for all kids, the age and rate of change will differ significantly from child to child.

Children learn to read best when the materials they read are **authentic and challenging**. The old textbooks and the latest "decodable-text" products all are designed to offer near-perfect materials for beginning readers by limiting length and controlling vocabulary, but this intention backfires. These synthetic stories are often harder for kids to read than seemingly more complex and uncontrolled literature. This is because logic or playfulness or sheer interest are often sacrificed in the effort to control linguistic features, thus rendering the story unreadable. In other words, the fake easy stuff is harder to read than the real hard stuff. Of course, there's nothing too new or shocking about this—it always has been somewhat peculiar for adults to "control reading vocabulary" for six-year-olds who know and routinely use words like *pterodactyl, tyrannosaurus,* and *Jurassic.* We must not belittle the powers of emerging readers any more than we patronize young speakers. If we respect what kids can do with language, they'll not only tell us a lot, they'll also choose whole, real books for themselves.

Wise reading teachers are **student-centered**, encouraging kids to follow their interests and choose their own books regularly. One of the insights from family literacy research is that in the ideal parent-child bedtime episode, the child, not the parent, picks the book and sets the pace for reading and talking. Learning to read, like learning anything else, is driven by curiosity and interest on the part of the learner; if these elements are missing, the motive for learning is absent. In school, when teachers always and only choose the stories or books to be read, motivation is sacrificed for most students most of the time.

Literacy is **socially** constructed and socially rooted. While there are obviously some solitary moments in the reading and writing process when the reader or writer bends her head over a page, still the beginning motive and ending payoff for most literacy work is profoundly social. In the "real" world, people read and write for some social purpose, to get or give information from or to someone else, for some real reason. The traditional school approach to literacy has cut kids off from this social connection and purpose for literacy, rendering too many reading activities into solitary, alienating exercises. Instead, children grow better amid rich and regular interaction, in classrooms where **expression** and **collaboration** are the norm, where there are many chances to read and write and talk with other readers.

Of course, classroom reading instruction itself is a complex social enterprise with powerful relationships and meanings. For just one example, students traditionally have been grouped in three levels for reading by some measure of "ability," past reading achievement, or intelligence. We now recognize that this practice is unnecessary and often destructive: the research on such tracking shows that it invariably harms the achievement and attitudes of the children assigned to the middle and low groups, while proving little or no benefit for even the highest ranked group. Today we seek a more heterogeneous classroom, not just for the **democratic** model it offers, but also for the genuine richness and stimulation that a diverse class of readers provides. Teachers are perfecting classroom structures and strategies—like Marianne Flanagan's Literature Circles—that make tracking irrelevant and unnecessary. Such activities are inherently individualized; when kids group themselves, flexibly and temporarily, no one needs to be classified and segregated. Everyone benefits and everyone can work in the same room.

The progressive approach also stresses that reading is a **cognitive** process. Not only do growing readers need to develop a repertoire of cognitive strategies for predicting, monitoring, and evaluating texts, they also need to practice metacognition. Kids need to become **reflective,** actively examining the meanings they construct from what they read, as well as noticing their own reading processes and strategies. This is one reason why journal keeping and portfolios are both such important tools in Best Practice classrooms. Both of these structures invite students to reflect regularly—keeping track of what one reads and writes, jotting down responses and plans, reviewing one's own history and accomplishments as a reader, and pondering the nature of one's own thinking processes.

EXEMPLARY PROGRAM

A Day in the Life of a Developmentally Appropriate Whole Language Kindergarten

Lynn Cherkasky-Davis

Foundations School
Chicago, Illinois

We begin at the beginning, with a program that encompasses young children's entire day at school. The account is in the words of Lynn Cherkasky-Davis, of the Foundations School in Chicago, a school that serves students from extremely poor neighborhoods. A visitor knows when he or she is approaching Lynn's room because the kids' work overflows out the door and down the hallway. A metal cabinet full of narrow drawers with a child's name on each serves as the class mail system. A huge bulletin board is encrusted with materials—not the usual neat rows of kids' essays or drawings because it couldn't possibly hold it all. Instead, there are ceiling-to-floor charts listing books the class has read in two categories: "real" and "make believe." A "brick wall" of reading is composed of colored squares with the title of a book someone has read on each and an inscription above stating, "This brick wall is under construction. Hopefully, it will take a lifetime to complete. Welcome to our community of readers." One section holds letters from parents, the mayor, visiting teachers, letters from the kids to visitors, and "letters to an absent teacher." Several projects hang in thick clusters, each grouped together on a ring. One is a science project, "Fish or Not Fish," with a news article about whales and dolphins, and the kids' own research on sea animals. Another, on math, includes a read-aloud book, *Fruit Salad*, plus charts and graphs comparing the numbers of each kind of fruit the children brought in to make fruit salad. A book on a particular theme—*In My Bed*—is grouped with kids' versions of similar stories and maps of their bedrooms. But there's plenty more going on *in* the room, as Lynn will tell you.

The children enter the classroom for family-style breakfast at 8:45. They "sign in" outside the door, thereby taking their own attendance. The first day of school, the children may draw their "portrait" as signature or may choose a color and shape to use as "theirs" until they are able to sign their names or parts thereof. From the first day, children use writing for authentic purposes, never for isolated tasks. We sign up for photographs, learning centers, literature preferences, activity helpers, field-trip participation, etc.

Following breakfast, the children blend into the rest of the classroom for family reading. Children may read alone in pairs or in small groups. Volunteer parents, a part-time teacher aide, and I read with the kids. We listen to them picture read, approximate read, or actually read—whatever stage they're at. Children may listen to literature tapes while following along in books, or read from charts, content-area books, big books, literature sets, songbooks, poetry, library books (with their mandatory library cards), magazines, literature from home, and/or materials written by other children (or themselves). Our reading period illustrates the cooperative and collaborative nature of the classroom. The students are comfortable risk takers who, without hesitation or embarrassment, will simply tell you what they can't read or need help on. But they don't stop there because they've learned how to gather context clues and continue on with their story. While the myriad of reading activities goes on, I am a participant as well as an evaluator, making note of further instruction particular children need.

Calendar activity comes next, and we address many content areas: math, language arts, science, and social studies. We tally, seriate, categorize, classify, write, pattern, order, and rhyme, as well as develop number, pattern, place value, and time sense. We classify the days as rainy, sunny, windy, etc., count them up, discuss the groupings, and so on. The children take the lunch tally and record the day's weather. They are empowered to do all "housekeeping business," following patterns set by children before them.

Several times throughout the day I read to the children. The books are alternately of my choosing (on a theme or particular subject matter) and the children's. Discussion follows. Another reading activity is Author's Circle. When a student has gone through all the writing-process steps and a work is ready for publication, he or she comes to "Author's Circle." Today Shanika read a book she wrote. The class was interested in her title page and how she produced the book, as well as the story and illustrations. Shanika explained her writing process clearly and her sequencing of information. She called for questions and comments when she finished "reading" her story, and the children eagerly verbalized their thoughts and feelings.

The rest of our day is spent in a literate, "hands-on," problem-solving environment. The children circulate to various learning centers—some of their own choosing, some as a result of teacher and child evaluation. Teacher planning underlies all the activities, but they are all child-centered, and the children construct their own knowledge. The classroom is set up to provide opportunities for children to explore, discover, experiment, and create their own sense of their kindergarten world and tasks.

Let's tour the classroom to view some of these activities as they're organized in thematic centers. We have a home and family center where children role-play, write shopping lists (while consulting peers and other class resources for color sequencing and correct spellings) and family stories. I am consulted as a last resource. Today I observed Daniel trying to figure out how to spell *hamburger*. He asked a peer who replied, "I don't know. Research it in our 'food text set.'" Not finding it there, Daniel flipped through previous lunch menus, looking for "H" and "A", two letters he was sure about. He found "Ha" and knew it was the word he was looking for. Daniel has been encouraged to be self-sufficient, self-directed, and resourceful. He could construct what was unfamiliar from the familiar.

Continuing our tour, we find the science center filled with things to manipulate and experiences to create and re-create. In the transportation center, children can build "cities" in conjunction with the construction site adjacent to it. They map their designs, post signs, and write speeding tickets. They may also explore various means of travel and building.

Around the corner from the manipulative shelves and math materials are art materials, musical instruments, and easels in the fine arts center. Back-to-back are the writing table and publishing and book-binding cart. At the typewriter and resource desk (the only desk in the classroom), the kids experiment with reading and writing connections. Here they keep writing portfolios and "works in progress," and conduct conferences with peers. These are but a few of the learning centers at which the children can work.

What ties all these centers together are books, books, books, and writing, writing, writing! Out in the hallway you will find the kids' mailboxes. Children write to each other, to me, parents, the principal, volunteers, upper graders, and anyone else. Today, two children wrote a publisher, explaining that the tape for "Goldilocks" does not match the words in the book in two places. In the mailboxes one will find some of the "letters" and stories written in full sentences with just about perfect spelling. Others combine functional spelling, letter strings, recognizable words, and pictures. Some may be pictures only, but interestingly, each is addressed, dated, and signed by its author in clear letters. On the walls around the room, the writing that the children do fills so much space that we're continually in trouble with the fire marshall. One chart shows how each child is progressing with various tasks surrounding the bedtime story parents are expected to read to them each week. In another area, pocket folders hold projects kids have done as part of their "Book of the Month" club. Each kid has a folder with his or her name and picture and a list of the books selected. Charts list things in various categories—"Films We Have Seen," titles of books about families, books about food, etc. Another display lists various items, one hundred of which children brought for counting—one hundred noodles, one hundred beans, etc. There are so many charts that some must be rolled up and pinned. This leaves room for others and allows us to unroll them when we need to take a look at them.

Looking around my class today, I saw that Lakita and Jinae were busy in the writing center. Jinae had written a story, and Lakita was her peer reviewer (yes, even in kindergarten!). She posed such questions as, "Did you leave spaces between words? What kind of letter must your sentence begin with? Check your punctuation. You need to research the spelling of that word." (The children follow my style of integrating phonics instruction into reading and writing.) With that, Jinae got up from the writing table and went to the housekeeping/grocery area where she thumbed through menus, recipe cards, shopping lists, books, magazines, and the class lunch menu to figure out the spelling of the word in question. She committed the word to memory but knew that it needed an "s" at the end to make it plural. This she doublechecked with her peer reviewer. (The previous phonics lesson of "More Than One" had not been an isolated lesson, but was a natural part of a story we wrote as a class. The plural "s" was introduced during the story where it was needed. Thereafter, it will be pointed out often in books we read. All letters and sounds are learned in this context of real literature.)

When Jinae's writing process was completed, another classmate was summoned to do final editing. This kindergarten child followed a checklist the class devised earlier in the year. "Do the illustrations match the print? Are the pages numbered and ordered? Is it ready to be bound?" At this point, Jinae signed up for a writing conference with me during the next learning-center time, to fine-tune her work and decide on the binding (as it is a multiple-page story). She will then go to the publishing center and, with the help of a parent volunteer, bind her work. After completion, Jinae is ready for Author's Circle. Anyone who collaborated on the story will join in.

My eyes scanned the room. Donald was in the math center making three-part patterns and recording them. He was using unifix cubes, chips, and colored toothpicks. Another student was checking him. Donald put his findings in his math journal and went on to seek out books in our class library that will reinforce his patterning (although books, like writing materials, abound at all learning centers). Donald has integrated math and reading. I noted this behavior in my anecdotal records. That, with his recordings, will go into his evaluation portfolio. Using this and my "kid-watching" guide, we will evaluate his progress, needs, and desires.

Moving about this small room, which has no front or back but is fluid in its space, I discovered several children moving ahead with what had begun, earlier in the week, as a teacher-directed, whole-class activity on categorization. The kids often take off with such activities and go as far as they are currently able. Today Antoine, Octavius, and Carla had taken books out of the classroom library and were categorizing them by "books about school," "books about home," or "books about food." They went one step farther and noted that some books fit into more than one category and some fit into neither. Carla wandered off to the beanbag to read one of the books about food she thought looked interesting. She then decided to make a "text set" with other books on cooking and placed them in the kitchen area. Meanwhile, the two boys continued to list the books in their appropriate categories. Octavius called Nicky over to read the list with him. Nicky then decided to categorize his own list. He chose another section of books and classified them according to "real" or "make-believe." He took a survey of classmates to discover and graph how many preferred fact over fiction and vice versa. When I left him, he was graphing his findings.

It was time to clean up for lunch. Later in the day, we wrote in our journals, used a guided imagery activity during writers workshop, did shared reading, listened to each others' bedtime stories during Literature Circle, followed guided reading, sang, and worked on problem solving during a whole-group "hands-on" math lesson. Following this, children broke into small groups (by interest, not ability) to delve further into the new math concept with parent volunteers. After they recorded their discoveries in their math journal, the children were free to return to the learning centers.

Patrice sat in the rocking chair by the post office drafting a letter to her pen pal. She needed to spell *spaghetti*. She went to the recipe box and child-written menus in the kitchen/housekeeping area (a popular spot today). She asked her friends for help and seemed satisfied. Seeing that I was busy with another child, she consulted her classmates first. Although she knows she can come to me after she has exhausted all other resources, she did not this time. However, I looked at the letters to her pen pal and saw, "We eight bus spgte pasta." (We ate busghetti, spagetti, pasta.)

When the second learning-center time was over, we used what I had learned from the children during the day for our culminating lesson. We brainstormed a list of food categories: meats, liquids, junk, pasta. Of course, under the pasta category, we listed spaghetti. Several purposes and subject areas were served here: consensus building, reading, writing, speaking, listening, science, nutrition, and setting another research base. This chart will be kept at an appropriate spot in the classroom, available as a resource.

At 2:15 we completed our daily diary. Children got coats and signed out. Patrice quickly went to the "out" mailbox, carefully opened the envelope to her pen pal, and did something to it. The bell rang and she didn't have time to reglue or tape her envelope. I told her I'd do it. Patrice gave me a hug, filled out her exit slip, and ran to meet her auntie.

The children are home. For the first time since 8:30, it is quiet. I read the student exit slips (I too am a learner!) and review and alter my plans for the rest of the week: (1) Upper-grade Reading Buddies will visit; (2) parent volunteers will reinscribe the stories children dictated into the tape recorder; they will illustrate, order, and enumerate pages to ready them for "read-aloud" or publication; (3) children will direct and act out stories they have written for the preschoolers; (4) the class will design covers for books they bind and sell to authors from other classes; (5) favorite literature will be discussed, compared, and contrasted for Books of the Month club; (6) we will do an author study of Stephen Kellogg; (7) scientific experiments, readings, and recordings regarding plants will take place; (8) we'll begin our study of Black authors and illustrators for age-appropriate literature; and (9) a new learning center will be introduced. My lesson plans are a hodgepodge.

There is never enough time. I read Patrice's exit slip. This is her "lesson plan." It says: "Today: I speled my letter write [sic]. Tomorrow: I want to write a store [story] book." I read the letter she has written her pen pal before sealing it. It says, "We eight bus, spgte, pasta" as before, but she has crossed it out. (The children do not erase, knowing I like to see the steps in their writing process.) It now says: "We eight spaghetti." No reading series, ditto page, isolated skill drill would have accomplished this.

Creating a literate, problem-solving, risk-free, higher-level critical thinking, encouraging environment for all twenty-five Patrices, taking into account their individual needs, desires, and learning styles—this is the embodiment of Best Practice in any developmentally appropriate classroom, not just kindergarten, but preschool through grade 12. Best Practice is not vase-filling. Rather, it is fire-lighting.

Works Cited

Anderson, Richard C., Elfrieda H. Hiebert, Judith A. Scott, and Ian A. G. Wilkinson. 1985. *Becoming a Nation of Readers: The Report of the Commission on Reading*. Washington, DC: National Institute of Education.

Bracey, Gerald W. 1997. *The Truth About America's Schools: The Bracey Reports, 1991–97*. Bloomington, IN: Phi Delta Kappa Educational Foundation.

Braunger, Janet, and Jan Lewis, 1997. *Building a Knowledge Base in Reading*. Portland, OR: Northwest Regional Educational Laboratory.

Daniels, Harvey. 1996. "Whole Language: What's the Fuss?" *Rethinking Schools*. (Fall).

Farr, Roger. 1986. *Reading Trends and Challenges*. Washington, DC: National Educational Association.

Foorman, B., D. J. Francis, T. Beeler, D. Winikates, and J. M. Fletcher. 1997. Early Interventions for Children with Reading Problems: Study Designs and Preliminary Findings. *Learning Disabilities,* 8, 63–71.

Harste, Jerome C. 1989. *New Policy Guidelines for Reading: Connecting Research and Practice.* Urbana, IL: National Council of Teachers of English.

International Reading Association and National Council of Teachers of English. 1996. *Standards for the English Language Arts.* Urbana, IL, and Newark, DE: International Reading Association and National Council of Teachers of English.

Moffett, James. 1988. *Storm in the Mountains: A Case Study of Censorship, Conflict, and Consciousness.* Carbondale, IL: Southern Illinois University Press.

National Center on Education and the Economy. 1995. *New Standards: Performance Standards, English Language Arts, Mathematics, Science, Applied Learning.* Washington, DC: National Center on Education and the Economy.

Texas Reading Initiative. 1997. *Beginning Reading Instruction: Components and Features of a Research-based Reading Program.* Texas Education Agency.

Suggested Further Readings

Allen, Janet, and Kyle Gonzalez. 1998. *There's Room for Me Here: Literacy Workshop in the Middle School.* York, ME: Stenhouse.

Atwell, Nancie. 1998. *In the Middle: Writing, Reading, and Learning with Adolescents.* (Second Edition.) Portsmouth, NH: Boynton/Cook.

Avery, Carol. 1993. *And with a Light Touch: Learning About Reading, Writing and Teaching with First Graders.* Portsmouth, NH: Heinemann.

Bayer, Ann Shea. 1990. *Collaborative-Apprenticeship Learning: Language and Thinking Across the Curriculum K–12.* Mountain View, CA: Mayfield.

Clay, Marie. 1993. *Reading Recovery: A Guidebook for Teachers in Training.* Portsmouth, NH: Heinemann.

Cunningham, Patricia. 1995. *Phonics They Use.* New York: HarperCollins.

Fountas, Irene, and Gay Su Pinnell. 1996. *Guided Reading: Good First Teaching for All Children.* Portsmouth, NH: Heinemann.

Goodman, Kenneth. 1996. *On Reading.* Portsmouth, NH: Heinemann.

Hindley, Joanne. 1996. *In the Company of Children.* York, ME: Stenhouse.

Hyde, Arthur, and Marilyn Bizar. 1984. *Thinking in Context.* New York: Longman.

Raphael, Taffy, and Kathryn Au, eds. 1998. *Literature-based Instruction: Reshaping the Curriculum.* Norwood, MA: Christopher-Gordon.

Rief, Linda. 1992. *Seeking Diversity: Language Arts with Adolescents.* Portsmouth, NH: Heinemann.

Rhodes, Lynn, and Curt Dudley-Marling. 1996. *Readers and Writers with a Difference. A Holistic Approach to Teaching Struggling Readers and Writers.* Portsmouth, NH: Heinemann.

Routman, Regie. 1994. *Invitations: Changing as Teachers and Learners K-12.* Portsmouth, NH: Heinemann.

Shannon, Patrick. 1990. *The Struggle to Continue: Progressive Reading Instruction in the United States.* Portsmouth, NH: Heinemann.

Short, Kathy, Jerome Harste, and Carolyn Burke. 1995. *Creating Classooms for Authors and Inquirers.* Portsmouth, NH: Heinemann.

Weaver, Constance. 1994. *Reading Process and Practice: From Socio-Psycholinguistics to Whole Language.* Portsmouth, NH: Heinemann.

Reading Resources on the Internet

The International Reading Association is the largest and most influential reading society and cocreator of the literacy standards. For association news, research bulletins, publications, and conference announcements, visit **http://www.ira.org.**

Although a K–12 organization, the membership of the NCTE is predominantly middle and high school teachers, and NCTE is the top source of information on reading, literature, and writing for secondary students. **http://www.ncte.org.**

The Center for the Study of Reading at the University of Illinois was an original partner in creating the national literacy standards. For its activities and research reports, visit **http://www.uiuc.edu.**

Literature teachers of all grade levels, and especially teachers facing censorship issues, rely on the American Library Association at **http://www.ala.org.**

RECOMMENDATIONS ON TEACHING READING

Increase	Decrease
Reading aloud to students	Exclusive emphasis on whole-class or reading-group activities
Time for independent reading	Teacher selection of all reading materials for individuals and groups
Children's choice of their own reading materials	Relying on selections in basal reader
Exposing children to a wide and rich range of literature	Teacher keeping his/her own reading tastes and habits private
Teacher modeling and discussing his/her own reading processes	Primary instructional emphasis on reading subskills such as phonics, word analysis, syllabication
Primary instructional emphasis on comprehension	Teaching reading as a single, one-step act
Teaching reading as a process:	
Use strategies that activate prior knowledge	
Help students make and test predictions	
Structure help during reading	
Provide after-reading applications	
Social, collaborative activities with much discussion and interaction	Solitary seatwork
Grouping by interests or book choices	Grouping by reading level
Silent reading followed by discussion	Round-robin oral reading
Teaching skills in the context of whole and meaningful literature	Teaching isolated skills in phonics workbooks or drills
Writing before and after reading	Little or no chance to write
Encouraging invented spelling in children's early writings	Punishing preconventional spelling in students' early writings
Use of reading in content fields (e.g., historical novels in social studies)	Segregation of reading to reading time
Evaluation that focuses on holistic, higher-order thinking processes	Evaluation focus on individual, low-level subskills
Measuring success of reading program by students' reading habits, attitudes, and comprehension	Measuring the success of the reading program only by test scores

3

Best Practice in Writing

How Writing Was

Steve Zemelman looks back on his own education in writing: "In third grade, we were assigned a geography project, and I chose Canada. I went home, pulled out the family copy of the *World Book Encyclopedia*—recently bought by my father for just such moments—and marked the passages I planned to use. I can still picture the maps with those tiny corn plants and coal cars that showed the products of various regions. I meticulously traced a map of Canada, complete with corn plants and coal cars, and put my mother to work typing up the passages direct from the encyclopedia. 'Are you *sure* this is how you're supposed to do this?' she asked diplomatically. I told her it was just fine and began designing the cover. I don't know what the teacher really thought, but I received the expected "E" for excellent. We were shown no models of what a good report might look like, had no audience for our work, generated no particular questions that we wanted our research to answer, and received no help getting started. It's no surprise that we simply copied from encyclopedias.

"On another occasion, we were to write about a family event. I innocently described the exhilaration I felt when my father drove at high speeds on family road trips. This clearly violated the teacher's sense of propriety and she humiliated me before the entire class with a lecture about my shocking disrespect for the law."

"Oh, yes: there were also all the boring routines—endless worksheets and sentences to be copied fifty times off the board, equating writing with punishment. The purpose of book reports was simply to prove that you read the book, so even if the reading was enjoyable (*Winnie the Pooh* and *Wind in the Willows* were my favorites), the reports were just a job to be dispensed with as quickly as possible. Otherwise, writing meant 'spelling quizzes.' I was good at those, which is no doubt one of the reasons I felt comfortable when I became an English major and then a teacher. And it meant 'handwriting.' As a lefty, I was regularly ridiculed, told that I held my pencil wrong, and that my script was hopeless. I really don't know why I didn't come to hate writing as most of the other kids did."

Writing the New Way

Although Pat Bearden is now a consultant for the Center for City Schools, the classroom where she taught until recently was a second/third-grade "split" in an urban school. The children there range from some who are highly verbal and acclimated to school routines to a few who angrily resist and occasionally children who appear to sleep much of the time. The neighborhood is made up of small single-family bungalows, but the residents are poor and working-class people. It is not unusual to be approached for a handout as you park your car outside the school, and children talk of the violence they see and fear around their homes. The building, however, is a newer cinder-block structure, with brightly painted hallways. Pat participated in extended inservice programs on teaching writing, and is now an accomplished teacher leader.

Pat never would have allowed the sad waste of time that was the "Canada" project to get started in the first place. From the beginning, Pat resolutely wanted to try new techniques for teaching writing, most of them aimed at giving **kids** ownership of their own work. As she introduced more writing activities, her classroom developed in unexpected directions, and the results surprised and pleased her. One major technique used by Pat and many other teachers involves journal writing in a workshop-style setting.

Here's what we observed on a typical day: As the kids come chattering back from gym, they can be seen getting to work on their journals. Children move around the room to find comfortable positions for working. Three boys join a visitor at the back table. Two girls scoot underneath another table to share their writing—they are supposed to read to a partner once they've finished a piece. Two others settle in a hidden corner, planning excitedly.

When it's time to share work aloud, everyone demands a turn. Danyelle offers to share hers, and Cherisse giggles nervously. "There are parts the boys aren't allowed to hear," Danyelle warns. She begins to read her piece, an explanation of how to play "Girl Talk," a game that adult non-TV fanatics may never have heard of. When she reaches a crucial spot, all the girls in the room jump up and point menacingly at the boys: "COVER YOUR EARS!" The boys instinctively obey, Danyelle plunges on, and the girls scream deliriously. Everyone is laughing, including Pat.

Later, on a more serious note, David reads a piece about why various kids in the room make him angry, ticking off a list of insults and conflicts that occurred out on the playground. The children listen solemnly and discuss the justice or injustice of each charge. David is writing *for* himself, *to* the class. Later, Cherisse is found upset, at the back of the room, and David comes over to see what's wrong. She opens her journal to a page of captioned cartoon squares with a stick-animal in each. "These are my pets," she says. "They've all died." The teacher, briefly at a loss as to what to say next, quietly says, "It's hard being a child, isn't it?" David and Cherisse nod their heads gravely.

These children are discovering how writing connects with their own lives and extends in many directions. In the events described above, writing serves many purposes, including entertainment, explanation, persuasion, and personal expression. It is a valued channel for human pleasure, negotiation, and feeling, rather than just a classroom exercise. The children are likely to remember this basic writing lesson long after they've forgotten the day-to-day events of this classroom.

What is the teacher's role in this writing workshop? Sometimes Ms. Bearden would simply sit and write along with the kids—after all, if writing is important, adults should be doing it too. Often she could be seen circulating among the children to monitor the stages of each one's effort and to see who needs immediate help. Then she'd spend a few minutes each with several children, her responses attuned to particular needs. If a child can't think of a topic, Pat asks questions about what is occurring in the child's life at present, such as places visited, stories read, events that evoked a feeling. If a piece is supposedly "finished" but needs revising, she asks what part the child likes best and what aspect of writing he wants to improve. Pat can press the issue because each child has a folder where all writing is kept, along with a sheet that lists elements the child has mastered and several the child and teacher have agreed to work on next.

How does the teacher help children improve mechanics and spelling? She stresses that in the journals and first drafts, children should focus on ideas and hold off on corrections until later—this is their "sloppy copy." Because most beginning writers actually worry *too much* about correctness, she tells them to draw a "magic circle" around words they are unsure of, so they can comfortably take care of corrections later. Then every few weeks, each child chooses a favorite piece from his or her folder to revise and polish for publication and a grade. Children work on revising in pairs, consult classroom editing "experts," and learn to look for correct examples in the surrounding environment of books and posters. Before an editing session, Ms. Bearden will choose one element that she considers most needed in the children's work and gives a focused "mini-lesson" on it.

Publication is a vital activity in this classroom. Every day, children take turns reading for a few minutes at the end of each writing session. The walls are covered with the kids' writing, including interviews of one another with mug-shot photographs attached, written responses from adult guests and famous people the class has written to, and a student-of-the-week bulletin board where each child gets a turn at displaying his or her best work, family photos, bios of favorite music stars, and other materials displaying their special interests.

Ms. Bearden uses evaluation carefully to promote learning, and does not let it overload her or discourage the children. She uses the "responsibility sheets" in the children's writing folders to keep track of the aspects of writing that children have learned (including both mechanics and processes). She holds evaluation conferences with children after they've finished and polished up their pieces to discover what the children perceive they've improved and learned, and she closely "grades" only the polished pieces that are turned in once every two to four weeks. Even on those, she actually marks just samples of a few items, so the writers can focus on patterns of errors and look for some themselves instead of having the teacher do all the work.

Qualities of Best Practice in Teaching Writing

The blossoming of research and pedagogical experiment on writing has created a clear and consistent picture of an effective writing program. Following are some of the main characteristics and strategies employed in a classroom like Pat Bearden's. These practices are supported by a body of research generated in the past thirty years, a key summary of which is found in George Hillocks' *Research on Written Composition*, and which we previously reviewed at length in *A Community of Writers* (Zemelman and Daniels 1988). These ideas most recently have been affirmed in *Standards for the English Language Arts*, created by the IRA and the NCTE (1996), the twelve main principles of which appear on pages 29–30. These exemplary writing activities have been further elaborated in the NCTE's *Standards in Practice* series (1996), four volumes that take readers into primary, intermediate, middle school, and high school classrooms where writing is part of an integrated approach to literacy education (Crafton 1996; Smagorinsky 1996; Sierra-Perry 1996; Wilhelm 1996).

All children can and should write.

> A preschooler recites a story from her "pretend" writing and then repeats it nearly word-for-word much later, as her parents chuckle over her "cute" imitation of adult behavior. But it's more than that. The constancy of meaning she associates with written symbols shows that the child not only comprehends what literacy is, but is already practicing it.

Most children have been writing long before they reach kindergarten. Beginning writers can make meaningful marks on paper, starting with drawings and moving through their own imitation writing, to more conventional messages that can be understood by a widening range of audiences.

Children of all backgrounds bring with them to school extensive involvement in literacy, although the particular cultural patterns of language use can vary widely—not just in grammar or pronunciation, but also in purposes and occasions for particular kinds of talk. Teachers can hope to succeed with children from many cultural backgrounds only if they seek to build on these strengths and then explicitly help children widen their repertoires. Therefore, it is vital that teachers listen to children and learn the particular language abilities and needs they bring to school, rather than assume that the teachers' own language styles and customs are universal.

Writing should not be delayed while reading or grammar is developed first; rather, experimenting with the ingredients of written language is one of the prime ways of advancing reading achievement and mastering the conventions of language. Children of all grades need sufficient writing time to fully complete and reflect on communicative tasks, for writing is one of the most complex and important of academic abilities. However, it can be incorporated readily as one of the tools for learning other skills, rather than merely competing for time during the day.

Teachers must help students find real purposes to write.

> Just before Halloween, Ms. McWilliams' class has talked over various versions of folk stories they've heard about a ghost named "Bloody Mary." Now they've decided to write up the many ghost stories they've collected from their families and friends, to produce a Halloween play. All protest vigorously when writing time is over for the day.

When the topic matters to them, children work hard to express themselves well, and are willing to invest time and effort in crafting and revising their work. The best language-learning occurs when students attempt actual communication and then see how real listeners/readers react. Arbitrarily assigned topics with no opportunity for choice fail to give students practice in this most crucial step of writing. Meaningful writing tasks bridge the cognitive demands of school and the issues of students' cultures and developing personalities. If the writer has no real commitment to the topic or the audience, he or she cannot interpret feedback effectively to learn about how words communicate between people.

Students need to take ownership and responsibility. Writing means making choices. The more choices teachers make, the fewer responsibilities are left for students. For a significant percentage of writing activities, students should choose their own topics. When revising, students must be helped to decide which pieces are worth continued work, to look critically at their work, and to set their own goals.

Yes, but ... does this mean that teachers don't teach? Many students don't know how to do these things!

In fact, there's as much or more teaching to do than before, but it's focused on higher-level thinking abilities. Because students don't automatically know how to make their own choices or to critique their own work, good teaching means helping students learn these true authoring processes. Teaching techniques to promote real authorship and good decision making include:

- modeling topic choosing and self-evaluation processes using the teacher's own writing
- brief one-to-one conferences between teacher and student (effective, however, only if the teacher asks real questions about the student's thinking process and ideas, rather than just telling the student what to fix, or using "read-my-mind" queries)
- small-group collaborative work and peer evaluation (which requires training students to work together constructively and meaningfully)

Effective writing programs involve the complete writing process.   Many children, having never seen skillful writers at work, are unaware that writing is a staged, craftlike process that competent authors typically break up into manageable steps. Teachers must help children enact and internalize the stages of writing by using classroom activities appropriate to each stage. The stages many teachers focus on are:

- selecting or becoming involved in a topic
- pre-writing—considering an approach, gathering one's thoughts or information, mapping or diagramming plans, free-writing ideas
- drafting—organizing material and getting words down
- revising—further developing ideas and clarifying their expression for a particular audience
- editing—polishing meaning and proofreading for publication

Teachers can help children recognize that the process varies between individuals and between various writing tasks. Just as with other crafts, not all pieces are worth carrying through all stages, and children can learn from focusing on just one or two stages for a given piece of writing. If they save their revising and editing efforts for their best pieces, the work will be most meaningful and they are most likely to put real effort into it.

Teachers can help students get started.   Support begins from the very start. Children can be helped to develop abundant ideas about their own topics—or, when topics are teacher-assigned, to generate plenty of ideas and connections between the topic and the students' own questions. Lists of these topics and questions can then be kept in students' folders or on wall charts so that students can get started on successive writing tasks on their own. Skillful teachers help student writers gather and organize material for writing through such pre-writing activities as:

- memory searches
- listing, charting, webbing, and clustering raw ideas
- group brainstorming
- free-writing (a specific process for free probing of thoughts)
- large- and small-group discussion and partner interviews
- reading and research on questions students generate

Teachers help students draft and revise.

> "Is this your first draft or did you revise it already?" Lakesha asks her part-
> ner as they sit down in a corner to read each other's work. For these chil-
> dren, revising writing is a regular activity, and they've learned to ask lots
> of questions to find out what stage the writing is at and what needs the
> writer perceives **before** they begin discussing a piece.

Successive stages in the writing process often are ignored in traditional
approaches. Children need to realize that good writing usually does not come
from doing it once quickly and forgetting about it. Teachers can model revision of their own work and conduct group revising of anonymous samples
from previous years so that students see what the process is like. Children
need instruction in how to revise their work. By using role-plays, modeling,
and group problem-solving activities, teachers can illustrate a number of
complex thinking processes:

- reviewing one's work and comparing what one has said to the
  intended meaning
- seeing the words from the point of view of a reader, who may have
  a different point of view and may not know all that the writer does
  about the topic
- being aware of various styles and strategies for explanation that can
  be used to clarify ideas—usually learned through reading and seeing ways that other writers do it
- generating multiple options for expressing an idea and choosing the
  one most appropriate for what the writer wishes to express

Revision is about thinking and communication, not just fixing up mechanical
details. Simply telling how to fix a piece may achieve a better piece of writing,
but it doesn't teach the child the thinking process involved in revising. Once
the teacher has modeled revising processes, she can promote meaningful
revising most by asking real questions about the topic and the process of
thinking about it, questions that very often open up alternatives for the writing.

Grammar and mechanics are best learned in the context of actual writing.
Grammar should be integrated into the later stages of the writing process and
connected with writing in which students have built some investment. When

work that writers care about is going public, they want it to look good and to succeed. In contrast, research has shown for decades that isolated skill-and-drill grammar lessons simply do not transfer to actual writing performance. Beginning writers in primary grades should be encouraged to use invented spelling, so they'll develop fluency and not waste half the writing period waiting for the correct spelling of a word.

"Yes, but . . . don't we owe it to children to help them succeed in our culture by teaching correctness?

As with other aspects of writing, a shift in philosophy does not mean that the teacher doesn't teach about this vital concern. Rather, the aim is to make the teaching efficient and effective, something that most teachers will agree traditional grammar teaching has not achieved. Brief focus lessons can be conducted during the editing phase, when correctness is more likely to matter to the writer (if, that is, the writing has a communicative purpose and destination) and doesn't interfere with motivation or the development of ideas. Specific grammar and mechanics lessons then can be efficiently centered on items appropriate to the kind of writing students are doing, or on needs that the teacher has observed the students actually have.

Grammar elements actually need reteaching less often than we think. When young children get a lot of practice reading and writing, their spelling gradually moves more and more toward conventional forms, even without direct spelling lessons. Teachers can use strategies that promote student responsibility. For example, students can keep lists in their writing folders of the elements of grammar and mechanics they've mastered, so they can remind themselves to proofread rather than wait for a teacher's complaints.

Students need real audiences and a classroom context of shared learning.

A teacher and three junior high writers listen to a fourth read her narrative about the months she spent in bed recuperating from a broken back. She knows it lacks an ending and everyone makes weak suggestions. Finally, she talks more about the experience and declares, "I was never so happy as the day I came back to school." The whole group cheers with delight as they realize she's found her ending—not through directives or criticism, but through supportive talk and listening.

Publication of student writing is vital: making bound books, cataloging student works in the school library, setting up displays in classrooms, in school hallways, at the local library, in neighborhood stores, or even placing class anthologies in local doctors' and dentists' waiting rooms. The old idea that the teacher is the only legitimate audience robs students of the rich and diverse response from audiences that is needed to nurture a writer's skills and motivation.

But connecting student writers with a wider community means more than just sending letters and books to people. Within the classroom itself, building a supportive context for working collaboratively and sharing writing is perhaps the most important step a teacher can take to promote writing growth. In fact, if the students don't experience their classroom as a constructive place where it is safe to try new approaches and say what they really believe, then even the most sophisticated, up-to-date "writing-process" techniques are likely to fall flat. On the other hand, when students hear and read one another's work in a positive setting, they are inspired to try new topics and learn new writing strategies. When they listen to each other's compositions, students discover, by examining their own reaction, what readers need to know in order to understand what writers intend.

Teachers build this kind of interactive learning context through lessons about listening and respecting other people's ideas, and through guided practice working responsibly in small groups on collaborative projects, as well as peer critiquing. The teacher must be sure to model respect and supportive questioning in her own conferences with children as well. Then, in collaborative groups, children can readily learn to give responses that lead the writers to critique themselves and figure out their own improvements. This approach yields much more learning than does direct advice about how to "fix" a piece because the writer experiences the actual problem solving. Writing comes to have greater value because it serves to promote learning and friendship by helping to build a classroom community. This community, in turn, becomes the most powerful motivator available for further efforts at carefully crafted communication.

Writing should extend throughout the curriculum.   Students value writing and use it more when it becomes a part of many other learning activities. Writing is, in fact, one of the best tools for learning any material because it activates thinking. Brief, ungraded writing activities should be used regularly in all subject areas to activate prior knowledge, elicit questions that draw students into the subject, build comprehension, promote discussion, and review and reflect on ideas already covered.

Writing for the study of other subjects need not absorb large amounts of class time or create an impossible paper load. Instead, spontaneous, exploratory efforts can easily be used to make learning tasks more engaging and more efficient. Such activities include:

- First Thoughts—two- to three-minute free-writes at the start of a new topic or unit to help students realize what they already know about a topic

- K-W-L Lists—charts of what students know about a topic, what they want to know (questions or curiosities they have) and then, later, what they've learned

- Admit Slips and Exit Slips—a few sentences on a notecard handed in at the *start* of class, summarizing the previous day's work or reading, or stating something learned (or not understood) to be handed in at the *end* of class

- Dialogue Journals—in response to material read or discussed, students write and react to each other's ideas in pairs, or between student and teacher

- Stop-N-Write—brief pauses during teacher presentations or reading periods when students can jot down responses to ideas, questions they have, or predictions about what is coming next

Teachers can collect these but should read them quickly to learn which concepts are understood and which need further explanation. Students simply receive a "check" to monitor the work or, better yet, a similarly informal prose response from the teacher. (For more about these writing-to-learn activities and their artistic alternatives, see Chapter 8.)

Effective teachers use evaluation constructively and efficiently.   Good teachers know that masses of red marks on a page discourage children and don't really provide effective help for learning how to revise or proofread. They also remember the research indicating that writers grow more by praise than criticism. Better strategies for evaluation include:

- brief oral conferences at various stages of the work
- folder systems for evaluating cumulatively
- focusing on one or two kinds of errors at a time
- official grading of only selected, fully revised pieces
- student involvement in goal setting and evaluation, using reflective portfolios and having regular teacher conferences

---

Yes, but . . . won't all this additional writing and revising and conferencing take more time than a teacher can possibly give?

Students need to write a lot, so much that teachers couldn't possibly mark every error in every paper. However, research strongly shows that the traditional intensive marking of student papers doesn't promote improvement. Instead, a brief conference, or marking a sample paragraph for just one type of problem, results in more real learning. The child then can take more responsibility for making the improvements in the rest of the paper. Students can periodically submit their best revised piece for in-depth evaluation. Thus, different types of evaluation—brief/informal versus extensive/formal are employed to suit particular purposes. Good teachers aim for learning within the *child,* not just achieving a correct manuscript.

Along with more selective marking of papers, the teacher can keep a sheet in each child's folder listing skills and processes the child has learned, plus brief notes on broader aspects of growth. Such record keeping allows for flexibility and individualization, helps the child reflect on his or her progress, focuses on actual learning rather than just the written product, and yet maintains clear accountability for both students and teachers.

Growth in writing always means trying something new and making mistakes in the process. Students must feel trust in the teacher and the situation to take that risk, and evaluation practices should support this necessary condition for learning.

How Parents Can Help

Because the most efficient and powerful language learning humans ever experience—learning to speak as babies—occurs at home and with complete naturalness, home should also be a place where writing is encouraged. Parents can best do this by reenacting the same sort of "scaffolding" they unconsciously used to promote their children's first language learning. Detailed study of early language learning shows that this parental support is characterized by **playfulness** and **closeness**, focus on **meaning** rather than language forms, **modeling** of adult language, regularity and **predictability** of language activities, growth of shared **terminology** for talking about language, and **role-reversal** in which children take the lead to ask questions and make decisions. First and foremost, there should be **pleasure** and **closeness** associated with children's writing at home. Writing done at school or at home should be celebrated and enjoyed, just as families celebrate first words, clever remarks, engaging stories, and other oral-language achievements. Playful notes can be exchanged on the refrigerator, slipped under a closed bedroom door, or included in the child's lunchbox.

The focus should be on the **meaning** of children's writing. Parents can support good teachers' efforts to help children become invested in and take responsibility for the ideas they have. It's best for parents not to respond first or primarily to a grade (whether good or bad) or red marks on a school paper, but to read what the child wrote and take an interest in it. Writing can be given meaning at home by using it for real purposes—chores completed, birthday-present lists, grocery lists, vacation itineraries, labels in family photo albums, invitations, letters to grandparents (encourage them to write back so children get a response), requests to companies for free information and brochures.

Parents can **model** this practical literacy for their children. When a letter goes to Grandma, two sheets can be written at the same time, one from the child and one from an adult in the house—and the two can talk over what they're deciding to say. Reading stories aloud at bedtime also provides models: it's pleasurable and immerses children in the language of good writers, which can increase children's motivation for both reading and writing.

Parents can make literacy regular and **predictable** at home. A special corner with writing implements and a convenient flat surface, regular times for writing and/or reading, ritualized note-leaving, letter-writing, and word-game times all help children to see literacy as a stable and dependable part of their life that becomes a treasured memory of childhood as they grow older. Gifts on holidays and birthdays—such as a desk lamp, blank-page diary, dictionary, computer, or publishing software—can further reinforce the regularity of writing. This ritualizing of writing will lead naturally to special family **terminology** that allows parents and children to further personalize writing and talk over the various activities associated with writing and publishing: book, author, character, ending, illustration, chapter, layout, caption, and headline.

At the same time, it's good for parents to let the child take the lead and to be open to **reversal** of parent-child roles. Children will want to make decisions about what to read and write, how long to work on a project, whether to display or abandon it—and will take more ownership of their writing when they have this control.

Parents should urge that writing be given a high priority throughout their child's school, and should look for and ask about the kinds of teaching practices described in this chapter. When possible, parents should visit their children's classes to help with publishing projects, to tell about the role of reading and writing in their work, or to serve as writing coaches and audiences. Good teachers will organize as much of this involvement as possible.

What Principals Can Do

Obviously, as an instructional leader, a principal will try to encourage state-of-the-art teaching of composition in his or her building. The principal can let teachers know it's valuable to use language arts/reading time to conduct a daily writing workshop, to have journal writing, or to adopt other promising practices. In classroom visitations, a principal should evaluate congruently: if teachers are using a process approach, one will see non-presentational, highly individualized, student-centered workshop activities in which the teacher mostly takes a facilitator/editor role. For long-term development, principals must help teachers get time to talk about writing together, exchange ideas, work on joint projects, think and grow as a faculty. And in the short term, it's important to make sure classrooms have all the supplies and materials needed to create a true writing-workshop atmosphere: plenty of paper, pens, folders, notepads, scissors, blank books, and even computers, printers, scanners, and the software to make complex kid-written books.

Principals also can work at the district level to align the curriculum guide and any standardized testing program with the process approach (i.e., get kids' noses out of dusty grammar drills and into creating whole, original, polished texts). Similarly, principals can help teachers communicate with parents. It's best to do this proactively, to let them know how writing is valued and how it is being taught. Then, when necessary, principals can react to complaints or concerns, defending teachers from skeptical parents and communicating the goals of the program.

Along with this larger leadership role, the principal also should be a model and an encourager and celebrator of literacy, as an adult and professional in the school. The principal can be a writer, writing and sharing writing in the school community. He or she can be an audience for students, read kids' work on the walls and in classrooms, and let the authors know their words have been appreciated. Every school can have a principal's mailbox, so that the leader of the school can enter into active correspondence with the kids.

The principal can make certain that writing is incorporated into special school events and programs. Space and occasions can be created for displaying and sharing written work noncompetitively. The principal can help children and teachers find outlets for "publishing" writing beyond the school building, can help find community sponsors for writing projects, can support kids' efforts to print a magazine, and can even buy postage stamps for letters and pen pal projects. And even though there's never enough time, principals can read the research, scan the journals, pass along ideas and articles to teachers, and order books that teachers request for their own growth.

EXEMPLARY PROGRAM
Writing Workshop in High School

Diane Clark and Rebecca Mueller
Lake Forest High School
Lake Forest, Illinois

Clumps of teenagers gather in small pockets of intent conversation. The room pulses with the rhythm of their chatter, punctuated with laughter, spiked with argument over voice and tone—the sounds of writers at work. Next door in the resource center, three office-style cubicles attempt to contain the spill-over sounds of teachers and students, head-to-head in preoccupied dialogue. Two boys fidget in the outer area, sheaves of paper in hand, pencils tapping, as they watch the clock and wait. A third student pops her head into a cubicle in search of feedback on a poem she recently submitted to the literary magazine. The period ends and harried but exhilarated teachers gather notes and papers, mentally shifting gears into the cadence of the next class.

Such a scenario is a typical occurrence throughout the day at Lake Forest High School (LFHS), where students and teachers are carving new roads of insight into reading, writing, and learning. Our interest and investment have changed the learning environment within English classes and, even more significantly, the writing culture of the school at large. At the core of the change are kids who care about their writing, who have learned that real writing comes from the heart, and who have discovered the power of an informed listener to help shape the impact of their message. Students here have discovered the intimate connection between the process and the product, the rhythm of roles between writer and reader.

Things were not always so. Ours was a traditional, literature-based curriculum, embedded in thematic integrity and enhanced by a carefully sequenced analytic writing program. As a result, students were highly successful readers of assigned literature and writers of significant, in-depth analysis. But a key element was absent from the equation, an element too powerful in its potential to ignore: authenticity. The reading and writing of our students was being guided by teachers' experiences and interests, not those of the learners. Compelled by the research of the last decade, we began to investigate possible avenues into the student experience, ways in which we could bring literature and writing into the hearts and minds of our kids.

Some experimentation during the 1993-94 school year led the English Department to propose an integration of our traditional English program with a student-centered workshop in reading and writing. Guided by Nancie Atwell's (1998) principles of *ownership, time, and response*, we drafted the basic elements of the proposed program. First, and most critical, was the revision of the teacher's classload to accommodate the increased demands of student-centered instruction. Instead of five classes, teachers would have four, with the fifth period devoted to individually scheduled student conferences. Class size would be held at twenty for all reading-writing workshop classes in English I, II, and III and the writing-centered senior electives.

As part of the traditional strand of the program, students would study the required literature—four to five significant works and a sampling of poetry and short stories—and would continue the required analytic writing experience. Within each semester, fourteen in-class workshop days would be created for students to read self-selected books, and another fourteen for them to write on topics and in genres of their own choosing. Teacher-student conferences held both in class and during the extended conference time would afford opportunities for in-depth exploration of the students' current work. The focus of conference and workshop instruction would be the craft of the writer and strategies of the reader as key components in artful, effective communication. Students would be expected to complete at least three to five polished pieces of writing during writing workshop, to make significant progress as readers, to reflect extensively on their growth, and to complete portfolios as a culminating demonstration of their learning. Based on findings of published research and results of our own pilot program, the Board of Education endorsed the proposal in the spring of 1994 and granted us a three-year trial implementation. Our real work had just begun.

For twenty-eight days of the semester, then, our classes took on a dramatic new spin. For half those days, students entered the classroom, grabbed a floor pillow or curled up in a corner and pulled out their latest book, its title likely suggested by a friend, parent, or Barnes and Noble clerk. Following a "status report," a brief statement of their week's progress, they zeroed in on their books and were silently engrossed for the remaining time, jolted from their other-world absorption only when reminded it was time to go. At planned intervals, and in unplanned moments as well, they shared their enthusiastic observations in letters to their teachers and conversed with their classmates about reading, their book-talk often overflowing into the hallways on the way out the door. This was reading workshop.

For the other half of the workshop days, students were engaged as writers. Following a status report similar to that in reading workshop, a brief mini-lesson typically was presented. It often dealt with a writing strategy such as "show-don't-tell" or sharpening focus, or offered a student model of writing for sharing and discussion. Beyond these first fifteen or twenty minutes of teacher-directed activities, the period was theirs to perform any one of multiple tasks that real writers pursue, depending on their stage in the process. Some gathered in pairs for peer conferences or joined their writing group of three or four to discuss their latest revisions. A handful went to the computer lab to work or the library to research their topic. Others sat at desks and drafted, brainstormed, topic searched, or edited. Some wore headsets to keep their focus and some paged through literary magazines for inspiration. The teacher circled the room, checking drafts, answering questions, hearing parts of stories or whole drafts, making suggestions, and keeping the noise to a productive level. Scheduled conferences with the teacher also were conducted. A few students were able to complete them during the class period, while others signed up to confer during lunch or study hall when schedules of teacher and student were compatible. If the sign-up sheet was already jammed, a before- or after-school conference became the only other option. Near the end of the year, the hectic pace only quickened as portfolio completion became the theme and the words *revision, reflection, selection,* and *editing* became the background music. This was what writing workshop was all about.

Four years and a number of minor modifications later, it is gratifying to report not just the success of our experiment, but a revolution in our practices as teachers and learners. This revolution has demonstrated to us the power and potential of student-centered learning. Foremost among its benefits is the level of caring students exhibit about their writing. Where before the writers who really cared were the few seniors taking creative writing or the handful producing the literary magazine, now they are regular freshmen and sophomores who come early and stay late to squeeze in conferences with their teacher before a piece is due. Early in the program, one conference per piece was required. Now that students realize the value of the teacher's individual attention, conferences not only are required, but desired. Before, most students cared about their writing to the extent that it impacted their semester grades. Now, students have grown used to the idea that writing workshop pieces tend to be ungraded, pencil-graded (an interim grade), or graded only as components of the portfolio. Yet, they are still willing to complete multiple drafts to create pieces that impact the reader. In fact, most students would probably be upset if their efforts were reduced to a simple grade. They value the teacher's response because it is authentic and personal.

Caring about writing is an outcome, a later stage in the maturation of writers, determined by several factors. The first is the freedom of expression that writing workshop offers. When initially given free reign in their choice of topics, freshmen students often write pieces that would win John Grisham or Tom Clancy look-alike contests, with predictable plots and clichéd characters. With experience and ongoing instruction in strategies such as Lucy Calkins' writer's notebook (1990) or Donald Murray's writing territories (1996), students learn that good writing is experiential, coming from the heart. Building an atmosphere of trust in the classroom encourages students to take the risk of exploring subjects in which they are emotionally invested. As their writing brings them closer to the point of truth, the sense of risk increases. Yet, so too does their understanding of the impact of honest words on a reader. Students wrestle with the dilemma of sharing their most effective pieces—those with personal significance and authentic voice.

Today, risk taking and publication are at all-time highs at Lake Forest. The annual writing contest of the Illinois Association of Teachers of English (IATE) has always produced a handful of winners from Lake Forest High School. In the spring of 1993, for instance, the year before our new program was adopted, six IATE entries, representing five authors, were award winners. This past year, 1997, we had a record twenty-nine award-winning pieces from twenty-four different authors. Five years ago, the literary magazine staff consisted of ten to fifteen dedicated souls; today, we have an active enrollment of more than eighty and the number of submissions has more than tripled. In 1996, our *Young Idea* magazine won a series of first-place awards: from Merlyn's Pen, the Golden Pen Award; from Columbia University, the Gold Crown Award; and from the NCTE, its highest recognition. In addition, interest in writing has spilled into the popular culture of the high school in the form of a student-inspired poetry rap group. Managed totally by students, "Prozac and Cornflakes" boasts lively and well-attended weekly poetry sessions. The writing culture of LFHS indeed reflects growing participation by kids who care.

This emotional commitment to writing also evolves through immersion in the writing process, an experience that the writing workshop structure invites. Through this holistic, complex, and sometimes messy learning experience, the writing process becomes more than a mysterious term that teachers define on an overhead or in a handout. It becomes real. Through it, the student becomes less the viewer of the completed painting and more the artist giving line, shape, form, and color to the details of the picture. The process of composing, as well as the writing workshop structure that immerses the student in that process, depicts the essence of student-centered learning. This happens gradually. Exploring the murky waters of experience in a writer's notebook, a student searches the depths to find a chest filled with memories, thoughts, and ideas. Sometimes the chest is intact and sometimes the contents are spread across the water's floor. Examining the treasures engages the writer in an inquiry process that includes questions, talk with peers and teachers, new insights, and continual writing, all of which are encouraged by the workshop structure. A topic emerges with a sharper focus, sometimes through threading together bits and pieces, sometimes through study of a single item. In re-creating this discovery for others, the writer moves from the sphere of experience to the sphere of language, the craft of writing. He uses every resource the workshop structure offers to meet the challenges of the task. The student surfaces not only with a sense of accomplishment, but also with another bag of treasures, this time the collection of learning experiences, the expertise and confidence, that fortifies him as he goes on to his next writing adventure. The process becomes a method that he applies to all writing experiences, academic or otherwise, in English class and outside of it.

This immersion in the writing process leads to improved craftsmanship and a deepening sense of pride. In the third and fourth years of the writing workshop curriculum, teachers observe the growing sophistication of the writing and adapt the instruction to meet the students' needs. In earlier stages, mini-lessons tend to focus on such subjects as vivid description, effective use of dialogue, or engaging introductions. Instruction in the junior and senior years turns to the topics of focus, voice, compression of poetic language, manipulation of structure to reinforce meaning, and the use of transitions as conceptual connecting devices. Individual teacher-student conferences during four years of workshop also offer many teachable moments where specific writing strategies can be modeled, discussed, and then embraced as part of the writer's growing repertoire of techniques. Student conferences also become a vehicle for growth. As students listen to the work of their peers, they cultivate the discerning ear of student-as-critic.

As part of the process, students gain an understanding of how a writer grows. "It allows me to sort out and make sense of things in my life. . . . It has given me the confidence to explore as a writer and has shown me that I can write if I work hard at it." Allowing students the freedom to explore personal experiences gives writing a power previously unknown to them. "Writing workshop is important, not only as a tool in developing writing, but it's really the only creative outlet for emotions or ideas you've got during the school day. I realize that perhaps the key issue is to become a better or more rounded writer, but it's also a place to step back and get a grip on what's going on around you. If good writing comes out, that's all the better." For many, writing workshop touches personal truth. "I've learned that writing too can serve as a way to cope. . . . Poetry has been a safe way for me to say those things that are too terror-filled for verbal communication. It has saved me." For others, the approach takes down social barriers. "Writing workshop makes a classroom more comfortable. You are on a more personal level with your peers, a level I like." But saying it best is the girl who moved to Lake Forest last fall from a traditional high school in California: "Kids here don't know what they have. Writing at most schools is a chore. Here at Lake Forest, it's a sport."

Students are not the only ones feeling the impact. A by-product of student-centered learning is the changing classroom role of the teacher from center stage to backstage, or at least to the wings. As demonstrated by the comments of our department colleagues, teachers are coming to see themselves as advisors, valued for their expertise and objective point of view. In this newly defined role, the interaction between student and teacher is dynamic, the lesson plans are fluid and changing, and the learning of both student and teacher is ongoing. "That's what happens in the conferences. You know the students and you push them, and you can see in their eyes that they are moved by what they have done." Such interactions can dramatically heighten the sense of community and mutual respect within the classroom. As one teacher puts it: "Conferences knock down walls. The relationships I create with my students individually intensify our rapport as a class." This new teaching relationship is invigorating, challenging, and most important, renewing. "Despite the drain on my time and energies, I'd feel oddly refreshed. My teaching changes from moment to moment to meet the needs of students—it's forever interesting." But most of all, the authenticity of the student-centered approach is what strikes us to the quick. "Real kids. Real writing. Real teaching."

The intensity of the day is past, and the teachers are left alone in their classrooms, drained yet exhilarated. Desks littered with papers remind them of the students' productivity and the continuing demands on their time. A glance at the calendar reveals a packed conference schedule tomorrow, a set of rough drafts to return, journals to read, and lessons to plan. "So much to do, so little time," echoes and re-echoes in the mind. Yet so much has been accomplished—a partnership in learning, a renewal in teaching, an authenticity in voice. The writing culture of the school has been changed through days like these, through the joint efforts of the students and teachers to make the mystery of writing a reality.

EXEMPLARY PROGRAM
Third-grade Writing at Hendricks Academy

Barbara Morris
Center for City Schools
Chicago, Illinois

After twenty-nine years of teaching in my own classroom in Chicago, working as a special-education teacher, and running workshops for the Illinois Writing Project, I "retired" from the public schools to become a teacher-consultant for National-Louis University's Center for City Schools. In my new job, I have the opportunity to work with colleagues as they develop and implement Best Practices in their classroom.

In the fall of 1995, I began working with several teachers at the Hendricks Academy on the South Side of Chicago. Located just a few blocks west of the Dan Ryan Expressway, near the Robert Taylor Homes public housing projects, Hendricks is an all–African American school whose student body is 98 percent poverty level. Over the past three years, I have spent one day a week in Hendricks classrooms observing, modeling strategies, and having conversations with the teachers. I began mainly in the primary classrooms, moving up with the children, so that now most of my work is with third- and fourth-grade classes. I've tried to support the writing program for these children and their teachers amid the many other priorities and pressures that Hendricks or any other city school faces.

One teacher I've worked with recently is Tina Glenzinski, and her story says a lot about how the Hendricks teachers are growing and experimenting with writing. Last spring, Tina asked me to help her implement some new writing strategies in her third-grade classroom. As a new teacher, she was eager and open to trying anything. We started with reading stories aloud and inviting kids to write short "reader-response" entries in journals. The students were attentive and willing to write. As she and her students became comfortable with this daily writing, Tina wanted to create a full-scale writing workshop. This was challenging. To get things started, I suggested that she use some fairy tales to prime the pump, reading the children several versions of the same tale. But just about the time Tina was ready to begin the writing workshop, the city-wide standardized testing program took precedence. She had to spend so much time preparing students for the Iowa Test of Basic Skills and Illinois Goal Assessment Tests that writing workshop was cut out. After the spring testing season finally ended, we returned to response journaling and tried the "stretch-to-sketch" strategy (Short 1994), which uses both writing and drawing to extend literary response. Tina was pleased with incorporation of these strategies and the progress her students had made. We agreed to try the fairy-tale–genre study in the fall.

When I walked into Tina's new third-grade class this September, I heard students say, "Hi, Ms. Moooris! I remember you used to read to us and let us write." Many of these smiling faces were students I had worked with in their previous grades but had not seen for a year or more. Tina was eager to implement the fairy-tale writing unit we had talked about last spring. Because this would be her and the children's first large-scale writing project of the year, we wanted it to be a carefully guided experience. While the long-range goal was a more "pure" writing workshop where kids would choose their own topic, we felt it was safer to begin with a carefully staged activity that picked up on Tina's and the children's love of literature and literary response. So Tina decided to organize a fairy-tale workshop.

Over two and a half weeks, Tina read the children several versions of the Cinderella story after their regular daily silent reading time. She started with the original version, followed by Frances Minter's *Cinder-Elly*. After hearing the first two versions, the students were put in groups of four to discuss the elements of stories and create notes they could refer to as the reading continued. They discussed similarities, differences, and the parts they liked best. Still, at this point, Tina was a little disappointed in their lack of enthusiasm. She needed to do something to perk them up. So she created a crown for herself and told her students they could make their own to wear during the read-aloud time. The kids made tall ones and small ones, decorated with everything from sparkles to torn paper. This was the spark they needed. Now there was a gathering of kings and queens for each day's read-aloud time.

One day, Tina read two poems instead of another book: "In Search of Cinderella" by Shel Silverstein and "Glass Slipper" by Judith Viorst. The boys really connected with the last line of "In Search of Cinderella," which goes, "I've started hating feet." They started chanting this phrase at the girls, who indignantly responded with Viorst's closing line, "He's not nearly as attractive as he seemed the other night. So I think I'll just pretend that this glass slipper feels too tight." This spontaneous call-and-response battle of the sexes added pep and movement. They started strutting around to the rhythm and asked for the poems to be read daily. This was more of the excitement Tina had been looking for.

.   Over the course of the next three weeks, Tina shared all or parts of many different Cinderella stories from around the world, including:

Cinderella, retold by Amy Ehrlich

Cinder-Elly, by Frances Minter

The Golden Slipper: A Vietnamese Legend, retold by Darrell Lum

Mufaro's Beautiful Daughters, by John Steptoe

The Egyptian Cinderella, by Shirley Climo

Cinder Edna, by Ellen Jackson

Princess Furball, by Charlotte Huck

Soot Face: An Ojibwa Cinderella Story, retold by Robert D. San Souci

Yeh Shen: Cinderella Story from China, retold by Ai-Ling Louie

The Korean Cinderella, by Shirley Climo

Princess Cinders, by Babette Cole

By now, the children had been immersed in literature for two and a half weeks, and it was almost time for them to write their own stories. But first, to be sure that they would take the writing process seriously, Tina read the picturebook *What Real Authors Do* by Eileen Christelow. This wonderful story tells about two children's authors with different styles and interests, but who both use the same writing strategies and terminology. These terms— *draft, edit, proofread, revise, publish*—helped Tina define the steps in the writing process and also became the children's spelling words for the week. Tina taught a mini-lesson for each step, creating a model that hung on the bulletin board for easy reference.

Finally, the children brainstormed some of the elements they might use in their stories. Just like the authors who had created the many Cinderella story variations they'd heard, the kids listed possible choices for characters, settings, opening lines, problems, solutions, shoes (instead of glass slippers), and vehicles (instead of pumpkin carriages). Tina wrote their suggestions on chart paper that she left up for reference. Among the children's possibilities:

Shoes

Penny loafers

Hush Puppies

high heels

gym shoes

K Swiss

Glass slipper

Nikes

Lugz

Transportation

bike

car

CTA

parade

limo

convertible

motorcycle

landcruiser

horse

dog

BMW

cab

carriage

train

horse

broom

snowmobile

garbage can

Cadillac

Firebird

Now the children's mouths were watering at the idea of writing their own versions of Cinderella. They were chomping at the bit. When Tina finally said, "Now you can write!" all you could hear was "Yes, Yes, Yes!" They wrote and wrote and revised and rewrote and eventually published their first stories. I was so excited to see those students I had known since first grade writing with such energy and excitement. Many of them rushed up to me pleading to read their story. Is writing supposed to be this much fun? The children certainly thought it should be.

As their drafts developed, students were put in peer-editing groups, using an evaluation sheet for content and a checklist for mechanics. Tina had conferences with each child after the second draft, each lasting about fifteen minutes. The conferences were long, but the students had written much more than Tina anticipated; the rest of the kids worked productively while she conferenced. After final corrections, they were ready to publish. Tina guided them through the decorating of their covers, designing title pages, and the rest. Finally, they eagerly signed up to debut their books at "Author's Chair" sharing sessions. Before the first books were read, though, Tina had some discussion with the children about ways that a helpful audience responds to stories. As I looked at their faces during the sharing, I realized these were truly happy children who were deeply pleased with what they had accomplished.

Milton Dockins' story shows how all the ingredients of this assignment came together in the third graders' work:

Cinder Selly

By, Milton Dockins

Dedicated to

My Family

My class, and

Miss Glenzinski

Glenzinski Publishing

© 1997

Long, long ago there lived a girl named Selly. She had two cruel stepsisters named Kelly, and Velly. Selly had one brother named Relly. He was nice and never treated Selly badly. Selly always wore an old and dirty dress. She worked almost all day doing things like washing dishes and cleaning her sister's dresses. Selly never got that much sleep when she had to do a lot of chores. One day Selly didn't feel like doing her chores. When the stepsisters saw that their dresses weren't clean, they went and said to the stepmother "Selly didn't clean our dresses". They started to yell at Selly. Selly ran, and ran, and ran. Selly stopped. Selly sat under a big, big apple tree and started sobbing. Out of no where, out came Angel. Angel was Selly's Fairy Godmother. Angel was wearing a blue dress with stars on it. She asked Selly "Why are you crying?" Selly said, "I'm crying because no one loves me anymore. There is a big Basketball game at my school and I can't go." "Then it is done" said Angel. "But what am I to wear?" With a Flick of her silver wand, Selly's old dress changed into a red and orange jump suit. On her feet were a pair of gold and sliver Jordans. But Angel wasn't through with her magic. Selly said "How shall I get to the basketball game?" With a flick of her wand a green bike with blue stripes appeared. Angel asked Selly to make a promise. That you will be back at 1:00 A.M? So off went Selly to the basketball game. Selly had a lot of fun in the first half. So half time was the time when you go to the washroom and get pop. Selly went to the wash room and she looked at her watch and saw that it was 12:45. So Selly said to her self "I will stay 5 more minutes." So she stayed 10 more minutes watching prince play that she forgot all about the time. Selly told the team bye and went out the door. Selly grabbed her bike and started to ride, but when she was riding she lost one of her Jordans. Selly could not stop now so she kept riding her bike. It was too late! Her gear had vanished. So poor Selly had to walk back home. Selly got back home and she put on her old and dirty rags.

She went on the front porch and started to sob. When her sisters came from the basketball game Selly was still sobbing. Selly asked her sister Velly and Kelly how was the game? They just looked at Selly and laughed. So Selly just went in the house and started to do her chores. The team's best player prince was looking all over for Selly, but as prince was looking he found Selly's Jordan. He got an idea to draw the shoe on a peice of paper. On it he worte if you lost your Jordan call 555-6789. It worked too. He had hundreds of girls calling, but the right one never called. So when Kelly called Selly was doing the laundry. The prince arrived and rang the door bell. Velly answered the door and said "Hello", Prince said "I am here to try on the gold and sliver Jordon, Velly said "Why come right in and have a seat." First Velly tried on the shoe. Velly's foot was too fat. Next it was Kellys turn to try it on. Kelly's foot was too small. Selly was doing laundry when she heard a commotion. Selly ran to see what it was about. So Selly ran down stairs when the sisters saw Selly they said to "go back to your laundry". But the prince said "You look like someone I've seen before. Please try on this shoe." Guess what? It fell right onto Selly's foot. Next Selly put the other on and they lived happily ever after. The END!

While it was obviously special, Milton's story was typical of the whole class. Every child's work was well-structured, elaborate, detailed, full of personal voice, carefully edited, and reverberating with the structures and conventions of fairy tales. (Obviously, Tina will want to do some mini-lessons on paragraphing soon!) As a consultant who visits schools throughout the region, I knew that these pieces compared favorably with the writing of third graders anywhere. What made it possible for these children—for whom many people hold such low expectations—to write so well? In structuring this lesson, Tina followed many of the principles of Best Practice in writing.

Above all, she gave children extensive prewriting experience, immersing them deeply in rich literature so that they would have plenty to write about. She reversed the traditional pattern of writing assignments where the teacher issues marching orders and then leaves the children alone to gather and shape material. Tina showed kids a clear, staged process of composition, and then provided help at every step along the way. She left children plenty of real choices and room for originality within her careful modeling and guidance. She made the process social, collaborative, energizing, and fun, inviting the students to meld their own interests and culture with the fairy-tale world. The "Cinderella Workshop" was a quite demanding unit, but these kids enjoyed the challenge and took pride in their efforts. As Brittany put it: "We worked hard but the stories are sooooo good!"

Works Cited

Atwell, Nancie. 1998. *In the Middle: Writing, Reading, and Learning with Adolescents.* (Second Edition.) Portsmouth, NH: Heinemann.

Calkins, Lucy McCormick. 1990. *Living Between the Lines.* Portsmouth, NH: Heinemann.

Crafton, Linda. 1996. *Standards in Practice: Grades K–2.* Urbana, IL: National Council of Teachers of English.

Hillocks, George. 1986. *Research on Written Composition: New Directions for Teaching.* Urbana, IL: National Council of Teachers of English.

International Reading Association and National Council of Teachers of English. 1996. *Standards for the English Language Arts.* Urbana, IL, and Newark, DE: International Reading Association and National Council of Teachers of English.

Murray, Donald. 1996. *Crafting a Life in Essay, Story, Poem.* Portsmouth, NH: Boynton/Cook.

Short, Kathy, Jerome Harste, and Carolyn Burke. 1994. *Creating Classrooms for Authors and Inquirers.* Portsmouth, NH: Heinemann.

Sierra-Perry, Martha. 1996. *Standards in Practice: Grades 3–5.* Urbana, IL: National Council of Teachers of English.

Smagorinsky, Peter. 1996. *Standards in Practice: Grades 9–12.* Urbana, IL: National Council of Teachers of English.

Wilhelm, Jeffrey D. 1996. *Standards in Practice: Grades 6–8.* Urbana, IL: National Council of Teachers of English.

Zemelman, Steven, and Harvey Daniels. 1988. *A Community of Writers: Teaching Writing in the Junior and Senior High School.* Portsmouth, NH: Heinemann.

Suggested Further Readings

Allen, Janet, and Kyle Gonzalez. 1998. *There's Room for Me Here: Literacy Workshop in the Middle School.* York, ME: Stenhouse.

Anson, Chris, and Richard Beach. 1995. *Journals in the Classroom: Writing to Learn.* Norwood, MA: Christopher-Gordon.

Avery, Carol. 1993. *And with a Light Touch: Learning About Reading, Writing, and Teaching with First Graders.* Portsmouth, NH: Heinemann.

Calkins, Lucy McCormick. 1994. *The Art of Teaching Writing.* Portsmouth, NH: Heinemann.

Chancer, Joni, and Gina Rester-Zodrow. 1997. *Moon Journals: Writing, Art, and Inquiry Through Focused Nature Study.* Portsmouth, NH: Heinemann.

Fletcher, Ralph. 1996. *A Writer's Notebook: Unlocking the Writer Within You.* New York: Avon.

———. 1993. *What a Writer Needs.* Portsmouth, NH: Heinemann.

Fulwiler, Toby, ed. 1987. *The Journal Book.* Portsmouth, NH: Boynton/Cook.

Graves, Donald. 1983. *Writing: Teachers and Children at Work.* Portsmouth, NH: Heinemann.

———. 1994. *A Fresh Look at Writing.* Portsmouth, NH: Heinemann.

Graves, Donald, and Bonnie Sunstein. 1992. *Portfolio Portraits.* Portsmouth, NH: Heinemann.

Harwayne, Shelley. 1992. *Lasting Impressions: Weaving Literature into the Writing Workshop.* Portsmouth, NH: Heinemann.

Heard, Georgia. 1995. *Writing Toward Home.* Portsmouth, NH: Heinemann.

Hindley, Joanne. 1996. *In the Company of Children.* York, ME: Stenhouse.

Hubbard, Ruth Shagoury. 1996. *A Workshop of the Possible: Nurturing Children's Creative Development.* York, ME: Stenhouse.

Johnson, Donna, and Duane Roen, 1989. *Richness in Writing: Empowering ESL Students.* New York: Longman.

Lane, Barry. 1993. *After the End: Teaching and Learning Creative Revision.* Portsmouth, NH: Heinemann.

Macrorie, Ken. 1984. *The I-Search Paper.* Portsmouth, NH: Boynton/Cook.

Porter, Carol, and Jannell Cleland. 1995. *The Portfolio as a Learning Strategy.* Portsmouth, NH: Boynton/Cook.

Rhodes, Lynn K., and Curt Dudley-Marling, 1996. *Readers and Writers with a Difference: a holistic approach to teaching learning disabled and remedial students.* Portsmouth, NH: Heinemann.

Rief, Linda. 1992. *Seeking Diversity: Language Arts with Adolescents.* Portsmouth, NH: Heinemann.

Romano, Tom. 1995. *Writing with Passion: Life Stories, Multiple Genres.* Portsmouth, NH: Boynton/Cook.

Spear, Karen. 1988. *Sharing Writing: Peer Response Groups in English Classes.* Portsmouth, NH: Boynton/Cook.

Taylor, Denny, and Catherine Dorsey-Gaines. 1988. *Growing Up Literate: Learning from Inner-City Families.* Portsmouth, NH: Heinemann.

Writing Resources on the Internet

The only truly national staff development effort in any subject area, the National Writing Project shares reports of outstanding practice, research bulletins, and a wide range of publications. Visit **http://www-gse.berkeley.edu.**

The National Council of Teachers of English is the most authoritative source for information on the teaching of writing. For association news, research bulletins, publications, and conference announcements, visit **http://www.ncte.org.**

A very special resource, especially for teachers of poetry and creative writing, is the Teachers and Writers Collaborative at **http://www.twc.org.**

RECOMMENDATIONS ON TEACHING WRITING

Increase	Decrease
Student ownership and responsibility by: —helping students choose their own topics and goals for improvement —using brief teacher-student conferences —teaching students to review their own progress	Teacher control of decision making by: —teacher deciding on all writing topics —suggestions for improvement dictated by teacher —learning objectives determined by teacher alone —instruction given as whole-class activity
Class time spent on writing whole, original pieces through: —establishing real purposes for writing and students' involvement in the task —instruction in and support for all stages of writing process —prewriting, drafting, revising, editing	Time spent on isolated drills on "subskills" of grammar, vocabulary, spelling, paragraphing, penmanship, etc. Writing assignments given briefly, with no context or purpose, completed in one step
Teacher modeling writing—drafting, revising, sharing—as a fellow author and as demonstration of processes	Teacher talks about writing but never writes or shares own work
Learning of grammar and mechanics in context, at the editing stage, and as items are needed	Isolated grammar lessons, given in order determined by textbook, before writing is begun
Writing for real audiences, publishing for the class and for wider communities	Assignments read only by teacher
Making the classroom a supportive setting for shared learning, using: —active exchange and valuing of students' ideas —collaborative small-group work —conferences and peer critiquing that give responsibility for improvement to authors	Devaluation of students' ideas through: —students viewed as lacking knowledge and language abilities —sense of class as competing individuals —work with fellow students viewed as cheating, disruptive
Writing across the curriculum as a tool for learning	Writing taught only during "language arts" period—i.e., infrequently
Constructive and efficient evaluation that involves: —brief informal oral responses as students work —thorough grading of just a few of student-selected, polished pieces —focus on a few errors at a time —cumulative view of growth and self-evaluation —encouragement of risk taking and honest expression	Evaluation as negative burden for teacher and student by: —marking all papers heavily for all errors, making teacher a bottleneck —teacher editing paper, and only after completed, rather than student making improvements —grading seen as punitive, focused on errors, not growth

4

Best Practice in Mathematics

The Way It Used to Be

Many adults believe they have a clear sense of what mathematics is and why they despise it. These thoughts and feelings have been slam-dunked into them by their years in school, struggling with textbooks and teachers living a kind of mathematical mythology of memorizing math facts (orally and with flashcards); computing page after page of sums, differences, products, and quotients (with and without remainders); going to the chalkboard to work out the answer; trying to remember the rules and procedures such as "write down the 2 and carry the 1" and "invert and multiply"; and developing careful, step-by-step proofs (beyond a shadow of a doubt). These practices provide a continuing source of material for cartoonists and comedians. Even Pippi Longstocking derides the dreaded "plutification" tables.

Common myths about mathematics include a variant of the Marine Corps recruiting slogan: math is only for a few good men; most mere mortals (especially women) are not good at it. Other prevalent myths are (1) doing math means getting the one right answer, quickly; (2) mathematics is a collection of rules, theorems, and procedures to be memorized (and you might get to use some of them later . . . maybe); and (3) mathematics is really just arithmetic, working with bigger and more complicated numbers. Finally, many parents and teachers assume that teaching math involves steadily working through the textbook, page by page, assigning sheets of drill exercises from the workbooks or worksheets for practice.

These ideas are fundamentally wrong; teaching practices and textbooks that directly or subtly perpetuate them continue to delude the American public into maintaining the mythology. Perhaps the saddest outcome of this situation is that each year a significant percentage of children come to believe that they are incapable of doing math. Teaching the mathematics that was needed by shopkeepers of the nineteenth century through stultifying drill and memorization has caused anxiety and loathing in a large portion of schoolchildren. The successive elimination of children at each grade level from enjoying and understanding mathematics is like a strainer that allows only a few to continue with confidence and power. By high school, when students can start avoiding math courses, each year only about half continue. By college, just a trickle of those who began counting buttons and beans in first grade take more mathematics than required, and a mere drop of these students elect to major in mathematics in college.

It does not have to be this way. And in a growing number of classrooms in the United States today, it isn't.

Teaching Mathematics a Better Way:
Five Teachers Show How

Sally Netherville

Sally Netherville's district has made a commitment to a hands-on approach to learning mathematics. She has no textbook, no workbooks; instead, she and the other primary-grade teachers have developed a set of activities for their students. She has a truckload of specially designed "math manipulatives"—a vast assortment of colorful, durable plastic materials with accompanying teacher resource handbooks. The children usually work in pairs or groups of three with the manipulatives on a variety of tasks: counting; arranging materials in groups of two, three, four, five, or ten; sorting and categorizing in various ways (e.g., by shape, size, or color). The children make designs and patterns with some materials. They are building a sense of the base-ten number system by gathering some materials into groups of ten. When they get ten groups of ten, they trade them in to the teacher for a special "one hundred prize."

Sally carefully prepares bags and boxes of materials, arranges the students in working groups for the activity, and explains the tasks for them to do. She supervises their work while walking around the room, occasionally stopping to provide a suggestion to a group. Frequently, the materials lend themselves to further exploration by the children, and Sally encourages them to go beyond the task she has "choreographed" so they might discover facts, relationships, and patterns on their own. Then she guides the students' work to make explicit connections to the most important mathematical ideas she wants them to know.

Jan White

Jan White's financially strapped school district failed to pass a tax referendum for quite a few years. So, unlike Sally, Jan does not have a roomful of commercially produced materials for her first graders. But both she and her principal believe they must provide students with hands-on experiences in counting, grouping, sorting, and the like. Jan rarely uses the outdated textbook provided by the district. Instead, she has become the self-proclaimed "queen" of recycling. She, the children, and their parents collect materials for their own manipulatives: plastic screw-on caps, pop-top tabs, washers, nuts and bolts, ceramic tiles, and so forth. Jan hounds businesses in the community for donations of leftover materials and containers. She is vigilant at garage and alley sales for leftover toys, blocks, and games that she can use. Often she buys odd lots of generic commodities and foods for manipulatives, such as dried beans, rice, and toothpicks.

Pam Hyde

Pam Hyde teaches third grade in a school whose principal has supported a lively, hands-on approach to teaching mathematics by purchasing one of the new curriculum programs developed with support from the National Science Foundation (NSF). The program has many engaging and mathematically rich activities for students. In her school, Pam has the latitude to supplement these activities with tasks, problems, or math work that fits what she believes her students need.

In one typical activity, Pam arranges six balance scales around her classroom, organizes the students into six cooperative groups, and gives each group a plastic bag with four different brands of bubble gum. She asks the students about their experiences with bubble gum: How big can they make bubbles? How long do they chew it? What are its ingredients? Then the students must predict how much of the bubble gum is sugar. Is it more than half or less than half of the weight? She records their predictions.

The students weigh each piece of gum in their bags with the two-pan balance scales by placing centimeter cubes that each weigh one gram into one pan and a single piece of gum in the other pan. They record how many grams each piece weighs. Next, each student chews a piece of gum for about five minutes and then weighs it. The resulting weight is always less than the original weight. Students record these data and Pam leads them in a discussion that compares the pre- and post-chewing weights for each brand. There are differences among the students for the same brand. She asks them to explain why this might be so. There are marked differences among brands. One of the brands was "sugar-free"; its post-chewing weight was more than half its original weight, but not by much. The brands with sugar show dramatic weight differences pre- to post-chewing, definitely less than half. Pam again asks the students to hypothesize what would account for these differences.

This is one of several activities that Pam and the third-grade teachers of her school use with the balance scales to give students a strong sense of quantity, gram weights, measuring, and the concept of half of a quantity.

Students also are getting firsthand experience with doing science and mathematics together. Another version of this activity is done by teachers in the upper grades of the school in which students use their data to calculate the specific *percentages* of sugar or sugar-substitute lost during the chewing. They will be more precise with the scientific experimentation, investigating the effects of the different chewing times and other factors.

Pam also uses the balance scales for the students to determine what part of a one-hundred–gram bag of peanuts consists of shells. Students predict, remove the shells, return them to the bag, and weigh the shells alone. They eat the peanuts. In this activity, the weight of the shells in grams is compared to an initial pile of peanuts with a total weight of one hundred. Pam uses this activity with others to help the children think in terms of parts of one hundred, building up experiences that will provide a foundation for concepts of two-place decimals and percentage. She will also have the students repeat this experiment with one-hundred–gram bags of various nuts to investigate differences among these foods. The upper-grade teachers in her school have their students do analogous experiments with bananas and oranges: initially weighing the food intact and then weighing the peel or skin. Because the comparisons between these part and total weights involve "messy" numbers (i.e., the total will not be one hundred grams), students use calculators to determine percentages.

Carole Malone

Carole Malone teaches mathematics to all ninety sixth graders at her school, using the textbook only three days a week. On other days, she uses activities from resource books that address the same topics and concepts as the text, but in ways she feels are better. One day each week, she arranges "Math Labs" in which small groups of students work on tasks, problems, or investigations designed to address major themes suggested by the National Council of Teachers of Mathematics (NCTM).

For instance, in a measurement lab, students are given a metric tape measure (with centimeters and millimeters marked) and a dozen or more cylinders of different sizes (e.g., soup can, hockey puck, and plastic medicine bottle). Their task is to measure and compare the lengths across and around each cylinder. They make lists showing these two measurements for each cylinder (e.g., 4.3 centimeters across and 13.7 centimeters around). Next, Carole asks them to estimate how many times bigger the around measurement (the circumference) is than across (diameter) the circular base of the cylinder. Students can readily see that it is a bit more than three times longer. With calculators, students compute what three times as long would be. Then they divide the circumference by the diameter to see exactly what this ratio is for each cylinder. Because the measurements are in centimeters, students can enter these figures directly into the decimal-based calculator. The ratios don't vary too much among the cylinders; they are between 3.1 and 3.2 (unless students measure incorrectly). Students often are surprised that no matter how much the cylinders differ in size, this ratio is always the same (except for approximations in measurement). They will have determined empirically the nature of *pi*, the constant ratio of the circumference to the diameter of any circle.

Jerry Cummins

When Jerry Cummins' freshman math students at Lyons Township High School begin studying algebraic expressions, they do so through an energetic, collaborative process of writing-(and talking)-to-learn. Jerry usually starts things out by putting a board-game number-spinner in a student's hands and an expression on the board—for example, X + C. Jerry asks the volunteer to spin the spinner, yielding a random number between one and nine. If the number is three, Jerry then fills in the variable X + 3. Now he asks a few volunteers to offer a verbal phrase, a statement of some real-world situation to which this expression might refer. A typical response might be "A person's age three years from now" or "The number of kids in this school plus three transfers." Once students get the idea, Jerry wants them to have plenty of in-class practice, so he uses a structure called "Roundtable." He introduces another expression, say "2X – B," and fills in "B" with another random number from the spinner, to yield "2X – 4." Then each student is asked to write down a phrase to go with this expression. After a minute or two, each student passes his or her paper to the left, where the next student reads the phrase and must generate another unique phrase. Then everyone passes and writes again, and finally a fourth time.

The fun grows as students become increasingly involved and original, trying to top each other with the plausible and relevant phrases. "2X – 4" becomes: "The promoter printed up twice the number of tickets as seats in the theater because the band was going to play two shows, minus four seats because the promoter was saving two seats for himself and his wife at each show."

Now it might be time to get teams of four students together to coauthor phrases and share these with the whole group. Jerry puts "BX + C" on the board, spins random numbers for both B and C, and then gives the groups two or three minutes to collaboratively devise and write down the best phrase they can come up with. The groups pause to share, hearing a few other groups' phrases, and then they do another one. When everyone is warmed up, Jerry lets teams share with one other team, rather than with the whole group, so everyone gets the maximum "air time." Meanwhile, Jerry circulates through the room, observing, facilitating, and helping out.

A Look at the Standards Documents

Although the words *reading* and *writing* invite images of people **doing** these actions, the analogous term, *mathematics,* is oddly static. What is a truly comparable, dynamic word? *Mathing*? *Mathematizing*? Perhaps *problem solving* could carry the connotations of students actually doing mathematics, using mathematical knowledge, engaging in mathematical thinking, investigating situations with mathematics. The five teachers just described all have their students actively involved in doing mathematics so they can build their understanding of mathematical ideas, see the power and usefulness of mathematics in their lives, and feel confident in their own capabilities as "problem solvers." These are key themes at the heart of major reports from the National Council of Teachers of Mathematics (NCTM): *Curriculum and Evaluation Standards for School Mathematics* (1989), *Professional Standards for Teaching Mathematics* (1991), and *Assessment Standards for School Mathematics* (1995).

Taken collectively, these three documents offer a significantly broadened view of the nature of mathematics, what it means to know mathematics, how students can learn mathematics, and what kinds of teaching practices best foster this learning. It has been nearly a decade since the first NCTM standards document appeared. Its far-reaching ideas have stimulated the development of a dozen new curriculum programs funded by the National Science Foundation (NSF). Most commercial publishers of mathematics textbooks have incorporated these standards into their latest editions. Countless staff development programs have been conducted to help teachers learn new practices for the teaching of mathematics. To supplement the standards, NCTM also has published twenty-two "addenda booklets" that focus on mathematical topics and grade levels.

Yet all this activity is a work in progress. The NCTM continues to refine and elaborate on these ideas and standards. The *Standards 2000 Project* began work in the summer of 1997 to create one standards document that integrates the curricular content of mathematics with teaching and assessment. The mathematics curriculum will span four grade-level bands (pre-K– 2, 3–5, 6–8, and 9–12), replacing the three bands of the 1989 document. As in the original NCTM standards, this project involves work groups of mathematicians, mathematics educators, teachers, researchers, and curriculum developers. The final *Standards 2000* document will be released in the spring of 2000. Updates on this revision project, as well as the three standards documents, are available on NCTM's website (**http://www.nctm.org**).

Qualities of Best Practice in Teaching Mathematics

The following are the important and interrelated characteristics of the Best Practices of teaching mathematics embodied in the NCTM reports. A chart summarizing the suggestions for practices to be increased and decreased is at the end of the chapter.

The goal of teaching mathematics is to help all students develop mathematical power.   Students should develop true understanding of mathematical concepts and procedures. Teachers must help students build understanding and meaningfulness by using mathematical ideas and by thinking mathematically. They must come to see and believe that mathematics *makes sense,* that it is understandable and useful to them. In these ways, they can become more confident in their own use of mathematics. Teachers and students must both come to recognize that mathematical thinking is a normal part of everyone's mental ability, and not just confined to a gifted few. The field of cognitive psychology illuminates the fundamental principles of learning with true understanding that comprise the heart of the standards.

Teaching for mathematical power requires providing experiences that stimulate students' curiosity and build confidence in investigating, problem solving, and communication.   Students should be encouraged to formulate and solve problems directly related to the world around them so they can see the structures of mathematics in every aspect of their lives. Concrete experiences and materials provide the foundation for understanding concepts and *constructing* meaning. Students must truly create their own way of interpreting an idea, relating it to their own personal life experiences, seeing how it fits with what they already know, and how they are thinking about related ideas. In the process, they experience the enjoyment of a challenge, the excitement of success, and the development of a good self-image. Their curiosity, inventiveness, and willingness to persevere is increased in such an environment.

How well students come to understand mathematical ideas is far more important than how many skills they acquire.   Teachers who help children become mathematically powerful devote less attention to telling students about mathematics, assigning worksheets for computational practice, and requiring rote memorization. Instead, they employ activities that promote the active involvement of their students in doing mathematics in authentic situations. Such teachers use concrete manipulative materials regularly to build understanding. They ask students questions that promote exploration, discussion, questioning, and explanations. Children also learn the best methods for knowing when and how to use a variety of computational techniques such as mental arithmetic, estimation, and calculators, as well as reasonable paper-and-pencil procedures. When students possess such understanding, they are far more likely to study mathematics voluntarily and acquire further skills as they are needed.

Yes, but . . . shouldn't students know the math facts? Won't students do poorly on standardized tests if they don't?

Versions of these questions are asked frequently. At issue is not if students should "know math facts," but rather what it means to *know*, how one comes to know (or learns), and when. For instance, children in kindergarten are capable of memorizing the multiplication tables, just as they can memorize the names of the emperors of the Roman Empire. In what sense do they know or understand what they might repeat from memory? In what ways might they thoughtfully use this information? On the other hand, if children participate in activities that develop a strong sense of what is happening as quantities of objects are counted, sorted, grouped, regrouped, arranged, and arrayed, they can build up a profound understanding of number, operations, and computation. From such a foundation, remembering is not difficult at all. Memorizing without such experiences is dreadfully difficult.

Furthermore, through these active experiences, the teacher can help children's understanding evolve into two different types of formal mathematical knowledge: procedural and conceptual. Procedures for working with symbols such as "invert and multiply" can be learned without understanding the underlying concepts. However, knowing *when* (i.e., which situations) to use which procedure requires an understanding of the concepts. Both kinds of knowledge are extremely important to success on tests and life. Understanding the concepts of multiplication and division, their various forms, and how to think about the real-life situations in which it would be appropriate to use them is essential for learning many topics of higher mathematics. "Knowing" the math facts without true understanding of the underlying concepts guarantees serious problems with learning other concepts in the mathematics curriculum.

Once they have a good conceptual foundation for the meaning of the operations of addition and subtraction (and later, multiplication and division), students should memorize the basic facts so they are able to calculate mentally and estimate with ease. There are several excellent "strategies" for memorizing these facts that are based on understanding rather than on brute force, rote memorizing of what is not really understood. These "fact strategies" might include memorizing all the "doubles" together (e.g., 1+1=2, 2+2=4, and 3+3=6) or a "fact family" together (e.g., 4+6=10, 10−4=6, and 10−6=4). (See Van de Walle [1998] for a full elaboration of these ideas.)

Mathematics is not a set of isolated topics, but rather an integrated whole. Mathematics is the science of patterns and relationships. Realizing, understanding, and using these patterns is a major part of mathematical power. Students need to see connections among concepts and applications of general principles to several areas. As they relate mathematical ideas to everyday experiences and real-world situations, students come to realize that these ideas are useful and powerful. Students' mathematical knowledge increases as they see and understand how various representations (e.g., physical, verbal, numerical, pictorial, and graphical) are interrelated; to do so, they need experiences with each and with how they are connected.

Problem solving is the focus of a curriculum that fosters the development of mathematical power.   Broadly defined, problem solving is an integral part of all mathematical activity. Rather than being considered a distinct topic, problem solving should be a process that permeates the curriculum and provides contexts in which concepts and skills are learned. Problem solving means far more than the narrow "word" problems or "story" problems of yesteryear. Instead, problem solving requires students to investigate questions, tasks, and situations that they and the teacher might suggest. They create and apply strategies to work on and solve problems. Hyde and Hyde's *Mathwise* (1991) is devoted to showing how to incorporate problem solving into one's math teaching.

Students need many opportunities to use language to communicate mathematical ideas.   Discussing, writing, reading, and listening to mathematical ideas deepen students' understanding of mathematics. Students learn to communicate in a variety of ways by actively relating physical materials, pictures, and diagrams to mathematical ideas, by reflecting on and clarifying their own thinking, by relating everyday language to mathematical ideas and symbols, and by discussing mathematical ideas with peers.

A major shift in mathematics teaching has occurred with helping students to work in small groups on projects collecting data, making graphs and charts of their findings, and solving problems. Giving students opportunities for *reflective* and *collaborative* work with others is a critical part of mathematics teaching. Mathematical ideas are constructed by humans; students need to experience the *social* interaction and construction of meaningful mathematical representations with their peers and with the teacher. In *democratic* fashion, the teacher is not the sole owner and transmitter of knowledge; students and teachers are inquirers together. The students can and should initiate mathematical questions and investigations of interest and importance to them. Teachers need not always have "the answer" (for there may not be one). Teachers and students can investigate together without threat to the teacher's authority and control.

Yes, but . . . isn't this emphasis on problem solving, collaboration, and teacher facilitation just watering-down the curriculum? Doesn't it make for soft, fuzzy math?

Doing real mathematics requires problem solving. In the real world of adults, collaboration is the norm, even in situations requiring mathematical problem solving and decision making. Students are well served learning how to communicate their mathematical conceptions to others. Of course, a teacher can go too far in promoting discussion among students and withhold knowledge that he or she could readily share. The art of good teaching is knowing how to ask good questions to provoke optimal thinking among the students, knowing how to help students make connections among ideas that the teacher knows are related when the students can't see the link, and knowing how and when to pull ideas together in a coherent explanation that will solidify connections and understanding.

There are a number of parent groups (especially in California) that are opposed to the NCTM standards, particularly for these concerns. In letters to the editor and over the Internet, one can find distortions of what the NCTM standards actually say and horror stories of bad math teaching, attributed to the standards. No responsible mathematics educator has suggested "throwing the baby out with the bath water"; the NCTM standards speak of increasing and decreasing certain practices and topics, not "eliminating" them. It is a question of emphasis. Of course, changes in practices, minor or substantial, require good implementation and staff development. Consistent attention over years (not months) to developing teachers' capabilities for teaching mathematics in different and better ways is critical.

Reasoning is fundamental to knowing and doing mathematics.   Students must come to believe that mathematics makes sense, that it is not just a set of rules and procedures to be memorized. Therefore, they need experiences in explaining, justifying, and refining their own thinking, not merely repeating statements from a textbook. They need to make and defend their own conjectures by applying various reasoning processes and drawing logical conclusions.

Helping students to move among various ideas and their representations in meaningful steps is a major task of teachers. Facilitating students' growth in abstraction and generalization is best accomplished by fostering experiences and reflection, rather than by the teacher presenting and telling. Students discussing, making conjectures, drawing conclusions, defending their ideas, and writing their conceptualizations are a vital part of doing mathematics. Of course, the teacher will give knowledgeable feedback on their work.

Concepts of numbers, operations, and computation should be broadly defined, conceived, and applied.   Real-world, authentic problems require a variety of tools for dealing with quantitative information. Students must have many experiences in order to develop an intuitive sense of numbers and operations, a "feel" for what is happening in the different situations in which various operations might be used. For instance, two different conceptions of subtraction are involved when asked (1) If I have ten marbles and give you two, how many will I retain? versus (2) If I have three marbles and you have seven, how many more marbles do you have than I do? Teachers cannot afford to gloss over the differences in these two situations by simply invoking the procedures of subtraction to "find the right answer."

The concepts of geometry and measurement are best learned through experiences that involve experimentation and the discovery of relationships with concrete materials. When students construct their own knowledge of geometry and measurement, they are more able to use their initial understanding in applied, real-world settings. They develop their spatial sense in two or three dimensions through explorations with real objects. Measurement concepts are best understood through actual experiences with measuring and estimating measures. Furthermore, such experiences are especially valuable for building number and operation sense.

The understanding of statistics, data, chance, and probability comes from real-world applications. The need to make decisions based on numerical information permeates society and provides motivation for working with real data. Probability emerges from realistic considerations of risk, chance, and uncertainties. Students can develop mathematical power through problem formulation and solutions that involve decisions based on data collection, organization, representation (graphs and tables), and analysis.

Yes, but . . . what if the mathematics textbooks in the district don't support these Best Practices? Isn't this teaching too hard for teachers? Won't they just fall back on the outmoded textbook?

There is no textbook series nor single text at a particular grade level that comprehensively addresses the NCTM standards. Virtually all publishers of mathematics texts have attempted to move toward the standards. Groups of authors (and their books) have different strengths and emphases, as well as drawbacks. Looking for the right or even the best text to adopt is not the most important task facing schools. The textbook should not define the curriculum. Instead, each teacher should have a clear sense of the concepts and thinking to be addressed during the year, how they fit together, how they build on what has been addressed in the prior year, and how they are likely to be addressed at the next grade level in the subsequent year. Each teacher should teach a curriculum of activities in which students are doing mathematics: estimating, measuring, manipulating objects, drawing pictures, making graphs and diagrams, collecting data, and compiling lists and tables. The textbook should be a resource for the process.

Although this activity orientation may sound extreme, it is the only sensible direction because no textbook, as a form of print media, can provide all the stimulation required for mathematical learning. Even with a "good" text, each teacher must supplement the printed material with manipulatives and activities. To do so, teachers must realize what is lacking in the texts, what kinds of activities are best, and how to help students do them. Although this is not easy, teachers are quite capable of learning these new approaches to curriculum and instruction with good staff development. For more information on this issue, see the suggested further readings or visit the website we've developed for Best Practice mathematics **(http:// members.aol.com/mathwise2**).

A major purpose of evaluation is to help teachers better understand what students know and make meaningful decisions about teaching and learning activities.   A variety of assessment methods should be used to assess individual students, including written, oral, and demonstration formats, all of which must fit with the curriculum. All aspects of mathematical knowledge and its connections should be assessed and used to help the teacher organize teaching and learning activities. Standardized tests are better suited to evaluating programs than to assessing individual students.

Yes, but . . . aren't these Best Practices more appropriate for elementary schools than secondary schools?

These practices describe how humans learn, understand, and use mathematics; they apply, though in somewhat different ways, to learners of all ages and levels of development. In fact, the NCTM standards on instructional practices for grades 9–12 are remarkably similar to those for the earlier grades. However, these practices are decidedly less prevalent in high school mathematics classes today than in elementary school classrooms. There may be many reasons for this state of affairs. Secondary teachers are subject-matter specialists who tend to focus on content—the structure of knowledge in their field—rather than on the processes of helping students understand. As students move up the grade levels, teachers expect certain skills and content to have been mastered and assume increased capability to deal with concepts and symbols of greater abstraction. Therefore, many high school teachers emphasize (often to the exclusion of all else) formulas, equations, and paper-and-pencil manipulation of symbols from the textbook. Students who cannot handle the pace and the high level of abstraction are judged incapable of learning algebra, calculus, or other branches of "higher" mathematics.

However, research on cognition has made it quite clear that abstract symbols, with all their power and generalization, are best used when the concepts underlying the symbols are truly understood. This understanding requires many varied experiences with particular situations and concrete referents (such as physical models and manipulatives). Best Practices in mathematics apply equally to elementary and secondary schoolteachers.

How Parents Can Help

Children have a great many opportunities to interact with older siblings, adults, and mathematical ideas before coming to school. In fact, research studies repeatedly have shown that young children begin schooling with some well-developed and effective problem-solving strategies. These processes help children figure out what they want to know *mathematically* about situations that mean something to them. For instance, a child can often judge perceptually whether he or she got half a candy bar (or at least about the same amount as his or her older brother). Also, many children use their fingers to count, keep track of quantities, or calculate needed amounts. Such methods are natural, developmentally appropriate, cognitive devices that work because they make sense to children. Unfortunately, instead of building on the home-grown strategies of five-year-olds, teachers often demand that the children abandon these devices in favor of more abstract manipulations of symbols on paper. The jump from working with fingers and concrete objects to symbol manipulation is often too great for children; it is a chasm they are not yet ready to bridge.

The Best Practices in mathematics teaching and learning described above make frequent mention of manipulatives, concrete materials, and real-world situations for optimal learning. These are the contexts that make understanding of mathematical ideas possible and provide a bridge to the more abstract symbolism that has maximal power and usefulness. Parents and the home environment of children of all ages can provide the richness of materials and opportunities for latent mathematical thinking to flourish. Mathematics and mathematical patterns are all around us: floor tiles and wallpaper; paintings and sculpture; coins and paper money; heights, weights, and ages of family members; combination pizzas; toys, games, and puzzles; shopping lists and recipes. The possibilities are limited only by adults' perceptions, willingness, and understanding.

In general, parents need only the desire to involve their children in talking and thinking about the meaningful and relevant mathematics they encounter each day. A good place to start is taking the time to figure out *together* how much of something is needed, rather than the adult doing all the thinking and then telling the child what "the answer" is. For instance, "How many days until my birthday?" should be an occasion for parent and child to look at the calendar together, count the days *in each intervening month,* and add them up, or simply count each day, one at a time. Real-life, authentic questions and tasks should be seen as opportunities to work with mathematics. Occasions for counting, sorting, and measuring abound in our lives.

Although video games have held children's attention for a number of years, there are many excellent games, toys, and cards that break through the flashing lights of the TV monitor. In fact, many children enjoy the different stimulation that physical sports and games offer beyond the passivity of the video medium. However, some have to be cajoled into trying something old-fashioned like Monopoly or playing cards. The inherent mathematics of such pastimes may or may not be obvious. However, the incidental learning (especially the number and operation sense) that comes from playing such games is pronounced. When students have a strong need to understand what is happening mathematically, they will exert effort and attention to do so. It is likely that three generations of Americans built their basic sense of what percentage means from landing on the Income Tax square of the Monopoly board.

In an analogous fashion, how many architects and engineers had their spatial sense nourished by blocks, Tinkertoys, and other three-dimensional building toys? Probably the most famous example is Frank Lloyd Wright, whose mother gave him a special block set at an early age. Parents should encourage children to build, create, explore, and arrange whatever toys and materials they can provide for their children. There is no lack of inexpensive materials in stores.

When adults state that they are not good at visualizing or have no sense of direction, how do they know this to be true? Perhaps they have had limited opportunities to work in relevant spatial mathematics. Even if there are inherent genetic differences in visual, perceptual, or spatial abilities, it is clear that experience, exposure, and practice with enjoyable, stimulating materials can enhance and develop anyone's capacity. In school, we have found that students who habitually do poorly at the drudgery of computational drill often excel with geometric and spatial manipulatives. They need to know that they are capable "mathematicians" in these legitimate areas of mathematics.

Our news media have repeatedly trumpeted the mathematical achievement and ability of Asians. Despite claims of genetic reasons for mathematical prowess, an inescapable conclusion has been drawn by many who have studied Asian families. In many Asian cultures, it is assumed that all children are inherently capable of learning and understanding mathematics. If they evidence a difficulty in understanding a concept, they are told, in effect: "You can understand it! Work harder! We will help you!" This message is fundamentally positive, self-affirming, and encouraging. "Mathematics is not so difficult that it is beyond you. It is within your grasp. You are capable!"

Contrast this message to the typical American parents whose child comes home with difficulty understanding the math topic of the day. "I never did understand this! I never was good at math! I guess you inherited my poor math ability! Call a friend and just write down the correct answer to your homework." Not only does the basic message tell a child that he is unlikely to ever be any good in mathematics, but it also lets the child off the hook. He or she does not have to try any more. "Give up, why bother?" In fact, it is socially acceptable in this country to say, "I'm no good at math. I can't balance my checkbook." Why is it socially acceptable to say such things while it is not okay to say, "I'm no good at reading; I can't make any sense out of the newspaper"?

Perhaps the best way for parents to help their children with mathematics is to send the clear message through their words and actions that mathematics is all around us, it is a vital part of our lives, and it is understandable with some effort. Let's do it together; it can be fun.

How Principals Can Support
Best Practice in Mathematics

There are several critical roles that a principal plays in the life of a school; each bears on the issue of supporting Best Practice in mathematics. The principal is the key figure in public relations for the school—the spokesperson for the school, its teachers, and programs—to the community and parents. Because new approaches to mathematics curriculum and teaching in many ways run contrary to conventional wisdom and popular beliefs in our society, the principal (and other district administrators) should be in the forefront *actively promoting* Best Practice in mathematics. She can explain and demonstrate new methods and materials, counter misconceptions and myths, and help build support at home for this new vision of mathematics.

Of course, the principal must educate herself to these monumental changes occurring in mathematics education. The NCTM reports and other related publications are an excellent source of information. These outline what the best minds in the country are saying about teaching mathematics so that students will learn with true understanding and capability. Administrators must read them, go to workshops to learn about them, visit classrooms where they are happening, and see for themselves what is possible and what must be done.

Many principals hold Parents' Nights to present new mathematics ideas, methods, and materials to parents. Some make videotapes of these presentations and send them home to parents who did not attend. Principals arrange for programs on evenings or Saturdays, at which teachers develop activities for parents and their children to do together. Then parents continue these activities and extensions of them at home. Teachers often train a small group of interested parents to take over this program, recapitulating the activities with another group of parents in a self-sustaining fashion. The principal provides a coordinating function: ensuring that announcements are made, the building is open, materials are available, and so forth. Thus, the principal sends a clear message that parents and teachers can work together on a vitally important area of children's experience.

The principal also sets a major tone in the life of the teachers, within school. We know many teachers who get excited about new ways of teaching mathematics by attending courses and workshops, only to return to a wholly unresponsive principal who neither understands nor values what they are trying. Students actively doing mathematics means increased discussion, movement, and noise. The principal must validate such dynamic activity as an essential part of doing mathematics.

Principals are often major determinants of budget priorities for the school and the district. The new approaches to mathematics require investments in people and materials. Staff development, courses, workshops, and other opportunities for teachers to learn more about Best Practices are essential. In addition, the principal can often effectively rearrange the available time within the school calendar for teachers to collaborate on trying these new practices, planning, sharing ideas and materials, and helping one another.

Similarly, the principal should find funds for mathematics materials, manipulatives, and resource books. Some schools have deliberately refrained from purchasing textbooks in the early grades in order to purchase manipulatives and teachers' resource guides instead. Principals play a coordinating role in ensuring the equitable and timely sharing of all materials. Some schools have a centralized location (e.g., the media center) for all mathematics materials checked out by teachers. Ideally, each teacher (or at least each grade level) should have the particular manipulatives they need to effectively teach the concepts of the curriculum; however, such arrangements are necessary when a school does not have sufficient manipulatives.

A final area in which the principal's leadership can be vitally important is assessment. If we believe the NCTM standards that assessment should primarily involve teachers' realizing what and how their students are truly understanding, principals and other administrators have a major job to do with the public and the boards of education. There must be a significant reorientation away from standardized achievement tests as the sole method of assessment for grouping and placement of individual students and for evaluating schools and programs. Teachers must begin to use a host of alternatives to formal paper-and-pencil tests to determine how a child is conceiving mathematical ideas. The principal's leadership can be invaluable in promoting the legitimacy of math journals and other written formats, as well as demonstrations and other oral formats through which students can portray their understanding and teachers can infer what might occur next in students' activities.

EXEMPLARY PROGRAM
Math Stations in Second Grade

Mary Fencl

Beye School
Oak Park, Illinois

A visitor kneels next to Lamaya at the "Tangrams" table in a second-grade classroom at Beye School. Lamaya and three other children are each trying to put together a puzzle consisting of various-sized triangles and one small square. They are supposed to form a larger square, but the solution is elusive. This is the sixth and last day for working on this particular set of "stations," or math problems, and Lamaya states readily that she's been avoiding the Tangrams table because "It's hard!" The children know they're not supposed to peek at each other's work, and even though everything is out in open view, they follow the rules.

The teacher, Mary Fencl, tells the visitor she will offer hints to keep the children from becoming discouraged. But it's clear that in addition to acquaintance with geometrical shapes, one of her purposes for this table is to help children learn to be patient and to keep on experimenting. "Play around with the pieces in as many ways as you can," she urges them. Later, when Lamaya shows frustration, Mary gives her an interesting hint. She places the two largest triangles together and draws the rest of the boundary for the final square on the formica tabletop with a marker pen. Lamaya then continues trying out various arrangements with a clearer definition of where she's headed, so that she's still using the process of "playing around," but in a slightly more supportive situation. After one more hint, Lamaya solves the puzzle, the kids and adults who are observing all applaud, and Mary remarks, "See, if you stick with something, it works out." Mary tells the visitor later that Lamaya came to the class from a more restrictive school and that while she's good at things like spelling, she has trouble taking initiative or being

creative. Mary hopes that experiences like the Tangrams table will help
Lamaya learn to experiment and take risks.

There are six "math stations" in the room, and on each day that they're
available, groups of children work at one of them. The class has math stations two days a week, so after three weeks everyone has had a turn at every
station and new ones are readied. Mary makes sure that several of the stations allow the children to review concepts they've studied earlier, several
are focused on topics presently being explored, and several deal with future
topics. During the other three days of each week, the current topics are covered in lessons from the textbook required by the district. However, the children especially enjoy the more unexpected activities on future topics, and
Mary says she learns a great deal from these. She discovers which explanations the children will need, where they will have difficulties, and which
concepts they are ready to tackle. And the children pick up the ideas through
experience, so the explanations will make more sense when they come.

Each day that math stations are scheduled, Mary reviews with the whole
class the activities at the stations before the children begin to work, so they
remember what to do. This preparation also serves as an efficient review lesson, and by the end of the cycle for a set of stations, she asks children to do
most of the re-explaining. Those who already have been to a table readily
describe it for those who haven't. For this three-week period, the stations are
as follows:

1. A board game using a die that has geographical directions on it—N,
    S, E, W. The object is to see how many rolls it takes for each player
    to move from the center of the board to the edge, "out of the city."
    The children are adding and working with directionality, which is
    currently a topic in social studies as well as in math.

2. Tangrams, using the puzzle described above. When the children
    complete the puzzle, they make a design with the same cut-out
    shapes to put up out in the hall.

3. Categorizing and Venn Diagrams. Children think up their own cat-
    egories for grouping cut-out figures of fish, from a large and vary-
    ing boxful. Then they lay two large wire loops on the floor with an
    overlapping area, to sort by categories that allow for some fish to
    fall into the mutually inclusive overlap (e.g., "spotted fish" and "fish
    with big fins," and then some that are both).

4. Averaging. The children carry out various timed activities—signing
    their names in cursive (helps with the recently begun process of
    learning it), jumping rope in the hall, dropping clothespins in a bot-
    tle, adding numbers on flashcards. The kids count the number of
    times they each complete a given activity within a three- or four-
    minute period, and then average the scores for the group for each

activity. This is a challenging concept for second graders, but Mary wants to see how far they can go with it.

5. Figuring Arrangements. Children work with three recipes—an ice-cream sundae with three ingredients, a four-layer cake, and a pizza with five ingredients. Colored-paper "layers" and cut-outs represent the various ingredients. The object is to see how many different ways they can rearrange the ingredients to make each food. For example, the sundae can have strawberry ice cream on top, choco-late in the middle, and fudge sauce on the bottom—or the fudge can go on top. They know there's a button on their calculator that will tell the answer (the factorial function), but they still need to write out all the permutations or combinations to see for themselves. Mary tells them that because the pizza can be arranged so many different ways (120), they'll need a "system" to get them all.

6. Lunch Menus. Here, a child gets $20 of play money and a copy of a restaurant menu. On a blank chart, the child writes his or her name and the names of the others in the group, and decides what will be ordered for each. Then subtotals are to be added up on the calcula-tor for main dishes, side orders, drinks, and desserts. Finally, the total bill must be tallied, which cannot be more than $20 for the whole group of diners.

Many of the activities are connected with other subjects the class is studying or interests the children share. As we've already mentioned, direc-tions had been a topic in social studies. Mary had noticed that the children struggled with translating physical orientation of one's body to lines and arrows on a map. The fish come from the "Lake Michigan" unit the class has been exploring in science. The food combinations turned into the making of real "pizza" (using English muffins) on a previous day. And the class **is** planning to go to the restaurant to celebrate the end of the school year, so each group will actually have to decide on their final choices for lunch.

As Mary reviews the stations with the children before each session, she urges the children to use a system for approaching each one, and offers a few hints about them: "Who used adding to figure out your restaurant bill as you went along? . . . Okay, did anyone use **subtracting**? How would you do that?" Mary also makes many other kinds of connections. When she gets to "categorizing," Mary pauses to ask the class about comparisons they've been making with two books they've read. Some elements are unique to one book, some to the other, and some are common to both. This clarifies the Venn Diagram concept, and also turns into a brief but spirited review of a couple of books the kids enjoyed.

When the review gets to the "arrangements" station, Dierdre volunteers to explain it, but then halts, laughs, and covers her face in embarrassment. "Did you do this station, Dierdre?" Mary asks. "Not yet, but I tried it at home after

Everett told me," she answers. Dierdre seems slightly worried, thinking she has cheated somehow, but the teacher's smile reassures her that there's nothing wrong with growing interested in something and doing it on your own.

As children go to work at the stations, the teacher circulates around the room providing help. One group sorting the fish does fine, but the other needs reminding to stay with the task. Some children using the calculators are confused because these calculators leave off final zeros that occur to the right of the decimal point. Because the kids are figuring dollars and cents, they don't realize at first that a total like "3.3" means "$3.30." The group working on averaging is so absorbed with the competition over who signed her name the most times in four minutes ("Ali" won with seventy-four, because she used the shortened version of "Alexandra") that they need reminding to continue with the next steps of adding and dividing. The kids at the Tangram table need hints at the right moments so they don't give up. When the room gets **too** noisy, the teacher clicks off the lights and very calmly reminds the children to keep the sound to a reasonable level. But in fact the period goes very smoothly and most children finish their tasks.

It's interesting to notice that while some of the stations require cooperative work, others are individually focused. The Venn Diagrams and permutations are cooperative; the lunch menus and Tangrams are individualized; and the averaging and the directions game are actually mildly competitive.

Even though Mary is using two days out of every week for math stations and only three on the book, her class has no trouble keeping up with other second-grade groups that spend the entire week on more traditional lessons and exercises. She finds the combination of textbook and activities handy, because the book organizes the topics and she can work gradually on expanding her hands-on repertoire. One of the more complex issues in all of the curricular areas we've described is how to make the transition from textbook to active inquiry, and Mary has solved it deftly.

Later, the visitor asks Mary about how she groups the children and provides the training they need to ensure that they use time well. Mary points out that the children love the variety and challenge of the math stations, and so it doesn't take much warning for them to get back on track if they've strayed. One secret, she says, is to start with group work immediately, at the beginning of the year. "If I don't start something right away, I'll never do it," she observes. The children were allowed to choose where they wanted to sit on the first day, and the groups that formed around the tables (desks are not separated or in rows) became their permanent groups. She found that the children quite naturally had formed groups with mixed ability levels and over the course of the year only a few changes were needed to solve behavior problems or achieve a better ability mix.

Mary admits that she didn't always enjoy math—"As a student, I hit the wall, myself, at about seventh or eighth grade." As a result, she didn't enjoy teaching it, either. However, as a special-education teacher before she took on her present assignment, she was driven by the desire to find something that would work for the children, since it was clear that traditional approaches to math did not. Then when she returned to the regular classroom, she specifically chose as one of her supervisory evaluation goals to develop the "math stations" approach, to force herself to make it work. "Now," she says cheerily, "math is my favorite subject!"

In fact, Mary's enjoyment of helping her students to **do** mathematics has led her to become one of the staff development teacher-leaders in her school district. Her principal, Susan Gibson, has encouraged teachers at Beye School to share ideas for teaching at the regular Wednesday after-school meetings. Ms. Gibson also arranged for eight teachers from Beye School (including Mary) to attend a district-sponsored staff development program in mathematical problem solving that we led. Since then, Mary has worked with other teachers to lead this program several times and frequently shares her methods and materials with teachers in her school and others in the district.

Works Cited

Hyde, A. A., and P. R. Hyde. 1991. *Mathwise: Teaching Mathematical Thinking and Problem Solving.* Portsmouth, NH: Heinemann.

National Council of Teachers of Mathematics. 1995. *Assessment Standards for School Mathematics.* Reston, VA: National Council of Teachers of Mathematics.

————. 1989. *Curriculum and Evaluation Standards for School Mathematics.* Reston, VA: National Council of Teachers of Mathematics.

————. 1991. *Professional Standards for Teaching Mathematics.* Reston, VA: National Council of Teachers of Mathematics.

Van de Walle, J. A. 1998. *Elementary and Middle School Mathematics: Teaching Developmentally.* New York: Longman.

Suggested Further Readings

Aichele, D. B., ed. 1994. *Professional Development of Teachers of Mathematics.* Reston, VA: National Council of Teachers of Mathematics.

House, P. E., ed. 1995. *Connecting Mathematics Across the Curriculum.* Reston, VA: National Council of Teachers of Mathematics.

Mokros, J., S. Russell, and K. Economopoulus. 1995. *Beyond Arithmetic: Changing Mathematics in the Elementary Classroom.* Palo Alto, CA: Dale Seymour Publications.

Parker, R. 1993. *Mathematical Power.* Portsmouth, NH: Heinemann.

Post, T. R., ed. 1992. *Teaching Mathematics in Grades K–8: Research Based Methods.* Boston: Allyn and Bacon, Inc.

Steen, L. A., ed. 1990. *On the Shoulders of Giants: New Approaches to Numeracy.* Washington, DC: National Academy Press.

Webb, N., ed. 1993. *Assessment in the Mathematics Classroom.* Reston, VA: National Council of Teachers of Mathematics.

Resources on the Internet

For materials, events, and other information from the National Council of Teachers of Mathematics, visit **http://www.nctm.org**.

For a variety of resources on Best Practice mathematics and links to a number of good mathematics websites, visit: **http://members.aol.com/mathwise2.**

RECOMMENDATIONS ON TEACHING MATHEMATICS

Increase	Decrease
TEACHING PRACTICES	**TEACHING PRACTICES**
Use of manipulative materials	Rote practice
Cooperative group work	Rote memorization of rules and formulas
Discussion of mathematics	Single answers and single methods to find answers
Questioning and making conjectures	Use of drill worksheets
Justification of thinking	Repetitive written practice
Writing about mathematics	Teaching by telling
Problem-solving approach to instruction	Teaching computation out of context
Content integration	Stressing memorization
Use of calculators and computers	Testing for grades only
Being a facilitator of learning	Being the dispenser of knowledge
Assessing learning as an integral part of instruction	
MATHEMATICS AS PROBLEM SOLVING	**MATHEMATICS AS PROBLEM SOLVING**
Word problems with a variety of structures and solution paths	Use of cue words to determine operation to be used
Everyday problems and applications	Practicing routine, one-step problems
Problem-solving strategies	Practicing problems categorized by types
Open-ended problems and extended problem-solving projects	
Investigating and formulating questions from problem situations	
MATHEMATICS AS COMMUNICATION	**MATHEMATICS AS COMMUNICATION**
Discussing mathematics	Doing fill-in-the-blank worksheets
Reading mathematics	Answering questions that need only yes or no responses
Writing mathematics	Answering questions that need only numerical responses
Listening to mathematical ideas	
MATHEMATICS AS REASONING	**MATHEMATICS AS REASONING**
Drawing logical conclusions	Relying on authorities (teacher, answer key)
Justifying answers and solution processes	
Reasoning inductively and deductively	

(cont.)

RECOMMENDATIONS ON TEACHING MATHEMATICS (cont.)

Increase	Decrease
MATHEMATICAL CONNECTIONS Connecting mathematics to other subjects and to the real world Connecting topics within mathematics Applying mathematics	**MATHEMATICAL CONNECTIONS** Learning isolated topics Developing skills out of context
NUMBERS/OPERATIONS/COMPUTATION Developing number and operation sense Understanding the meaning of key concepts such as place value, fractions, decimals, ratios, proportions, and percents Various estimation strategies Thinking strategies for basic facts Using calculators for complex calculations	**NUMBERS/OPERATIONS/COMPUTATION** Early use of symbolic notation Complex and tedious paper-and-pencil computations Memorizing rules and procedures without understanding
GEOMETRY/MEASUREMENT Developing spatial sense Actual measuring and the concepts related to units of measure Using geometry in problem solving	**GEOMETRY/MEASUREMENT** Memorizing facts and relationships Memorizing equivalencies between units of measure Memorizing geometric formulas
STATISTICS/PROBABILITY Collection and organization of data Using statistical methods to describe, analyze, evaluate, and make decisions	**STATISTICS/PROBABILITY** Memorizing formulas
PATTERNS/FUNCTIONS/ALGEBRA Pattern recognition and description Identifying and using functional relationships Developing and using tables, graphs, and rules to describe situations Using variables to express relationships	**PATTERNS/FUNCTIONS/ALGEBRA** Manipulating symbols Memorizing procedures and drilling
EVALUATION Having assessment be an integral part of teaching Focusing on a broad range of mathematical tasks and taking a holistic view of mathematics Developing problem situations that require applications of a number of mathematical ideas. Using multiple assessment techniques, including written, oral, and demonstration formats	**EVALUATION** Having assessment be simply counting correct answers on tests for the sole purpose of assigning grades Focusing on a large number of specific and isolated skills Using exercises or word problems requiring only one or two skills Using only written tests

5

Best Practice in Science

Teaching Science the New Way—Elementary

The fourth graders are working with "mystery powders" this month. Chris Davis first asks her class to recall times when they've happened upon some material and don't know what it is. The kids think of quite a few—containers in the cupboard or freezer that have lost their labels, old medicines left in the bathroom cabinet, a parent accidentally pouring spoonfuls of salt instead of sugar into the cake batter, the time when playmates dared them to eat strange berries growing in the empty lot. They talk also about some aspects of the scientific method—how do you systematically find out what a substance is, or what it contains?

Chris doesn't just define the vocabulary terms, like *hypothesis,* or *scientific method,* but also asks the class to predict what they think the terms mean. What prior knowledge do they have about what scientists do? They realize that on TV they've seen representations of scientists mixing things into liquids and heating them, and they talk about what might happen when substances are treated in such ways. Finally, they learn that they'll be testing five "mystery powders" to discover what they are, and they make more pre- dictions about what these might turn out to be. The kids usually expect they'll be edible.

Now that the mental ground has been set, the children work in groups to identify their five powders. Dittoed guidesheets help them to keep on task and record their findings. They smell, touch, listen (as they stir the dry materials), look closely with magnifying glasses. They realize that while all the powders are "white," they don't really look the same up close. Some are crystalline, others not; some particles are larger, some finer. They try dissolving each in water, vegetable oil, and vinegar, and different things happen. Three disappear in the water. One fizzes in the vinegar. One mixture turns hard when left to stand for a while. They heat each powder and observe the results. They put a drop of iodine on each—and one turns black as a result. It takes a week of entire afternoons to complete all the testing. The groups decide their own order for testing, based on whether some facilities (e.g., the burners for heating) are in use or not. Because the children have had plenty of experience working in groups, they proceed with minimal teacher direction.

Then comes write-up, discussion, and comparison of their results, and the kids learn what the materials really are: sugar, salt, baking powder, corn-starch, and plaster of paris. After this, the kids get a new task: each group receives a bag of powder that is a *mixture* of the five substances, and they must determine their particular constituents. The final write-ups follow a scientific protocol that the students try out by first doing one collaboratively. The writing and revision work goes on during language-arts writing time.

The kids also write and share their reflections about what the unit has taught them. Chris is surprised and pleased when the children, on their own, talk about the value of working through a step-by-step procedure and using a process of elimination. "We can use this for math, too," they say, "especially when we get stuck." Finally, they list the questions they realize were *not* answered during the activity: *Why* did the baking soda fizz in vinegar? Why *does* iodine make cornstarch turn black? What was happening when some of the powders burned during heating? These will become topics for successive units later in the year. Some of the kids also decide, during art or language-arts time, to make safety posters about not playing with unknown substances, to be put up in their kitchen for the benefit of younger brothers and sisters. Altogether, the unit takes a month to complete. The lab times are lengthy, but time is actually saved because the kids don't have to clean up and set up as many times as they would with shorter work periods.

Teaching Science the New Way—Secondary

In San Antonio, Roger Robison's biology class begins its study of genetics by reading several articles about teenagers suffering from some debilitating conditions—diabetes, sickle-cell anemia, and a rare liver disorder that claimed the life of a student from their own school. The students discuss the articles and list their questions about these diseases: if they're inherited, will every child of the same two parents get the illness? Why don't the parents have it too? Exactly how are the diseases passed from parent to child? Is there any way, short of going childless, to prevent them or to protect future generations?

With these kinds of questions in mind, the kids head to the lab for an experiment. Each group of three students receives a pair of dishes with fungi growing in them. The fungi in one dish have spores of one color, and those in the second dish have another. Each group talks over what they think will happen when they crossbreed their fungi. Will the spores from the next generation of fungi be brown? Gray? A color in between? Some of each? In what proportions? The groups write out their predictions and their reasoning, and then after a lesson on sterile technique (so the experiment will be accurate), they breed their two fungi in a third dish and examine them two days later. Of course, the teacher has set things up a bit. As a result, the groups get differing results, compare them, and write out their own guesses about what is going on. It is at this point that they are ready to learn Mendel's laws.

Class sessions now focus on reading and information sharing on the principles of genetics that will explain the experimental results and also answer some of their questions about human genetic disorders. Student groups take turns studying sections of the textbook and then explaining them to the rest of the class. Roger provides additional explanatory and curiosity-provoking articles, plus suggestion sheets listing ways to promote class discussion, to help the groups plan their explanation sessions. One important job for each group is to explain how their information helps answer one or more of the questions the class first posed.

The study moves on to population genetics. The class conducts surveys of their own genetic patterns. How many class members are left-handed? Which ones can taste the chemical PTC? How many have index fingers longer than their ring fingers? How many cannot see certain colors? These are all inherited traits. If the students haven't already stumbled on certain questions, Roger poses them for people to write about in an "admit slip" at the start of a class period: If sickle-cell anemia is an inherited trait, why is it more common in the Black population? If most people with cystic fibrosis die as teens, before they can have children of their own, then why does the gene for it still occur? Answers are found by working through the text together.

While this whole-class study has been going on, the students also extend their initial discussion of genetic disorders by brainstorming and gathering information (e.g., calls to hospitals and doctors, finding news articles) to identify other diseases and related genetics topics they might inquire about: Tay-Sachs disease, Down syndrome, the work of genetics counselors at hospitals, purposes and problems of inbreeding pets and farm animals. Ultimately, everyone chooses a topic to investigate further, with most working in groups of three or four.

As their classroom study continues, the students carry out interviews to get information on the topics they've chosen to investigate. Students visit hospitals, interview patients who agree to cooperate, talk with March of Dimes officials. Then each group prepares an informational brochure about the disease they've studied. Finally, after reading each other's brochures (which will be displayed in the library or at local hospitals), they list further questions they now have. These often prove to be questions that can be answered through study of succeeding text chapters. Rarely is anyone bored during the genetics unit.

A Look at the Standards Documents

National concern about Americans' ignorance of science has increased sharply in recent years. Several well-publicized reports, both national and international, have suggested the science achievement of our students may be far behind that of children in most industrialized nations, and even in some Third World countries. These results may exaggerate the problem a bit— U.S.-educated scientists still lead the world in most fields of basic research and many areas of technology, and continue to collect more prizes than their colleagues from other countries.

Whether it's a crisis or not, the happy fact is that we now have reports from several national bodies that to a great extent agree on approaches, like those described above, that could make science education both more inviting and more effective. These reports, drafted by scientists as well as science educators, are striking in their nearly unanimous advocacy of the principles of progressive education that we outlined earlier. They call for making science learning experiential instead of lecture-oriented, cognitive and constructivist rather than focused only on facts and formulas, social and collaborative rather than isolating students from one another. The American Association for the Advancement of Science (AAAS) set the tone in 1989, by asserting:

> Teaching related to scientific literacy needs to be consistent with the spirit and character of scientific inquiry and with scientific values. This suggests such approaches as starting with questions about phenomena rather than with answers to be learned; engaging students actively in the use of hypotheses, the collection and use of evidence, and the design of investigations and processes; and placing a premium on students' curiosity and creativity. (5)

Along with goals for content learning, the 1989 report, *Science for All Americans: A Project 2061 Report on Literacy Goals in Science, Mathematics, and Technology*, includes a full section on "Effective Learning and Teaching," which outlines most of the principles set forth later in this chapter.

The *National Science Education Standards* (National Academy Press 1996) took several leaps further by *starting* with a set of teaching standards, moving on to standards for professional development for teachers and standards for meaningful assessment, and only then moving on to content standards for student achievement. Unlike many documents from other fields, rather than just arguing that higher standards for kids would mean higher standards for teachers and school systems, this report recognizes that better learning comes first and foremost from better teaching and better systemic support for good education. Within the content standards themselves, the document turns its asserted values into explicit standards for the classroom. The first content standards are about "Unifying Concepts and Processes." Then, standards for each grade level begin with a standard for "Science as Inquiry" and conclude with one for "Science in Personal and Social Perspectives" and one for "History and Nature of Science." Understanding large ideas and themes and developing inquiring habits of mind, in other words, are the central goals for teaching and learning science.

Unfortunately, not every standards document is this sophisticated. The AAAS *Benchmarks for Science Literacy* (1993) begins well enough with a larger perspective, through standards on understanding the "nature" of science, mathematics, and technology, and concludes, late in the text, with standards on "Common Themes" and "Habits of Mind," which emphasize the value of large ideas and of students' curiosity. But the attention to teaching that was so striking in *Science for All Americans* is gone. The authors stress that this will come in later documents, and that matters of order and separation should not be taken as significant; but, unfortunately, they are, as the contrast with the *National Science Education Standards* illustrates. Even more troubling, the *Framework for High School Science Education* (Aldridge 1996), which claims to be based on the *National Science Education Standards*, dispenses almost completely with the larger perspective. It dives immediately into the narrowest subject instruction issues and relegates "Unifying Concepts" and "Science as Inquiry" to a small section late in the document, headed "Science Applications and Processes."

We strongly recommend that teachers and schools seeking to reform and strengthen science teaching, as opposed to merely ratifying the status quo, make use of the *National Science Education Standards*. It's an extremely helpful document because it not only provides goals for high-quality science teaching and learning and for leading more students to enter science fields, but also shows us how to work toward those goals.

Qualities of Best Practice in Teaching Science

Students need opportunities to explore the significance of science in their lives.   For both the students who will study and use science in their careers and for all students who need to be well-informed citizens, the broad goal of a school science program should be to foster understanding, interest, and appreciation of the world in which we live. Along with building a knowledge base, science education should encourage students' natural curiosity, develop procedural skills for investigating and problem solving, consider the possibilities and limits of science and technology in human affairs, and build an understanding of the nature of science and technology as fields of inquiry themselves. Thus, at each grade level, the *National Science Education Standards* includes a separate standard for relations between science and technology and one on "science in personal and social perspectives."

Science study should involve doing science, that is, questioning and discovering—not just covering—material.

One San Antonio high school biology teacher begins the year by giving each student twenty-five acorns and asking students to observe everything they can about them. Then she asks if they float, something most didn't check. Some acorns float while others don't, and there are many possible reasons, so the students proceed to hypothesize about why. But this is only a prologue. Each student must then choose a topic to investigate, design his or her own data-gathering process, pursue it, and write up the results, a project that continues throughout the year while the rest of the biology study goes on.

While science has built a massive body of knowledge over the past few centuries, the essential spirit of science is one of *process*—of inquiry and questioning. Students learn this spirit by engaging in it themselves. If they are asked only to memorize information that is presented as already known, they are not being exposed to this questioning side of the discipline. As the *National Science Education Standards* asserts, "Learning science is something students do, not something that is done to them. . . . Emphasizing active science learning means shifting emphasis away from teachers presenting information and covering science topics" (20).

Science involves higher-order thinking and comparison and connection of phenomena from a variety of settings. Therefore, as repeated research has shown, lectures, front-of-the-class demonstrations, and rote memorization of explanations lead to very little long-term understanding or correction of misconceptions about the natural world. Much more effective is a "constructivist" approach, which means activating children's prior knowledge about a phenomenon, encouraging their questions about it, and helping them gather information hands-on and build their own concepts.

This approach does not negate or minimize the value of factual information in science. Rather, it seeks to ensure that students really understand and retain this knowledge, and that the information is seen in a larger context of thought and inquiry, because future scientific development may very well make particular explanations obsolete. In fact, if more students were involved in this stimulating and motivating kind of study, it's likely that more would be willing to continue with more demanding advanced courses and science careers.

However, not all hands-on laboratory activities present students with cognitive challenges. A "cookbook" approach can be as trivial as rote memorization of vocabulary lists. Therefore, teachers must organize and guide experiments so that the students engage in real problem solving—that is, they are helped to generate real questions, realize apparent contradictions between pieces of data, pose alternate hypotheses, gather information to test them, and analyze the meaning of the information.

Yes, but . . . hands-on activities are time-consuming, and involve expensive materials and special expertise that not all teachers have.

Most science educators already recognize the value of direct experimental activity, though many also acknowledge that they use it far less than they should. This approach does indeed take time, but science groups also urge that teachers shift to an in-depth exploration of fewer concepts, to allow a full process of inquiry to take place. We discuss this as a separate, major recommendation later. However, some steps, such as probing children's prior daily-life experience of a phenomenon and generating questions about it, or stopping to elicit alternate predictions or hypotheses about successive trials of an experiment comparing different materials, need not absorb large amounts of time. Even the simple addition of a few seconds of wait time between a question asked and answers sought from the class has been shown to increase students' learning significantly. The point of these steps is to help convert mechanical labs and class discussions into a real process of questioning and discovery.

For elementary teachers who are not experts in particular science areas, excellent resources are available that describe easy-to-do experiments using inexpensive, readily available, nontoxic materials (e.g., Vicki Cobb, *The Trip of a Drip* [1986] and *More Science Experiments You Can Eat* [1985]). The steps and objectives described in the following sections help a teacher to guide classroom experiments so that they are productive. And once a teacher comprehends the essential investigating process, she needn't be an expert with all the answers, but can be a fellow experimenter with her students—that is, a good *model* of scientific thinking.

Effective hands-on inquiry involves a series of steps that builds students' investigative skills.   Scientific inquiry for learning, while open-ended and flexible in many ways, involves a number of distinct steps and helps children acquire a range of process skills. Thinking about these can help teachers organize and guide experimental activities to ensure that in-depth learning takes place. The dividing lines within the process have been drawn differently by various science educators, but can be described generally as follows:

- **Questioning.** The teacher (and/or student) introduces a problem, incites curiosity, or invites recall of personal experience with a natural phenomenon. Students discuss and list what they know or think they know about it, and questions they have. Often a demonstration of contradictory or puzzling outcomes helps raise such questions.

- **Observation.** Students gather data, at first in an exploratory way to probe the question. They begin to propose hypotheses to explain variations they find. This leads to more focused observation to test the hypotheses.

- **Organizing Data.** This may overlap with observation. It focuses on looking for patterns and differences.

- **Explanation**. Students may be able to discern a cause or theory to explain differences. With more complex phenomena, reading, text-books, or a teacher's expert input will be needed—and by this stage welcomed.

- **Reflection**. Review of the process, obstacles, and how these were addressed makes students aware of the concepts, problem solving, and thinking processes they've learned in the course of the inquiry.

- **Taking Action**. Some topics with technological implications can result in responsible action in the larger community. Others lead to further scientific questions the students realize remain unanswered, thus encouraging students to continue learning.

Just as with stages in the writing process (see p. 60), these are not lockstep, one-after-the-other phases in some ideal "scientific method." A good teacher—or researcher—recognizes that at any stage, one may need to jump back to another, and that real science is a complex mixture of organized inquiry and intuitive play with ideas and possibilities. Students may realize their real questions or misconceptions only after they've begun to observe, or organize, or work out explanations for their data. By observing students carefully as an activity proceeds, a teacher can decide when to intervene to point out what has taken place thus far, when to guide students so they won't become bogged down, and when to stand aside so the students take more responsibility for their learning.

Instead of a single scientific method, science educators have come to realize that there are many process skills students learn as they carry out meaningful investigations. These include:

- posing questions
- defining operationally
- designing experiments
- inferring relationships
- controlling variables
- observing
- coping with limitations in instruments
- interpreting
- evaluating data
- making generalizations about findings
- responding to constructive criticism

- hypothesizing
- formulating models
- using space and time
- justifying decisions
- predicting
- measuring
- classifying data
- using mathematics
- collecting more data if needed
- communicating

These thinking skills are extremely important for students' success in other school subjects as well as science. Teachers can use such a list to determine whether an activity they wish to employ will in fact give students a rich learning experience in science.

Meaningful science study will aim to develop thinking, problem solving, and attitudes of curiosity, healthy skepticism, and openness to modifying explanations.   Just as in the newer approaches to mathematics, good science teachers have recognized that attitudes toward—and learning good strategies for—problem solving are especially important to their teaching.

A start-of-the-year activity used by Jim Effinger at Naperville North High School illustrates just how a problem-solving approach can excite students about biology. Jim brings donuts to class and asks what sorts of things people might do before they eat their donuts. Possibilities include choosing and inspecting your donut, saying a prayer, and sooner or later someone mentions washing hands. "Why do that?" Jim asks. The students decide that *getting rid of germs* is the main purpose.

"How could we test to see if washing really does the job?" Jim asks. The kids agree to give this a try, and Jim brings out Petri dishes, soap, and pans of water. Each student touches one Petri dish, then washes up, and touches a second one. They inspect the dishes the next day, to see what has grown. Invariably, the results are:

- sixty to seventy percent of the dishes show **more** bacteria after washing than before
- ten to fifteen percent are the same before and after
- fifteen to thirty percent have fewer bacteria after washing

The students are surprised and confused, and begin to hypothesize about the cause of these results—old versus new bars of soap, drying or leaving hands wet. They redesign more experiments following rules they've decided on to standardize their efforts and maximize the cleaning achieved and try again—only to get the same results!

The kids are now hooked, eager to discover what factor influences the difference in number of bacteria on their hands. But Jim tells them the experiment is taking too much class time. If they really want to continue, they'll have to come after school. They do, of course, and after trying out many variables (quick-thinking groups organize into cooperative teams, to try a number of factors at the same time), they finally discover the secret: *time*. A short scrub just loosens the bacteria, so that more end up on the dish. A long, eight-minute scrub (as doctors use) does indeed do the job. But far more than just finding an answer, the students have learned many important aspects of scientific thinking: to consider many possible causes for a phenomenon, to design ways to look for these causes, to plan and control their experiments so that additional variables are not introduced, and most important, to expect that their everyday beliefs and guesses may not always be correct.

More broadly, it is essential to encourage students' natural curiosity, sense of self-esteem, and confidence in approaching science study. Students should see themselves as active, responsible citizens who use their knowledge to take an active part in public debate on the technological choices that always balance gains and liabilities as they are introduced into our surroundings. The 1989 AAAS report, *Science for All Americans: A Project 2061 Report on Literacy Goals in Science, Mathematics, and Technology* emphasizes overcoming student anxieties, associating science with positive learning experiences, and especially helping minority and female students to feel that science is an inviting field.

Science education can build a knowledge base focused on essential concepts, rather than disconnected topics or bits of information.   Many of the national reports on science education observe that science curricula too often focus on discrete topics and present information, facts, and processes within these. Instead, teaching can be organized around broader unifying themes, concepts, and kinds of thinking. The *National Science Education Standards* (104) provides a concise group of five unifying concepts:

- Systems, order, and organization
- Evidence, models, and explanation
- Change, constancy, and measurement
- Evolution and equilibrium
- Form and function

By organizing material into themes around one or several of these analytical approaches, teachers can focus more readily on thinking skills, make connections between various specific topics, and identify clear learning objectives within a number of inquiry activities, so that children can even choose which ones to carry out and still work through all the essential concepts. The themes also make it easier for teachers to integrate science with reading, writing, and math and to explore technological implications of a science topic.

For example, an activity in which children collect seeds from nearby areas, examine them, and attempt to make them grow under varying conditions could be used in a number of ways. It could fit within a unit on **form and function** (the role of various parts of the seed); one on **change, constancy, and measurement** (influence of light, water, and chemicals on germination and growth); or **systems, order, and organization** (following the life cycle of the plant). Of course, the teacher would need to encourage observation, questions, and reflection to help make any of these themes explicit for the students. Then analogues for any of the concepts could be found elsewhere in the curriculum, in literature the children read and stories they write.

Students should explore fewer topics in depth, not skim many superficially.
Thoughtful teachers and national panels on science education have, over the
years, repeatedly stressed in-depth inquiry instead of wide coverage of science topics. The *National Science Education Standards* puts it most strongly:
"Emphasizing active science learning means shifting emphasis away from
teachers presenting information and covering science topics. The perceived
need to include all the topics, vocabulary, and information in textbooks is in
direct conflict with the central goal of having students learn scientific knowledge with understanding" (20–21).

The aim is for a larger number of educated citizens to be comfortable
with science and scientific modes of thought, to be more personally involved
with it, and thus more likely to continue studying it, either for career purposes or for informed decision making in a world that is affected ever more
deeply by scientific and technological choices. Achieving this attitudinal
development requires sufficient time to focus on a continuing process in
which students are deeply involved.

Some teachers, especially at the high school level, seek to cover lots of
material because "These kids will probably never study biology again and
this is their one chance to get it." Sadly, this becomes a self-fulfilling proph-
ecy. Many students experience minimal engagement with the topic and so
they discover little of its relevance to their lives or its ability to fascinate.
Conversely, kids who are actively involved in an extended cycle of questioning, experiential data-gathering, group discussion, and sharing of information
will be engaged, will want to learn more, and will be motivated to do so later
on, after the course is over.

**Yes, but . . . what about the growing number of state compe-
tency tests and the achievement tests for advanced students'
college entrance? Don't the students need to cover a large number of science topics to do well on these?**

Science education panels acknowledge that this is a problem, especially because the tests are focused on memorizing facts instead of
learning scientific thinking. The panels have argued for shifts in district, state, and national testing so that tests support the kind of science we ought to teach. Student performance on national tests has
shown declines in the past, so there seems to be little to lose. If so
many students don't fare well with superficial textbook and lecture
study, a shift to in-depth learning may well result in *better* standardized test performance. In one classroom experiment that demonstrated this connection, a group of remedial students used ethnographic interviews of local farmers and gardeners to learn about
factors that influenced plant growth. These remedial students, who

had consistently failed in all subjects, scored higher than all other classes in their school on the related textbook chapter test on plant biology (Heath 1983, 315–327).

Students grow out of misconceptions and naive theories only by actively engaging in investigation.   In our daily lives, all of us construct concepts that help us interpret familiar events. These ideas seem sensible, but with natural phenomena they are often incorrect. Because they appear reasonable to the student, such concepts are not readily changed, even when a more accurate scientific explanation is given by a teacher. Science teachers often have as objectives the clarification of such misconceptions. However, research studies show that much of the time, students memorize a new explanation without truly understanding it and still retain their basic misconceptions. Usually, it is only through a process of active questioning, encountering contradictory data, and investigating it that students can internalize more accurate scientific concepts and perceive their plausibility and usefulness.

In one earth science class, for example, the teacher helps students undo their confusion about the phases of the moon by using two tennis balls, each painted black on one side. Many high school students (and adults, no doubt) believe the moon's phases occur because the earth blocks sunlight, casting a shadow on the moon. The teacher hands each of two students a painted tennis ball, asks them to imagine one is the earth and one the moon; a window in the classroom represents the sun. Now the two students decide how to move to represent the "moon" tennis ball orbiting the "earth," with the bright side of the "moon" always facing the "sun," where its light originates. At the same time, other students take turns observing, positioning one eye as close to the "earth" tennis ball as possible. They immediately see the growing and shrinking crescent that the "moon" displays to them. The earth's blockage of light, they later learn, is the cause of the much rarer lunar eclipses. This is not an expensive or complex experiment, but it is well understood and remembered by the students.

Learning science means integrating reading, writing, speaking, and math.
When Georgeann Schulte's fourth graders study the desert, they use reading and writing in a wide variety of ways. They write letters to kids in Arizona, asking about how those children experience desert geography and desert life. They read *Desert Dog* by Jim Kjelgaard. Georgeann reads aloud Bird Baylor's *I'm in Charge of Celebrations*, which poetically celebrates the pleasures of closely observing in nature, and the children then find natural objects, creatures, and events to observe, after which they compose their own written celebrations.

It is not difficult to see how an effective science program involves a wide range of language and numeracy skills. Groups working on an investigation will use plenty of writing to list what they know, recall personal experience of the phenomenon, generate questions, keep track of data and variables in an experiment, compare hypotheses, plan presentations to the rest of the class, or write letters to outside authorities about technological implications of their learning. Students practice speaking skills when they work in groups, interview informants and visiting experts, and present results to the class. They read whenever they compare their written data and explanations. Once they are excited about a topic, students eagerly read and recount related information from textbooks, library materials, and news articles. Math is used in measuring, tallying, graphing, and averaging. Thus, teachers—especially those with self-contained classrooms—can readily integrate many parts of the curriculum in order to make time for extended science exploration.

Students need to consider issues of application of science and technology. While science education often neglects technology, or conflates it with science, the *National Science Education Standards* authors considered the topic so important to the education of informed citizens that they set a separate standard for it at each grade level. Technology addresses problems of human adaptation in the environment, while science attempts to answer questions about the natural world. And each, of course, influences the other. Students can be engaged in both these areas of thinking, and it is usually the technological questions that lead to major public issues—acid rain caused by industry and power plants; pollution in rivers, air, and food chains; depletion of natural resources; alternate energy sources. All technologies involve both gains and environmental costs, and most present various alternatives for solving a given problem. These impact wider systems in the process. Students can be encouraged to weigh technological questions in these terms, rather than simply label a technological development "good" or "bad."

At present, many elementary teachers do conduct units on ecology and conservation, providing picturebooks and articles on preservation of rain forests and endangered species. However, few present these as controversies or introduce the arguments of competing interests. We do not mean to imply that we side with the timber industry against the spotted owl. However, if students don't get an opportunity, early on, to sort through a series of arguments and counter arguments—which is usually what technological issues involve—they won't be able to effectively advocate for their ecological values later on. We've observed primary-level classrooms where children readily do this kind of thinking, if the teacher has encouraged thought and analysis rather than memorization.

Good science teaching involves facilitation, collaborative group work, and a limited, judicious use of information giving. When we consider the teacher's role in the science classroom, we must recognize that lecturing is not only unsupportive of hands-on investigation, but also that research shows it is strikingly unsuccessful at influencing students' science concepts. The teacher needs to model the same kinds of questioning and problem solving that he or she wishes the class to learn. Fortunately, this means a teacher need not have all the answers or be an expert in all areas of science. Instead, teachers can facilitate learning in a number of ways. They can offer tantalizing natural situations and puzzles that invite children to question. Teachers can observe student groups carefully to see what kinds of help they need, and provide guidance and information when students become stuck or discouraged. Teachers can analyze the activities launched in the classroom to understand the concepts and process skills involved, so as to reinforce these during evaluation and reflection sessions. In other words, the teacher still has an important role as expert and information giver, but uses it more strategically to promote lasting learning, and holds back when it would short-circuit students' own initiative and investigation process.

As for students' classroom roles, real-world scientists frequently work in groups, and top science educators stress the importance of group work in school. They recognize that discussion promotes thinking and problem solving by leading students to compare alternate ideas and solutions. When differences of opinion occur in a group, the students are naturally forced to elaborate their explanations and reasonings, and so these are made more explicit and tested against opposing arguments. Thus, students think out scientific explanations instead of just memorizing them. They realize the questions they have and are motivated to seek answers from the text or the teacher because they desire to settle the passionate arguments that develop. As a result, they also remember a lot more of what they've studied. Group work need not be confined to lab periods. Students can work together throughout entire units, with each group investigating a different question under the same theme or topic, and then reporting its findings to the class.

Yes, but . . . can teachers and students really adopt these teaching and learning approaches when they're so accustomed to the usual lectures, textbooks, memorizing, and test taking?

Fortunately, we have many more tools for applying new teaching methods than in the past. We needn't depend on intuitive trial-and-error approaches that can leave teachers and students floundering when they don't work well. For example, Johnson, Johnson, Holubec, and Roy provide very clear, practical, and effective methods for teaching children to work productively in small groups, in *Cooperation in the Classroom* (1991). This training takes time, of course, but as more and more teachers are using small-group work in various subjects and grade levels, increasing numbers of students will arrive in science classes already equipped to do it well.

Teachers don't always have the time or expertise to design their own more experiential science investigation units. However, materials are also available to help with this—for example, Wendy Saul and Jeanne Reardon's *Beyond the Science Kit* (1996), which guides teachers in leading thoughtful and active science inquiry activities with their students.

Meaningful assessment of students' learning in science must promote the objectives of a good science curriculum, and not undermine them. Testing in science classrooms often focuses on the body of knowledge in science, rather than the thinking and investigative processes or attitudes a student should acquire. If teachers are to promote experiential work and thinking skills in science, then assessment should stress these as well. Otherwise, teachers and students are being asked to do one thing but being held accountable for another. The *National Science Education Standards* writers chose to develop an entire set of standards just for assessment, so they could highlight the need to bring it more in line with up-to-date science teaching. They couldn't put the need more strongly:

> Rather than checking whether students have memorized certain items of information, assessments need to probe for students' understanding, reasoning, and the utilization of knowledge. Assessment and learning are so closely related that if all the outcomes are not assessed, teachers and students likely will redefine their expectations for learning science only to the outcomes that are assessed. (82)

The authors further stress the importance of opportunity-to-learn indicators, recognizing that we must hold districts and schools responsible directly, rather than blame students, when science learning is not adequate.

The *National Science Educations Standards* document also affirms the value of authentic assessments such as portfolios, interviews, performance tasks, and self-assessment. While it is difficult for formal pencil-and-paper tests to assess attitudes and thinking skills, informal but structured assessment based on teacher monitoring of group investigations can do this job very well. Teachers can use checklists to guide their observations, have students fill out self-evaluation forms, and in brief conferences, ask questions about why individuals or groups are proceeding in a particular way. Even written tests can be designed so that they focus on the *process* of finding an answer, rather than just the answer itself. Some questions can be designed so that they have more than one right answer, so as to recognize creative thinking and problem solving. Since assessment unavoidably influences curriculum, if we don't test for the real *doing* of science, our schools won't teach it.

How Parents Can Help

Kids are questioners. Every parent knows this, and we remind ourselves about it in endless cartoons and stories. Much as we can feel dogged by all the questions when the day has been long and dinner still isn't on the table, and much as we feel inadequate to answer them, we need to encourage children's questioning, for this is the real basis for scientific learning. Questions need not be viewed as a challenge to our parental authority, but rather as a chance to reinforce kids' natural desires to learn and to gain some control over the complex world around them.

Just as with teachers, parents don't need to be science experts or to invest in expensive microscope kits to encourage their children's interest in science. They can read aloud from the steady stream of newspaper reports on science discoveries and technological problems and advances. The flow of new information about astronomy and the origins of the universe, genetic engineering and the cure for AIDS, pollution and global warming, and similar topics continues to challenge the very foundations of much scientific thought. If parents and children don't understand what some of it is about, they can head for the library or ask a teacher to help the children decipher some of the mysteries.

Plenty of family activities can promote an interest in science—observing the habits of pet hamsters or guinea pigs, vacationing at the beach or in the mountains; visiting zoos, museums, and special exhibits. As with all the curricular areas covered in this book, children's independent reading is especially important. When gift-giving time comes and parents are selecting books, fiction is not the only choice. Parents can choose some of the excellent (and not necessarily expensive) children's nonfiction books about nature, health, and technology. Among these are Ruth Heller's books on wildlife, David Macauley's splendid architecturally illustrated books on how things work, and Alfred A. Knopf's "Discovery" series, which covers everything from diamonds to dinosaurs. And we can avoid gender differences. If microscopes or computers **are** on the gift list, they should be given to girls as well as boys.

Parents should ask teachers and principals about how science is taught in their schools. Are there in-depth, hands-on study units? Are the kids encouraged to ask questions, develop hypotheses, and interpret the data, or is the process primarily lecture, workbook pages, and cookbook experiments? What kinds of learning do the tests emphasize? Parents don't need to be scientists or education experts to ask these questions and to evaluate the answers they get. Communities tend to get the kind of education they demand.

What Principals Can Do

First and foremost, the principal can model an inquiring, problem-solving spirit in the school. When issues arise—rules of behavior, uses of space— he or she can distribute questionnaires to learn what is really happening and can solicit suggestions from students. When unusual natural or biological events occur—violent storms, mold infestations, measles outbreaks—classes can be invited to investigate them and prepare explanatory displays. Anyone who's in charge of a building like a school, which depends for its proper function on many interlocking technological systems—heat, ventilation, electricity, roofing, insulation, traffic, communications, waste disposal—can always share experiences with "scientific" and technical decision making.

Effective professional development is vital for helping teachers—particularly those elementary teachers who have limited science backgrounds—to adopt meaningful, conceptually and experientially rich science explorations. Staff development can be provided not just in science itself, but also in connected areas like collaborative learning and writing across the curriculum. Teachers need help developing integrated curriculum activities that use time efficiently by connecting with all the subjects taught in the school day. Subject-area specialists, of course, will need less help with the content of their teaching, but usually can use support for adopting new classroom techniques, and sufficient planning time to incorporate these appropriately into their teaching plans.

Developing extended thematic units takes hard work, and too few published materials are available to supply ready-made plans. Principals can work to gain resources for after-school and summer curriculum design time for teams of teachers. Teachers need to be given responsibility for inquiry and development, if they are to encourage it in their students.

The principal can help build community understanding and support of kids' inquiries. School-wide science fairs often gain considerable community attention, although they also require plenty of planning and hard work by the staff, and are most productive when they don't depend on competition as a motivator. More daily ongoing support can be developed through letters to parents and contact with neighboring hospitals, industries, universities, botanical gardens, zoos, and other facilities that can provide visiting experts and data sources for inquiring kids.

Materials can be expensive. New computer "hypercard" programs are available that provide complex sets of data for students to explore, following their own lines of questioning—but good software is costly and creates the need for newer, more powerful hardware. At the elementary level, textbooks have been shown to be particularly ineffective in promoting science learning. If the district can afford extensive science materials, the principal should lobby for judicious selection, so that resources aren't wasted on systems that don't really teach much—especially when the same funds could be used for effective inservice training in active science inquiry methods, or for a good library of books for independent nonfiction reading. However, if the district cannot afford lots of new materials, the principal can seek help from community businesses and parents to obtain the simpler supplies that can support many excellent classroom experiments.

Testing is perhaps the issue on which principals feel most caught in the middle. Communities expect the kids to do well on standardized tests and principals especially believe they are judged by performance on these.

Principals can keep in mind, however, that American students, in general, are not performing very well on tests of science knowledge anyway, and a more interactive curriculum is likely to promote a better understanding of science concepts than traditional approaches. Furthermore, faculties that are developing better science curricula can be asked to create assessment activities that reflect their goals so that more meaningful information on students' learning is being provided to the community, whatever the standardized tests show. The *National Science Education Standards* provides valuable justification for adopting more valid science assessments.

For all of these issues, the *National Science Education Standards* provides very persuasive ammunition, for it sets forth in separate chapters clear standards for professional development for teachers, standards for school science programs, and standards for the support that should be offered by regional and state agencies. The document recognizes, more than many, that calling for meaningful standards in science teaching and learning means calling for significant change. As the authors assert in outlining their goals, "Students could not achieve the standards in most of today's schools. Implementation of the *Standards* will require a sustained, long-term commitment to change" (13).

EXEMPLARY PROGRAM
Literature Circles in Intermediate Science

Jacqueline McWilliams Chappel

Carnegie School
Chicago, Illinois

Carnegie School, on the South Side in Chicago, is just south of the University of Chicago and the wide "Midway" that cuts an east-west swath across the area close to Lake Michigan. Most of the University and the professional-intellectual Hyde Park community lie North of the Midway; Carnegie serves the much poorer, racially segregated neighborhoods to the south. Jackie's students were full of energy and ideas, and she worked gently but insistently to keep them on track, listening to one another, and using their time well.

When Jackie Chappel taught a fourth/fifth-grade "split" at Carnegie, she adapted for science a strategy—Literature Circles—that she originally employed for reading. This was especially efficient because the children had already learned how to use the activity in one setting and didn't need separate training to employ it efficiently in another. The overlap also helped the children realize that effective group-learning strategies can be extended to any sort of inquiry, and that the many subjects taught during the day are all interconnected. As we will see, Jackie used topics and issues from throughout the curriculum to reinforce the principles involved in the cooperative work of Literature Circles. This unit not only integrated reading, writing, and science, but also put special emphasis on learning to generate questions leading to further study. We'll first describe the Literature Circle structure itself, and then explain how Jackie applied it to the study of biology.

Jackie learned about Literature Circles in her search for effective strategies to share as a staff development workshop leader. As Harvey Daniels describes in *Literature Circles: Voice and Choice in the Student-Centered Classroom* (1994), Literature Circles are student-led, small-group discussions of a book that all group members have read. The teacher briefly reviews the books children may choose from, each child reads one book of his or her choice, and participates in a discussion group with others who chose the same book. Prior to the first time children try this, they practice a number of different roles for contributing to the discussion groups—Discussion Director, Illustrator, Connector, Word Wizard (for vocabulary), and so forth. The children carry on the discussions themselves, with the teacher monitoring the groups' work. Gradually, the children learn to have good discussions without depending on the roles. Frequently, the groups will be required to create an outcome reflecting their reading—a poster, perhaps, a presentation to the rest of the class, a project. We've described in more detail how this strategy works in practice in Marianne Flanagan's classroom (see Chapter 1).

Many teachers worry that their children "just don't work well in groups," and Jackie testifies that several background pieces are crucial to their success, in reading or in science. First, throughout the year, she stressed with the children the importance of self-government, negotiation, and democratic problem solving. When children came to her with a disagreement, she asked them to find a way to negotiate and work it out on their own. She asked students to divide up tasks or decide which groups will work with which books, and explained that if they couldn't reach compromises, the choice would revert to the teacher. Discipline problems with the groups were reduced significantly. "They would come back to me later and brag about how they solved their problem," she says. The very content of the curriculum provided repeated occasions for stressing these values and processes. Every story has a conflict, Jackie points out, so during discussions of literature, talk often centered on how conflicts were resolved in constructive ways. The neighborhood violence that frequently showed up in these kids' journal entries occasioned yet more talk about alternate ways to solve problems.

The teacher still must work patiently on discipline as the children carry on their discussion groups. Talk, noise, and movement are a natural part of the process, and children need to learn boundaries between productive noise and distraction. Teachers unfamiliar with cooperative groups may envision only the extremes—complete control and silence or letting kids go and watching the chaos. Instead, when the noise verged on the nonproductive, Jackie reminded her children that the work was important and the aim was to learn together effectively. "You have to keep your eye on everything," she says, "but the kids really do keep working."

Now for the science application of this strategy. Jackie used the science Literature Circles early in the fall to generate science questions the children could pursue throughout the year. The focus was biology. Some hands-on experimentation established important concepts about scientific inquiry that would come up in the reading. In a short mini-lesson on the scientific method, Jackie introduced the concept of "hypothesis," using the verbal formula, "I believe that if I do X, Y will occur." The children then experimented with dried beans, employing an activity suggested by the school's science department head, Raymond Gardner. The kids used pins to test the permeability or brittleness of the beans, eventually discovering that the beans change when soaked in water. The children listed as many conclusions and further questions as they could, in light of their data. One obvious conclusion: if the beans were soaked in water, they could be penetrated. Other conclusions that began to reach farther afield:

- The longer a bean is soaked, the softer it gets.
- The bean has an outer membrane, which becomes wrinkled when soaked.

Questions the kids asked:

- Why do the beans get soft?
- Could the beans still grow after we've poked holes in them?
- Could just part of a bean grow into a plant?
- Does a bean have different parts inside?

Hypothesizing, posing questions, drawing inferences are then steps in scientific thinking the children will be encouraged to use as they read. Jackie explains how she developed the idea from here, using discussion circles for children to further their science study:

> I had some short (thirty pages), easy-reading, science-related books published by Troll Associates, and I chose five of them—*Ecosystems and Food Chains, Human Body, Birds, Fossils,* and *Plants, Seeds, and Flowers.* They weren't the most exciting science books, but they were what I had available and they proved to be good enough, because the excitement came from the way the kids worked with them. We had been talking for months about eating healthy foods, and four of these books formed a nice sequence linking the natural world with children's health. I added the *Fossils* book as an alternative because I knew it would appeal to many of the children for a change of pace. I decided to name the activity "LSC" for "Literature, Science, and Children."
>
> Using the time period from 9:30 to 11:30 each morning, with a short break at 10:30, one full round of this LSC activity took about a week to complete. This represents a large chunk of the school day, but since we were doing plenty of reading, writing, **and** science, while at the same time achieving a good, continuous stretch of concentration, I had no trouble justifying it in my own mind or with the principal. First, I asked the students to form groups based on their choices from among the five books. Each of the five groups that emerged then selected a method for reading the book, (e.g., silent reading, taking turns with oral reading, choosing a leader to read to the group). The only restriction was that the decision be collaborative.

After the initial reading of a book by each group, I visited each group and did a second reading of the book aloud to them. Then each member of the group developed questions about the book to ask the other group members orally. Most of the questions at this stage tended to be factual "review" questions about information found in the book, rather than higher-level hypothesizing or inference questions. This was understandable because the children were new to my approach and simply followed the questioning patterns they had absorbed in their previous years of school. Together, the children then worked on answers to their questions.

The next task was for a member from each of the five groups to explain his or her group's book to the entire class. After that, students responded in writing to the book read in their group, focusing on any aspect that caught their interest. They could choose to do this individually or collaboratively. Time was allotted for sharing those writings with the class and for classmates to respond.

Later, I rotated books so that eventually all five were studied by all five groups of students. The entire project covered a period of five weeks. This might seem like a lot of repetition, but the oral reports reflected children's differing styles, and emphasized different aspects of the books, each time around. And the repetition helped kids begin to grasp the larger science thought processes I was teaching—problem posing, hypothesizing, observing, using materials, drawing conclusions.

Because Jackie found that the children were not yet generating very thought-provoking questions, she added a step to help them learn this process more explicitly. Once they had finished all the books, she asked the groups to brainstorm new questions they had about health, growing plants, birds, ecosystems, and fossils. This took some work, because school had accustomed the children so thoroughly to considering only questions that could be answered by their reading selection. But after some modeling, the groups worked intensely and produced a number of questions they wished to pursue further. Some could be answered through more reading:

- What is the oldest bird?
- How was the archaeopteryx discovered?
- How did the human body develop?

A few could be researched by classroom experiments:

- What are some relationships between plants and insects?
- How do muscles move the bones in your skeletal system?

And some were more about the nature of the concepts themselves:

- Why are there ecosystems and food chains?
- Why are we a part of the food chain?

All of these questions required elaboration, refinement, or narrowing of focus in order to become topics the kids could easily explore during the year. However, the children were now on their way to a more inquiring approach to science. Many completed special projects on their chosen topics during the course of the year.

After the circles project was finished, Jackie noticed a marked effect on the students' general reading abilities and interests. The predictability and repetition helped children become comfortable with the words and ideas. A number of her kids began meeting at the library to do further reading about the topics together after school—in a neighborhood where such a step is nearly unheard of. When the children reflected on the value of working in groups, they remarked: "It helped me remember a lot of the information." "I liked asking questions." And especially gratifying: "I felt good because I realized some of my questions didn't have answers in the book, and some of the other kids had the same questions!"

Works Cited

Aldridge, Bill G., ed. 1996. *A Framework for High School Science Education.* Arlington, VA: National Science Teachers Association.

American Association for the Advancement of Science. 1993. *Benchmarks for Science Literacy.* New York: Oxford University Press.

American Association for the Advancement of Science. 1989. *Science for All Americans: A Project 2061 Report on Literacy Goals in Science, Mathematics, and Technology.* Washington, DC: American Association for the Advancement of Science.

Cobb, Vicki. 1986. *The Trip of a Drip.* Boston: Little Brown.

———. 1985. *More Science Experiments You Can Eat.* New York: Harper and Row.

Daniels, Harvey. 1994. *Literature Circles: Voice and Choice in the Student-Centered Classroom.* York, ME: Stenhouse Publishers.

Heath, Shirley Brice. 1983. *Ways with Words: Language, Life, and Work in Communities and Classrooms.* New York: Cambridge University Press.

Johnson, David W., Roger T. Johnson, Edythe Holubec, and Patricia Roy. 1991. *Cooperation in the Classroom.* Edina, MN: Interaction Book Company.

National Academy Press. 1996. *National Science Education Standards.* Washington, DC: National Academy Press.

Saul, Wendy, and Jeanne Reardon, eds. 1996. *Beyond the Science Kit: Inquiry in Action.* Portsmouth, NH: Heinemann.

Suggested Further Readings

Beisenherz, Paul, and Marylou Dantonio. 1996. *Using the Learning Cycle to Teach Physical Science: A Hands-On Approach for the Middle Grades.* Portsmouth, NH: Heinemann.

Bruer, J. T. 1993. *Schools for Thought: A Science of Learning in the Classroom.* Cambridge, MA: MIT Press.

Doris, Ellen. 1991. *Doing What Scientists Do: Children Learn to Investigate Their World.* Portsmouth, NH: Heinemann.

Harlen, Wynne. 1992. *The Teaching of Science.* London: David Fulton Publishers.

Hein, George, and Sabra Price. 1994. *Active Assessment for Active Science.* Portsmouth, NH: Heinemann.

Hyde, Arthur, and Marilyn Bizar. 1989. *Thinking in Context: Teaching Cognitive Processes Across the Elementary School Curriculum.* New York: Longman.

National Center on Education and the Economy. 1995. *New Standards: Performance Standards.* Washington, DC: National Center on Education and the Economy.

Pfundt, Helga, and Reinders Duit. 1991. *Bibliography: Students' Alternative Frameworks and Science Education.* Kiel, Germany: Institute for Science Education.

Saul, Wendy, Jeanne Reardon, Anne Schmidt, Charles Pearce, Dana Blackwood, and Mary Dickinson Bird. 1993. *Science Workshop: A Whole Language Approach.* Portsmouth, NH: Heinemann.

Short, Kathy, Jerome Harste, and Carolyn Burke. 1995. *Creating Classrooms for Authors and Inquirers* (Second Edition). Portsmouth, NH: Heinemann.

Science Resources on the Internet

The American Association for the Advancement of Science has a major general-interest website at **http://aaas.org.** Its offspring, *Project 2061,* more focused on schools and standards, is at **http://www.enc.org.**

The documentation from the National Committee on Science Education Standards, as well as other valuable science and math information, is offered by the North Central Regional Educational Laboratory at **http://ncrl.org/sdrs.**

The National Science Teachers Association offers association news, research bulletins, publications, and conference announcements at **http://www.nsta.org.**

The National Biology Teachers Association offers association news, research bulletins, publications, and conference announcements at **http://www.nabt.org.**

The American Association of Physics Teachers Association offers association news, research bulletins, publications, and conference announcements at **http://www.aapt.org.**

RECOMMENDATIONS ON TEACHING SCIENCE

Increase	Decrease
Hands-on activities that include: —students identifying their own real questions about natural phenomena —observation activity, often designed by students, aimed at real discovery, employing a wide range of process skills —students hypothesizing to explain data —information provided to explain data only after students have engaged in investigation process —students' reflection to realize concepts and processes learned —application, either to social issues or further scientific questions	Instruction based mainly on lecture and information giving Dependence on textbooks and lockstep patterns of instruction Cookbook labs in which students follow steps without a purpose or question of their own Questions, concepts, and answers provided only by the teacher Students treated as if they have no prior knowledge or investigative abilities
Focus on underlying concepts about how natural phenomena are explained	Memorizing detailed vocabulary, definitions, and explanations without thorough connection to broader ideas
Questioning, thinking, and problem solving, especially: —being skeptical, willing to question common beliefs. —accepting ambiguity when data aren't decisive —willing to modify explanations, open to changing one's opinion —using logic, planning inquiry, hypothesizing, inferring	Science approached as a set body of knowledge with all answers and information already known Attempts to correct student misconceptions by direct instruction
Active application of science learning to contemporary technological issues and social choices	Isolation of science from the rest of students' lives
In-depth study of a few important thematic topics	Superficial coverage of many topics according to an abstract scope-and-sequence
Curiosity about nature and positive attitudes toward science for all students, including females and members of minority groups	Sense that only a few brilliant "nerds" can enjoy or succeed in science study
Integration of reading, writing, and math in science units	Activity limited to texts, lectures, and multiple-choice quizzes
Collaborative small-group work, with training to ensure it is efficient and includes learning for all group members	Students working individually, competitively
Teacher facilitating students' investigative steps	Teacher only as expert in subject matter
Evaluation that focuses on scientific concepts, processes, and attitudes.	Testing focused only on memorization of detail, ignoring thinking skills, process skills, attitudes

6

Best Practice in Social Studies

Social Studies a New Way: Post-Holes in History

In the usual American high school, the task of drawing on many parts of the curriculum for holistic learning activities presents a much greater challenge than in the lower grades because subjects are departmentalized and the day divided into short, discontinuous pieces, while at the same time teachers feel pressed to "cover" an impossible range of knowledge. Here is how one high school teacher strives to overcome these limitations, to turn his classroom into an active place where students take responsibility and make choices about topics they will study in greater depth.

It's Wednesday, and Wayne Mraz' U.S. History class at Stagg High School is in the library to begin research for group reports on the 1960s and the Vietnam War. Some groups are clear about their topics and have begun looking for books and articles. Others are still struggling to understand what they're really after. One pair, Greg and Jim, has chosen the phrase "Guns versus butter," which labeled the 1960s debate over use of resources for war or for domestic social needs. Wayne conferences with them for a few minutes. What are their reactions to what they've learned about the Vietnam War? "My father was there," Jim muses. "He says it was just a huge waste. It didn't do any good for anyone, and a lot of his friends got killed." The boys decide they want to focus just on weapons, literally the "guns" side of the equation. "So how do you relate your basic feeling about the war to the weapons?" Wayne asks. Gradually they begin to list some issues—the cost of the weapons, the situational advantages held by the Viet Cong, the limitations on what the military was permitted to do, the problematic nature of the most powerful unused weapon, The Bomb—all items mentioned in the textbook but not really thought through in the students' heads until now. On a scrap of paper, the students begin drawing a cluster to see how the issues are connected, and Wayne moves on.

Why does Wayne call his course "Post-Holes"? He explains that instead of a myriad of dates, names, and events, he wants students to grasp a limited, carefully chosen set of major issues and turning points upon which they can construct in their own minds an understanding of U.S. history. If they've got the post-holes, they can build the rest of the structure themselves. Wayne rarely gives a lecture. Instead, most of the turning points, or "post-holes," are explored in two-week units, each of which builds up to and centers around reports by collaborative groups. By the time the students reach the 1960s unit in May, they're well practiced at working together, using clustering or time lines as visual guides for presenting ideas, and teaching and learning with one another.

Wayne takes several days at the beginning of the unit to start the students exploring the period and considering possible topics for their investigations. The first day typically begins with an "admit slip." The students have been asked to read sections on the sixties and the war in their regular textbook, and they are to identify ten key words on a slip of paper to get in the door of the classroom. In September, some kids end up sitting on the hallway floor to fill out their admit slips, but by now everyone knows and follows the routine. Wayne checks the slips for interesting highlights to share with the class, and goes on to list and talk through some possible topics for reports. Typical topics for the sixties:

- Guns vs. butter—the "Great Society"
- The 1968 Democratic Convention
- The Civil Rights Movement
- The U.S. military doctrine of "flexible response"
- Tensions between domestic and foreign policy
- The return of Richard Nixon

Students add in topics of their own, such as "Music of the Sixties" and "Films About Vietnam." Within several days, the groups will have to choose their topics, but right now there's time to think and explore.

The next day, everyone brings in a seventy-five–word summary of an article from the library about the sixties, or one written in that period if they can get to the microfilm collection at the nearby community college. Again, highlights are shared. Working in their groups of three, students make charts listing things they think they know about the period and questions they have. These lists will give direction to their reading and perhaps spark some particular interest or curiosity that will influence the groups' choices of report topics.

The rest of the hour is spent watching portions of a video, "Homefront During the Vietnam War." Wayne doesn't sit passively and let the students snooze while the VCR runs, however. Every few minutes, he pauses the tape and poses a question or points out a connection between what they're watching and some idea that has come up during these first two days of the unit.

The period concludes with the groups quickly filling out a form to reflect on what has taken place thus far in the unit, and how the groups are working.

For a few minutes of the third day, the introductory activities continue as before. The students arrive to hear a Simon and Garfunkel tape bringing them sounds of the sixties. They complete short summaries of articles of their choice from a collection that Wayne has handed out, and then watch and talk through a few more minutes of the videotape that was begun the day before. Then it's off to the library to begin researching possible report topics. As Wayne circulates among the groups while they sift through articles and information banks, he learns which groups have settled on their topics and which ones need help. By the end of the period, all the groups have usually focused on something. They know they'll need to work outside class to do most of the research, but ordinarily one more class period is spent in the library with Wayne's guidance as the groups work.

A few of the groups are ready to give their reports on Friday, and the weekend provides time for the rest to finish. Monday and Tuesday are devoted to the balance of the presentations. An observer might wonder what leads the students to draft their reports so quickly, and whether such promptness allows for sufficient thought and learning to go into them. But Wayne has done much to ensure that the reports are productive for both authors and listeners. The entire first week of the year is spent on thinking strategies and logical problem solving. Wayne believes this is most crucial. Then there's the regular practice: this is not a once or twice a year exercise. By the time the class reaches the 1960s, everyone has completed and presented at least a dozen reports. In addition, he finds that having students frequently prepare visuals—clusters, time lines, flowcharts—gets the groups into the habit of organizing their thinking. Teachers also worry about covering the material required by district curriculum guides, but Wayne estimates that 85 percent of the major events and concepts he would have discussed in more conventional lecture format are dealt with in the reports. And, of course, students remember the material more permanently because the reports are their own.

Wednesday is test day. Each group has already prepared one essay question and five multiple-choice questions on their own group's topic. Wayne circulates among the groups, helping them craft fair and interesting questions. For the test, each group draws an essay question out of a hat (of course, if they get their own, they must draw again). All the students in a group thus get the same question, but work on their answers separately. Everyone answers all the multiple-choice questions, plus one or two items Wayne adds in. The group that originated a given essay question are the people who grade it. As homework, each student must not only evaluate the essay of one other, but must also provide a written rationale for the grade awarded. Wayne adjudicates discrepancies and unfair evaluations, and on the final day of the unit the evaluating groups meet with the corresponding essay writers to discuss the evaluations.

Wayne has discovered that this approach to testing results in a great deal of learning. Students feel responsibility to listen to the reports since they will have to answer questions on one of them. Much thinking goes into the question drafting, evaluation, and rationale writing. The students hold conferences with one another after the test to go over their answers and their reasons for grading each other as they did. Students who find it hard to accept a teacher's response about an unclear explanation give much more credulity to their peers' observations about the same problem. Sometimes it takes several periods just for the groups to talk through their evaluations with one another.

What does a pair-conference on test results look like, when it's going well? On one particular day, two students in the basic-level class, Rob and Javier, were observed talking over Javier's test.

Rob: Where was your theme—you know, where you come out and explain what you are really . . .

Jav: (*Discouraged*) I guess I didn't have one.

Rob: Yes, wait a minute, you did, look right here!

Jav: I guess it's just a little spread out.

The boys then proceeded to open several books to compare Javier's answers with the texts and with the cluster-chart left on the wall from the group's presentation. But it doesn't take long for them to become reengaged in the actual topic:

Jav: Yours was pretty good . . . If I had more time, I would have put down more information.

Rob: Well, there was more about Martin Luther King, anyway. (*Jav laughs as he notices numerous spots where he scratched out words.*)

Rob: When you're writing, you get all excited, and you get into it, and you don't realize.

Jav: (*Rereading his paper*) I got the wrong date for when Malcolm X was assassinated. You know, one big difference was that even when they bombed his [King's] house, he didn't get angry.

A Look at the Standards Documents

As in the other major school subjects, good social studies teachers have long used creative and powerful strategies to make topics come alive for kids, and national commissions and task forces have repeatedly drafted recommendations for reform of less successful classrooms. Unlike the other subject areas, however, social studies recommendations have been subject to sharp debate, and as a result, a progressive consensus has not emerged to the degree that it has in science, math, and literacy. Before we proceed with recommendations for Best Practice, we need to examine this debate.

The big questions were recognized in one of the field's earliest reports, "Building a History Curriculum," by the Bradley Commission on History in Schools (1988, 24):

- Should history be taught as activity, as "something you do," or as cultural heritage?
- Should the history curriculum be driven by our cultural diversity as Americans or by our common, mainly Western, political heritage?
- Should social history, concerned with the ordinary people and daily issues, play the primary role, or should it be political history, concerned with "elites" and decision-making?
- Should we stress facts or concepts? Chronology or case studies? Narrative or thematic history?

A further layer of disagreement arises from the fact that "social studies" is not one discipline but combines many, with each competing for time in the curriculum. Each discipline's standards document begins with a manifesto declaring its work to be the most essential to the future of our democracy. Only the *Curriculum Standards for Social Studies* published by the National Council for the Social Studies (1994) attempts to integrate the various fields—history, geography, economics, political science, sociology—but defenders of these subjects view this effort with suspicion.

Another important question centers around the value of controversy and commitment itself. The Bradley Commission report argued that "By its nature, history is not wishful, or partisan, or proselytizing," but provides the facts for informed decision making (26). In contrast, even a most narrowly focused document like the *National Standards for United States History* (1994) says:

> History opens to students the great record of human experience, revealing the vast range of accommodations individuals and societies have made to the problems confronting them, and disclosing the consequences that have followed the various choices that have been made. By studying the choices and decisions of the past, students can confront today's problems and choices with a deeper awareness of the alternatives before them and the likely consequences of each. (1)

The 1994 NCSS *Expectations of Excellence: Curriculum Standards for Social Studies* goes further, viewing social studies as preparation for, and even direct participation in, social and political action in the community, stating that "Social studies students need to learn to make choices after weighing their personal expectations, along with the pros, cons, responsibilities, and consequences of those choices for themselves and others" (4).

These differences are understandable. While all of public schooling in this country has been used as a vehicle for promoting social stability and obedient citizenship, social studies offers the main occasion for explicitly instructing children in traditional values and behaviors. At the same time, it also offers the best opportunity in the curriculum for questioning those values, examining ways our society has failed to live up to its principles, and preparing future citizens to work for change. Thus, the subject is bound to engender debate.

The clash is especially harsh and repressive, however, because the most outspoken voices are those of conservatives able to attract media attention—the Gablers in Texas, Phyllis Schlafly in the Midwest, Diane Ravitch and William Bennett in Washington, DC, and E.D. Hirsch with his ubiquitous cultural literacy merchandise. The 1992 draft version (titled *Lessons from History*) that preceded the *National Standards for United States History*, for example, was roundly attacked by Ravitch and others for including too much emphasis on Native Americans, Blacks, and other minorities, and too much attention to failures and atrocities committed over the course of U.S. history. The U.S. Senate, as a result, voted ninety-nine to one to repudiate the document. That draft included some valuable features, including a list of "Habits of Mind" linked with each historical topic, a series of larger themes in American history, and strategies for thoughtful and creative teaching. The new version reduces the focus on the errors in our past, and relegates the pedagogical help and "Habits of Mind" to a set of five separate "Standards in Historical Thinking" that are never linked to specific content. Considering the studies and news reports that endlessly bemoan Americans' lack of historical knowledge, this loss of focus is tragic. Fortunately, more courageous reports such as the NCSS *Curriculum Standards for Social Studies* have maintained more of a balance.

We'll be up front about where we stand in this debate. While disagreement is no doubt unavoidable, the harshness of the conservative attacks have made advancement in the teaching of social studies far more difficult than for the other subject areas. Rather than address the need to involve students more actively so they do indeed learn the facts that advocates say are important, the history and geography standards simply call for more "coverage," more content, more time spent on their subject. It's the safest possible, purely additive approach to reform—"Let's just do more of the same thing that isn't working." Yes, a need for more in-depth, active learning is mentioned in the documents' introductions, when they genuflect toward citizens' need to make informed social and political decisions. But when the documents go on to simply list hundreds of facts and topics as essential for student competence, it's clear what matters most.

In fact, the argument to just do more ultimately leads nowhere. If teachers attempted to cover everything for all the social studies fields, they'd teach nothing else all day. "Take time away from literature or math, and emphasize 'my' field above any of the other social sciences," each commission seems to imply.

The history and geography documents never seem to recognize what educators in other fields have come to understand, namely that teaching must promote lifelong learners, students who continue reading and writing and observing on their own, to fill in the inevitable gaps left in *each* of the subjects in school. Particularly in social studies, this is the only way to prepare the informed, responsible citizens that the field's experts say we need. Even the students who dutifully memorize all the assigned content in all the grades, outlined on all the scope and sequence charts, will soon need to inquire further on their own, for the focuses of social concern inevitably shift from decade to decade.

As the early draft "Lessons from History" report admits, panels have been advocating more "active learning" for the social studies since the Committee of Ten recommendations on American education in 1892—more than one hundred years ago. But we won't achieve this goal by simply reshuffling the scope and sequence charts. Students don't become self-motivated learners by listening to civics lectures for twelve years. They do it by *regularly* practicing the kind of inquiry, evaluation, decision making, and action they'll be called upon to exercise later.

Fortunately, the debate is not all on one side. Within almost every report there are bright spots of real reform, newer thinking about how students learn, and practical ways that teachers can more creatively and effectively help. Standard 1 of the *National Standards for History for Grades K–4*, for example, focuses on family history, a powerful means for helping students of all grade levels link their own lives and interests with school (1994). All the standards for the early grades are, in fact, thoughtfully conceptual, illustrated with creative curricular activities, and integrated with excellent readings in literature. Standards for Grades 5–6 and 7–8 retain a bit of this quality. It's in high school that the documents endlessly march through topics for teacher lectures and student research reports and essays.

The NCSS *Curriculum Standards for Social Studies* report is far more effective at linking content with instruction. The standards are organized around ten themes:

1. Culture

2. Time, Continuity, and Change

3. People, Places, and Environments

4. Individual Development and Identity

5. Individuals, Groups, and Institutions

6. Power, Authority, and Governance

7. Production, Distribution, and Consumption

8. Science, Technology, and Society

9. Global Connections

10. Civic Ideals and Practices

The document's "performance expectations" provide broad but concrete requirements for important content, illustrated with descriptions of integrated classroom activities for bringing about the required performances.

In its introduction, the document outlines four perspectives for approaching these themes: a personal, an academic, a pluralist, and a global perspective. Four learning skills are addressed: (1) acquiring information and manipulating data; (2) developing and presenting policies, arguments, and stories; (3) constructing new knowledge; and (4) participating in groups. Finally, the introduction lists principles of teaching and learning to be practiced in bringing social studies content to the classroom. Social studies teaching and learning are powerful, the document asserts, when they are:

- meaningful
- integrative
- value-based
- challenging
- active

This list is clearly supportive of the one we provided in the introduction to this book.

What we do, then, in our recommendations in this chapter, is to draw on the most forward-looking ideas and arguments in the recent national reports, those most in touch with the research about children's learning and constructivist teaching, those most confirmed by the thinking and demonstrations and achievements we've observed in outstanding social studies classrooms.

Recommendations for Best Practice in Teaching Social Studies

Students of social studies need regular opportunities to investigate topics in depth. Complete "coverage" in social studies inevitably results in superficial and unengaging teaching, like painting a room—covering plenty of square feet but only one-thousandth of an inch thick. Thus, every one of the national reports recognizes that real learning involves in-depth understanding of the complexities of human existence. *National Standards for United States History* urges "the use of more than a single source: of history books other than textbooks and of a rich variety of historical documents and artifacts that present alternative voices, accounts, and interpretations or perspectives on the past." *Expectations of Excellence: Curriculum Standards for Social Studies* also highlights this need:

> *Instruction emphasizes depth of development of important ideas within appropriate breadth of topic coverage and focuses on teaching these important ideas for understanding, appreciation, and life application. . . .* The most effective teachers . . . do not diffuse their efforts by covering too many topics superficially. Instead, they select for emphasis the most useful landmark locations, the most representative case studies, the most inspiring models, the truly precedent-setting events, and the concepts and principles that their students must know and be able to apply in lives outside of school. . . .

Yet there are many separate social studies fields—history, geography, sociology, anthropology, psychology—and each field includes many topics, all of which seem important. Therefore, teachers of social studies have no choice but to accept the fact that under *either* approach—thin coverage on everything or depth for a few areas—students won't really learn it all in twelve years of public schooling. Covering less in more depth not only ensures better understanding but increases the likelihood that students will pursue further inquiry of their own at later times.

Students need opportunities to exercise choice and responsibility by choosing their own topics for inquiry.   Particularly because social studies is meant to prepare students for *democratic* citizenship, active engagement is necessary in a good classroom. Social studies teachers can learn that student choice need not mean chaos, or an impossible paper load, or avoidance of important content. Good teachers lay out lists of significant topics to choose from, give mini-lessons on how to make intelligent choices of what to study, and conduct brief negotiating conferences with groups of students as they design and focus their topics. This not only increases students' engagement, but teaches them an important academic skill needed for doing research projects in upper grades and college—how to judiciously choose topics for reports and papers.

Social studies teaching should involve exploration of open questions that challenge students' thinking.   Along with more time and detail on a topic, in-depth study means going beyond the learning of information to consider some of the hard but meaningful questions brought up by just about any study of human social existence. Reports and panels have been recommending this approach for many years, but abstract and brief prescriptions are not enough to help teachers change—just as they aren't enough to help students learn. To enact this principle, teachers need to learn how to generate questions that invite discussion, rather than those that merely check to see if students read the chapter *or* those that just lead the class to the teacher's own chosen conclusions.

Another teaching skill needed for this exploratory, open approach is conducting constructive group discussion. Teachers can learn to use brief learning-log jotting and small-group preparatory tasks so that students are ready to contribute to a larger class session. Climate-setting activities are essential so that students learn to respect one another's differing opinions and to trust that their ideas will not be ridiculed when expressed openly. After a good discussion, student-made follow-up reports and wall charts—or at the very least, end-of-class reflective log entries—can solidify learning so the ideas shared do not simply evaporate when class ends.

To make real the concepts being taught, social studies must involve students in active participation in the classroom and the wider community. This can be thought of as yet another way to achieve depth. *Expectations of Excellence* goes to considerable length in its supplementary statement on "Powerful Teaching and Learning" to describe the possibilities, including variety of materials, field trips, collaborative learning, and increasing individual responsibility for learning. The text even describes a constructivist approach:

> *Students develop new understanding through a process of active construction.* They do not passively receive or copy curriculum content; rather, they actively process it by relating it to what they already know (or think they know) about the topic. Instead of relying on rote learning methods, they strive to make sense of what they are learning by developing a network of connections that link the new content to preexisting knowledge and beliefs anchored in their prior experience. Sometimes the learning involves conceptual change in which students discover that some of their beliefs are inaccurate and need to be modified.

However, because social studies groups and educators also agonize so extensively about covering every historical period or field subtopic, resulting in overstuffed district curriculum guides, teachers often despair at finding time to organize and include such activity.

Yet the task need not be overwhelming. Many of the concepts in sociology, economics, and politics have obvious embodiments right in the individual school building—issues of personal freedom versus the good of the community, relations between various cultural groups; questions of governance, authority, and decision making. Children of most ages can debate an issue, draft letters and proposals, seek actual changes in school procedures, or set up committees to accomplish some new goal. Wide student participation in these matters will, as an additional benefit, contribute to the social health of the school.

Active involvement can easily reach outside the school walls as well. For information gathering, representatives of many social and governmental organizations are happy to visit classrooms to talk about their work. Parents who work in relevant fields make willing resource people. Genuine responses from community leaders to students' letters, proposals on community projects, and real advocacy are usually long-remembered by students as rich and exciting learning experiences.

Yes, but . . . how can a teacher find the time to prepare such projects if individuals or groups of students are working on different issues and there's no textbook for any of them?

A thematic approach, as outlined in Tarry Lindquist's *Seeing the Whole Through Social Studies* (1995), certainly makes student participation easier to include in the curriculum. Walter C. Parker, in *Renewing the Social Studies Curriculum* (Association for Supervision and Curriculum Development 1991), recommends a number of programs and units that provide teachers with workable materials and directions for participatory activities. Many more are described in Stephanie Steffey and Wendy Hood's *If This Is Social Studies, Why Isn't It Boring?* (1994) and David Kobrin's *Beyond the Textbook: Teaching History Using Documents and Primary Sources* (1996). When teachers take a thematic approach to the subject, they find that many of the concepts, skills, and topics listed in their social studies curriculum guides are automatically covered.

Social studies should involve students in both independent inquiry and cooperative learning, to build skills and habits needed for lifelong, responsible learning.   Once significant topics are chosen, social studies classes can most easily generate active participation if projects use cooperative learning. Children who have not had previous experience with small-group learning will need training in how to work collaboratively and productively. However, this in itself is a significant social studies topic worth exploring, and the training will be valuable for students throughout their schooling and in their adult working lives.

It is wise to establish a balance between individual and group work. Some children learn more readily in one setting, some in another, and so variety helps reach them all. Children need skills and confidence for pursuing topics on their own as well. A "classroom workshop" structure, in which students research topics of their own choosing while the teacher holds brief one-to-one conferences, is a highly efficient way of immersing the children in individual study. These two organizational structures—cooperative small groups and classroom workshop—are also essential tools for making a non-tracked, heterogeneous classroom work (see Chapter 8 for descriptions of these strategies).

Social studies should involve students in reading, writing, observing, discussing, and debating to ensure their active participation in learning. Reports and studies all recommend active learning, but teachers and planners often picture writing, discussion, or group work as time-consuming add-ons to the material that is supposed to be covered. They imagine essays that take days for kids to write and nights for teachers to grade. But many valuable activities can be brief and informal, moments to help students focus, consider a problem, or reflect on the meaning of the material. Students can write for two minutes at the beginning of the period to recollect main points from the last night's homework or the ideas covered the day before. They can stop in the middle of the class to talk for five minutes in pairs or threes about possible solutions to a particular problem. They can reflect on a notecard what they've learned or still have questions about at the end of class, and turn in their responses so the teacher can see what's getting through and what isn't. Integrating modes other than lecturing and quizzes means using those modes as tools for learning, to advance the subject matter itself.

Social studies learning should be built on students' prior knowledge of their lives and communities, rather than assuming they know nothing about the subject.   It is usual media practice to bash schools and students by periodically running features on how little geography or history kids know, or parading the bloopers they may write for short-answer quizzes (never mind the vagueness or lack of thought in some of the quiz questions). Yet young children constantly listen far more closely to adult conversation than we like to acknowledge, and they sense the problems, issues, and paradoxes in the community, the school, and their families much more sharply than we realize. When we do take notice, many of us find this phenomenon alternately cute and threatening.

We do far better to find out just how much children *do* know about the social world around them and build our teaching on that. By drawing out and then building on this prior knowledge that children bring to school, we can help them discover how social studies concepts are close to, and relevant to, their lives, and not just abstract words to memorize. Just as in the physical sciences, social studies are about phenomena to be explored, not just answers to memorize.

Of course, it is common sense to expect that children grasp more social studies concepts as they move up the grades, since older children are more sensitive to social interactions around them and more aware of a wider world with all its complexities. Traditional social studies curricula have followed an "expanding environments" formula for elementary grades, starting with the family and working outward. More recently, however, educators have developed ways to introduce young children to history, geography, and other topics in forms they could grasp. The *National Standards for History for Grades K–4* shows some recognition of the significance of children's prior knowledge. However, the earlier 1989 NCSS document, *Charting a Course: Social Studies for the 21st Century,* puts it most strongly:

> First, students at all ages know more about the world than is readily apparent. Much of that knowledge represents out-of-school learning. . . . Quite young students have rudimentary concepts of some of the critical ideas in social studies: spatial and temporal ordering, authority and power, the nature of groups, cultural differences, scarcity, and many others. . . . In particular, the notion that students cannot deal with social studies abstractions until Grade 4 is clearly discredited.

Social studies should explore a full variety of the cultures found in America, including students' own backgrounds and understanding of other cultures' approaches to various social studies concepts. The acrimonious debate over "our common heritage" versus study of individual ethnic groups has sadly obscured much of the real meaning in the latter option. First of all, minority children are not the only ones who have been cut off from their own history. Most students in any age group or social stratum know very little of the various historical and political developments that affected their own families and forebears. History, politics, economics, culture, folklore—all could become more meaningful to students through interviews about events and experiences in the past, with parents, grandparents, neighbors, and other adults they know. It is particularly important to explore the cultures of the children who are present in the classroom because children of minority backgrounds so often see school subjects as disconnected from their own lives and worlds. Once this connection is made, study of other cultural groups can create an understanding of the common struggles and aspirations of various groups, and an appreciation of their rich particularity. Far from engendering divisiveness, this approach helps eradicate it.

What is especially crucial is *how* these things are studied. We've observed children endure profound boredom as a teacher lectured and demanded memorization on the principal grain crops exported from various African countries. Such methods do not reconnect children with their own history but simply alienate them from it once again. In contrast, when students can make choices, discover facts that they find significant in their own family backgrounds, and share and contrast them with mutual respect, they will not only feel pride in their own heritages. They will also become more excited about history and geography and culture in general—and perhaps even be able to critique and evaluate aspects of their own past, as well as to honor them.

Social studies should eschew tracking of students because it deprives various groups of the knowledge essential to their citizenship. The *National Standards for United States History* document is eloquent on this matter, at least in its introductory statement:

Standards in and of themselves cannot ensure remediation of the pervasive inequalities in the educational opportunities currently available to students. The roots of these problems are deep and widely manifested in gross inequities in school financing, in resource allocations, and in practices of discriminatory "lower tracks" and "dumbed-down" curricula that continue to deny large sectors of the nation's children equal educational opportunity. ... Every child is entitled to and must have equal access to excellence in the goals their teachers strive to help them achieve and in the instructional resources and opportunities required to reach those ends. Nothing less is acceptable in a democratic society.

More and more educators and school systems are now contemplating the social and racial implications of tracking and realizing that they must find alternatives. Research studies indicate that tracked classes really do not even benefit high-track students as much as once claimed, but they do systematically discourage and slow down the lower-achieving ones. Particularly in social studies (though this thinking applies to many other subject areas as well), students of various backgrounds can benefit by hearing from one another.

Yes, but . . . how can a good classroom simultaneously meet the needs of students with differing achievement levels, particularly as students move up the grades?

The answer is found in how the classroom is organized. Traditional lectures and quizzes are the least adaptable to heterogeneous grouping because the teacher offers only one version of the material for everyone. Small-group work, with children of differing levels in each group, is much more successful, as long as children are trained to take an active role. When small groups are working, the teacher isn't "delivering" information to the unenlightened. Instead, kids talk through and argue over the ideas, which results in better learning. The teaching that the stronger students provide for the less prepared benefits them both—the old saw being quite true, that the teacher of a subject often learns more than his or her students.

The other effective structure for a part of each day or week in a nontracked setting is the "classroom workshop." This structure has been described most thoroughly for literature and writing, but it's important to consider here, as a way to make nontracked social studies classes work in the upper grades. As we describe in Chapter 8, in a classroom workshop, every student has a list of topics he or she is interested in reading and/or writing about, worked up through individual and group brainstorming and negotiation or encouragement by the teacher. At the start of workshop time, each student reports in a phrase what he or she will be working on—a verbal contract that commits the student and tells the teacher who is on track and who needs some help. Students can sign up for conferences, and once the class gets down to work the teacher circulates around the room for *brief* one-to-one sessions. In these, the teacher leads the student to solve his or her own problem rather than simply giving directions or answers. Brief moments can be taken at the beginning or end of the session to conduct "mini-lessons" on concepts or processes for getting work done, based on what the teacher observes the class or subgroups may need. Near the end of the period, one or two individuals share something they've done, and every few weeks everyone turns in a written product. Student folders allow the teacher to survey students' work-in-progress regularly and quickly.

This may sound like a complex structure, and it does take training, both for teachers and kids. But it uses time very efficiently, allows students to work at their own levels and to make choices according to special interests, and teaches them responsibility, something surprisingly missing from traditional classroom structures. Teachers at all grade levels, in every socioeconomic setting, have found the classroom workshop highly effective. Once again, not every historical period or geographical location can be covered—and, indeed, the teacher may not use workshop every day. But students' commitment becomes very strong, the learning acquires depth, and all the students in the room can be challenged and helped, whatever their achievement level. We describe this strategy in some detail here because we know that only when decision makers can visualize a workable approach will they support the changes needed to achieve a nontracked classroom for social studies or any other subject area.

Social studies evaluation must reflect the importance of students' thinking, and their preparation to be lifelong responsible citizens, rather than rewarding memorization of decontextualized facts.   In the history class described at the beginning of this chapter, Wayne Mraz has each small group of students compose a test question, evaluate the answers written by individual students from another group, and then review the answers with the test takers, one to one. This may take longer than a traditional quiz, but a tremendous amount of learning goes on. Evaluation in Mraz' classes is not just time spent checking on students; it's another occasion for learning.

Because the stated goal of social studies education in every one of the national reports is not just acquisition of information, but also preparation for democratic citizenship, it's pretty obvious that evaluation in social studies should serve that goal. How can evaluation in social studies encourage this, recognize it when present, and help students reflect on their own progress toward doing it well?

Perhaps more than in any other subject, evaluation in social studies must involve reflective **dialogue** between teacher and student. Yes, we can ask students to show they have inquired deeply into a subject, through detailed sharing of their knowledge. But on every occasion for evaluation, there should also be questions about what the student considers to *be* a good historian (or history book, or student of geography, or observer of folk traditions); questions on *how* one learns about families or governments or economic systems; and questions on the significance, the implications, the human issues within the material studied. The answers to these questions need to be valued by extending discussion out from them, rather than leaving them as final statements that are graded and then forgotten.

However, if students are to feel truly free to speak their minds, we must have many occasions when their thoughts and ideas are *not* evaluated along with the times when they are. Students should be able to select some of the essays and products they will submit for evaluation, out of a larger portfolio, so they have some zone of safety for expression that may seem risky, tentative, or unresolved.

Finally, to mirror the democracy for which social studies aims to prepare our population, students can participate in setting the standards by talking together about what makes a good paper/answer/project and how to evaluate it. In fact, the issue of meaningful evaluation of students' education is a very worthy social studies topic in itself.

How Parents Can Help

Because we are all social beings, helping children to learn about social studies at home is especially easy and natural. The most effective approach is to model social involvement. If a parent participates in community activity of some kind, even for small time periods, children will come to see such activity is important. They'll be curious and will naturally begin to learn about how things work and what the problems are in the community. Also valuable for learning about the nature of the community, as well as for fun and togetherness in a family, are trips to museums, historical societies, ethnic fairs, interesting neighborhoods, and historically or culturally significant sites in the surrounding regions.

For awareness of national politics, social issues, and history, it's important to subscribe to or bring home newspapers and news magazines. Parents and kids can read articles together and then discuss them, with the parents encouraging children to talk first so adult opinions don't overpower them before they begin to consider an issue.

On a more immediate level, parents can share family history, memories, and customs to help children value heritage and realize how the family's experiences are a part of the history, geography, and culture of the world that surrounds it. Visits to other places family members live or originated from can help to make this realization vivid. To help make the economic world more understandable, adults can share with children the satisfactions, problems, and issues involved in work-lives. Of course, these are all forms of knowledge that also help make a family close-knit and supportive of one another.

In relation to formal school social studies, parents can let teachers know that they're available, to the extent that time permits, to share with students their experiences with work, community groups, and political efforts. Teachers need connections with the larger school community to illustrate for students the reality of the social studies material they are exploring in class. It's also especially important for parents to let school officials know they support the concept of mixed ability levels in social studies courses (and other areas too). School staff often worry that the public won't understand if the school begins to adopt a more equal and interactive approach to learning.

What Principals Can Do

Given the pressure for wide coverage in areas like history and geography, and the unfortunate lack of real learning that occurs when teachers give in to this pressure, it is especially important for the principal to step in and help by lobbying for more meaningful curriculum guides at the district level. Also, encouraging teachers to sort through the many topics and parts of the social studies curriculum, to select a few for focused study—either for individual classrooms, or grade-level or school-wide special units—can help move them toward Best Practice in social studies. The principal can also support meaningful classroom learning by building confidence among teachers that if they encourage children to think honestly about real social concerns in class, he or she as principal will help the community to value and appreciate the effort.

Best Practice in social studies calls not just for classroom activity, but also for development of the entire school community. If students learn about democracy, government, and relations among social groups in the classroom, but find their lessons irrelevant or contradicted in their own surroundings, then they're likely to regard their learning as pointless. Therefore, the principal must help teachers build the school into a model community—not "model" in the sense of "perfect," but as an example, a school in which students can participate actively in decision making, in developing norms and expectations, and in planning special study units and other school-wide learning activities. Teachers and kids can be encouraged not just to participate, but to reflect on what takes place and find connections with the topics they've studied in classes. This way, kids can see how the social structures, issues, and interactions they study are reenacted in the microcosm of their own locale.

It's particularly valuable, both for modeling group interaction and for the health of the school itself, to develop mechanisms to help social and ethnic groups relate positively in the school. In many communities, it may be important to develop mechanisms by which students can help arbitrate conflicts or deal with tensions or misunderstandings that may arise between individuals or groups.

Principals can use their influence to help move a school or district away from the tracking that separates social groups and deprives some students of experience and learning that would benefit them. This means not just working for policy change, but providing staff development so that teachers can learn how to individualize learning through classroom-workshop activities and collaborative learning.

EXEMPLARY PROGRAM
Getting to Know You Culturally

Yolanda Simmons
King High School
Chicago, Illinois

Patricia Bearden
Metcalfe Magnet School
Chicago, Illinois

Our colleagues Pat Bearden and Yolanda Simmons are sisters who've taught in different Chicago schools, at different grade levels. They've designed a multicultural cross-disciplinary unit they conduct in very similar ways for three different audiences—Pat's third graders, Yolanda's high schoolers, and groups of teachers and parents in inservice programs. The learners at all three levels find it involving and rewarding. The biggest difference in the activity between the three groups is simply the time allotment—high schoolers work longer on the whole project than either the younger kids or the adults. We'll describe the activity as it plays out in a high school classroom.

Day One. Students choose partners and conduct three-minute interviews with one another, taking notes on the following questions:

- Where were you born?
- Who were you named after and what does your name mean?
- Where do your ancestors come from within the United States?
- Where do they come from outside the United States?
- When and why did they leave to come to their present home?
- Have you or anyone in your family researched your family history?

150

While the students are working, Simmons circulates around the room taking Polaroid pictures of each kid. She also makes sure she has a bit of information of her own about at least one student. Students then take a minute or two to review and select from their notes in preparation for oral presentations.

Next, each student introduces his or her partner "culturally." Simmons provides a model by doing the first introduction, giving some of the information briefly:

> This is John. He was born here in Chicago on the South Side, and he was named after his great uncle. His family comes from Macon, Georgia, where he used to visit every summer when he was small. He loved his grandmother's cooking, but hated the farm work he had to do. He doesn't know anything about where his family came from before that, but he wishes he did. Mee-ee-eet John Coleman!

Everyone applauds. As the introductions proceed, Simmons records the place-of-family-origin information in two columns—origins inside and outside the United States—using newsprint paper on the wall.

Meanwhile, however, as the students begin to realize that they don't have answers to some of these questions, Bearden and Simmons introduce an information-gathering step—interviews with parents or grandparents. The class brainstorms interview questions and everyone takes them home to obtain data on their family's history.

Day Two.   The students obtain from each other answers to questions where information was missing, and then complete and edit one-page written versions of their interviews, with space left on each page for a photograph. These are pasted on, and someone with artistic talent is drafted to make a cover. Overnight, Yolanda photocopies the interviews to produce a class book, and everyone receives a copy the next day. The kids immediately check their own photographs and moan that they don't do the owner justice. But they save and browse through this information about their peers for weeks.

Day Three.   Working in groups of four, the students tally information from the interviews to develop a class profile for each question that was asked originally—each group focusing on one question. The groups prepare posters charting their results, showing percentages and using visual representations. Then at the end of the period, using a journaling activity to think through the options, each student chooses one ancestor he or she has heard about to be the focus of his or her research and study.

Day Four.   The students come into class to find newsprint sheets taped to the walls, with the headings "English," "Language Arts," "Math," "Social Studies," "Science," "Phys. Ed.," and a few blank sheets. Students are told to gather next to the sheets according to their strongest interests, with the option of also using the blank sheets to create their own categories—often "Dance," "Music," and "Home Economics/Foods." Their task is now to look for patterns on the tally sheets and to brainstorm research questions about some of the issues revealed in the profiles, as they relate to each subject area. The students warm to this work, for it offers a rare opportunity to share control of the curriculum. Simmons remarks that no subject area seems to go without a few devotees in each class. Some typical questions the kids put on their chart:

- English—Who were some famous authors from this place, and what did they write during the time your chosen ancestor lived?

- Language Arts—What are some slang terms teenagers used during the time period?

- Social Studies—What historical events impacted the life of your chosen ancestor?

- Science—What are some of the diseases that occurred at this time in the area where your ancestor lived?

- Math—What are the population statistics, comparisons among them, and trends, for various ethnic groups in this area and time period?

Days Five and Six.   These are spent in the library. Each group chooses one of the research questions listed on their chart (the charts are brought to the library beforehand and hung up so the students can consult them), and looks for answers to that question for each place of family origin in the United States in their particular group. The kids work on their research with help from Simmons and the librarian. Yolanda has been delighted to see low-achieving students work intently in their groups, and some even skipping lunch to continue their search.

Day Seven.   The students bring in their research reports and each group compiles an information book on their subject area. These books are kept as references in the classroom, reading material that the students can study on other occasions when they do reading of their own choice.

Days Eight and Nine.   Each group gives an oral report to the class, using family pictures, graphics, home videotapes, family members as guest speakers, and so forth.

Day Ten.   At the end—and also at various points all along—the students "debrief" their research work in short discussion sessions. Among the important questions Yolanda poses are "How did you feel when you were doing _____ ?" and "Why do you think we included that step?" The students especially enjoy this reflecting, and find the latter question the most thought-provoking. Such reflection adds to students' sense of ownership of the curriculum because they are asked to evaluate it. It also strengthens their learning by making them aware of the processes they've learned that lead to success in school. Many go on to write up their thoughts on these reflection questions as extra work on their own.

Clearly, this unit of study starts students thinking about multicultural issues, but it also does much more. It integrates all of the subject areas of school and applies them to topics of real interest in the students' lives. It involves interviewing, writing, researching, working individually, in pairs and small groups, and giving oral reports to the whole class. It honors students' own knowledge and backgrounds, but also helps them discover much that they did not know about their own past, in aspects of geography and history that are actually quite traditional academically. It builds a classroom rapport that helps students become a serious community of learners, as well as a class that achieves a level of intergroup understanding sorely needed in many locales. It requires an extended piece of time—two weeks—but provides a powerful springboard to many other social studies topics, either in traditional areas or farther afield.

Works Cited

Bradley Commission on History in Schools. 1988. *Building a History Curriculum: Guidelines for Teaching History in Schools.* Bradley Commission on History in Schools.

Crabtree, Charlotte, Gary B. Nash, Paul Gagnon, and Scott Waugh, eds. 1992. *Lessons from History: Essential Understandings and Historical Perspectives Students Should Acquire.* Los Angeles: National Center for History in the Schools.

Kobrin, David. 1996. *Beyond the Textbook: Teaching History Using Documents and Primary Sources.* Portsmouth, NH: Heinemann.

Lindquist, Tarry. 1995. *Seeing the Whole Through Social Studies.* Portsmouth, NH: Heinemann.

National Center for History in the Schools. 1994. *National Standards for History for Grades K–4.* Los Angeles: National Center for History in the Schools.

———. 1994. *National Standards for United States History.* Los Angeles: National Center for History in the Schools.

National Commission on Social Studies in the Schools. 1989. *Charting a Course: Social Studies for the 21st Century.* Washington, DC: National Commission on Social Studies in the Schools.

National Council for the Social Studies. 1994. *Expectations of Excellence: Curriculum Standards for Social Studies.* Washington, DC: National Council for the Social Studies.

Parker, Walter C. 1991. *Renewing the Social Studies Curriculum.* Washington, DC: Association for Supervision and Curriculum Development.

Steffey, Stephanie, and Wendy Hood. 1994. *If This Is Social Studies, Why Isn't It Boring?* York, ME: Stenhouse Publishers.

Suggested Further Readings

Banks, James A., and Cherry McGee Banks. 1989. *Multicultural Education: Issues and Perspectives.* Boston: Allyn and Bacon.

Brown, Cynthia. 1992. *Like It Was: A Complete Guide to Writing Oral History.* New York: Teachers and Writers Collaborative.

——— . 1994. *Connecting with the Past: History Workshop in Middle and High Schools.* Portsmouth, NH: Heinemann.

Galt, Margot Fortunato. 1992. *The Story in History: Writing Your Way into the American Experience.* New York: Teachers and Writers Collaborative.

Geography Education Standards Project. 1994. *Geography for Life: National Geography Standards.* Washington, DC: Geography Education Standards Project.

Loewen, James. 1995. *Lies My Teacher Told Me: Everything Your American History Textbook Got Wrong.* New York: Simon & Schuster.

National Center for History in the Schools. 1994. *National Standards for World History.* Los Angeles: National Center for History in the Schools.

Simons, Elizabeth Radin. 1990. *Student Worlds, Student Words: Teaching Writing Through Folklore.* Portsmouth, NH: Boynton/Cook.

Sleeter, Christine E., ed. 1991. *Empowerment Through Multicultural Education.* Albany, NY: State University of New York Press.

Tunnell, Michael O., and Richard Ammon. 1993. *The Story of Ourselves: Teaching History Through Children's Literature.* Portsmouth, NH: Heinemann.

Young, Katherine. 1994. *Constructing Buildings, Bridges, and Minds: Building an Integrated Curriculum Through Social Studies.* Portsmouth, NH: Heinemann.

Social Studies Resources on the Internet

The National Council for the Social Studies offers association news, research bulletins, publications, and conference information at **http://www.ncss.org.**

The National Geographic Society has an elaborate website that features a variety of lesson and unit plans for teachers on topics like ecology, resources, and wildlife. **http://nationalgeographic.com.**

The Smithsonian Institution, "America's Treasure House for Learning," offers resources and materials that support historical studies. **http://si.edu.**

The National Center for History in the Schools developed the current national history standards. **http://www.sscnet.ucla.edu/nchs.**

RECOMMENDATIONS ON TEACHING SOCIAL STUDIES

Increase	Decrease
In-depth study of topics in each social studies field, in which students make choices about what to study and discover the complexities of human interaction	Cursory coverage of a lockstep curriculum that includes everything but allows no time for deeper understanding of topics
Emphasis on activities that engage students in inquiry and problem solving about significant human issues	Memorization of isolated facts in textbooks
Student decision making and participation in wider social, political, and economic affairs, so that they share a sense of responsibility for the welfare of their school and community	Isolation from the actual exercise of responsible citizenship; emphasis only on reading about citizenship or future participation in the larger social and political world
Participation in interactive and cooperative classroom study processes that bring together students of all ability levels	Lecture classes in which students sit passively; classes in which students of lower ability levels are deprived of the knowledge and learning opportunities that other students receive
Integration of social studies with other areas of the curriculum	Narrowing social studies activity to include only textbook reading and test taking
Richer content in elementary grades, building on the prior knowledge children bring to social studies topics; this includes study of concepts from psychology, sociology, economics, and political science, as well as history and geography; students of all ages can understand, within their experience, American social institutions, issues for social groups, and problems of everyday living	Assumption that students are ignorant about or uninterested in issues raised in social studies
	Postponement of significant curriculum until secondary grades
Students' valuing and sense of connection with American and global history, the history and culture of diverse social groups, and the environment that surrounds them	Use of curriculum restricted to only one dominant cultural heritage
Students' inquiry about the cultural groups they belong to, and others represented in their school and community, to promote students' sense of ownership in the social studies curriculum	Use of curriculum that leaves students disconnected from and unexcited about social studies topics
Use of evaluation that involves further learning and that promotes responsible citizenship and open expression of ideas	Assessments only at the end of a unit or grading period; assessments that test only factual knowledge or memorization of textbook information

7

Best Practice in Visual Art, Music, Dance, and Theater

As elsewhere in America, the hallways of many Chicago elementary schools tell a sad story. Rows of identical children's artworks stretch down the corridors, neatly hung in class sets: thirty matching pink valentines on white doilies, thirty cute cut-out Thanksgiving turkeys, thirty leaping leprechauns with the same yellow pipes puffing the same grey smoke. Usually the only thing that distinguishes one of these products from the next is the signature at the bottom (often done with a flourish that hints at much greater possibilities) and the degree to which each child can stay inside the lines. Often, these clone galleries originate with seasonal art projects offered up by teacher magazines, complete with photocopy masters and instructions for the students: "Attach cottonball here." "Now, color the beak yellow."

Meanwhile, across town, Linda Voss' third graders nervously climb off the school bus at Clinton School, in a strange Chicago neighborhood far from their own homes. They have come to meet Eleanor Nayvelt's students, who until now have been unseen cross-city pen pals. Linda and Eleanor have embarked on a family history project that will bring these children, recent Russian immigrants from Clinton, and African American and Hispanic children from Washington Irving, together to explore their own stories of movement and change and to link these stories with U.S. and world history. In addition to meeting local curriculum mandates, Linda and Eleanor hope their students will confront, explore, and perhaps overcome the worrisome stereotypes that they've already begun to express about other races and cultures as they live in their separate communities and attend ethnically segregated schools.

The young visitors are led quietly up the stairwell to the Clinton library, where Eleanor's students are waiting in a big circle of chairs, with an empty seat next to each child. With some hesitation, the Irving kids filter into the room, taking the alternating seats and carefully not staring at the Russian children beside them. After a few welcoming comments, the teachers introduce Cynthia Weiss, a mosaicist and painter who works with the Chicago Arts

Partnerships in Education (CAPE). Cynthia gently explains that she is there to help everyone get acquainted with one other person, their pen pal. She passes out black construction paper and pastel markers to everyone, inviting students to doodle a bit to get the feel of the medium. For practice, she asks the kids to try to blend a color that exactly matches their own skin tone.

Then Cynthia asks pen pals to pair up, one from Irving and one from Clinton, and to carefully, patiently look at each other. Suddenly, the thing that everyone was avoiding a minute ago (but really wanted to do) has become the assignment. Cynthia talks a few minutes about different approaches to portraits, and then turns the children loose to portray each other in pastels. The kids look each other over, many shyly, and slowly begin to draw. Thus begins a study of immigration, ethnic history, U.S. and Chicago history, with pairs of children of vastly different heritages facing and drawing each other.

Twenty minutes later, an extraordinary set of pair portraits has been created, signed, and hung around the room: "Vasily by Rebecca," "Rebecca by Vasily." As artwork, the quality of many portraits is astounding: faces are vibrant, lively, colorful. Many of the children could be picked out of a lineup by these accurate renderings. On the other hand, even after Cynthia's skin-tone demonstration, some children of color have depicted their Caucasian pen pals as stark ice-white, while some of the Russian kids have drawn their African American partners with outsized lips and pitch-black skin. The pre-existing images that children carried with them to this meeting are manifest in the artwork. Linda, Eleanor, and Cynthia know they were right to start this project; everyone has much to learn.

On and off over the next couple of months, the children work in their own classrooms, and also meet several more times, using art to explore and connect their heritages and to relate that heritage to the wider stories of immigration to and within the United States. They choreograph dances to express key events, creating performances that combine traditional cultural elements with of-the-moment rock-and-roll favorites. These dances occur in front of stage sets designed and painted by the children. They write and publish stories, poems, and nonfiction pieces about their family and community history. As a culminating project, each student makes a large collage of his or her home, using colored construction paper and a snapshot of himself or herself, which they trim and place somewhere in the collage. Some kids perch themselves on the roof of their apartment building, a few peer through windows, while others wave from the stoop.

Finally, the Clinton and Irving kids get back together to see what they've got. Looking at the rows of colorful houses, one student suggests, "Let's make a neighborhood." Everyone puzzles over how to form all these homes into a community. The teachers carefully try to stand back, letting students find their own direction. After some discussion, the kids decide to create a huge square, with everyone's house around it. But what to put in the middle? The Russian kids want to put the ocean in the center to represent their journey to their new home in America. But what about us? the Black kids ask. Our people came from Mississippi and Alabama. Within moments, the village square takes shape: on the right, a wavy ocean filled with ships and planes; on the left, a railroad track, connecting Chicago to the American South.

Linda and Eleanor's children have come a long way, in more than one way. Starting with sweet but stereotypical portraits of each other, they have now created a symbolic integrated community that honors everyone's individual and group story. It has been quite a journey. They may not have learned every name and date in U.S. history, and they are probably not permanently vaccinated against prejudice. But this hasn't been about leapin' leprechauns or identical turkeys either. They have had the kind of learning experience that only real arts can provide: they've encountered and grappled with serious ideas in ways that are deep, personal, and transformative. They and their teachers will never be quite the same.

The Arts in School and Society

The arts have long led a marginal existence in American schools. Historically, visual art, music, drama, and movement have been looked upon as frills, extras, or add-ons. In the workaday parlance of many elementary schools, the arts are "the specials"—those intervals during the week when the *real* teachers get a well-earned break while someone else takes the kids off their hands. In the words of arts educator Arnold Aprill, this is "art as recess, not resource." In this typical model, the building's one or two art specialists see each class of children once or twice a week for half an hour, and rarely does that instruction have a chance to achieve intensity or continuity. In secondary schools, the arts rarely are considered part of the core curriculum at all, and usually can be taken only as electives. In Chicago, for example, the Board of Education requires four years of English, three years each of math, science, and social studies, and only one year each of music and art. For students in upper-track college preparatory programs, the exclusion of the arts can be even more pronounced: counselors recommend taking more "challenging" courses, and tracked grading systems award fewer GPA points for "A's" in music and art than in more academic subjects.

Lately, the role of the arts in public education has weakened even further. The national back-to-basics fervor and mania over reading test scores have pushed the arts even farther into the background. Since 1990, forty-four states have slashed arts funding, and schools have suffered these cuts severely. The amount of time devoted to school music experiences is down 29 percent since the baby boomers went to school. Arts teachers have been let go, programs dropped, and time allocations distorted, while class loads for the surviving arts specialists swell to ludicrous numbers. In Boston schools, the average music teacher now serves eight hundred students; in Denver, the ratio is one to seven hundred. In its report *Creative America,* the President's Committee on the Arts and Humanities bluntly describes the arts programming of the average American school as "impoverished or nonexistent" (1997, 17).

Of course the arts are marginalized in the wider culture as well, so their limited role in public schools merely parallels the lack of esteem the arts are accorded in American society at large. As detailed in the same *Creative America* report, our country offers mild and inconstant support for the arts. Philanthropy in support of arts institutions is sometimes lavish, sometimes sporadic and niggardly. Censorship constantly looms, and seems to drive the most conspicuous public discussions about art. A handful of well-funded major arts institutions uphold the high-culture art forms—opera, painting, and ballet—and the activity that they mainly support is *viewing*. Community arts organizations, which may explore the more experimental or popular arts forms, involve more everyday people and working artists, and support *doing* as well as viewing, are struggling perennially at the brink of extinction. We are simply a country that is ambivalent about the arts; we show a mild reverence for certified fine art, but don't put much importance on everyday art-making by our citizens, young or old.

But then, the unstable place of art in our culture is not so unusual. Art and artists have always been independent and somehow apart. Although throughout human history and across diverse cultures some art has always been harnessed to glorifying the existing culture, many artists have been critics, renegades, and reformers. These artists don't preserve traditions, they transgress them—holding up various kinds of mirrors to society, culture, and art itself. Often, they paint quite unpretty pictures. One job of such artists is to redirect the path of a culture, not to revere it.

So while we grieve the undersupport of the arts in our educational system, we would never want its reformist power to be tamed or muted by its incorporation into public education. We want to bring art to children in its full-strength formulas: robust, powerful, idiosyncratic, critical, and more than a little bit dangerous. If we have to leave these attributes outside the classroom door, we would do better to leave art out of the curriculum altogether.

Standards Come to Arts Education

While arts educators have lost many battles over school staffing and budgets, they have also been spared from some of the entropic wrangles that afflict the "basic" school subjects. Until lately, art, music, theater, and dance teachers were largely unaffected by clarion calls for more standards, benchmarks, targets, assessments, accountability measures, standardized tests, and international achievement comparisons. The arts have been a break for everyone. For the kids, they offer an occasional hiatus from the relentless passivity of "real" subjects, a rare invitation to learn by playing, a chance to do something and make something tangible, to have some fun. And arts teachers were compensated for their heavy loads and low academic clout by having some fun with kids themselves, by being exempt from micro-management via state mandates and by not having to march students toward unjust screening tests.

Accordingly, the literature on "art standards" is thinner, newer, and more contradictory than the documents covering recognized core school subjects like reading, writing, mathematics, science, and social studies. When the push for national standards in the early 1990s belatedly offered arts educators a chance to make their case, the results were rough and imperfect. The major document, *National Standards for Arts Education: What Every Young American Should Know and Be Able to Do,* was created by a consortium of professional associations in visual art, music, dance, and theater (Consortium of National Arts Education Associations 1994). In spite of some problems we address shortly, *National Standards* provides an adequate base for describing Best Practice in the arts. It makes a strong case for the inherent value of the arts in public education, in the growth of well-educated people, and in the building and improvement of a culture. It defends the value of the arts as disciplines, while asserting that hearing about, studying, or appreciating art is not enough. Students need to draw, paint, make, choreograph, design, play, sing, act, and direct real artworks throughout their schooling. By high school graduation, the report recommends, young people should be able to communicate at a basic level in all four art forms, and should develop to the proficient level in at least one chosen medium.

The document also has some shortcomings. Understandably, the four coauthoring professional organizations transparently lobby for more time and money for their own subject area in schools, for more work and better working conditions for their members. Tired of their ancillary place in school curricula, the groups pitch for more teachers of art, music, drama, and dance; more contact hours with students; and more equipment and materials. Unfortunately, the authors elected to buttress their case by making art sound just like any other school subject, depicting it largely as a fixed body of content that can be transmitted to students in comfortably academic ways. Of course, there's nothing wrong with studying the history of art, the biographies of pioneers, the facts and figures concerning different art forms in America and around the world. But such factual knowledge only comes alive as it informs a living, ongoing conversation that students are having, and that is anchored in the constant reality of making art. This balance reminds us of the Best Practice approach to reading: we want students to write their own stories, poems, and articles, but also to be constantly informed through wide reading and active discussion of other authors, from Shakespeare to their own classmates.

In some of the Commission's recommendations, the subject matter hardly sounds like art at all. Fourth graders are to "accurately answer questions about dance in a particular culture and time period (for example, 'In

Colonial America, why and in what settings did people dance? What did the dances look like?')" (25). In middle schools, students are expected to "read whole, half, quarter, eighth, sixteenth, and dotted notes and rests in 2/4, 3/4, 4/4, 6/8, 3/8, and alla breve meter signatures." High school students are to "create and answer twenty-five questions about dance and dancers prior to the twentieth century" (57). In these low moments, the *National Standards* document inadvertently endorses content it wouldn't even take a practicing artist or musician to teach; lectures and textbooks would be sufficient to transmit these mundane cultural subskills.

Ironically, in its urgent attempt to sound rigorous and academic, the *National Standards* document actually falls short by not being ambitious, challenging, or visionary enough. We can expect far more of children than answering factual recall questions about the history of different arts disciplines. And we can expect a far greater and broader contribution by the arts to students' intellectual development in school. Several other recent reports are beginning to fill this gap, raising our standards for thinking about arts education, across the curriculum and up through the grades.

For example, when New York's Educational Priorities Panel (Connell 1996) studied a group of struggling inner-city elementary schools that raised their standardized test scores dramatically and got off the city's academic "probation" list, panel researchers made a surprising discovery. Even though probation status focused urgent attention on the "basic" reading and math content appearing on achievement tests, many of the schools that got off the list had actually *increased* their arts programming. These successful schools, the report said, were distinguished by "a strong arts program that was infused through the instructional program and that included most of the students in the school." These schools used art as a lever to enhance students' learning across the curriculum, and included media as disparate as opera, rap, and fabric art. "In all eight schools," the report concluded, "these programs were not add-ons or treated merely as classes to be held so as to give regular teachers their forty-five minutes of preparation time . . . the arts, at least in these schools, were a strategy for improving learning" (13). Given that increased basic-skills test scores were the sole criterion for getting off the New York City probation list, this story has implications for schools around the country.

So why would students' academic performance improve as a result of arts involvement? At the most basic level, arts activities make school more motivating and attractive. The Educational Priorities Panel was not afraid to invoke the F-word in explaining this phenomenon—because art is **fun,** they reasoned, students attend school more regularly and are more engaged and attentive. Logically enough, when students come to school and pay attention, they learn more across the whole day and across all subjects. Further, many arts activities involve tactile, active learning that can connect with the many children for whom the old, sit-in-your-seat-and-listen style of teaching is ineffective. We now have an ample body of research and documentation of multiple learning styles and intelligences (Gardner 1983) that explains why kids would score higher in basic skills, and why whole schools might even get off the probation list, with the help of more intensive arts programming. Indeed, the failure of schools to teach in such multiple modalities, to offer invitations to students of different cognitive styles, actually deprives many children of their right to learn basic academic skills.

In secondary schools, the arts seem to have the same capacity to enhance academic skills, engaging students and integrating the curriculum. A recent University of California at Los Angeles study of twenty-five thousand middle and high school students showed strong correlations between the arts and a number of important outcomes (Catterall 1997). Students with more intensive arts involvement during their adolescent years have significantly better school grades; achieve higher standardized test scores in reading, writing, and mathematics; have higher levels of persistence in school; report less boredom in school; are more likely to be involved in community service work and rate it as important; have greater self-esteem and confidence; and make time for their artistic and community interests by watching less TV than their classmates.

These correlations hold up strongly for disadvantaged and minority students, even though they are currently far less likely to have arts-rich childhoods. While many education pundits believe that poor kids in low-achieving schools should get extra doses of knuckle-knocking "basics" and fewer "frills" such as art, this report counsels just the opposite. As the study's author concludes: "The arts do matter—not only as worthwhile experiences in their own right for reasons not addressed here, but also as instruments of cognitive growth and development and as agents of motivation for school success. In this light, unfair access to the arts for our children brings consequences of major importance to our society."

Many more studies are piling up that show the power of the arts to strengthen learning across the curriculum. The College Board reports that students with high arts involvement score better on the SATs (President's Committee 1997). A Rhode Island study of first graders who participated in a special visual arts and music program demonstrated that their reading and mathematics skills increased dramatically compared to students without this enhanced curriculum (President's Committee 1997). In Chicago, the Whirlwind Performance Company documented significantly increased Iowa Test of Basic Skills (ITBS) reading scores for students who participated in a fourth-grade drama program (Parks and Rose 1997). The President's Committee on the Arts and Humanities summarizes these kinds of studies by embracing multiple-intelligences theory: "Researchers are demonstrating that there are many ways that children learn: teachers can reach students through their spatial, musical, kinesthetic, and linguistic 'intelligences.' Educators observe that students develop creative thinking through the arts and transfer that capacity to other subjects. Studies also show that when the arts are a strong component of the school environment, dropout rates and absenteeism decline" (1997).

So the case for the arts is well-documented and conclusive, across age levels and subject areas. Clearly, students need far more arts experience than they are getting. But there's a danger here—a theoretical and practical trap that the National Consortium fell right into. Lobbying for more instructional time for separate arts discipline instruction in schools is not the only answer. At a practical level, we cannot allow the national movement for standards, in art or any other subject, to be simply additive. Reform does not mean larger and larger time allocations for any subject that can make a case for itself: more time for math, more time for art, more time for drivers' education. Instead of waging these craven and unwinnable turf wars, educators should be using time in new, more powerful ways. We need synergy, overlap, integration.

The project described at the beginning of this chapter, in which Linda Voss and Eleanor Nayvelt's students used music, dance, visual art, and drama to help students learn history, is the prototype of the new role of the arts in education. Indeed, the arts are the prototypical "integratable" subjects; music, dance, visual art, and drama have a rightful place in every field of human inquiry. We don't have to steal time away from reading, math, or science to do art; art helps us to do science, math, and reading—to explore them, express them, and connect them.

Qualities of Best Practice in the Arts

Students should do art, not just view art.   From the earliest preschool years, children have a powerful urge to make art. We don't have to "assign" children to draw with markers, chant jump-rope rhymes, share dramatic monologues, make theatrical faces, or dance—often, better than their parents. Artistic expression seems to be wired into children's genes. Therefore, the first job of teachers and other adults is to get out of the way and let kids express and experiment. We need to provide tools, materials, equipment, models, examples, coaching, and plenty of time. Grown-ups don't have much trouble taking this role until about third or fourth grade, when they start thinking maybe they should make the kids put away the crayons and songs and get serious. While it is probably okay to "get serious" about math or science for part of the school day, it is most definitely not okay to put away art or the exploratory, playful spirit that drives it. As kids get older and the curriculum gets more overstuffed with content-area mandates, smart teachers incorporate art activities into integrated curriculum units. Students who are reading a novel can show their understanding by illustrating critical scenes, acting them out, translating them into movement and dance, or creating background music for them. In every subject, doing the arts can provide new ways of exploring and expressing ideas about practically anything—the Civil War, triangles, photosynthesis, or *To Kill a Mockingbird.*

The arts should be integrated across the curriculum, as well as taught as separate disciplines.   As *Creative America* and other reports assert, the arts have value both in themselves and as useful tools of thought and connection throughout life. That means schools with exemplary arts programs will have a balance of arts discipline teaching and arts integration across the curriculum. This balance is both theoretically grounded and highly pragmatic. Practically, the school day is unlikely to get much longer, nor will there suddenly be huge increases in time allocations for arts teaching in American schools. But there are infinite opportunities for weaving artistic thinking and expression into the whole rest of the curriculum. Ideally, the arts take a central place in broad, interdisciplinary inquiry projects that teachers and students plan together, and that extend over long chunks of time. After all, life is integrated, not divided into separate-subject events. Real-life projects and problems tend to be interdisciplinary, and the arts can be a lever for understanding, connecting, or sharing inquiries into them. School should be organized in the same way, preparing students for that real, complex world.

Children need to exercise genuine choice, control, and responsibility in their art making.   This chapter's opening image, of hallways decorated with identical children's art, symbolizes the way schools too often turn art from a creative process into an obedience ritual. Indeed, why would any child care about "art" after a few years of mandatory matching leprechauns, especially if she is also being graded on the caliber of her copying? Choice is an integral part of artistic thinking. Real artists choose their own subjects, materials, media, and audiences. They decide how to begin, when something is valuable, when something should be abandoned, when something is ready for an audience. In school, students should be helped to learn how to exercise the same kinds of choices.

This means that there should be plenty of "free" art time, when students have authority for deciding what kind of art or music or drama or dance they want to make, and responsibility for carrying out their choices, under careful teacher guidance. In some school subjects, like reading and writing, we call this student-directed segment of the day "workshop," and it alternates with equally important teacher-guided lessons. Elsewhere during the daily or weekly schedule, whole classes can pursue more focused, teacher-directed art activities. For example, after reading a short story, everyone can make a torn-paper collage that represents an interpretation of one of the characters. As long as students have real choices within such assignments, deciding within the teacher's parameters what to represent and how to represent it, this kind of artmaking provides an excellent balance for open-ended workshop time.

Students should be helped to nurture their special talents and to find their strongest art form.   Every student's education should assist in the lifelong quest to discover and develop one's strongest, most powerful modes of expression. If we take seriously the theory of multiple intelligences (or even if we simply go back to the American educational platitude about developing each child's full potential), we realize that people have different strengths, gifts, and talents. If there are indeed seven intelligences, as Howard Gardner claims, then arts clearly tap into many of them. This means schools must not just tolerate, but celebrate and extend children's various talents, inviting them to explore a wide range, make selections, and gain lots of practice in their areas of greatest strength and highest potential. A straightforward approach to this is taken by the Key School in Indianapolis. During the morning, every student pursues what looks like a normal elementary or middle school program. Then, after lunch, everyone goes off to study their chosen, usually strongest, intelligence. The musical kids get out their horns and blow, the writers make poetry, the kinesthetic kids go outside and run, the artists paint and sculpt. This is one school—one of very few schools—that organizes itself so that all children actually do find success and develop their talents.

The arts should be used as a tool of thinking.   While students need plenty of chances to create final, polished artworks, the arts should also regularly be employed as tools for the exploration of ideas, without being pushed to final, edited, and exhibited forms. These informal, tentative, exploratory applications of the arts can help kids engage and grapple with ideas in any subject area. For example, teachers often ask students to keep a learning log in which they write notes about their learning. Instead, teachers can have students keep a sketchbook, where they can still jot words—*or* sketch pictures, make diagrams, map ideas, or create unique combinations of words and graphic elements in response to class activities. Another example is the strategy called "say something," in which students are asked to give an immediate verbal response after hearing a presentation, reading a story, or conducting an experiment (Short, et al., 1996). Adding the artistic choices, students can "draw something," "dance something," "sing something," "act something" after any content lesson. These kinds of expression are not refined, formal artworks; rather, they are spontaneous, along-the-way uses of art as a tool of thinking. But when teachers add these different media to the instructional mix, many more students' learning styles are engaged, and more students can comprehend and remember what they study.

Students should experience a wide variety of art forms.   Music, visual art and dance should be included throughout students' schooling. To begin with, all children will naturally participate in certain art forms in their own homes and communities, and they can be invited to bring these into school. These art forms should be welcomed, honored, and studied, whatever they are: folk dance, cartooning, teen zines, hip-hop music, or "playing the dozens," the dueling insults game. Teachers and schools should be careful not to judge or disvalue children's enjoyment of art forms considered "lowbrow." Any of these popular or childhood art forms could be the base upon which a lifelong artistic involvement is built.

But it is also the job of teachers and schools to widen the range, to introduce children to the wondrous variety of arts from around the world and back through time. This certainly includes the traditional "high culture" art, which can be encountered more than just reverentially. It is worth remembering that Shakespearean drama was popular entertainment in its day, that Oscar Wilde toured English coal-mining towns giving boisterously received readings, and that in the nineteenth century, many American symphony orchestras played parties and weddings. School should also expose children to arts from a wider range of cultural and ethnic groups, and arts that represent people around the world. And "experience" does not just mean observing these diverse forms, but trying one's own hand at them. Kids should try a Polish folk dance, make a portrait after the style of Frida Kahlo, perform a scene from Shakespeare, memorize and recite a set of haiku. As a result of this wide exposure and experimentation, students will gain an informed acquaintance with many exemplary artworks, not as arbitrary ingredients on a list of "cultural literacy," but as a natural byproduct of becoming artistic thinkers and students of cultural history.

Students should have opportunities to share their work.   Young artists should be provided safe and encouraging venues to perform, exhibit, or publish their work, both what they create during the study of specific arts disciplines and the products completed within wider interdisciplinary inquiries. During the steps of the creative process as such artworks are being created, there should be routine, informal, noncritical collaboration among student pairs, teams, and groups, paralleling the way that cooperative groups work to gradually create objects or events in many "real" art forms. When works move toward a more final, potentially public form, teachers can help students set up exhibitions or performances that reach a wider audience of other students, parents, and community members. These occasions are not provided mainly for competition, ranking, or scoring students against each other, and certainly not for putting a few students on stage and silencing others. In the adult world of professional art, there may be a place for competition; in public schools, the fundamental job of teachers is to ensure that all children have chances to advance successfully through whole cycles of art making, over and over throughout their school years, and to provide real, supportive audiences.

This means that when teachers help students publish class magazines, everyone's best story is included; when plays are produced, there are parts for everyone; when dances are created, there are roles for all; when collages are hung, everybody's goes on the wall. Schools may periodically sponsor selective, competitive programs, but the main work of arts education is helping everyone grow, not encouraging some and prematurely excluding others. For everyone, these culminating experiences provide a natural and realistic kind of pressure to do one's best: to prepare carefully, to practice, to polish, to refine. And the main purpose of this sharing is the same for students as for grown-up artists: to connect with and learn from an audience.

Children should attend a variety of professional arts events.   Schools should take students to performances and exhibitions, as well as bring artists and performers to school. Especially for students in poorer communities, children's exposure to the arts may well depend on the school's taking this kind of action. But the annual bus trip to the symphony is not enough. A school's schedule of arts performances should be continuous and varied, and should include not just the major "downtown" institutions, but local community arts organizations, musicians, galleries, and dance and theater companies as well. These visits and performances should not be disconnected inoculations of culture or random treats; instead, they should be integrated into the ongoing curriculum of the school. Events should be chosen either because they fit an existing school theme or focus, or because an academic theme will be built around them. Making the most of any performance means starting well before the event, with students and teachers learning background information, reading, doing artwork, getting ready to actively engage the performance. Afterwards, it is important for students to respond, debrief, and critique, to connect the event to their ongoing studies. A valuable experience, where possible, is for artists to talk with students after a performance or during an exhibit, sharing candidly how they work and think. Even more valuable is conversation with artists *before* they perform, when they open up their own planning and preparation process, sharing their real creative struggles with students.

Artists should be present in schools and classrooms.   There's something special and different about people who have committed their lives to make their livelihoods as musicians, videomakers, dancers, actors, sculptors, artists, poets, storytellers, or painters. They can make special, sometimes magical, connections with young people that can contribute knowledge, motivation, and inspiration to growing artists. Therefore, children need chances to meet, observe, and work with adult artists in their school. While one-shot performances and traditional residencies are helpful, even better are genuine long-term partnerships between the school and community arts organizations, providing sustained, intensive arts experiences for children, coplanned with the regular teachers and integrated into the school's overall curriculum. This model transforms the artist from a transient celebrity to a long-term consultant and deeply involves the classroom teacher as a co-artist, as well. This powerful model has been pioneered by the Chicago Arts Partnerships in Education (CAPE), funded by several local foundations, and now replicated around the country and throughout Great Britain.

All schoolteachers, not just art specialists, should be artists in their classroom.   Teachers can open up their own creative processes to student view, modeling their artistic choices and struggles. If we expect students to take risks and grow artistically, their teachers must be willing to do the same, demonstrating how a grown-up grows. This is no different from the demand that teachers read with their students, explore science with them, be a fellow writer with them. Still, this requirement frightens many working teachers whose own artistic explorations may have been shut off in childhood, and who don't feel the least bit like artists in any medium or genre. The fact that our culture tends to label artists as "gifted" rather than credit them as largely self-made practitioners who studied long and hard to develop their "gift" adds to this feeling among teachers and other citizens that they are not worthy to participate. But we do not ask regular classroom teachers to be professional-caliber artists, but simply to act as ordinary citizens who use the tools of the arts to explore ideas and express themselves. Like students, teachers will probably be on a quest to find and enhance their strongest and most preferred arts discipline, as well as trying to grow into others.

How Parents Can Help

A good arts education begins when loving parents respond to their infant's earliest expressions—gurgling, smiling, babbling—with delight, amazement, and the predisposition to see it all as meaningful. "Did he just say 'Daddy'? I'm sure he said 'Daddy'!"

The sometimes comical tendency of parents to dote on their children's earliest utterances, however meaningless they sound to outsiders, is an important factor in child development. This intense reciprocal relationship is integral to kids' learning to talk: they need to have their verbalizations responded to, extended, and shaped. And this establishes the pattern of expression and response: children learn from their earliest days that there's a conversation going on, that they are part of it, and that they are expected to have something important to add. Later, a natural extension of this phenomenon is the refrigerator door, where parents proudly post their young children's first attempts at visual art. Note how supportive and entirely uncritical parents are inclined to be about these tentative artworks. They don't mark them up with red pens, critique them, or publish scathing reviews. Instead, they look at the three-legged blue horse, get a tear in their eye, hug the kid, and get out the Scotch tape. This has nothing to do with parents holding "low standards"— it means that parents intuitively realize that the crucial developmental tasks at this stage are fluency and love of art, not refining advanced skill. Indeed, elementary schoolteachers could learn a few things from this family dynamic.

It is no less true for being a platitude: parents should immerse their offspring in the arts. The recent brain research pointing to the importance of early and diverse stimulation of young minds only adds validation to the wisdom of providing children an arts-rich childhood. And art begins right at home. Parents and kids can draw, paint, and sing together at home, for their own sake or along with other activities. Parents can involve children as they pursue their own artistic activities, practicing piano, sewing, painting, reading novels. Although TV viewing is condemned by many educators and child-development experts alike, it is an inevitable part of the artistic landscape, and parents may mitigate its banality and passivity by watching with their children; guiding them to better choices; renting tapes of quality children's films; and helping kids to discuss, understand, and evaluate what they are watching. Even better, parents and children can produce simple videos together. Nothing helps children understand that media are consciously created more powerfully than shooting and editing their own films or tapes. Although only the most affluent families currently have this capability, with the advent of cheaper home-computer-based video-editing systems, costs should plunge and access increase.

In taking children to arts events and activities outside of home, parents should follow their own tastes and passions. If it is blues music you love, sneak the kid into a club and keep him up late. It is far better for parents to take children to see performances they personally care about than to dutifully drag children to events they do not genuinely enjoy, just in the name of cultural development. If you are going to fall asleep in your seat at the opera, don't drag yourself or your children there. (But do send them with a friend or relative who really loves opera.) What is most important is for the child to see the adult engaged, involved, and moved by an art form, and to be in conversation with him during and after the event. At the same time, is not very good modeling to write off unfamiliar art forms without trying them, without giving them a chance. After all, people of deep artistic sensibility tend to be eclectic and curious, and so parents will be setting a good example if they take their children along as they venture into some new and different art forms.

Probably the most powerful family arts experience is when parents and children make art together. When Steve Zemelman's young son began playing the piano, it drew Steve back into music after a twenty-year interval, and he was soon able to play for and with Daniel. Among Harvey Daniels' most treasured memories are playing punk-rock guitar with his son and serving in his daughter's Motown backup band, mostly down in the family basement, and a couple of precious times on stage.

Even as we expose children to a wide range of art forms, it is important that we help them to be empowered, not awed, audiences. That means, on the way home from the movie, play, or concert, parents should invite kids' response and critique. Families should share ideas: what they liked, what they didn't, and especially, trying to express *why* a given element did or didn't work. Children learn from these conversations the implicit criteria of successful performance in different art forms: believability, balance, detail. It is important to raise active consumers of the arts who have developed their own taste and judgment. Such young people are far more likely to become serious arts patrons.

Aside from these spiritual supports, there are plenty of very tangible things parents can do, like buying lots of art supplies and materials, from markers to leotards to instruments to graphics software programs. In deciding what to supply, parents should mainly follow their children's interests or their own predictions of what might be welcome. Making a list and shopping for art supplies together makes a wonderful family outing, whether the destination is a fabric store, an art supply house, a music store, or an office supply warehouse. As children show particular interests and abilities, out-of-school lessons or classes can extend their exploration of arts—if the child is ready and eager for them. While private instruction is one option, many community centers and park districts also offer free or inexpensive classes of high quality.

All children are artists and performers to some extent, and these recommendations apply to all young people. But what if your child shows special talent in the arts? Then parents are called upon to do more and make more choices, and perhaps more sacrifices. Steve faced this happy dilemma with his son Dan, identified at a young age as an extraordinarily promising pianist. When he was about nine, the family came to the inevitable fork in the road: should Dan enter the world of intensive competitions, making music the main focus of his life, or instead simply develop his talent in a more relaxed, noncompetitive way? Following Dan's inclinations and their own, with the guidance of a wise teacher, the family opted for the latter path, deciding that for this particular person, a more balanced life was the right choice. Even though in the fifteen years since, Dan Zemelman studied and developed in many other areas, he now makes his living as a jazz pianist.

Having said all this about the arts at home, we caution against overweening parental arts mentoring. Many young artists have been permanently bruised by forced dance lessons, pressure to win awards, or premature public performances. Remember the findings of the Educational Priorities Panel: the arts work powerfully for kids because they are fun, and a lot of that fun comes from making your own choices and finding your own voice. It's not much fun to live out someone else's artistic agenda or to be dragooned into unpleasant or ill-timed commitments. Let the child lead, and when he or she evinces an interest, offer every opportunity you can: lessons, materials, visits, coaching, and audiences.

What Principals Can Do

Just as with all the other school subjects we cover in this book, the starting point for principals is to feel and act like artists themselves, modeling for the students in their building how one highly visible adult does art, thinks about art, responds to art, uses art. But this is a tall order. Most American school principals, like most teachers, scarcely think of themselves as artists. On the contrary, they often feel artistically incompetent, intimidated, and self-conscious. They are full of self-deprecating excuses. "I can't draw" we've heard more than one principal say. "But I can hardly carry a tune" others moan. This art avoidance sounds a lot like the sentiment we encounter when we ask teachers to share their writing with students, except that the art phobia seems even more severe and widespread.

But no one expects school principals to be professional-level musicians or sculptors. That's *not* the kind of modeling we are asking them to do. Instead, the task is simply to be an everyday, arts-involved adult who is willing to open up his or her artistic thinking for kids, at whatever level of development it has reached, to help students see how grown-ups use and value and grow with art. In short: find your own strongest art mediums and share them with children, when you can make a natural contribution to the ongoing curriculum. Visit classrooms and read your poems or someone else's poems, show your pictures, play the piano. Talk about the paintings or music or films you love. Lead a field trip to your favorite gallery or theater company, and talk about your involvement. If you are a graphic artist, pour some of that artistry into the school newsletter.

One of the best principals we know, Jim Balotta of Landis School in Cleveland, finally shared his Elvis impersonation during a whole-school assembly last spring, which needless to say, brought down the house. Some might argue that this ain't exactly art, but that's not how it seemed to those of us in the audience. What we saw was an influential adult taking a big risk, putting himself on the line as a performer in front of five hundred kids. He rehearsed, he wrote, he practiced, he hesitated, and then, finally, he did it (really well, too). Jim's performance was structurally just as valuable as if he had recited a Shakespeare soliloquy or played some Chopin.

Once a principal takes the steps of becoming a growing artist right along with the children, many other decisions and choices will come naturally. Here are some of the key supports that a principal-artist can provide:

1. **Help your teachers become artists.** Many teachers are art-phobic too, just like principals, and they need chances to recover the shamed and silenced artist inside. There's one main way teachers can accomplish this rebirth: making art alongside a patient and generous artist who can help them recover their curiosity and confidence. Some of the most powerful, transformative staff development experiences we have ever attended are teacher workshops led by the phenomenal artists of the Chicago Arts Partnerships in Education, who help damaged grown-ups become arts-loving, arts-doing teachers. In your school, arrange and fund staff development that lets teachers rediscover their own joy in art. After all, no teacher is going to add extensive classroom activities in a domain of knowledge that is anchored in personal failure and discomfort. The first step toward an arts-rich curriculum is developing teachers as artists.

2. **Be an audience for students.** View kids' work on the walls and in classrooms. As teachers schedule culminating performances and exhibitions, attend as many as you can. Don't worry too much about saying "the right thing" or giving elaborate critiques. Being a fully engaged audience, simply being a witness in the moment, is a powerful demonstration that the students' work is being taken seriously. Give children constructive feedback as they are ready for it, bearing in mind that you are viewing "first drafts," and that for young artists, fluency and productivity are more important than perfection. Far better than prizes or awards are individual notes, written by the principal and delivered to kids in their classrooms, telling them how you responded to pieces of art or performances you viewed. You don't have to judge or praise; just tell kids where the art took you, how it made you feel, what thoughts went through your mind. The more you can link your response to specific details or elements of their artwork, the more you will be helping them to understand "what works."

3. **Make sure classrooms have all the supplies and materials needed to support the arts.** Because art supplies can be costly, the principal's legerdemain with budgets may determine what kids can do. If you have arts-specialist teachers in the building, you need to supply them with the instruments, paint, tape recorders, and other equipment they need. If you are going to infuse arts through the curriculum, the classroom teachers need serious inventories of art materials as well. The most empowering way to provide this is to let the teachers list and order the needed materials, within actual budget constraints. Or take a cue from our friend Madeleine Maraldi, and send groups of teachers and students to the supply store together with a blank school check. You can also encourage teachers to visit local scrounging sites, recycled materials centers, or other sources of cheap art stuff. Funding for professional performances and long-term artists-in-the-school programs may require special central-office or external grant funding, which the principal may be especially skilled at applying for. Space is another resource that many arts require: space with the right kind of light, with the necessary sinks, with enough room to move, with room for an audience, and so forth. Because space is often at a premium in chronically underfunded public schools, the principal may need to be the procurer of arts space inside the building, and also may need to connect with neighborhood partners who can offer performance or studio space.

4. **Celebrate the arts in your school, building special events around them, and incorporating them into other school programs.** Invite

professional and community artists to perform or exhibit at the school. If possible, make the school a gallery, a studio, a rehearsal space. Create many occasions for displaying and sharing student work noncompetitively. Everyone needs an audience, not a contest with few winners and many losers.

5. **Involve parents and families in school arts programs.** Obviously, they are natural audiences for all kinds of school art events. Parents can also teach or perform when their skills match the curriculum; they can bring in their saxophone, brushes, or tap shoes and give demonstrations. When younger children need lots of help with complex or messy art projects, a few extra parent hands can be a real blessing. As always, before parents are used as classroom volunteers, they attend a training meeting first, at which teachers show them what is and what isn't part of their role. There are many other ways parents can help, from donating scrounged art material to hanging kids' art shows. Even the warhorse "picture lady" program has some merit, where different volunteer parents visit classes with a large copy of a favorite artwork, talking to students about the piece and the artist, starting a conversation and answering questions about Monet, Klee, or Wyeth. At Elm School in Milwaukee, families are given art assignments over the summer, and in the fall there's a gallery where everyone displays their work. In one project, parents and kids brought in line-drawing self-portraits, which were transferred to stained glass and installed in a huge archway window leading into the school library.

6. **Rethink the role of the arts specialists in your building.** If you have art or music teachers who are seeing eight hundred children a week, as in Boston, maybe a new model is in order. Invite the specialists to partner with some teachers—the second-grade team, the middle school faculty—to design, implement, and teach long-range integrated curriculum projects together. Instead of trying to teach overwhelming loads of students a little art or dab of music in not nearly enough time, let specialists infuse the arts into studies of ecology, history, or literature. If this seems like too big a commitment to make, try a two-week pilot arts-integration program and see what happens. Let the faculty evaluate the results and decide whether to extend it. This doesn't need to be an all-or-nothing deal. The art specialists can alternate: twenty weeks a year doing discipline-based instruction and twenty weeks co-teaching in integrated projects.

7. **Use your role as instructional leader, supervisor, and evaluator to let teachers know that the arts matter.** In your classroom visitations, evaluate congruently: if teachers are incorporating the arts,

let them know they are on the right track. When they are not, make suggestions, offer resources, link them up with teachers who are farther along. Try to root out the bureaucratic anti- or mixed messages about art that afflict most schools. In Chicago, for example, the mandatory lesson-planning forms have separate boxes for every subject, mapping them in priority order from reading, with its roomy boxes at the top of the list, on down to the arts, which get smaller, separate spaces at the bottom. Documents like this work against arts and against curriculum integration. Design new forms that honor the arts and invite interdisciplinary work. Then recycle those old forms, so they can be reborn as blank paper ready to carry more sensible messages.

8. **Work at the district level to support the arts programming across the curriculum.** In most school systems, the arts are in a constant battle to maintain their funding and their place in the curriculum, so it is vital that a few principals be arts advocates. If you can testify about the impact of the arts in your school, do so. If you can pass along articles documenting the academic value of the arts, copy away. If you can refer a fellow principal to an artist who works well with students, great. Even better, you can create a partnership among two or three other buildings to support ongoing arts projects, giving each other more resources and wider audiences to work with.

9. **Nurture continuing growth and emerging peer leadership among your staff** by sending volunteer teachers to workshops, courses, art courses, summer institutes, or teachers-training-teachers events. Support your outstanding and committed teachers by giving them a chance to lead, to share with colleagues.

10. **Help teachers get TIME** to talk about arts integration together, exchange ideas, work on joint projects, and think and grow as a faculty.

EXEMPLARY PROGRAM
Teachers, Artists, and Parents as Partners at La Escuela Fratney

Marcia Pertuz, Janet Larscheid, and Sandra Hays
La Escuela Fratney
Milwaukee, Wisconsin

Marcia: Imagine a class of urban seven- and eight-year-olds on a trip to the Milwaukee airport being more excited by the art displayed in a shop window than by the airplanes. These same children identified Frank Lloyd Wright furniture on an art museum tour before the docent had a chance to introduce it. The names Pablo Picasso, Francisco Mora, Jacob Lawrence, Georgia O'Keeffe, and Frida Kahlo were part of their everyday vocabulary, as in: "I still have to finish my Mary Cassatt piece." How did these kids get so turned on to art and artists? Although it was not part of our master plan for the school year, a series of happy events led to art becoming a major focus in our second grades last year at Fratney School.

La Escuela Fratney is a two-way bilingual immersion school in Milwaukee that serves a diverse population of children from both Spanish- and English-language backgrounds. Each grade level has two classrooms, with two teachers sharing about sixty students. One teacher creates an English print-rich environment and the other does the same in Spanish. Children are taught about 45 percent of the time in their second language. Most teachers at Fratney have chosen to have the children address them by their first names.

Sandra: As part of the September "Parents' Open House," my daughter Katharine's teachers, Janet Larscheid and Marcia Pertuz, handed out a sheet describing the Milwaukee Public Schools (MPS) standards for art education in the second grade. A cursory look at that document revealed the ambitious depth and scope of the proposed art curriculum. But a moment later, Janet and Marcia explained that there would be no art teacher at school that year because the money budgeted for that position had been reprogrammed. I felt chagrin because I realized that my daughter and her classmates would be denied the richness of an art experience for a whole year.

Upon rereading the MPS art curriculum document, I realized that my years-ago college minor in art history might be a springboard for helping in the classroom. I could use the art experience my daughter had enjoyed at her marvelous preschool as a paradigm for working with my daughter's teachers. Her first art teacher, Mary Tooley, encouraged even the youngest children to work with various art media and produced results beyond what one would believe possible from such young children. Mary would talk about one piece by a specific artist, tell the children a related story, and then have the children draw their interpretation of that artist's work. Due to my schedule, I knew I could not be in the classroom each week, but I could arrange to present eight or nine artists over the course of the school year.

Janet: After we told the parents about the art teacher being cut, Sandra responded with a five-page letter telling how she could help us. She had been pleased to hear that we wanted to place a strong emphasis on art, and wrote: "I am especially happy to know that these young children will be introduced to the vocabulary of art aesthetics and criticism, in addition to pursuing their own artwork. Additionally, it is gratifying to see two native Wisconsinites, Georgia O'Keeffe and Frank Lloyd Wright, heading the list of famous artists to be studied this year. I would be happy to present programs on some, perhaps all, of the artists."

To say Marcia and I were thrilled is an understatement. We were astounded at Sandra's depth of thinking and commitment, and her willingness to help create a year long study on art history, with a strong cross-cultural perspective and hands-on experiences. We immediately responded with a resounding "YES!" and began planning with her for the year. Sandra, we decided, would guide the study of O'Keeffe and Wright, along with the Hispanic artists Pablo Picasso, Frida Kahlo, and Diego Rivera, and the Impressionists (with emphasis on Mary Cassatt and Vincent van Gogh). I would take the lead role in exploring Jacob Lawrence and the "Great Migration" series, Cree Indian George Littlechild, and Kiki, a German artist/ illustrator living in and greatly influenced by the Mexican culture. Marcia would support the exploration of Hispanic/Latino art. Our plans also included bringing in other parents and community members as resources, and making multiple visits to the Milwaukee Art Museum, the Indian Summer festival, and the Milwaukee Public Museum. Our enthusiasm for the planned program was surpassed only by the children's as they became increasingly knowledgeable and excited.

Marcia: Sandra used a very successful technique when introducing the artists and their work to the children. She would focus on just one or two distinctive concepts for each artist. For example, with Frida Kahlo she stressed the concept of still life; with Mary Cassatt she talked about her use of family members for subjects and the way she filled the space with the figures, leaving very little background. The children would then execute their own paintings or drawings in the style of that artist or using those concepts.

The first artist Sandra presented was Georgia O'Keeffe, bringing in books and large flowers to share with the children. After her talk, the children used markers and white paper to create a picture in the style of Georgia O'Keeffe. They were spectacular. We displayed them in the hallway along with some examples of O'Keeffe's work. When we saw the beautiful quality of the work the children were producing, we realized that we were onto something very special. These were too significant to just send home, so we decided to laminate them and create a book for each child at the end of the year.

Sandra: Our study of Georgia O'Keeffe's "Still Life with Flowers" was one of the highlights of my experience with these second graders. I brought real sunflowers into the classroom so the students could see for themselves the colors, textures, and motion of the flower that they would be drawing. The children were eager to touch and smell the real flowers, absorbed the information about a famous native daughter, internalized their experience, and then produced the most incredible sunflower still lifes vibrating with golds and greens against a deep blue background.

Janet: To show the children the range of O'Keeffe's and other artists' work and their development over time, I bought postcard books of the artists' work, took them apart, mounted them on large construction paper in chronological order, and laminated them. These were then posted in the classroom and were also durable enough for the children to carry around and examine.

Journal writing was the first thing we did every day. One assignment was to list seven or eight pictures by an artist or features they noticed in the art from the classroom display and books. Another day, students would list several features within a single picture. Watching the children arrive in the morning was like watching an opening in an art gallery. They would walk up and down, examining and discussing the display of artworks. I would overhear children helping each other to see concepts that Sandra had talked about, spontaneously using the vocabulary she had introduced. It was interesting listening to their explanations about the art: One small group examining "Vincent's Bedroom" by van Gogh noted that the colors were a bit different in the two examples I had for them; one was a postcard, one was a large print. In one, the colors were more vivid. Their theory was that the first people moved out and the next people refurbished the furniture and the floors. Their discussion included wondering whether or not when people move they leave the furniture behind.

Janet: The Milwaukee Art Museum was one of the few art institutes in the country to display Jacob Lawrence's magnificent "Great Migration Series." Marcia and I went to hear Lawrence speak, and then used his stories, a book on his work, and a portfolio of prints from the series to prepare our students for visiting the exhibit. Each child chose one of the panels to study carefully and later try to paint, after reading and discussing the artist's life and works. At the museum, we had four wonderful docents, two of them able to speak to some of our children in Spanish, to guide us through the exhibit. Children listened carefully, often able to answer each other's questions because of their background knowledge. They observed details with which they were familiar and identified with their particular panel, as well as with all sixty.

The children had their own exhibit prominently displayed on one of the school's bulletin boards for all to see. Under each panel was the story of poverty and discrimination and the hopeful migration of Southern Blacks to "a better world" in the North. Our students not only knew the story; I believe they felt it. They learned that art can convey important messages and historic events. Later in the year, we compared this African American migration to the forced movement of many American Indians.

Molly, an African American student, took pride as she wrote: "Jacob Lawrence painted the Great Migration. He used dark colors and outlined things in light colors. He did a lot of research about the migration of African Americans. He paints the actual things, not like an imaginary dragon." Contemplating Lawrence and his work, another student stated, "His mother and father were part of the Great Migration. He started with the darkest colors and went to the lighter. When his mother learned about better jobs up North, she left her children in foster homes when he was young. He drew mostly geometric shapes off the Oriental rugs that decorated his house. Jacob was the oldest of the children in his family. He mostly painted no face features."

Sandra, of course, accompanied us on our excursion to the museum along with parents representative of the different racial backgrounds of our students. To watch her interact with the children, as she crouched down to their eye level while they sat on our rugs, was a wonderful experience. Whichever artist she discussed, she never talked down to the kids. On the contrary, she used the grown-up terminology of the art world. She expected the children to understand and learn, and they did. Her warmth, patience, and enthusiasm for her subject drew in every student. They eagerly responded to her questions, "oohed" and "aahed" when she showed pictures of or by the artists, and kept creeping closer to her until they were almost on her lap. Her daughter, Katharine, of course, was always at her mother's knees or side. She proudly held the books as her mother explained an artist's technique or use of color and shape.

Marcia: As the year progressed, the children wrote about each artist, using notes from their journals. We then typed them up and included them in their book of artists. One day a boy asked, "Why are all the good artists dead?" This gave us the perfect segue to look at artists in our immediate community. Again, the parents of students were able to help. We visited Al Blankschien, a neon artist, at his studio one block from the school. Al is the father of one of our students and fascinated them with his demonstration. As the children left, each told him one thing they would remember about their visit. Cathy Liptack, the mother of one of our students and a graphic artist, brought in her portfolio. She explained how she has used her son Max and his friends as models for magazine work she has done. The use of parents as examples reminded the students that artists are everyday people too.

Sandra: I was delighted that my art presentations were a hit with the second-grade students, the teachers, and the administrators at La Escuela Fratney. That year I shared in an enthusiasm, a collaboration, and a cooperation with my daughter's teachers that was unique. I have often tried to delineate the reason, but I always come back to personal compatibility and synchronicity of events. Those same second-grade students who are now in the third grade still become very excited when I walk into their classroom and they eagerly ask, "Are we going to do art today?"

The art program was designed around the MPS second-grade curriculum, the Hispanic emphasis of the school, and my own interest in several artists. The goal was to increase their aesthetic and critical appreciation of art, both of the famous artists and of the students' own personal artistic vision. Since I am not an artist, it was not my intention to teach the children the techniques of drawing or painting. I wanted them to begin to appreciate art and have fun creating their own. I wanted them to look at the work and see what was going on in it: color, mass, movement.

The program was successful beyond my wildest hopes because both Janet and Marcia were enthusiastically supportive. They hung artwork in the room before and after my presentations, they researched the artists on their own, they provided books for the children to read before and after my presentations, and they expanded the program to include artists with whom I was not familiar. But most important, they created a museum within the classroom and in the adjacent corridor, filled with the work of these exceptionally talented second-grade students. The north end of the second floor at La Escuela Fratney became an archive for a year's worth of artwork.

Janet: Reflecting on our year, I feel it was truly a catalyst for a lifetime appreciation of fine art, history, the performing arts, and many cultures for our students. Children saw themselves mirrored in multicultural literature and in the faces and drawings of the artists and performers. They wrote about their experiences from the heart, and through their actions and enthusiastic responses, we realized that children—all children—really love learning and are capable of understanding more at ages seven and eight than many credit them.

All of these wonderful educational experiences would not have happened without such a tremendous collaboration of parents, teachers, community members, special artists, district personnel, and the state through its funding. The African proverb that says it takes a whole village to raise a child was truly realized that special year. Our student B.J. summed the whole project up for me when he wrote: "The most important thing about me is that I am a great artist. When I grow up, I want to be an artist. I like drawing all kinds of things. I learned from the masters like Botticelli, Cassatt, da Vinci, Monet, Picasso, Rembrandt, van Gogh, Michael Angelo, and Frida Kahlo."

Works Cited

Catterall, James. 1997. *Involvement in the Arts and Success in Secondary School.* Los Angeles: The UCLA Imagination Project.

Connell, Noreen. 1996. *Getting Off the List: School Improvement in New York City.* New York: Educational Priorities Panel.

Consortium of National Arts Education Associations. 1994. *National Standards for Arts Education: What Every Young American Should Know and Be Able to Do.* Reston, VA: Music Educators National Conference.

Gardner, Howard. 1983. *Frames of Mind: The Theory of Multiple Intelligences.* New York: Basic Books.

President's Committee on the Arts and Humanities. 1997. *Creative America: A Report to the President: The President's Committee on the Arts and Humanities.* Washington, DC: The President's Committee on the Arts and Humanities.

Parks, Michaela, and Dale Rose. 1997. *The Impact of Whirlwind's Reading Comprehension through Drama Program on Fourth-Grade Reading Scores.* Chicago: Whirlwind Performance Company.

Short, Kathy, Jerome Harste, and Carolyn Burke. 1996. *Creating Classrooms for Authors and Inquirers.* Portsmouth, NH: Heinemann.

Suggested Further Readings

Brandt, Elizabeth Feldman. 1996. *Power in Practice: The Arts Education Development Project.* Philadelphia: Pew Charitable Trusts.

Claggett, Fran, and Joan Brown. 1992. *Drawing Your Own Conclusions: Graphic Strategies for Reading, Writing, and Thinking.* Portsmouth, NH: Boynton/Cook.

Darby, Jaye T., and James Catterall. 1994. "The Fourth R: The Arts and Learning." *Teachers College Record* 96 (2) (Winter): 299–328.

Edwards, Betty. 1979. *Drawing on the Right Side of the Brain.* Los Angeles: Tarcher.

Ernst, Karen. 1994. *Picturing Learning: Artists and Writers in the Classroom.* Portsmouth, NH: Heinemann.

———. 1997. *A Teacher's Sketch Journal: Observations on Learning and Teaching.* Portsmouth, NH: Heinemann.

Fowler, Charles. 1996. *Strong Arts, Strong Schools: The Promising Potential and Shortsighted Disregard of the Arts in American Schooling.* New York: Oxford University Press.

Grant, Janet Miller. 1995. *Shake, Rattle, and Learn: Classoom-Tested Ideas that Use Movement for Active Learning.* York, ME: Stenhouse.

Heller, Paul. 1996. *Drama as a Way of Knowing.* York, ME: Stenhouse.

Hubbard, Ruth Shagoury, and Karen Ernst. 1996. *New Entries: Learning by Writing and Drawing.* Portsmouth, NH: Heinemann.

Moline, Steve. 1995. *I See What You Mean: Children at Work with Visual Information.* York, ME: Stenhouse.

Morrison Institute of Public Policy and the National Endowment for the Arts. 1995. *Schools, Communities, and the Arts: A Research Compendium.* Tempe, AZ: The Morrison Institute of Public Policy and the National Endowment for the Arts.

Olson, Janet L. 1992. *Envisioning Writing: Toward an Integration of Drawing and Writing.* Portsmouth, NH: Heinemann.

Page, Nick. 1996. *Music as a Way of Knowing.* York, ME: Stenhouse.

Robinson, Gillian. 1996. *Sketch-Books: Explore and Store.* Portsmouth, NH: Heinemann.

Roe, Betty, Suellen Alfred, and Sandy Smith. 1998. *Teaching Through Stories: Yours, Mine, and Ours.* Norwood, MA: Christopher-Gordon.

Sklar, Daniel. 1992. *Playmaking: Children Writing and Performing Their Own Plays.* New York: Teachers and Writers Collaborative.

Whitin, Phyllis. 1996. *Sketching Stories, Stretching Minds: Responding Visually to Literature.* Portsmouth, NH: Heinemann.

Zakkai, Jennifer. 1997. *Dance as a Way of Knowing.* York, ME: Stenhouse.

Art Resources on the Internet

The Music Educators National Conference was the lead organization in the consortium that created the national standards, and offers association news, research bulletins, publications, and conference announcements from **http://www.uwec.edu/student/mused.**

The National Arts Education Association offers papers, news releases, and links to state arts organizations. **http://naea-reston.org**.

ArtsEdge offers a website of arts-advocacy materials, research studies, and key links. Visit **http://www.artsedge.kennedy-center.org.**

Just as decorative as its new building in California is the website of the Getty Education Institute for the Arts, offering news of the establishment art world and Getty's own doings at **http://artsednet.getty.edu.**

Under construction as this book goes to press, but soon to offer rich examples of the arts as a lever of whole-school change will be the site of CAPE. Search: **Chicago Arts Partnerships in Education.**

BEST PRACTICE IN TEACHING ART

Increase	Decrease
Art making; more doing of art, music, dance, drama	Studying other people's artworks
Student originality, choice, and responsibility in art making	Art projects that require students to create identical products or closely mimic a model
Stress on the process of creation, the steps and stages of careful craftsmanship	Concern with final products and displays that smothers learning about process
Art as an element of talent development for all students	Art as an arena for competition, screening, awards, and prizes for a few
Exploration of the whole array of art forms, from Western and non-Western sources, different time periods, cultures, and ethnic groups	Exclusive focus on Western, high-culture, elite art forms disconnected from a wide range of art making
Support for every student's quest to find and develop personal media, style, and tastes	Cursory dabbling in many art forms, without supporting a drive toward mastery in one
Time for art in the school day and curriculum	Once-a-week art classes that lack intensity
Integration of arts across the curriculum	Restricting study to separate arts discipline instruction
Using art as a tool of doing, learning, and thinking	Art as body of content to be memorized
Reasonable classloads and work assignments for arts-specialist teachers	Overloading arts specialists with excessive classloads
Artists in schools, both as performers and as partners in interdisciplinary work	Arts experiences provided only by school arts specialists
Long-term partnerships with artists and arts organizations	One-shot, disconnected appearances by artists
Teacher, principal, and parent involvement in the arts	Art-phobic, noninvolved school staff members running arts programs for students

8

Classroom Structures for Best Practice

In the past six chapters, we have presented dozens of recommendations from important national bodies and shared stories from many exemplary classrooms. Now the questions arise. What holds all these recommendations and classrooms together? What's happening in common among all those teachers from Lynn Cherkasky-Davis to Wayne Mraz, from kindergarten to high school, from rural to inner-city schools? What's the same about Best Practice, whether in reading, writing, math, science, or social studies? Is there a short list of fundamental classroom activities or structures that characterize Best Practice teaching across all boundaries?

We've already asserted that one common ingredient of Best Practice is a **philosophy**—a set of harmonious and interlocking **theories about learning**. Whether consciously or intuitively (or a little of both), all the teachers we have visited in this book subscribe to a coherent philosophy of learning that is child-centered, experiential, expressive, reflective, authentic, holistic, social, collaborative, democratic, cognitive, developmental, constructivist, and challenging. Similarly, the professional societies and research centers whose reports we summarized subscribe to the same fundamental views of learning and teaching.

So all these teachers and organizations believe something in common. But what are these practitioners **doing** with children that brings the philosophy alive? How do teachers enact, implement, and live out their theory? Although the classrooms we described so far may look quite diverse, under their varied surfaces are a few recurrent structures, basic ways of organizing kids, time, materials, space, and help. Actually, these exemplary teachers often are orchestrating a surprisingly **small** number of key activities in their search to embody Best Practice. Among these basic structures are:

Integrative Units

Small-group Activities

Representing-to-Learn

Classroom Workshop

Authentic Experiences

Reflective Assessment

Most of these structures are simple, familiar, and well proven. While these elements can profoundly shift the classroom balance from teacher-directed to student-centered learning, many of them are actually quite easy to implement; they are easy to begin, easy to slot into the existing teaching day, easy to experiment with incrementally. Indeed, far from requiring teachers to master a huge inventory of newfangled, technical instructional methods, Best Practice largely means returning to some old, perhaps prematurely discarded approaches, and fine tuning them until they work. But these simple activities are also very powerful: they can effectively take the teacher off stage, decentralize the classroom, and transfer responsibility for active learning to the students in any subject.

These six key structures each contain within their design the management features necessary to make them work. But many of them do require careful training of students, and the more complex a structure is, the more time and training it will require—happily, of course, the learning and social skills acquired with this training are valuable in themselves. Many of these key structures are the subject of recent articles or whole books that explain in detail how they can be adapted for different subjects and grade levels. Indeed, our own corps of teacher-consultants has recently written a book on these special strategies: *Methods That Matter: Six Structures for Best Practice Classrooms* (Daniels and Bizar 1998). In the next few pages, we offer a few comments on each structure; between the sources listed here and the recommended readings in Chapter 10, we point the way to detailed information and guidance about many of these structures.

Integrative Units

From the earliest days of elementary school to the waning moments of high school, American children typically study a sadly disconnected assortment of facts, ideas, and skills. In the typical first-grade reading program, children are presented with a year long series of reading "stories" sequenced according to the supposed reading skills that they teach, rather than their meaning or theme. This means that kids may jump from a basal story about fairies in a castle to one about Daniel Boone on the frontier, to another about talking robots in outer space—without any sense of order, connection, or transition among them. At the other end of the educational system, secondary schools are **designed** for incoherence: students' days are chopped into seven or eight segments guaranteed to be discontinuous with each other. A kid may start the day with forty minutes of Greek history in social studies class, then move to English to read some modern American poems, then shuffle off to science where the refraction of light is presented, and then move along to math to do problems connected to no aspect of life whatsoever.

In Best Practice schools and classrooms, teachers refuse to accept this randomness. They believe that content does matter and that for school to work, it must make sense to students—ideally, make sense all day long. Therefore, coplanning directly with the students, teachers identify a few big subjects of interest and importance, and then build extended units around those topics. In elementary grades, we know teachers who've built multi-week chunks of curriculum around topics such as Whales, Exploring, Castles, Australia, Fairy Tales, or Homes. In a whales unit, for example, the children might read (and hear read aloud) lots of different whale stories, build a library of favorite whale books, do a whale readers' theater, study the biology of whales, work in research teams to investigate different kinds of whales (e.g., blue, killer, and beluga), go to the aquarium and observe real whales (in Chicago's Shedd Aquarium, you actually do this), write and illustrate whale stories and reports, do whale mathematics (calculating the days of gestation or the quantity of plankton a baleen whale eats daily), and, of course, do lots of whale art. When teachers design such thematically coherent activities, they usually find that they can quite easily fit in many of the old, mandated curriculum elements; these topics simply come up in a different way, at a different time, and in a different order. But the main benefit of such teaching is that it provides children with the choice, continuity, order, challenge, and genuine responsibility they need to both enjoy school and stay engaged with the work.

Extended lessons like these are often called "themes" or "integrated units," denoting their multidisciplinary nature, but we use the term *integrative* to take the definition one step farther. Often, thematic units are designed by teachers (or published in teacher magazines) and then delivered to students, without kids having any voice or choice in their development. If the teacher guesses right, and lots of kids really are interested in whales, this can be a big step ahead of the old, disjointed curriculum. But it's even better practice to involve students much sooner—identifying topics, developing questions to be pursued, planning the inquiry, dividing up tasks, gathering information, and sharing in the whole process—right from the start.

This kind of integrative curriculum, as developed by James Beane (1997), does more than cross subject areas: it makes students real, responsible partners in curriculum development. Integrative curriculum is designed around real concerns students have about themselves and their world. Inquiries begin with a complex series of brainstorming and listing activities designed to gather students' questions and issues. From these lists of topics, units of the curriculum are developed collaboratively by teachers and students. If needed, teachers can later "back-map" from students' genuine questions to many of the mandated ingredients in district or state curriculum guides. If young people say they want to study racism (as they often do), teachers can plug in plenty of history, math (compiling statistics from racial-attitude surveys), and science (the literature of scientific racism, from phrenology to mental measurement), along with plenty of reading, writing, researching, and representing skills.

Curriculum integration often seems easier in elementary schools, where teachers may have the same thirty kids all day long. Aside from district rules and controls (which may present formidable obstacles), if a self-contained elementary teacher decides to start integrating the curriculum, her own good-will and resolve can actually get it done. Perhaps this is why some elementary teachers have always taught thematically, and why this approach is now growing so rapidly as an element of Whole Language, problem-, and project-based teaching. But in high school, things are a little tougher. Creating a truly integrated curriculum for any one student would require the cooperation of six or seven teachers who have no mandate to cooperate nor history of doing so, who have no common planning time, and who each still have on their desks a weighty scope-and-sequence document for their own segment of the school day—a curriculum that they probably have spent many increasingly comfortable years delivering.

Still, in high schools there are many ways teachers can move toward integrated, thematic instruction. If schools are ready to make moderate institutional reform, they can follow the pattern of Wasson High School in Colorado, where students now take four classes a day instead of eight, allowing kids and teachers to focus more carefully and deeply during ninety-minute class periods. At our own Best Practice High School in Chicago, we timeshare: Tuesdays and Thursdays are block-scheduled integrated curriculum units; Mondays and Fridays are scheduled as regular seven-period, separate-subject days; and on Wednesdays, students attend their community internships.

Even where there's no school-wide sanction for innovation, teachers still can reform their own forty-five-minute slice of the school day, reorganizing material into more meaningful, coherent, even integrative chunks. If the textbook presents a jumbled or arbitrary sequence of materials, the teachers can rearrange it, finding and identifying organizing themes that the curriculum writers didn't notice or mention. Teachers can help kids by identifying and stressing the few "big ideas" that strand through the welter of seemingly disparate material often presented to students.

For example, at Stagg High School (see Chapter 6), the history teachers decided that the old curriculum presented far too many disparate facts, and so the department went on a two-day retreat to hammer out a limited number of major themes in U.S. history. As the teachers now testify, this was one of the longest and loudest weekends of their professional lives, but they came back with a list of sixteen themes (they called them "post-holes of history") for a whole year's course. This provided every teacher with about two and a half weeks to approach each theme in a way that worked for their own students, even though everyone was still operating within the old bell schedule and framework. The Stagg faculty simply insisted that history make sense to their students.

Sometimes, two secondary teachers can get together to provide integration across more than one period of the day. For years, this has been done in American Studies programs, in which history and literature are taught in a combined, two-period, team-taught class. As a next step, several schools we've worked with have begun projects where a group of seventy-five kids and three teachers get a half-day together to pursue a big topic: at Stagg High School, one pilot group studied U.S. history, literature, and German—an approach that, among other things, highlighted the often overlooked Germanic origins of American colonial culture. Although curriculum integration in high schools is especially problematic, there's increasing hope as schools around the country break down the barriers of student and teacher scheduling, departmental boundaries, ability-grouping, and subservience to standardized test scores.

As helpful as thematic approaches to curriculum can be, teachers also need to be careful not to overload them. Academic subjects are so rich and extensive that in the course of one unit or semester or year, there's simply too much material for anyone to learn in any deep or significant way. Indeed, one of the most counterproductive elements of traditional American schooling has been its relentless emphasis on "covering the material" in a prescribed curriculum guide. Typically, such a mandated curriculum is an overstuffed compendium of facts, ideas, dates, concepts, books, persons, and ideas—a volume of material so enormous that no one thing in it can ever be understood if all of it must be mentioned. There's simply not enough time for deep study, and so each ingredient in the curriculum can only be "covered" in the sense that a wall is covered with a microscopically thin layer of paint. Among the many manifestations of the "coverage curriculum" are lecture-style classes, with emphasis on student notetaking, followed by multiple-choice tests stressing temporary memorization and factual recall.

In Best Practice classrooms, teachers realize that every child needn't study every possible topic, and that not everyone has to study all the same topics. Indeed, it is good educational practice (and solid preparation for adult life) to be part of a community where tasks and topics are parceled out to work groups, task forces, teams, or committees. When teachers jigsaw the curriculum, they seek natural ways to divide a given topic, assigning small groups of students to investigate the different parts, each team bringing back its piece of the puzzle to the whole group later on. In U.S. history, for example, not every student needs to learn about every Civil War battle. (Indeed, if everyone had to study every battle, the only choice would be for the teacher to simply talk as fast as she could.) Instead, a Best Practice teacher might let groups of kids each pick a single battle to study—Antietam for one group, Gettysburg for another, Bull Run for a third, and so on. Then the kids' job is to really dig in with reading and researching and talking, taking time to carefully explore and grasp the events involved, pursuing a deep understanding of their particular battle. Later, when the class comes back together, each group has a responsibility to share the highlights that emerged from their study. To pull the whole experience together, the teacher helps students find the similarities, differences, connections, and key concepts in the subtopics all have studied. In following this procedure, everyone learns one subject in detail, while still gaining a familiarity with related topics by way of reports from other classmates.

A final comment: the old "coverage curriculum" dies hard. Because the rote memorization of multiplicitous facts was so much a part of every American adult's education, many grown-ups still confuse factual recall with a good education. This craving for coverage has even given rise to a multimillion-dollar cottage industry. Under the banner of "cultural literacy," E.D. Hirsch and his collaborators are selling the nervous parents of America a series of books that list "What Your First (Second, Third, or Fourth) Grader Needs to Know." These banal handbooks reiterate what the old school curriculum used to say: that everyone should study the same things at the same time, and that a satisfactory outcome of schooling is the mere recognition of certain key words.

The durability—indeed, the marketability—of this "curriculum of superficiality" is a real challenge to school reformers. The bung-full curriculum has many defenders who use words like *rigor* and *standards* when they defend their view. Yet this advocacy of comprehensive coverage by self-appointed cultural guardians is actually deeply ironic, since their model of curriculum actually breeds disrespect for learning. After all, everyone involved in traditional schooling, teachers and students alike, will testify with remarkably little embarrassment that students normally forget virtually everything they "learned" in school. Yet, we who want to **raise the standards of learning** by insisting that students study a finite number of topics in much greater depth are labeled "permissivists." This is clearly a long and deeply rooted cultural struggle, one that won't be settled for generations—but it is wise for school reformers to be aware of its dynamic.

Suggested Further Readings

Beane, James. 1993. *A Middle School Curriculum: From Rhetoric to Reality.* Columbus, OH: National Middle School Association.

———. 1997. *Curriculum Integration: Designing the Core of Democratic Education.* New York: Teachers College Press.

Boomer, Garth, Nancy Lester, Cynthia Onore, and Jon Cook. 1992. *Negotiating the Curriculum.* London: Falmer Press.

Davies, Ann, Colleen Politano, and Caren Cameron. 1993. *Making Themes Work.* Winnipeg: Peguis.

Five, Cora Lee, and Marie Dionisio. 1995. *Bridging the Gap: Integrating Curriculum in Upper Elementary and Middle Schools.* Portsmouth, NH: Heinemann.

Lindquist, Tarry. 1995. *Seeing the Whole Through Social Studies.* Portsmouth, NH: Heinemann.

Manning, Maryanne, Gary Manning, and Roberta Long. 1994. *Theme Immersion: Inquiry-Based Curriculum in Elementary and Middle Schools.* Portsmouth, NH: Heinemann.

Messick, Rosemary, and Karen Reynolds. 1992. *Middle Level Curriculum in Action.* White Plains, NY: Longman.

Short, Kathy G., Jean Schroeder, Julie Laird, Gloria Kauffman, Margaret J. Ferguson, and Kathleen Marie Crawford. 1996. *Learning Together Through Inquiry: From Columbus to Integrated Curriculum.* York, ME: Stenhouse.

Springer, Mark. 1994. *Watershed: A Successful Voyage into Integrative Learning.* Columbus, OH: National Middle School Association.

Steffey, Stephanie, and Wendy Hood. 1994. *If This Is Social Studies, Why Isn't It Boring?* York, ME: Stenhouse.

Stevenson, Chris, and Judy Carr. 1993. *Integrated Studies in the Middle Grades: Dancing Through Walls.* New York: Teachers College Press.

Tchudi, Steven, and Stephen Lafer. 1996. *The Interdisciplinary Teacher's Handbook: Integrated Teaching Across the Curriculum.* Portsmouth, NH: Heinemann.

Vars, Gordon. 1993. *Interdisciplinary Teaching in the Middle Grades: Why and How.* Columbus, OH: National Middle School Association.

Small-group Activities

Best Practice means big changes in the way classrooms operate. Across all content areas, the new curriculum calls for much less teacher presentation and domination, far more active student learning, and constantly shifting, decentralized groupings. In Best Practice classrooms, students work together effectively in small groups—in pairs, threes, *ad hoc* groups, and long-term teams—without constant teacher supervision. Teachers all across the country have been discovering and adapting the powerful versions of collaborative learning described by William Glasser (1990), David and Roger Johnson (1991), Sharan and Sharan (1990), Robert Slavin (1985), and others. They have been reassured and excited by research showing that, even using the customary standardized measures, students of all grade levels show significant achievement gains across the curriculum when they are organized into collaborative groupings and projects. It works.

But we must be sure to apply these effective collaborative structures to an elevated conception of curriculum. Too often, the trendiest cooperative learning applications are merely study teams that harness the power of social learning to help kids memorize the same old curriculum content. In fact, kids **can** teach each other dates and facts and formulas quite effectively when they study as a group, but why bother? Far more powerful and appropriate uses of collaboration occur when students set up and pursue group investigations, read and discuss novels in literature circles, or generate their own crafted pieces of writing with the input of peer response and editing groups. Following are listed a few structures for collaborative learning that move kids toward higher-order thinking.

Partner/Buddy Reading.   Paired reading activities with many variations. Two students may take turns reading aloud to each other from a story or textbook, either passing a single book back and forth, or with the listener following the text in her own copy. Pairs can read the same section outside of class and join to discuss the reading, or they can jigsaw the text, reading different sections and sharing their respective pieces of the puzzle.

Peer Response and Editing.   Ongoing groups in which students give diplomatic and critical feedback on drafts of each other's writings. Training students to help each other with their work requires both management tools (e.g., how to talk quietly, developing a "twelve-inch voice" so that everyone in the room can hear his or her own partners) and process skills (i.e., how to pose questions that help an author make her own decisions, instead of just giving criticism).

Reading Circles/Text Sets.   Groups of four or five students choose and read the same article, book, or novel. After doing their reading outside of class, they prepare to play one of several specific discussion roles, and come to the group with notes to help them take that job. Circles have regular meetings, with discussion roles rotating each session. When they finish a book, the circle may report briefly to the whole class; then they trade members with other finishing groups, select more reading, and move into a new cycle (Daniels 1994).

Study Teams.   Where it is necessary for kids to memorize voluminous or complex material, Slavin's "Team Games Tournament" and related strategies help students bring energy to the task. These structures help kids form interdependent groups that parcel out tasks, share the work, stop to help members who fall behind, and provide an interlocking reward system where everyone gets maximum benefits if everyone in the group succeeds. (One caution: if such team strategies merely harness collaborative learning to an archaic, irrelevant, teacher-dominated curriculum, they are certainly a mundane application of Best Practice.)

Group Investigations.   One useful legacy of the 1960s is the wide assortment of group inquiry models developed in different fields, including the Biological Science Curriculum Study, the Social Science Curriculum Project, and the Group Investigation Model (all described in Joyce 1986). In the common structure of these models, a learning cycle begins when the class encounters or identifies a problem for study. As a first step, the whole class discusses the topic, shares its prior knowledge, generates hypotheses, poses questions, sets goals, and makes a plan for studying the topic. Roles and tasks are parceled out to different groups of students based on their curiosities and skills. Then the inquiry proceeds in the small groups, with the teacher serving as facilitator and resource along the way. When the investigations are completed, the teams reconvene to share and discuss their findings.

Centers.   This form of small-group work is usually thought of as relevant mainly for elementary teachers, though we see many secondary applications as well. Centers are learning stations set up by the teacher around a classroom, where students can visit and explore ideas in an organized sequence. Centers are meant to replace passive whole-class presentations with active exploration by individual kids and small groups, and include an element of student choice, in that kids can decide when to visit each center, traffic permitting. Back in the "open classroom" movement of the 1960s, some schools tried to have centers be the *main* teaching device, and teachers often imploded from stress. They tried to "teach" kids all day by setting up independent-learning centers that were engaging and active, that somehow covered the curriculum, that coordinated with each other, that kept kids busy for roughly the same amount of time each, that allowed for record keeping and grading, and that didn't make too big a mess.

Today we still recognize the importance of a decentralized classroom, but balance is our watchword: we know that kids learn best across a school day that provides a rich mixture of different activities, from quiet individual work to energetic collaboration. Centers still have a place, not as the main vehicle for instruction for most of the day, but as a natural element of differentiated classroom space and a varied schedule. We know many elementary teachers—like Lynn Cherkasky-Davis, whom we visited in Chapter 2, and Mary Fencl in Chapter 4—who routinely have four or five centers in their room, rotating in new ones periodically, and who schedule between forty-five minutes and one-and-a-half hours a day of "center time" when kids can explore these. We also know some high school teachers who don't think centers are just for the little kids, who believe that creating some functional subareas around the room makes an ideal environment for teenagers who welcome settings where they can work alone or with a few friends. In a high school classroom, a computer can be a kind of center; so is the table at which writers meet to conference over their work or where teams meet to work on their research.

As teachers set up an environment in the classroom, differentiated space is needed both to create some nooks for privacy and some areas defined by purpose; some are temporary and some are permanent. Good centers should be natural. A writing center might be mainly a supply depot with a variety of paper, pens, markers, tape, Wite-Out, and a table for editing. A reading center would include a classroom library of enticing books of various levels of difficulty, hand-published books by other students, comfortable corners for reading, and a table and chairs for quiet group discussion. Listening centers, with a couple of tape recorders and a good collection of tapes, offer kids a chance to listen to books read aloud (either familiar ones or ones they can't yet handle independently) or to hear interviews with favorite authors. Math centers can present a variety of manipulatives and problem-solving activities, so that as students cycle through all of them over a period of weeks, they are involved in a variety of tasks—required to do some review of previously taught ideas, some work with topics currently being discussed, and some challenging inquiry into more advanced concepts. A science center might be the location where a classroom pet is kept, along with books about that creature, and a set of observational activities to be recorded in each child's learning log. A room with centers offers kids variety in the day, a chance to engage content actively, natural occasions for quiet talk, opportunities for *ad hoc* collaboration, and the responsibility for making choices. Centers also put the teacher in a helper-observer role, providing a splendid time to give help to kids who need it and to observe carefully the ways in which different kids approach the work of different centers.

Teachers who want to successfully implement all these promising new student-centered small-group activities may need to begin with some whole-class training first. If students are inexperienced with small-group structures, the starting point may be developing a productive, interdependent, cooperative classroom community. After all, if the climate isn't right, small groups will fail, and instruction inevitably will regress toward the old teacher-centered, lecture-test model. At the whole-class level, teachers must help students to join in effective, democratic meetings during which the group can brainstorm ideas, set goals, make plans, learn new structures for working, solve problems, and evaluate their own work. While this kind of session may sound routine, most teachers are experienced in giving whole-class presentations and instructions, not in chairing meetings that invite genuine interchange and decision making by the students.

William Glasser (in Joyce 1986) outlined a recurrent cycle of classroom meetings that builds both content learning and democratic involvement. The class (1) meets regularly to talk about its own learning activities and social processes; (2) identifies learning goals or group problems; (3) prioritizes its goals or problems; (4) proposes and discusses alternative courses of action; (5) makes a formal, group commitment to action; and (6) regularly meets to share and review the outcomes of group decisions. While this pattern of whole-class meetings obviously can nurture the socioemotional development of the classroom community, its academic uses are just as vital: at these meetings, students can decide what to study, divide into working groups, plan how and when to report their learnings with others, and more.

If students have difficulty functioning in a participatory whole-group democracy, teachers need artful strategies to build comfort, familiarity, and fluency with the procedures. For sessions when a class is planning a project or investigation, the teacher can use brainstorming, asking people to call out options or stages in the work, listing them all, and then having the class order or prioritize them afterward—a simple, well-known, but under utilized strategy. If participation isn't proving sufficiently widespread, a resourceful teacher will ask students to talk in pairs for a minute to make their own lists and then request one idea from each person. Meaningful discussions of a topic in any course can be started effectively by having students write brief learning-log entries on an open-ended question (e.g., "What do you think was going through the character's mind when he said that?"; "What are some of the pros and cons President Lincoln might have considered as he thought over his decision about emancipation?").

Whole-class meetings are also important for sharing completed work that students are proud of or that they want more input on, to help them revise further. Many elementary teachers end their daily writing workshop time with ten minutes for a few students to occupy the "author's chair," read their work aloud, and call on peers who ask questions, offer specific praise, or explain where they felt confused. A whole class can profitably talk through the qualities that characterize an effective lab explanation, report, or small-group presentation—so that the class participates in setting criteria for meaningful evaluation. And when a unit or project is finished, a science teacher can help her class internalize the underlying concepts and become more effective learners by outlining together not only the major ideas explored, but also the activities the class used, and how people overcame various obstacles and solved problems in the course of their learning.

Suggested Further Readings

Cohen, Elizabeth. 1986. *Designing Groupwork: Strategies for the Heterogeneous Classroom.* New York: Teachers College Press.

Daniels, Harvey. 1994. *Literature Circles: Voice and Choice in the Student-Centered Classroom.* York, ME: Stenhouse.

Girard, Suzanne, and Kathleen Willing. 1996. *Partnerships for Classroom Learning: From Reading Buddies to Pen Pals to the Community and the World Beyond.* Portsmouth, NH: Heinemann.

Glasser, William. 1986. *Control Theory in the Classroom.* New York: Harper & Row.

Glazer, Susan Mandel. 1997. *The Literacy Center: Contexts for Reading and Writing.* York, ME: Stenhouse.

Hill, Bonnie Campbell, and Nancy Johnson. 1995. *Literature Circles and Response.* Norwood, MA: Christopher-Gordon.

Hill, Susan, and Tim Hill. 1990. *The Collaborative Classroom: A Guide to Cooperative Learning.* Portsmouth, NH: Heinemann.

Johnson, David, Roger Johnson, Edythe Holubec, and Patricia Roy. 1991. *Coopera-
    tion in the Classroom*. Edina, MN: Interaction Book Company.

Samway, Katharine Davies, and Gail Whang. 1995. *Literature Study Circles in a
    Multicultural Classroom*. York, ME: Stenhouse.

Samway, Katharine, Gail Whang, and Mary Pippitt. 1995. *Buddy Reading: Cross-age
    Tutoring in a Multicultural School*. Portsmouth, NH: Heinemann.

Sharan, Yael, and Shlomo Sharan. 1992. *Expanding Cooperative Learning Through
    Group Investigation*. New York: Teachers College Press.

Spear, Karen. 1987. *Sharing Writing: Peer Response Groups in the English Class*.
    Portsmouth, NH: Boynton/Cook.

Representing-to-Learn

Many teachers are already familiar with the notion of *writing-to-learn*, developed in the 1970s and 1980s by teacher-authors like Peter Elbow (1973) and
Toby Fulwiler (1987), and widely disseminated in National Writing Project
inservice programs. The idea is simple: writing can be a tool of thinking as
well as a finished product. There are many quick and simple writing activities that help students to encounter, probe, explore, and remember the content of the curriculum. While schools typically act as though finished, polished compositions are the only form of worthwhile writing, modern learning
theory shows us that when students act on information by using informal,
spontaneous writing, they actually understand and recall more of what is
taught in school.

Since the early days of writing-to-learn, we've discovered that writing
down *words* is not the limit of this activity: drawing, sketching, jotting, mapping, and other artistic and graphic representations are equally valuable—and
when combined with words, in strategies like clustering, semantic mapping,
or cartooning, can powerfully leverage students' thinking about the curriculum. Indeed, research is quickly accumulating (see Chapter 7) that documents the contribution that artistic expression offers to the development of
basic-skills learning in subjects like math, science, and literature. So, to
acknowledge this important broadening of writing-to-learn, we've renamed
the category *representing-to-learn* (Daniels and Bizar 1998).

Representing-to-learn strategies help overcome the passivity of the traditional classroom, making students more active and responsible for their
own learning. Teachers of all subjects and grade levels can have students
keep sketchbooks or learning logs, in which students regularly do short,
spontaneous, exploratory, personal pieces of writing or drawing about the
content they are studying. Instead of filling in blanks in worksheets and jotting short answers to textbook study questions, students respond to fewer,
broader, more open-ended prompts: What would have changed if Lincoln
were shot six months earlier? What are the advantages of an indicator over

a meter? What are three questions from last night's reading that we ought to discuss in class today? In logs, teachers ask students to react, record, speculate, compare, analyze, or synthesize the ideas in the curriculum. Students aren't writing to be graded on grammar or artistic ability, but rather to pursue ideas and try out thoughts. These notebooks are a way of running your mind, monitoring your thinking, and making reflection habitual and concrete. This is writing and drawing for thinking, not as a polished product.

As a cognitive tool, learning logs can work for learners in any content field. After all, whatever the subject matter, learners can always jot down their responses, record their own prior knowledge, probe their own thinking patterns, map predictions, diagram connections, or sketch plans for what to do next. When they are shared, notebooks also open a private channel of communication between the teacher and each student. In learning logs, teachers report, students will often share things that they would never announce out loud, thereby providing teachers a new and valuable kind of feedback.

Teachers also **use** student representing-to-learn products in class, reading them aloud, feeding them into group discussions, parceling them out to teams for review or action. Many teachers, like our friend Wayne Mraz, assign "admit slips" and "exit slips," short bits of writing used to start and end a class. Others run classroom conversations about a topic—a poem or a Civil War battle or a chemical process—conducted entirely in notes that students pass back and forth, formally called "dialogue journals." For teachers who use these representing-to-learn strategies regularly, the compiled entries become an increasingly thick record of what each student has done and learned.

One of the surprising and pleasant side effects of representing-to-learn is that the classroom is **quiet**. While many people anticipate chaos in progressive classrooms, the opposite is often the case. For example, if you visit the kind of reading workshop described by Nancie Atwell (1998) and implemented by teachers around the country, what you typically will find is a room full of teenagers working quietly, without overt supervision, for forty-five minutes at a stretch. Students will be reading novels of their own choice, which they will occasionally put aside at a good stopping place to write a "literature letter" to the teacher or a designated student partner. Or they may draw their own vision of a scene from a story in response to a "lit letter" received from their partner. In this quiet but hard-working classroom, the teacher and the students are all industriously reading books and using special kinds of writing and drawing to channel their responses and enhance their comprehension.

Although these logs are often called journals, they are *not* diaries. Some teachers are wary of trying journals because of the confessional connotations of that word, but academic journaling (which we prefer to call learning logs, notebooks, or sketchbooks) is expressly for recording and advancing subject-matter learning in school. Other teachers worry about implementation problems, perhaps because they have seen too many ill-advised English teachers trudging home from school on Friday afternoon, lugging a sky-high stack of student spirals that they "have to" respond to over the weekend. But learning logs needn't increase the workload of either students or teachers. They are supposed to **replace** textbook study questions, ditto sheets, or other low-level, memorization-oriented activities. Students should spend the same amount of time working and teachers the same amount of time responding, with everyone engaged in higher-order, more valuable thinking. In fact, many teachers find that when the students' representing-to-learn pieces are used as the starting point for class activities and discussions, they don't even need to collect and read the work separately; hearing the ideas discussed aloud provides plenty of feedback about what kids are thinking.

Some teachers wonder whether their content is too technical or their students are too young for notebooks to work. We have seen learning logs effectively integrated into everything from preschool classes, where kids draw their entries, to animal husbandry courses at a technical college. Other teachers worry that if students are assigned learning logs in all school subjects, they will either become confused or "burn out" from the overuse of this teaching novelty. One answer to this: in Terrie Bridgman's first-grade class at Baker Demonstration School in Evanston, Illinois, the six-year-olds are keeping a math journal, a reading journal, and a personal "news" journal within the first few days of school, with gusto and without any confusion. On a deep level, treating representing-to-learn as a gimmick makes no more sense than labeling **reading** in every class a fad. Effective teachers, as well as theorists, are finally recognizing that writing and drawing are rightful bookends to reading, too-neglected tools that help students actively process their encounter with ideas to deepen their engagement with the curriculum.

Suggested Further Readings

Anson, Chris, and Richard Beach. 1995. *Journals in the Classroom: Writing to Learn.* Norwood, MA: Christopher-Gordon.

Bayer, Ann Shea. 1990. *Collaborative-Apprenticeship Learning: Language and Thinking Across the Curriculum K–12.* Mountain View, CA: Mayfield.

Calkins, Lucy. 1990. *Living Between the Lines.* Portsmouth, NH: Heinemann.

Claggett, Fran, and Joan Brown. 1992. *Drawing Your Own Conclusions: Graphic Strategies for Reading, Writing, and Thinking.* Portsmouth, NH: Boynton/Cook.

Countryman, Joan. 1992. *Writing to Learn Mathematics.* Portsmouth, NH: Heinemann.

Edwards, Betty. 1979. *Drawing on the Right Side of the Brain.* Los Angeles: Tarcher.

Ernst, Karen. 1994. *Picturing Learning: Artists and Writers in the Classroom.* Portsmouth, NH: Heinemann.

———. 1997. *A Teacher's Sketch Journal: Observations on Learning and Teaching.* Portsmouth, NH: Heinemann.

Fletcher, Ralph. 1996. *A Writer's Notebook: Unlocking the Writer Within You.* New York: Avon.

Fowler, Charles. 1996. *Strong Arts, Strong Schools: The Promising Potential and Shortsighted Disregard of the Arts in American Schooling.* New York: Oxford University Press.

Fulwiler, Toby, ed. 1987. *The Journal Book.* Portsmouth, NH: Boynton/Cook.

Heller, Paul. 1996. *Drama as a Way of Knowing.* York, ME: Stenhouse.

Hubbard, Ruth Shagourny, and Karen Ernst. 1996. *New Entries: Learning by Writing and Drawing.* Portsmouth, NH: Heinemann.

Isaacs, Judith Ann, and Janine Brodine. 1994. *Journals in the Classroom: A Complete Guide for the Elementary Teacher.* Winnipeg: Peguis.

Moline, Steve. 1995. *I See What You Mean: Children at Work with Visual Information.* York, ME: Stenhouse.

Olson, Janet L. 1992. *Envisioning Writing: Toward an Integration of Drawing and Writing.* Portsmouth, NH: Heinemann.

Page, Nick. 1996. *Music as a Way of Knowing.* York, ME: Stenhouse.

Parsons, Les. 1994. *Expanding Response Journals: In All Subject Areas.* Portsmouth, NH: Heinemann.

Rico, Gabrielle. 1985. *Writing the Natural Way.* Los Angeles: Tarcher.

Robinson, Gillian. 1996. *Sketch-Books: Explore and Store.* Portsmouth, NH: Heinemann.

Romano, Tom. 1995. *Writing with Passion: Life Stories, Multiple Genres.* Portsmouth, NH: Boynton/Cook.

Whitin, Phyllis. 1996. *Sketching Stories, Stretching Minds: Responding Visually to Literature.* Portsmouth, NH: Heinemann.

Worsley, Dale, and Bernadette Mayer. 1989. *The Art of Science Writing.* New York: Teachers and Writers Collaborative.

Zakkai, Jennifer. 1997. *Dance as a Way of Knowing.* York, ME: Stenhouse.

Classroom Workshop

Undoubtedly the single most important new strategy in literacy education is the reading-writing workshop. As Donald Graves, Nancie Atwell, Lucy Calkins, Linda Rief, Tom Romano, and others have explained, students in a workshop classroom choose their own topics for writing and books for reading, using large scheduled chunks of classroom time for **doing** their own reading and writing. They collaborate freely with classmates, keep their own records, and self-evaluate. Teachers take new roles, too, modeling their own reading and writing processes, conferring with students one-to-one, and offering well-timed, compact mini-lessons as students work. In the mature workshop classroom, teachers don't wait around for "teachable moments" to occur—they make them happen every day.

The workshop model is simple and powerful. It derives from the insight that children learn to read by reading and write by writing, and that schools in the past have simply failed to provide enough guided practice. It recognizes that kids need less telling and more showing, that they need more time to **do** literacy and less time hearing about what reading and writing might be like if you ever did them. Even the term *workshop* harks back to the ancient crafts-place, where not only did products get produced, but education went on as the master craftsman coached apprentices.

In school, a workshop is a long, regularly scheduled, recurrent chunk of time (i.e., thirty minutes to an hour or more) during which the main activity is to **do** a subject: reading, writing, math, history, or science. Workshops meet regularly, at least once a week; in many classrooms, students have workshop time every day. A defining element of a true workshop is **choice**: individual students choose their own books for reading, projects for investigating, topics for writing. They follow a set of carefully inculcated norms for exercising that choice during the workshop period. They learn that all workshop time must be used on some aspect of working, so when they complete a product, a piece, or a phase, they aren't "done" for the day. Instead, kids must begin something new, based on an idea from their own running list of tasks and topics, or seek a conference with the teacher. While there are regular, structured opportunities for sharing and collaborating in a workshop, students also spend much time working alone; there are other times of the day when teachers set up collaborative group or team activities.

Today, pathfinding teachers are beginning to extend the workshop model outward from reading and writing, where many have already found success, into other parts of the curriculum—establishing math workshops, science workshops, history workshops (e.g., Saul et al. 1993). Teachers are adapting workshop because they see that deep immersion is the key to mastery, whatever the subject: they want kids to **do** history, **do** science, **do** math.

Following is a generic schedule for a single forty-five-minute workshop session that could happen in any subject, just to show one way that teachers commonly manage time and activity.

Five Minutes: Status of the Class Conference. Each student announces in a few words what she will work on this session.

Thirty Minutes: Work Time/Conferences. Students work according to their plan. Depending on the rules and norms, this may include reading or writing, talking or working with other students, going to the library, making telephone calls, using manipulatives or microscopes. The teacher's roles during this time are several. For the first few minutes, the teacher will probably experiment, read, or write herself, to model her own doing of the subject. Then the teacher may manage a bit, skimming through the room to solve simple problems and make sure everyone is working productively.

Then the teacher shifts to her main workshop activity: conducting one-to-one or small-group conferences with kids about their work, either following a preset schedule or based on student sign-ups for that day. The teacher's roles in these conferences are to be a sounding-board, facilitator, and coach—rarely a critic or an instructor.

Ten Minutes: Sharing. In many workshop sessions, teachers save the last few minutes for students to discuss what they have done that day. Writers may read a piece of work aloud, readers may offer a capsule book review, math students show how they applied a concept to a real-world situation, scientists demonstrate a chemical reaction, social studies teams report the results of their opinion survey.

Obviously, the workshop classroom is not an entirely new phenomenon. Its decentralized, hands-on pattern, with kids "doing" the subject rather than just hearing about it, is familiar to teachers of art, science, home economics, physical education, and other "doable" subjects. Of these fields, however, only art has traditionally allowed for any measure of student choice in the work. The commitment to student autonomy and responsibility is rooted more in experiments with independent study, classroom contracting, the open classroom, and learning laboratories. This new vehicle for student-centered learning—the workshop classroom—works because it addresses the shortcomings of prior experiments: it gives both students and teachers clear-cut roles to perform, it provides for careful balancing of social and solitary activities, and it respects the necessity of detailed training for students to work purposefully in this decentralized format.

Conferences are the heart of the workshop. In a very real sense, they are the main reason we go to all the trouble to set up the norms, structures, and processes of workshop in the first place. What we're trying so hard to create is time and space to sit down with kids, one at a time, and work for a few minutes on just what each student needs. Sadly, these conversations are still too rare in American schools. In spite of decades of research confirming the impact of teacher-student conferences—from Jerome Bruner's scaffolding research in the 1960s to this year's headlines about "Reading Recovery" tutoring—most American students still spend their school day deployed in groups of thirty, listening to the teacher or doing seatwork. Ironically, most teachers will readily agree that a one-minute private conversation with a child, timed at just the right moment and targeted precisely to that kid's own work, is often more effective than hours of whole-class instruction. But still, few teachers are reorganizing their day to make more one-to-one exchanges happen.

Why haven't conferences caught on more widely? There are several sticking points. Tradition, as usual, provides a first layer of resistance. Teachers' formal training, as well as their own experience as students, strongly conditions them to think of teaching as a one-on-thirty rather than a one-on-one activity. Experienced teachers already possess banks of lesson plans, some of them developed and polished over years, for teacher-centered classroom activities that seem to work. These treasured whole-class lessons are ready to use, and they don't carry the risks and uncertainties that are inevitably part of anything new.

The second level of reluctance involves classroom management: teachers worry about "what to do with the other twenty-nine kids" while they hold conferences with individual pupils. This is a reasonable concern: until teachers can get a classroom of students working productively without constant monitoring, they won't feel clear to introduce decentralized activities like conferences. This, of course, is one of the main reasons why it is so important to establish the workshop structure described above—not only does it provide practice time in key curriculum areas, but it also creates the basic frame within which conferences can occur. And, working farther backward, building a productive workshop depends on the initial climate-setting, group-building activities we talked about earlier.

The other worry of teachers is that they won't know what to say to a child in a conference. Many think that to have an effective conference, they must first study the learner's work and then ask "the right questions"—or have the right advice ready to give. For teachers just starting to consider instituting such one-to-one conversations, this sounds like a lot of work. But good conferences do not necessarily require extensive teacher preparation. In writing instruction, for example, we have found that kids who have regular three-minute "process conferences" with their teachers gain significantly in writing achievement, even when the teacher does not read the papers or give advice in those conferences.

So what kinds of things can the teacher say? Three simple questions can start a conference in any subject: (1) What are you working on? (2) How is it going? (3) What do you plan to do next? For each of these key questions, teachers will gradually develop some subprompts or helping questions, but the three basic queries serve just fine for starters. In such a process conference, it is not the teacher's job to tell or teach or offer instruction; the task is to help the student talk and to listen. In fact, such process conferences actually can help teachers avoid one conferencing problem that they may not worry about, but should: dominating the student. Too many teachers, when they first begin conferencing, simply offer a kind of knee-to-knee lecture, talking at the student for three or four minutes. The simple, three-question process conference transfers the conversational responsibility from teacher to student, providing the teacher with a good implicit reminder to keep quiet.

How do such short "content-free" conferences actually promote the learning of content? Process conferences work because they teach a habit of mind. They help students learn how to reflect on their own work, to review their own progress, to identify their own problems, set their own goals, and make plans and promises to themselves about steps they are going to take.

As we regularly hold conferences with students, leading them through the pattern of where-am-I-and-where-do-I-want-to-go, we are truly modeling a way of thinking for themselves; we are holding out-loud conversations with kids that they can gradually internalize and have with themselves.

Implementing the workshop classroom, with its core of individual conferences, can be a real challenge for teachers. The structure itself violates the expectations of many students, administrators, and parents, it competes for time with the official curriculum, and it often contradicts teachers' professional training and their own childhood experience in school. Nor do students always take smoothly and effortlessly to the workshop model: on the contrary, implementation can be bumpy, tricky, and slow, even for dedicated teachers in progressive districts. Yet, when the workshop starts to work, it turns the traditional transmission-model–classroom upside down: students become active, responsible, self-motivating, and self-evaluating learners, while the teacher drops the talking-head role in favor of more powerful functions as model, coach, and collaborator.

Suggested Further Readings

Allen, Janet, and Kyle Gonzalez. 1998. *There's Room for Me Here: Literacy Workshop in the Middle School.* York, ME: Stenhouse.

Atwell, Nancie. 1998. *In the Middle: New Understandings About Writing, Reading, and Learning.* Portsmouth, NH: Boynton/Cook.

Avery, Carol. 1993. *And with a Light Touch: Learning About Reading, Writing, and Teaching with First Graders.* Portsmouth, NH: Heinemann.

Brown, Cynthia Stokes. 1994. *Connecting with the Past: History Workshop in Middle and High Schools.* Portsmouth, NH: Heinemann.

Harwayne, Shelley. 1992. *Lasting Impressions: Weaving Literature into the Writing Workshop.* Portsmouth, NH: Heinemann.

Hindley, Joanne. 1996. *In the Company of Children.* York, ME: Stenhouse.

Hubbard, Ruth Shagourny. 1996. *A Workshop of the Possible: Nurturing Children's Creative Development.* York, ME: Stenhouse.

Jorgensen, Karen. 1993. *History Workshop: Reconstructing the Past with Elementary Students.* Portsmouth, NH: Heinemann.

Rief, Linda. 1992. *Seeking Diversity: Language Arts with Adolescents.* Portsmouth, NH: Heinemann.

Ross, Elinor. 1996. *The Workshop Approach: A Framework for Literacy.* Norwood, MA: Christopher-Gordon.

Saul, Wendy, Jeanne Rearden, Anne Schmidt, Charles Pearce, Dana Blackwood, and Mary Dickinson Bird. 1993. *Science Workshop: A Whole Language Approach.* Portsmouth, NH: Heinemann.

Zemelman, Steven, and Harvey Daniels. 1988. *A Community of Writers: Teaching Writing in the Junior and Senior High School.* Portsmouth, NH: Heinemann.

Authentic Experiences

Virtually all the standards documents that have been published over the past decade entreat teachers to "make it real," to involve students in tangible, genuine, authentic, real-world materials and experiences. This challenge is problematic in several ways. To begin with, school itself isn't "real," in the sense that schools are purposely separated from the rest of life and people and work and community. If we want to make education "real," we have to somehow overcome that segregation, either by sending bits of the world into schools or bringing the kids out into the world. Well, that's okay; the school-house door does swing both ways. But the "how" part is tricky. After all, realness or authenticity isn't exactly a teaching *method,* but rather a condition. So, as we address this issue, we acknowledge that the structure we are calling "authentic experiences" is asymmetrical with the other five learning methods on our list. But it is worth the difficulty to sort this out. In every story of powerful, transformative learning we've heard (or shared in this book), there's almost always the crucial detail that students were working on something that felt real.

A story in the National Science Education Standards provides one vision of "real." In Ms. F's classroom, a lesson on collecting data and conducting research began when she noticed the kids' fascination with the earthworms living in an empty lot next to the playground. She suggested that the students figure out what kind of habitat the worms required. The kids eagerly spent a few days examining the living conditions of the earthworms in the empty lot before creating a similar environment in a terrarium, away from the sun and filled with soil, leaves, and grass. Ms. F. ordered some worms from a biological supply house, and the students put them in their new home. For two weeks, students observed the earthworms and recorded their behavior, and began listing questions they wanted to answer. How do they have babies? Do they really like the dark? How big can they get? How long do they live? Children formed into small groups to decide together which question they would be most interested in exploring. The groups were given time to decide how they would conduct their investigations and by the following week, the research was under way.

The group that chose to investigate the lifecycle of earthworms had found egg cases in the soil, and while they waited for the eggs to hatch, they read some books about earthworms to add to their knowledge base. Another group wondered what earthworms like to eat and offered test foods. Two other groups wondered what kind of environment earthworms preferred, and they experimented by varying moisture, light, and temperature.

This authentic scientific inquiry started with the interest and natural curiosity of the students and taught them much more than just stuff about earthworms. They became researchers: gathering data, manipulating variables, asking questions, discovering answers, and asking more questions. The students worked collaboratively, just as grown-up scientists join in a collaborative enterprise that depends on the sharing of ideas and discoveries.

This exemplary activity actually included several kinds of "realness." Ms. F. began with a real expressed interest of the children; she involved them in real research, doing what real scientists do, in a complete but simplified form; she gave them real responsibility and choice, helping them divide into teams and jigsaw the inquiry; and obviously, she had them working with very real worms. Notice that part of the realness came from getting outside the school walls, while other aspects of realness came from importing things into the classroom—like worms! The following chart outlines some of these key kinds of authenticity. Keeping in mind that school can be made more lifelike, we first mention steps toward authenticity that can be inside school, followed by ways of taking students out into the community.

Making Learning Authentic

INSIDE SCHOOL

- Let kids in on curriculum planning, choosing topics and readings, making schedules, keeping records.
- Develop broad, interdisciplinary, thematic units based on student concerns.
- Use tangible, tactile materials, artifacts, and live demonstrations where possible.
- Favor learn-by-doing over learn-by-sitting-there-quietly-and-listening.
- Follow news and current events, connecting them with curriculum.
- Include activities that connect with students' multiple intelligences and cognitive styles.
- Let students subdivide content, form groups, and conduct team projects.
- Assign real, whole books, rather than synthetic texts created by basal publishers.
- Use primary source documents, not just textbooks, to teach history, science, etc.
- Invite in speakers, experts, and interview subjects from the community.
- Bring in parents to give presentations, conference with kids, create materials.
- Mix children through multiage grouping, cross-age projects, buddy programs, and mainstreamed special education.

- Schedule time in flexible blocks that match the curriculum.
- Stress student goal setting and self-assessment.
- Have frequent one-to-one conferences across the curriculum.
- Offer frequent performances, fairs, and exhibitions, inviting parent and community audiences.

BEYOND SCHOOL

- Give homework assignments that require interaction with family and community.
- Share student work through parent and community newsletters, displays, and events.
- Display student artwork or research projects in off-campus settings.
- Plan regular field trips and attend arts performances that support the curriculum.
- Visit, study, and investigate local government, services, and businesses.
- Get involved in community issues: recycling, safety, programs for kids.
- Launch family and community history projects.
- Join in a community beautification or art project.
- Take children on outdoor education, wilderness, ecology, and adventure programs.
- In conjunction with integrative units, have fact-finding tours; students take notes, make observations, or conduct interviews.
- Conduct survey or opinion research, by mail or in person.
- Develop volunteer relationships with local agencies, nursing homes, and hospitals.
- For older students, create regular student service or work internships.
- Support student service clubs and groups that reach out to the community.
- Invite students to suggest, plan, and evaluate outreach projects.

At the secondary level, school often seems especially unreal, cycling stifled adolescents through endless forty-five–minute chunks of disconnected irrelevance. At the new Best Practice High School (BPHS) in Chicago, the teachers are committed to making classroom time as authentic and engaging as possible, within the boundaries of state and city mandates. But we also knew from the start that we wanted the kids out in the community, doing something of value, at least once a week. Finding 140 meaningful, reachable, and supervised internships the first year—and 260 this year—was a feat that required the full-time, year-round efforts of a talented certified teacher. But it worked. We found spots that matched each of our kid's interests—in museums, hospitals, banks, social service agencies, arts programs, business offices, zoos, and elementary schools. They spend every Wednesday morning at these sites doing real work under the mentorship of one or more staff people from the host institution, keep weekly logs, and debrief their experiences when they return to their advisory period at BPHS.

These placements are helping our young people face genuine issues about what it means to work, to see what kind of problems adults encounter on the job and how they address them, and to begin thinking about their own career options. One group of students has been apprenticed to a delightful group of guerrilla television producers called Community TV Network. Each week, the students spend Wednesday morning with Sree Nallamothu from CTVN. For most of last year, she taught them the mechanics and the art of video production, using real school events as subject matter for their training. This was handy for our brand-new school, because we urgently needed someone to document our first steps and missteps. Once kids had mastered the basics and went on a few shoots around the building, they went to the CTVN studio to learn how to edit videotape, add music and sound effects, create titles, and the rest. As this book goes to press, the team has just been commissioned to make a video documentary about Mabel Manning, a local hero who served the homeless of our school's community and tended a famous neighborhood garden for many years. Because of CTVN's reputation around town, there's a good chance the kids' program will find a real audience, and may air on local broadcast TV. This is what we mean by making school real.

Suggested Further Readings

Chancer, Joni, and Gina Rester-Zodrow. 1997. *Moon Journals: Writing, Art, and Inquiry Through Focused Nature Study.* Portsmouth, NH: Heinemann.

Horwood, Bert, ed. 1995. *Experience and the Curriculum.* Dubuque, IA: Kendall-Hunt.

Kraft, Richard J., and James Kiesmeier, eds. 1994. *Experiential Learning in Schools and Higher Education.* Boulder, CO: Association for Experiential Education.

London, Peter. 1994. *Step Outside: Community-Based Art Education.* Portsmouth, NH: Heinemann.

McVey, V. 1989. *The Sierra Club Wayfinding Book.* Boston: Little, Brown.

Nabhan, Gary, and Steven Trimble. 1995. *The Geography of Childhood: Why Children Need Wild Places.* Boston: Beacon Press.

Saul, Wendy, and Jeanne Reardon, eds. 1996. *Beyond the Science Kit: Inquiry in Action.* Portsmouth, NH: Heinemann.

Shor, Ira. 1987. *Freire for the Classroom: A Sourcebook for Laboratory Teaching.* Portsmouth, NH: Boynton/Cook.

Stephens, Lillian. 1995. *The Complete Guide to Learning Through Community Service: Grades K–9.* Des Moines, IA: Allyn and Bacon.

Wigginton, Eliot. 1985. *Sometimes a Shining Moment: The Foxfire Experience.* Garden City, NY: Anchor Press/Doubleday.

Reflective Assessment

In Best Practice classrooms, teachers don't just make up tests and put grades on report cards. They are less interested in measuring students' recall of individual facts or use of certain subskills than in how they perform the authentic, complete, higher-order activities that school aims for: reading whole books, drafting and editing stories or articles, conducting and reporting a scientific inquiry, applying math to real problem solving. Because progressive teachers want deeper and more practical information about children's learning, they monitor students' growth in richer and more sophisticated ways. More and more, teachers are adopting and adapting the tools of ethnographic, qualitative research: observation, interviews, questionnaires, collecting and interpreting artifacts and performances. They use information from these sources not mainly to "justify" marks on a report card, but to guide instruction, to make crucial daily decisions about helping students grow. And above all, they see the main goal of assessment to be helping students set goals, monitor their own work, and evaluate their efforts. Nothing more conclusively marks the well-educated person than the capacity to run one's own brain, have clear self-insight, and follow through on projects.

Many teachers now keep anecdotal, observational records, saving a few minutes each day to jot notes about students in their classes—some call this "kid-watching." Instead of numbers, letters, or symbols, teachers create written descriptions of what students are doing and saying. Some teachers put these observations on a schedule, tracking five particular kids on Monday, another five on Tuesday, and so forth. Some watch just one kid per day; some simply jot notes on any kids who show noteworthy growth, thinking, problems, or concerns on a given day; others prefer to record observations of the class as a community. The common feature of these observational records is that teachers save time for regularly recording them, they develop a format that works for them, and they consistently use these notes both to guide their instruction and to communicate with parents and others about children's progress.

Teachers also use students themselves as self-observers in increasingly powerful ways. In face-to-face interviews, written questionnaires, or learning logs, teachers ask kids to record and reflect on their own work (e.g., books read, experiments conducted). In Best Practice classrooms, it is common for students to have periodic "evaluation conferences" with their teachers, where both parties use their notes to review the child's achievements and problems over a span of time, and then set goals for the upcoming weeks or months. In a curriculum that values higher-order thinking as well as individual responsibility, such self-evaluation teaches multiple important lessons.

One of the most promising mechanisms for authentic evaluation is the student portfolio, a folder in which students save selected samples of their best work in a given subject. The practice of keeping such cumulative records has many benefits. First, of course, it provides actual evidence of what the child can do with writing, math, art, or science, instead of a mark in a grade book—which represents, after all, nothing more than a teacher-mediated symbolic record of a long-discarded piece of real work. These portfolio artifacts also invite all sorts of valuable conversations between the child and the teacher, children and peers, or kids and parents: How did you get interested in this? How did you feel while you were working on this? How did you solve the problems you encountered? What would you tell another student about this subject? What are you going to do next? The process of selecting and polishing items for inclusion in the portfolio invites students to become increasingly reflective about their own work and more skillful at self-evaluation.

When teachers try to add these new, more productive forms of evaluation to their classrooms, they will run into a time crunch unless they either subtract some old assessment activities or overlap the new assessments with something else. A good starting point is to review all the forms of evaluation underway in the classroom, terminating those that don't usefully steer instruction, advance kids' learning, teach students to self-evaluate, or produce artifacts worth saving. For many teachers, this may mean grading far fewer busy-work dittos, workbook pages, study questions, and worksheets. Instead of tabulating the errors in stacks of identical fill-in-the blank worksheets, teachers instead can spend their precious evaluation time responding to each kid's whole original reports or stories, perhaps writing a personal note of response that gives guidance, as well as modeling solid adult writing.

The other key to implementing better assessments is to overlap assessment with instruction, instead of always relying on evaluations that occur separately, after the work is done (and when it is too late for students to improve their product or learn from the assessment!). Many progressive forms of assessment are integral to learning itself. Reading and writing conferences are a case in point; when sitting down to talk with a child about her writing, the teacher can simultaneously and seamlessly gather information about the child's development as a writer. As the teacher jots down a few notes following each conference, a powerful record of growth is created. Similarly, when students and teachers together design scoring rubrics for class presentations, science experiments, or persuasive essays, they are explicitly being taught the ingredients of a successful performance, right along with creating a mechanism to evaluate their efforts.

All these adjustments mean that teachers are making a time trade: they're not spending any less time on evaluation, but they're also not spending more. They're differentiating their assessment efforts, looking at children's growth in a wider variety of ways. They are committed to the principle that the most valuable assessment activities are **formative**, aimed at understanding a child's development and making instructional decisions about that child. **Summative** evaluation, the process of converting kids' achievements into some kind of ranked, ordinal system that compares children to each other, needs to happen far less often, if at all.

Suggested Further Readings

Azwell, Tara, and Elizabeth Schmar, eds. 1995. *Report Card on Report Cards: Alternatives to Consider.* Portsmouth, NH: Heinemann.

Cambourne, Brian, and Jan Turbill, eds. 1994. *Responsive Evaluation: Making Valid Judgments About Student Literacy.* Portsmouth, NH: Heinemann.

Graves, Donald H., and Bonnie B. Sunstein, eds. 1992. *Portfolio Portraits.* Portsmouth, NH: Heinemann.

Herman, Joan, Pamela Aschbacher, and Lynn Winters. 1992. *A Practical Guide to Alternative Assessment.* Alexandria, VA: Association for Supervision and Curriculum Development.

Hill, Bonnie Campbell, and Cynthia Ruptic. 1994. *Practical Aspects of Authentic Assessment: Putting the Pieces Together.* Norwood, MA: Christopher-Gordon.

Johnston, Peter H. 1997. *Knowing Literacy: Constructive Literacy Assessment.* York, ME: Stenhouse.

Porter, Carol, and Janell Cleland. 1995. *The Portfolio as a Learning Strategy.* Portsmouth, NH: Boynton/Cook.

Purves, Alan, Sarah Jordan, and James Peltz. 1997. *Using Portfolios in the English Classroom.* Norwood, MA: Christopher-Gordon.

Rhodes, Lynn K., ed. 1993. *Literacy Assessment: A Handbook of Instruments.* Portsmouth, NH: Heinemann.

Rhodes, Lynn K., and Nancy Shanklin. 1993. *Windows into Literacy: Assessing Learners K–8.* Portsmouth, NH: Heinemann.

Wiggins, Grant. 1998. *Educative Assessment: Designing Assessments to Inform and Improve Student Performance.* San Francisco: Jossey-Bass.

Woodward, Helen. 1994. *Negotiated Evaluation: Involving Children and Parents in the Process.* Portsmouth, NH: Heinemann.

Can Teachers Still Teach?

All of these activities have one thing in common: they take the teacher off stage. They do not cast the teacher in the familiar role of information-dispenser, font-of-wisdom, expert/presenter/lecturer. In each of these key classroom structures, the teacher is somewhere farther in the background, acting as a moderator, facilitator, coach, scribe, designer, observer, model— everything **but** the standard, normal, stereotypical, conception of the teacher as . . . well, as a **teacher**. What gives? Does this mean that in the idealized, progressive Best Practice classroom the teacher never "teaches" in the old-fashioned sense of the word?

Not at all. But once again, balance is the key. It is fine for teachers to conduct whole-class presentations, to give information, to share and tell and even lecture—**some of the time**. But time-sharing is the key. In the traditional curriculum, we have catastrophically neglected the student-centered side of the "airtime" equation. Indeed, one of the key findings from classroom research across subjects is that students don't get enough time to try out, practice, and apply what teachers are talking about. Kids never get to do any science or any writing or any math, because the teacher is so busy **talking** that there is never any time to practice the target activity.

Because it is so deeply ingrained in our culture that teaching means talking at other people who are silent and inactive, we all must police ourselves very closely to make sure we don't regress to that old transmission model. That's one reason why this chapter may seem so unbalanced, giving almost all of its attention to the structures for student-centered classroom time. But teachers already know how to conduct whole-class presentations, probably all too well. It was highlighted in their professional training, it was the core of their personal experience as students, and it probably predominates in their on-the-job experience. Most American teachers simply don't need as much help conducting whole-class presentations as they do with, for example, facilitating a collaborative workshop. So teachers need to fill this gap, to correct this imbalance in their professional repertoire by equipping themselves with all the classroom structures they need to comfortably and safely get off stage, to provide and manage plenty of kid-centered time for practice and exploration.

With this extended disclaimer in place, we can return to the subject of whole-class, teacher-directed activities and see what's valuable about them. There are at least three reasons why teacher-centered, whole-class instruction can and should remain part of the school day. First and most important, teachers have great things to teach—they have knowledge, wisdom, experience, ideas, content that can be shared through whole-class presentations they design. All of us who teach have developed great units, favorite sequences of activities that engage students, year after year. We have worked to design and refine and enrich these units; they are our treasures, and we're not about to give them up. We also realize that as we present these favorite lessons, we are modeling for students our own passion for the material. Even if they don't understand or remember everything, we hope they'll catch our excitement about ideas.

On a more pragmatic level, some teacher-directed lessons are still necessary because most teachers work within a mandated curriculum. They are responsible for students learning (or at least briefly remembering) many required elements of an official syllabus of content. We argued earlier that some ingredients of the typical school curriculum can be learned incidentally, amid innovative, student-centered techniques. For example, kids who have regular writing workshops will acquire many English spelling and editing skills even though they are not taught them directly in teacher presentations or workbook drills. However, the average school curriculum still contains much other material that isn't learned collaterally through applied experience in the subject. In language arts, for example, all the writing workshops in the world will not teach students the names of the parts of speech. If kids and teachers are to be held accountable for learning about gerunds, subordinate clauses, and the like, the teacher will probably have to take the initiative to conduct such lessons.

Finally, as learners and as people, teachers deserve to feel safe and comfortable in school too. They need the security of doing something familiar for some of the day: we cannot expect teachers who have been trained and socialized to think of teaching as presenting to suddenly cast aside that whole model for the entire six-hour day. The fact is that teachers **will** continue to present whole-class lessons; the point is for them to get better at it and at the same time start doing it less.

Ways to Improve Teacher-directed Lessons

Because good teachers have been creating dramatic and effective individual performances for years, we'll just mention a few valuable examples here. One presentational activity that is especially powerful, but mistakenly neglected above the primary grades, is **reading aloud**. Great writers in every field and subject have hypnotized readers for as long as there has been print. Many of their writings were the very sources that inspired some teachers to enter the profession in the first place. So reading great writing aloud can be one of the most captivating and motivating presentational techniques a teacher can use. Quality children's literature new and old, primary source documents, insightful historical essays, passionate political arguments, biographical and auto-biographical accounts of key discoveries in math and science—all are capable of mesmerizing children, adolescents, and adults and drawing them into real engagement with the subject matter. National recommendations on teaching reading advise plenty of reading aloud by the teacher at all levels.

Another strategic way to think about direct teaching is the **mini-lesson**—a very brief explanation or demonstration aimed to help students with a skill or concept about which the teacher has observed many students having difficulties, at a time when they are actually in need of it. For example, children who are writing plays may need to understand quotation marks and paragraphing to separate characters' speeches from each other and from stage directions.

Mini-lessons can be given to a whole class before, during, or after more active, experiential activities—or offered to small, selected groups of students as others continue other work. Indeed, one of the fundamental insights of mini-lessons is that teachers' old-style presentations—we might call them maxi-lessons—often were simply too long and too overloaded to be effective. We now find that teachers can convey key content more effectively when they are very selective and present in quicker, smaller bites. Mini-lessons are an integral feature of the workshop classroom; teachers can draw out small groups of students who are struggling with a particular skill or topic, sit them at a table in the back of the room, and give a compact, focused five- or six-minute lesson—and send them directly back to work, where they will be immediately applying the concepts taught. This mini-lesson strategy obviously requires that the teacher be a sharp observer—but handily, the workshop structure itself provides the teacher with the time and the responsibility to monitor students' work closely through conferences and constant observation.

Demonstrations are a closely allied technique, and they are useful in plenty of situations beyond the science lab. A good writing teacher may revise a piece of her own work before the eyes of the whole class, using an overhead projector. Kids can ask questions about her choices as she works. Most students have never watched a competent adult at work on a piece of writing, and all too often their only visual image of the process is from some melodramatic movie in which a struggling poet rips pages out of a type-writer, crumples them, and shoots them despondently toward the wastebas-ket. Teachers can profitably demonstrate how they go about brainstorming a new writing topic, or choosing an appropriate book to read, how they figure out the meaning of a new word from context clues, or mentally sort through likely possibilities while working on a geometry proof.

In the most interactive classrooms, many teacher presentations become hybrids. Teachers invite questions and suggestions as the session proceeds. Students know their ideas are valued and they don't hesitate to take part. Teachers decide to offer an explanation to just the half or third of the class who need it, while others who don't can continue with more appropriate activities.

Conclusion

When we talk about the balancing between teacher-directed and student-centered activities, it always boils down to how **time** is spent. Teachers must design days, weeks, years that provide kids a rich alternation between different configurations, groupings, and activities. The schedule must be predictable so students can prepare, mentally and even unconsciously, for what is coming up. This predictability is especially important for poor children who may lack continuity in their life. The balance in a day's or week's activities must also include things that make teachers reasonably comfortable, and yet teachers need to be growing and challenging themselves too. In the end, school is more satisfying when everyone is growing and learning daily.

To work toward the goal of "Best Practice," to embody the changes recommended in the curriculum reports we have cited, most teachers need to enrich their classroom repertoire in two directions: (1) to set aside time and build classroom structures that support more **student-directed activity**, using the six key structures outlined in the past few pages; and (2) to make their **teacher-directed** activities both less predominant and more effective. We've seen that when teachers learn practical strategies to manage both of these modes of instruction, the curricular improvements they desire begin to take hold. As a final way of making clear this special kind of balance, we provide the accompanying chart of indicators of Best Practice. As teachers begin implementing the key structures outlined in this chapter, these are some of the things that start to change and grow and develop in their classrooms.

INDICATORS OF BEST PRACTICE

Note on the Arrows: In this chart, growth does not necessarily mean moving from one practice to another, discarding a previous instructional approach and replacing it forever. Instead, teachers add new alternatives to a widening repertoire of choices, allowing them to alternate among a richer array of activities, creating a richer and more complex balance (e.g., lecturing isn't discarded, but is done less as other, new choices become available).

Physical Facilities

Setup for teacher-centered instruction (separate desks) → Student-centered arrangement (e.g., tables)

Rows of desks → Clusters → Centers (varied learning stations for writing, computers, math, etc.)

Bare, unadorned space → Commercial decorations → Student-made artwork/products/displays

Few materials → Textbooks and handouts → "Stuff"—books, materials, manipulatives, pets, etc.

Classroom Climate/Management

Management by punishments and rewards → Order maintained by engagement and community

Teacher creates and enforces rules → Students help set and enforce norms

Students are silent/motionless/passive/controlled → Purposeful talk, movement, and autonomy

Students in fixed groups based on "ability" → Flexible grouping based on tasks and choice

Rigid, unvarying schedule → Predictable but flexible time usage based on activities

Student Voice and Involvement

Balanced with teacher-chosen and teacher-directed activities:

→ Students often select inquiry topics, books, writing topics, audiences, etc.

→ Students maintain their own records, set own goals, self-assess

→ Some themes/inquiries are built from students' own questions; "negotiated curriculum"

→ Students assume responsibility, take roles in decision making, help run classroom life

Activities and Assignments

Teacher presentation and transmission of material → Students actively experiencing concepts

Whole-class teaching → Centers and cooperative small groups → Wide variety of activities

Teacher in front, directing whole class → Teacher hard to find, working with groups

Uniform curriculum for all → Jigsawed curriculum; different topics by kids' needs or choices

Short-term lessons; one day at a time → Extended activities, multi-day, multi-step projects

Focus on memorization and recall → Focus on applying knowledge and problem solving

Short responses; fill-in-the-blank exercises → Complex responses, evaluations, writings, artworks

One-way assignments/lessons → Accommodation for multiple intelligences and cognitive styles

Language and Communication
Forced constant silence → Noise and conversation alternates with quiet time
Short responses → Elaborated discussion → Students' own questions and evaluations
Teacher talk → Student-teacher talk → Student-student talk
Writing: All channels are open (student-teacher, student-student, student-parent)
Talk and writing focuses on: Facts → Skills → Concepts → Synthesis, Evaluation

Time Allocations
Time allocations are BALANCED between:
    Teacher-directed and student-directed work
    Subject-specific lessons and integrated, thematic, cross-disciplinary inquiries
    Individual work/small-group or team work/whole-class work
    Intensive, deep study of selected topics/extensive study of wide range of subjects
Fundamental recurrent activities happen on daily/regular basis
    Independent reading (SSR, reading workshop, or literature circles)
    Independent writing (journals or writing workshop)
    Reading aloud to students
    Teacher-student and student-student conferences
Students can explain the time allocations and recurrent activities/procedures in their classrooms

Student Work and Assessment
Products created for teachers and grading → Products created for real events and audiences
Classroom/hallway displays: no student work posted → "A" papers only → All students represented
Identical, imitative products displayed → Varied and original products displayed
Teacher feedback is scores and grades → Teacher feedback is substantive, varied, and formative
Products are seen and rated only by teachers → Public exhibitions and performances are common
Teacher gradebook → Student-maintained portfolios, with self-assessments and conferences
All assessment by teachers → Student self-assessment an official element → Parents are involved
Standards set during grading → Standards available in advance → Standards codeveloped with students

Teacher Attitude and Initiative
Toward Students:
Distant, negative, fearful, punitive → Positive, respectful, encouraging, warm
Blaming students → Reasoning with students
Directive → Consultative

Toward Self:
Helpless victim → Risk taker/Experimenter → Creative, active agent
Solitary adult → Member of team with other adults in school → Member of networks beyond school
Staff development recipient → Chooses and directs own professional growth
Conception of Job Roles:
Expert, presenter → Coach, mentor, model, guide

Sources: Daniels, Harvey and Marilyn Bizar. 1998. *Methods That Matter: Six Structures for Best Practice Classrooms.* York, ME: Stenhouse.

Kohn, Alfie. 1996. "What to Look for in a Classroom." *Educational Leadership* (September).

Works Cited

Atwell, Nancie. 1998. *In the Middle: New Understandings About Writing, Reading, and Learning*. Portsmouth, NH: Heinemann.

Beane, James. 1997. *Curriculum Integration: Designing the Core of Democratic Education*. New York: Teachers College Press.

Bruner, Jerome. 1983. *Child's Talk*. New York: Norton.

Calkins, Lucy, 1995. *The Art of Teaching Writing* (Second Edition). Portsmouth, NH: Heinemann.

Daniels, Harvey. 1994. *Literature Circles: Voice and Choice in the Student-Centered Classroom*. York, ME: Stenhouse.

Daniels, Harvey, and Marilyn Bizar. 1998. *Methods That Matter: Six Structures for Best Practice Classrooms*. York, ME: Stenhouse.

Elbow, Peter. 1973. *Writing Without Teachers*. New York: Oxford University Press.

Fulwiler, Toby. 1987. *The Journal Book*. Portsmouth, NH: Heinemann.

Glasser, William. 1990. *The Quality School: Managing Students Without Coercion*. New York: Harper.

Graves, Donald. 1983. *Writing: Teachers and Children at Work*. Portsmouth, NH: Heinemann.

Johnson, David W., Roger T. Johnson, Edythe Holubec, and Patricia Roy. 1984. *Circles of Learning: Cooperation in the Classroom*. Alexandria, VA: Association for Supervision and Curriculum Development.

Joyce, Bruce, and Marsha Weil. 1986. *Models of Teaching*. Englewood Cliffs, NJ: Prentice-Hall.

National Academy Press. 1996. *National Science Education Standards*. Washington, DC: National Academy Press.

Rief, Linda. 1992. *Seeking Diversity: Language Arts with Adolescents*. Portsmouth, NH: Heinemann.

Romano, Tom. 1987. *Clearing the Way: Working with Teenage Writers*. Portsmouth, NH: Heinemann.

Sharan, Yael, and Shlomo Sharan. 1992. *Expanding Cooperative Learning Through Group Investigation*. New York: Teachers College Press.

Slavin, Robert, Sharan Shlomo, Karen Spencer, Clark Webb, and Robert Schmuck. 1985. *Learning to Cooperate, Cooperating to Learn*. New York: Plenum Press.

Instructional Resources on the Internet

The Association for Supervision and Curriculum Development publishes *Educational Leadership* magazine and a wide range of classroom-oriented books and materials. Visit **http://www.ascd.org.**

A prime source of curriculum integration ideas and materials is the National Middle School Association at **http://www.nmsa.org.**

For the daily doings of educators, school reformers, and related government agencies, *Education Week* online is the key source: **http://www.edweek.org.**

9

Making the Transition

Jan calls Steve one night to talk. She's been teaching many years, but suddenly it's all new. "You won't believe what's happening in my classroom! Since the books I ordered didn't arrive on time, I started with something else. We interviewed each other, just like you had always been telling me we could. It was unbelievable. We told stories about ourselves and our families, and everyone loved it. When the book did arrive, I couldn't even *pretend* I knew any more than the students did, since it was just published and I hadn't had a chance to read it myself. So we're reading and talking over each chapter together, instead of my telling them what they're supposed to get from it. They're thinking about it a lot more that way. We're trying out those notebooks Lucy Calkins said would work so well. The other day, one of the students started crying, and the rest of us just had to comfort her. Everything seems to really matter in that room."

Jan had been reading and working on a more student-centered curriculum for a long time. She'd been comparing ideas with Steve, and he'd appreciated her basic caring for her students and her openness to good teaching ideas. He had visited her class, modeled a few strategies, and suggested others. But he'd also wondered why the process she talked about wasn't as fully enacted as it might be in her teaching. Now suddenly she was ready to take some risks when the opportunity presented itself, and to help her students do so too. For Steve, it had been difficult to be patient, to accept the best Jan could do and not press too quickly for her to do more. He could tell in discussions when he'd gone too far, when the possibilities didn't connect with her own thoughts or put her on the defensive. Now, the waiting paid off, and Jan had made discoveries on her own. She also knew Steve had been waiting. "You've probably been doing this stuff all along, haven't you," she remarked sheepishly.

Why Change Is Difficult

Teachers, students, parents, and principals must go through many learning steps to make new approaches work. They need time and positive support as they grow. They need organizational structures and relationships that provide this support. And they have many questions that must be respected: *"What about the math facts?" "Do the kids still need phonics lessons?" "Can children really help each other and collaborate in small groups?" "How do we evaluate children's progress with this kind of teaching?"* If change is forced on them, not only will they rebel, but the act of force will contradict the very spirit of the change. The educational strategies described in this book are all based on helping children make their own choices, ask their own questions, and become invested in their own learning. *Forcing* teachers to adopt a new pedagogy with this approach, but without teachers' ownership, is indeed a disturbing contradiction. People always recognize this kind of discord at some deep level, even when they're not conscious of it, and resent its hypocrisy.

Many other complexities make educational change a tricky business. Much has been written about how the "culture" in a school building—as in most complex organizations—can support or discourage the kind of change Jan experienced. Sociological studies of teachers, such as Dan Lortie's *Schoolteacher* (1972), reveal how they spend most of their careers in cellular classrooms, isolated from one another and from administrators. The trial-by-fire initiation into teaching, the lack of time for interchange among staff, the sense of being "evaluated" rather than helped to develop—all lead teachers toward a protective isolation and defensiveness. Principals have the authority to mandate classroom actions, but their power to reward and punish can undermine the chance to nurture and coach. A principal's suggestions can easily appear to be critical, or teachers can feel threatened when a colleague tries something new: "Does this mean they think *my* way is old-fashioned? Will they become obnoxious with missionary zeal and try to force it on me?" This is not meant as an indictment. Each person becomes caught up in this system and is hard put to change without great effort and practice at new kinds of communication.

Mass testing is an increasingly problematic school structure that paradoxically reinforces the status quo. Much recent school reform has mandated tests with the intent of enforcing standards for student performance and pressuring teachers to do a better job. However, as any good teacher will testify, tests force teachers to drill students for the tests, which is not the same as really *doing* science or history or writing. When teachers are held accountable purely for students' scores, then the most engaging questions kids bring up spontaneously—"teachable moments"—become annoyances. Worse, many standardized tests focus on what is most easily testable, rather than the most important knowledge and abilities in a field; therefore, they undermine the most valuable teaching and learning. Unfortunately, it is usually much cheaper and easier to test rote detail rather than complex understandings or performances. As the *National Science Education Standards* document points out:

> Many current science achievement tests measure "inert" knowledge—discrete, isolated bits of knowledge—rather than "active" knowledge—knowledge that is rich and well-structured. Assessment processes that include all outcomes for student achievement must probe the extent and organization of a student's knowledge.

Ironically, in the effort to hold schools accountable for better performance, pressures to increase scores on standardized tests narrow and limit what schools can accomplish. Occasionally, the news media have critiqued standardized tests that simply don't *and cannot* test the learning we know is most important. Nevertheless, even educators who have read the articles and heard the research are reluctant to abandon the tests because of political pressures: "Isn't this accountability what the community demands? Will they understand if we try to explain that it's more complicated?"

Or consider textbooks. They get their share of casual bashing, but sit on a district committee deciding whether to purchase a new volume or to abandon textbooks in favor of primary sources or real science inquiry. Some committee members will recognize that most publishers superficially embrace new approaches only as camouflage for the same old ineffective strategies. However, the realists on the panel may ask, "What about the traditional teachers unprepared to go without a book?" Perhaps they know the district won't spend enough money on staff development to support the textless teachers. Perhaps they fear a backlash from more traditional teachers or administrators who are just waiting to capitalize on any disorganization that comes with change. Maybe the committee is even sensitive about forcing change on teachers involuntarily. But they also know that when they do choose a book, it will become one more limit that only the more adventuresome teachers will be willing to overcome. What should they do?

Achieving real change in the interlocking structure of a school district is a complex process, not readily accomplished by a few pronouncements or fancy new curriculum plans. Educational change at the turn of the millenium is a deep river filled with crosscurrents. Conservatives urge programs that march through lockstep curricula and dissociated skills exercises. Principals and politicians worry about standardized test scores, whether or not the test preparation teaches kids what they really need for success later. Some reforms seem aimed at teacher-proofing the classroom rather than building a corps of expert and caring nurturers of learning. At the same time, more comprehensive, progressive programs, such as the Comer Model (Comer 1980, Ramirez-Smith 1995) and the Coalition of Essential Schools (O'Neil 1995), have matured, have begun to examine their successes and failures, and have highlighted the value of teacher and student and parent voices. And in schools in all sorts of settings, some teachers doggedly resist *every* change that comes at them, whatever its stripe, while others energetically seek to learn and grow.

The Key: Teacher Empowerment

No matter how extensively legislatures and national panels attempt to control teaching, teachers must still learn and grow one at a time, and it's in their individual interactions with children that the children, too, learn and grow, one at a time. How can we truly facilitate teacher development, then, rather than draft inflexible curriculum plans and threaten schools with test results?

One first step is to learn from past mistakes. In many failed efforts such as "new math," teachers were the last to hear of the experiment, and the only change they were asked to make was in "content." An official goal of "new math" was for kids to become excited about mathematics and to develop understanding that would entice further learning, rather than create blockages and dislike of the subject. However, as critics pointed out, in many locations teachers were introduced to the program only at a final training and "delivery" stage. This left them uncommitted, feeling inadequate about the concepts, and they proceeded to deliver the material in a self-defeating way to children—so that ultimately nothing changed. To bring true reform to learning, we must involve teachers from the beginning, not just hand them new curriculum as an afterthought.

Teachers need to re-create their own understandings of how learning can work for children, and then they need to be involved in decision making. There are a host of reasons why this ownership is vital, and plenty of literature—including books about change in the corporate business world—to explain them. Why is it so crucial for teachers to "buy in" in order for change to take root?

1. The teacher working daily with students knows best what the specific needs, conditions, and obstacles are.

2. No matter what changes are prescribed from the outside, their success in the classroom depends on teachers' own choices and interpretations as they move through the school day. So if choice isn't involved sooner, it will inevitably come later, with less likelihood of positive commitment.

3. The most important changes needed in education are not superficial, but involve the teacher's deeply held beliefs, expectations, and relationships.

4. Many key changes involve giving responsibility and ownership to children, which will be undermined if ownership is not there for teachers.

Over the past decade, the centrality of teachers' role in decision making has been recognized by those researching and experimenting with school change. Ann Lieberman and Lynn Miller (1991) have written strong statements about collaborative leadership that redefines the relationship between teachers and principals. Henry Levin's (1988) "Accelerated Schools" concept features school-based governance with input from all parties—teachers, students, parents, administrators—and uses the strengths of the particular teachers who work in a building. In the Comer Model, the school planning team must include representatives from each group in the school, including various teacher teams, administration, staff, and parents (Ramirez-Smith 1995). John Goodlad (1994) describes the need for faculty dialogue and organizational "health" if schools are to escape from passive, uninspired classroom experience.

Given the many school reform efforts under way in recent years, we needn't prescribe one right structure or one best starting point. But perhaps, based on our own work with many schools large and small, urban, suburban and rural, we can identify some key ingredients for promoting change. Because the teacher is in a pivotal but too often neglected position, we focus on what can help a teacher improve instruction; then through this lens we can also see what is needed in the broader school setting.

How One Teacher Changed

Delois Strickland teaches second grade in an inner-city building, Woodson South School, with housing projects on one side and empty lots on the other, left from apartments burned or razed thirty years ago. She's no charismatic heroine of some pious movie about the valiant inner-city miracle worker who triumphs over all. She's also not the long-suffering, ineffectual martyr, the well-meaning but hopeless urban educator pictured by Tracy Kidder in *Among Schoolchildren* (1990). Delois is quiet, calm, loves children, and desires continually to improve her teaching. She's not burning herself out with overwork, but enjoys her profession. Like most good teachers, Delois can do at least three things at once. When a visitor joins her at lunchtime, she sits at her desk and chats uninterrupted while simultaneously preparing materials for an afternoon activity, receiving a steady flow of office messengers, and keeping a maternal eye on the kids who insist on hanging around.

Delois attended a thirty-hour workshop on teaching writing one fall and experienced many new possibilities. The teachers in the workshop interviewed one another and compiled a book of their portraits. They wrote about significant personal moments and shared autobiographical writing in small groups. They talked about journals where children could write what they chose without fear of being judged. They explored strategies for small-group work, practiced teacher-student conferences, debated about when grammar work obstructs children's writing and when it's more effective. They shared food, gossip, disagreements, frustrations, laughs, hopes. After eight weeks, they went off to apply what they had learned.

Delois tentatively started putting one or two new ideas to work. Her actions were courageous, considering the conservative tone in the building. Her first experiment was with children's journals. Delois understood that these special writings belonged to the children and were not to be graded. Her seven-year-old inner-city kids enjoyed the writing, were prolific and proud of their work, but there never seemed to be enough time in the day to fit journal writing in. A few enthusiastic weeks passed, and then she began to feel pressure to produce the formal essays the principal periodically collected from every class. Delois felt it was possible to teach writing for only two forty-five–minute periods per week at most, so after an initial burst of success, the journals languished on a shelf under the windows.

Delois' next step was to introduce an interviewing activity like the one teachers had enjoyed in the workshop. The children were to interview one another and write portraits to be accompanied by photographs and hung on the bulletin boards. At this point, Steve asked if he could visit as a participant observer. His main contribution at first was simply to encourage Delois and to help individual kids as they worked. Delois was very organized, helping the children brainstorm questions to ask one another and copying the list so everyone could reconnect after a two- or three-day interruption. The children followed the question list slavishly—but they were writing and having a grand time.

Delois wanted these papers to look good, particularly because other teachers in the building were watching her conduct what seemed to them a fairly radical experiment. Therefore, she decided to try individual conferences to help the children revise and polish their interviews. These second-grade interviewers had naturally tended to write down literal first-person answers the interviewees gave to their questions:

I like ice cream.
I have two sisters.
I will go to college . . . etc.

At first, Delois patiently explained to each child how to restate such sentences in the form, "Tyree likes ice cream." Steve realized that the kids had conflicting ideas about *whose* paper it was. Was the interviewer an author or a transcriber?—an understandable, in fact a very thoughtful, confusion for second graders. Meanwhile, kids waited impatiently in line to have their paper "checked" or fiddled in their seats if Delois shooed the line away. Finally, she asked Steve to intervene more actively to conduct a brief whole-class lesson on how to translate statements into indirect quotations. He also set up a conferencing sign-up list on the chalkboard and urged children to work on their journals while waiting for a conference.

Delois welcomed these refinements. Still, her conferences consisted essentially of proofreading, so the mood was dogged—kids would go back to their seats, try again and return once more to the teacher, hoping for deliverance. The papers were gradually cleaned up, but the tedious work spread out over several weeks and involved too little learning. Wouldn't it be better to have less revising and get on to some new writing topics and new skills? But Steve let this be. Perhaps, he thought, Delois had enough new ideas to digest for one year. Perhaps with the other teachers and the principal looking over her shoulder, this was as far as she could go right now.

Delois learned other valuable lessons that spring. Kids began very naturally to help one another. On a persuasive writing task, most children chose to write letters to their parents pleading for new bikes or other toys. Pieces grew longer. Struggling children made surprising advances. Writing seemed to be a positive, enjoyable activity. But how much, Steve wondered, did this depend on having a regular visitor in the room, an extra hand to provide lots of individual help? The children were hungry for attention and easily could have benefitted from twice as much. His presence was a luxury most classrooms couldn't afford.

The next fall, Delois requested help from Patty Horsch, a consultant with the literacy program at Chicago's Erikson Institute who was already working in the building. She had heard that Patty could help her reorganize and better use the materials in her classroom. By winter, the whole room looked different. On one side next to the windows was a large rug where small groups of children could be found quietly playing math games. Many new children's books occupied one set of shelves. The writing-center desks were cleared of old dust-gathering projects and restored to active use. Kids were industriously working on various tasks in small clusters everywhere. "My room used to be so disorganized that my children could never use what we had," Delois explained.

Patty convinced her to bring in her own children's books, which were much more interesting than the hand-me-downs crowding the shelves. Patty argued that if Delois were clear about rules and responsibilities, the children would treat the books with respect. A mobile hung next to the bookshelves stated on its dangling parts the rules about caring for books. Children took turns serving as classroom librarian. "They're reading much more and enjoying it more," Delois reported, "and they take good care of these books."

Horsch also modeled good teacher-student conferences. When Steve returned for a visit, Delois handed him an article about using conferences to help children take responsibility for writing instead of simply executing the teacher's corrections. "You ought to have teachers read this in your workshops," she urged. He smiled, knowing the very same ideas had been suggested in last year's sessions. If Delois wasn't ready to absorb those ideas then, she had made them her own now. She had even added the skillful variation of conducting conferences with groups of four or five children looking on, so they could learn more. The visitor asked, with a tinge of guilt, whether it would have been helpful to provide more forceful modeling the previous year. "No," she said. "I needed to feel my way. I was just starting then."

The children were writing far more—four to five days per week. "If you only write once a week you don't really get into it," Delois explained. "But if you enjoy it as a teacher, you'll do it more." Old restrictions and pressures no longer stopped her. Still another improvement: the teacher's aide in the room became much more involved. The previous year, the aide sat off to the side, doing busywork and occasionally scolding an overactive child. Horsch had arranged for the aide to get some training, and now she too was helping with conferences. Delois felt the aides should be included in all workshops for city teachers.

Delois was already thinking about her next innovations. She would use interviewing at the beginning of the year instead of waiting until winter. "That way, they'll get to know one another better right at the start," she explained—a good refinement, making the assignment more purposeful and natural. She'd start group conferences earlier too, because these build children's excitement about one another's writing. The logistics of journals needed to be handled better. Kids spent too much time stapling paper into the folders, so she planned to purchase spiral notebooks. Every little physical adjustment would mean better use of time. Reading, however, remained a frustration. The children read more, enjoyed it more, and even did better on practice tests. But they still had difficulty with the official subskills-oriented reading tests. "I guess I'm not a miracle worker," Delois sighed.

Five years further on, Delois Strickland is a busy and sophisticated teacher-leader in her school. For one thing, the school has charged ahead around her. A new, progressive principal has involved the building in a variety of school-reform efforts and networks, hired a new, energetic curriculum coordinator, and supported the continuing staff development work of the Erikson Institute. He encourages teachers to attend seminars and take risks to improve their techniques, finds resources to support their efforts, and participates in instructional planning sessions. Grade-level teams have common planning time plus a week of curriculum planning in the summer to continually evaluate their strategies and address areas that need further improvement. An after-school reading program adds an hour of extra instructional time three days a week. The teaching of reading combines good literature, student choice, and well-focused teaching of skills and strategies.

Delois Strickland has been able to greatly expand her expertise, refine and integrate her classroom strategies, and share ideas with other teachers within this structure. She's taken courses on "The Responsive Classroom," "Math Their Way," and technology usage in the classroom, and applies the approaches she has learned with great thoroughness.

On the day of his most recent visit, Steve watched Delois guide her second graders through "morning meeting," during which time the greatest behavioral problem came from the boys sitting next to the classroom library who kept pulling out books to read instead of "paying attention." We know teachers who would sell their souls for such a problem. These children, the least advanced of the three second-grade classes in the school, chose and read books eagerly during SSR, listened closely to a mini-lesson on prefixes and suffixes, participated actively as she conducted a prewriting brainstorm session for writing about the snowstorm that had occurred that morning, and then turned intently to their journals to write. As of December, this classroom of second graders who were very unsure of themselves at the start of the year was reading and writing daily, with skill and confidence and energy.

When children get into conflicts, Delois calmly but firmly reminds them about the values taught in their "character education" class—respect and dignity. Each child has a personally made, expandable spelling look-up notebook. The science center draws a steady stream of children to check up on the class snake and to try out the experiments with magnets that are laid out for them. Periodic thematic units throughout the year create great excitement for everyone. For example, one on "Children as Inventors," funded by a small grant from the Chicago Foundation for Education, helped the students connect more actively and thoughtfully to the history lessons Delois had been teaching on famous Black inventors.

Delois provides leadership not as an egoistic star but as a powerful example of excellent teaching and respect for children, working extensively with her grade-level team, giving of her time for extra school activities, and, as the principal testifies, speaking up when her strongest beliefs call for it. As a result of the larger team effort, Woodson South has taken its place as one of the 111 Chicago elementary schools posting substantial gains in reading scores during the past seven years of school reform in the city.

What Helps a Teacher

What are some conditions that facilitate the kind of evolution we've seen in Delois Strickland's teaching and in Woodson South overall? What helps spread improvements to teachers throughout a school system through support and respect, rather than binding everyone to a mechanistic, scripted curriculum? At first, Delois was intimidated by pressures from standardized tests and administrators. Later, she felt increasingly freer to follow her own judgment. How do we engender ownership and initiative in a setting built upon authority? In working with schools and teachers, and in reviewing the literature on school change (e.g., Darling-Hammond 1996; O'Neil 1995; Reitzug and Burrello 1995; Wasley et al. 1997), we've found that the following conditions and approaches help teachers grow and change. We describe them briefly and then return to each item to list specific ways that schools and districts can turn it into a reality. The first three categories focus on the external structural conditions in the school, the second three on the internal consciousness of individual teachers—though of course each aspect, internal and external, overlaps extensively with the other.

Teachers need regular time together.   Teachers need to talk, encourage, compare ideas, organize cooperation between classrooms, troubleshoot when things don't go as expected, and work out the conflicts that often come along with change. Unlike other professions, where planning meetings, "staffings," and conferences at fancy resorts are regular activities, teaching as it is organized in this country has shockingly little room for professional conversation. And because teachers' work is carried out almost entirely apart from colleagues, there's little daily time for informal exchange. Parents and community members who, at their workplace, spend many hours in cooperative tasks, in department and committee meetings (much as they may tire of those meetings) don't realize how little of this connectedness teachers enjoy. Linda Darling-Hammond (1996) points out that teachers in many other countries spend fifteen to twenty hours a week in the classroom and the rest of the time on planning, meeting with fellow faculty, continuing their education, contacting parents, and counseling students.

Achieving real instructional change calls for more than brief "inoculation" sessions for teachers once or twice a year. Deep inquiry into reading or math or science in an inservice program requires time to build group trust, experience model activities, discuss, disagree, rethink, and work out classroom applications. Teachers new to student-centered approaches usually try one thing at a time and gain confidence before moving on to another, so change requires several school years. It takes time to extend a new concept to all of one's teaching.

Teachers' change efforts must be supported by collaborative, social experiences and extensive, open discussion of issues.   Especially because teaching involves so much day-to-day isolation from fellow professionals, opportunities to work together and exchange views and information are essential. Collaborative work among teachers on tasks that have concrete results in classrooms builds supportive bonds. However, collaboration does not have to mean conformity. Nor should teacher leadership and decision making devolve upon a few senior teachers who are virtually promoted to become new supervisors. Rather, it's important to find a complementary role for each of the different abilities and interests in a group of teachers.

As new strategies are debated and tried out, there are almost always turf battles, complex organizational dynamics, strong emotions, and normal resistance to change. A study comparing five high schools in the Coalition of Essential Schools (Wasley et al. 1997) showed that when issues were aired in an atmosphere of mutual respect, changes and improvements went forward much more successfully than when they were repressed or dealt with either through angry confrontation or covert maneuvering.

Significant change needs leadership from the top, even while the support itself emphasizes teachers' decision making and initiative.   When Delois Strickland was trying out an interviewing activity with her second graders, many worked diligently but some grew noisy as she circulated to help individuals and pairs. What would the principal think if she walked by at that transitional moment? And with upcoming standardized tests, was it really acceptable to take so much time for writing while the other teachers were drilling their students for the big day? The previous year's scores were discouraging and the stakes were high. Delois needed to know where her principal stood.

This requirement may seem simple and obvious. Yet, it really asserts two seemingly contradictory things at once—the need for leadership and the need for the leader to support individual initiative. To be realistic, we are trying to introduce democratic and collaborative elements in organizations that remain pyramidal. We can try to alter the underlying style of operation in a school, but at base we are working with contradictions. And so the best staff development effort in the world can fail if school leaders do not consistently support the changes.

Perhaps this need for administrative support is especially strong in urban schools, where chaotic conditions in the neighborhood and the bureaucracy make it extra difficult for a teacher to carry out classroom changes. When the classroom population turns over because families frequently move, when books and materials don't arrive for months because of bureaucratic delays, when distant administrative offices announce sudden new requirements for testing or reporting every day—teachers need protection and help so they can feel safe to expand their repertoire. In this situation, a strong, encouraging principal who knows curriculum, welcomes innovation, and believes in teachers, and who does not him/herself impose sudden arbitrary requirements, is vital.

Schools and staff development programs must support and strengthen teachers' latent professionalism.   This is especially important if teachers are to take more decision-making roles. Teacher attitudes that must be encouraged include:

- viewing teaching approaches not just as private preferences or personality traits, but as strategies to be compared, analyzed, and then adapted to one's own style
- regarding a school staff more as a community and less as a hierarchy of leaders and led, senior people and juniors, etc.
- seeking improvement not because we are "deficient," but because in our work there's always more to learn, which is what keeps us fresh and energized for our kids

Most teachers originally entered the profession with enthusiasm and a desire to do something of value with their lives, and they are regularly reminded of that desire by the children sitting in front of them. So the internal impetus toward more professional attitudes is usually there, waiting to be reignited.

Staff development should be built around experiential activities, rather than theoretical lectures.   In our observation, both the strengthening of professional commitment and the initiation of new classroom strategies is most effectively initiated by inservice programs that feature concrete experiential activities, rather than starting with educational philosophy or research data (Zemelman and Daniels 1986). In the chapters on each curriculum area, we outlined how experts in every field have found that children's learning must be experiential and authentic, reflective and constructivist. Teachers need these ingredients just like kids do. Powerful experiential activities are not merely "demonstrations"; they immerse participants in fresh alternatives instead of just initiating debate about them.

To say that experiential learning is important for teachers is actually a controversial assertion. Much of the literature about school change comes from university academics, whose own careers have required them to stress theory and research. But classroom teachers' mental constructs, though often implicit and unconscious, must stand up to the rigorous test of everyday application. And so teachers especially need to directly experience models for what is possible in the classroom, to end the isolation that cuts them off from alternatives, and to help them work out the many details that go into a new classroom approach.

Teachers need to reflect, to analyze, to compare—to build knowledge and theoretical understandings about their work.   After experiential activity naturally comes reflection. Of course, within book covers the knowledge has been there for years—shelves full of reports about classrooms that work and research about what doesn't. However, because academic research is so often used in the educational world to prove one person's status higher than another's rather than to really improve schools, teachers often view "theory" with well-justified suspicion. This is just one more reason why teachers appreciate experiential activity first, as an inductive approach to theory. Yet when a teacher's natural curiosity has been tapped and when she is ready to digest and use the ideas, it's hard to stop her. Delois Strickland showed *us* the article about conferencing because the information became meaningful to her.

Getting Down to Business

Following are some ways in which schools and reform programs have created conditions to help teachers improve children's learning. All of these strategies help to work *with* teachers' resistance to change, rather than opposing it head on. Negative approaches, arbitrary mandates, and punitive labels engender resentment and quiet, passive resistance that, in the long run, can undermine any program. Because schools are such complicated social structures, and because many of the elements are extensive and intricate, we can only sketch some of the issues that must be addressed to make programs succeed, expanding a bit on the six needs outlined above, that teachers need as they attempt to change. Those interested in a particular program will want to consult the more detailed literature on it.

1. Time to Explore and Plan

Make a "concerns" list with any group of teachers and what invariably comes at the top? Time. Teachers need significant chunks of time with their peers if they are to plan serious changes in curriculum or school structure. The school system that fails to provide this time sends a clear signal that teacher participation is not really important. The few days before school begins in August are hectic with preparation, not a good time for reflection or massive changes in direction. Two or three inservice days scattered throughout the year, even on the same topic, amount to only a gesture. Brief before-school meetings do not permit concentration. More extended workshops are often held during the summer or after school hours when teachers must fight weariness after the day's work.

Find time creatively.   In many buildings in Chicago, the staff has restructured the school day. Children arrive fifteen minutes earlier each day, and are then dismissed one-and-a-quarter hours early one afternoon a week, or half-a-day early every two weeks, to gain cooperative planning time for teachers. It works out that kids and teachers spend the same total amount of time in school as before. In one school we'll never name, the PTA parents—totally illegally—cover classes one half-day each week so teachers can meet in curriculum workshops.

Another part of coping with time is finding funds to pay for extra committee work, consultants, or after-school inservice time. While schools are always short of cash, it's surprising how much money can be available if decision makers are clear about priorities. In Chicago public schools, for example, as much as 25 percent of a school's budget may actually be discretionary. While there are other legitimate needs to be met in each building, devoting some funds to pay for teacher planning time is often possible.

Take time for the long view.   Finding time means working with a longer-range view—easy to say, not always in evidence. Making "science" this year's theme for two inservice days doesn't do the job. The essential steps:

- organizing to study an issue
- conducting a needs assessment and finding internal or outside help
- building interest
- providing in-depth workshops
- identifying and training teacher-leaders
- providing classroom consultants for on-the-spot assistance

- sharing through follow-up sessions and informal peer support
- repeating the inservice and follow-up cycle to gradually spread the new approaches to more teachers
- revision of formal structures (report cards, for example) to support the changes

All this can take three to five years in a school or district. But if it includes teachers in the leadership and decision making, change can become broad and deep.

Taking time, in the long-range sense of coming to new realizations, sometimes means having patience. This is hard. A school may not be ready for change, perhaps because not enough teachers really seek it or the administration is ambivalent. An enthusiastic advocate can burn out in frustration and needs to know when it is better—at least temporarily—to focus on her own classroom and share ideas with just a few sympathetic friends. The effort to change ought not destroy the people initiating it. And sometimes it pays to wait. Many a principal or department chair has been known to come back a year or two later and ask blithely for help—because the problem, of course, hadn't really gone away.

2. Collaboration and Peer Leadership

It's easy to forget what social creatures we are, or how discouraging it is to be a lone risk taker. Most people would rather go along, or at least keep their differences quiet, than bear the group's disapproval. The "far-out" character who advertises his stance gets labeled, making it easy to protect the system from his successes—"Oh well, that's Wayne. He's good, but he's crazy."

The school culture can reinforce isolation as the accepted way to get along. In surveys, teachers say they hesitate to seek a colleague's help on a problem because they fear the word will spread and they'll be negatively evaluated by the principal. Conversely, taking leadership seems like joining with or seeking favor from the boss. Thus, while many schools attempt some form of faculty collaboration such as mentoring or peer coaching, the effort must be approached thoughtfully or it will break down.

Be sensitive to organizational dynamics and details.   Mentoring offers a good case study of complexities and pitfalls. A gathering of high school department chairpersons discussed the following realities: (1) *Time* (again!). Unless mentor and protegé have matching schedules, it is difficult for the two to get together. One chairperson coped by placing the new teacher in a room next to the mentor so that brief informal exchanges could occur. Teachers report that much gets said between neighbors during passing periods. (2) *Arbitrary pairings*. Personalities, styles, and needs differ. Some chairpersons let protegés make their own choice of mentors, after large-group get-acquainted sessions. Some realized that designating someone as a mentor gave the appearance of favoritism, engendering jealousy among others in the department. One solution was to plan the mentoring program collaboratively with the whole department. (3) *Evaluation.* In some locations, mentors are required to conduct evaluations of their protegés. This undermines the entire program because the new teachers are motivated to conceal rather than share the problems they encounter. Just as it requires thoughtful structure to make the classroom more interactive, so it does for a school faculty.

Effective collaboration depends on the whole school culture, not just an isolated program. Comparisons of schools where peer coaching was tried showed that it was most positively viewed in the buildings where a rich variety of regular exchange activities took place (Little 1988). Exchange can occur at a number of levels:

- one-on-one interchange for growth and improving classroom strategies
- wider communication and planning within departments or grade levels
- periodic reports on various initiatives at the building or district level
- formal instructional leadership roles, taken by a few, or shared widely

In the more successful buildings that were studied among the Coalition of Essential Schools, faculty met at length to compare the vision they had articulated with the strategies they were carrying out. In one school, regular reports from the superintendent and from various faculty groups kept the whole staff involved and informed. Any of these approaches can provide a starting place, but a key to success is using each to support the others.

Allow for differences.   Once teachers become more active, talk isn't automatically productive. Committees can bog down and factions wrangle. The problem is how to keep innovation going *without* alienating the more traditional teachers and turning a building into a battleground.

One way to ameliorate this is to avoid absolute mandates for an entire school or district, and to ask instead that each teacher choose among several improvements to work on. Successful reform in places like East Harlem involve multiple teacher groups, each organizing their own smaller "schools." Then, as we've emphasized repeatedly, each group needs to be kept well informed about the efforts and struggles of the other. When each group within a faculty learns to appreciate the strengths of the other, change is more likely for all.

Build mutual respect.   This is so essential to collaborative change that it simply must take priority over installing "correct" practices. A powerful tool for building cohesion among staff members is the gradual sharing of individual histories and past learning experiences. This opens communication and builds understanding so that teachers can live with their natural human disagreements. Group-dynamics theorists call this "maintenance" activity, and assert that every effective group needs plenty of it. Good administrators and staff development leaders incorporate such self-disclosure, sharing, and storytelling into just about any meeting or inservice session. In a session on lump-sum budgeting, for example, a good workshop leader began by asking participants to pair up and describe to each other the gains and tradeoffs resulting from a recent personal purchase. The talk led to principles for analyzing the budget process. But the one-to-one exchange was vitally important to build trust, to open channels, and to begin a conversation first.

3. Administrative Support for New Efforts

Any group working on change can be undermined and burn out as it encounters resistance and contradictions. We've watched districts adopt new tests that encouraged rote teaching of isolated skills, just as a staff development committee introduced a higher-order thinking-skills approach to the same subject. It's no surprise when teachers feel whipsawed and planners get discouraged. They need to know that the school administration is behind the new ideas—and yet also that programs won't be rammed down their throat. Districts must choose a few areas to work on and create a long-range development plan, instead of jumping from one inservice fad to another every year—yet teachers need choices and a strong role in drawing up that plan.

What are some steps that principals and other administrators can take to support teachers as they change? Following a recent study of effective principals by Ulrich Reitzug and Leonard Burrello (1995), we sketch out three areas, although we know they overlap a good bit: (1) nurturing a supportive school culture—developing the context in which risk taking and change can take place; (2) acting as a guide and a model, being an instructional leader and thoughtful questioner; and (3) supporting collaborative teacher groups to work on the effort. Within all of these, however, what matters most are the implicit messages of commitment, openness, and trust more than the formal structures that the principal sets up. What this really adds up to is building a healthy, adult, working community in an organization not well designed for it.

Nurture a positive school culture.   Because schools are such complex places, says school researcher Michael Fullan (1985), effective leaders cannot depend on just a few strategies, and instead need a broader "feel for the process." School administrators, he says, should learn from Hewlett-Packard Corporation's very successful policy of "management by wandering around."

Fullan speaks of the need for "intense interaction and communication." A principal who practices listening, who doesn't react defensively or jump to conclusions when events occur, who seeks as much feedback as possible will be able to gather information about how a new activity is going. Student achievement scores or surveys of classroom applications will never yield such information. One needs to discover the particular obstacles or supports at work, and it's hard to prescribe how to do this because the best information gathering is informal. Yet involvement must also be balanced with respect for teachers' autonomy and the sanctity of instructional time. As one teacher explained to a researcher:

> An administrator can walk in and interrupt what I am doing with any cockamamie thing. . . . He butts into my classroom with all sorts of nitpicky stuff. The message is clear. What I am doing is not important. The kids can pick this up. (Pfeifer 1986)

Teacher evaluation by principals can especially influence change in the classroom for good or ill. As Boston principal Kim Marshall (1996) explains, using frequent brief visits instead of twice-a-year formal ceremonies, making the teacher-evaluation process dialogical rather than just an awkward ritual, asking teachers to set goals for their own development and to write responses to the principal's comments, supporting experiments in which a teacher's performance may not be perfect the first time—all set the stage for change to flourish. Otherwise, it can seem safer for a teacher to quietly undermine a new program, rather than risk seriously trying it. Susan Ohanian (1985), teacher and freelance writer, vividly described the more unproductive approach to supervision:

> Once, while I presented for my supervisor a required lesson on *Julius Caesar*, a belligerent girl (whose attendance had improved dramatically since the appearance of self-chosen books) steadfastly read her novel. My department chairman leaned over and whispered to her, "Don't you think you should put that book away and pay attention to the teacher?" "Who the hell are you?" demanded the girl. "If she wants me to put it away, let her tell me." She went back to her book, and I continued my performance. Later, it was hard to convince my boss that the girl's devotion to that book was an excellent moment for me, much more valid than my gyrations. . . . For fifty minutes twice a year, we all pretend that school is what everybody outside the classroom claims it should be. No student even asks to go to the bathroom. (318)

Be a guide and a model.   Almost every national reform advocate calls for the principal to enunciate a vision of the school and of objectives embodied in any new effort, in order to help teachers set priorities. As long as he or she doesn't deny obstacles and realities, such rhetoric can help everyone maintain commitment. Henry Levin describes this role as "keeper of the dream." A principal's actions will be read very carefully as a school change initiative proceeds. The principal who protects the faculty from arbitrary district rules or bends a few to help a project along will prove her commitment.

The principal must model the attitudes the rest of the staff should adopt, learning new concepts to strengthen his or her understanding of effective curriculum and instruction along with everyone else. We know principals who regularly invite and answer letters from students throughout the school to encourage involvement and written communication. They are also the ones who attend inservice workshops with their teachers and take the risk of joining in all the activities, writing, and sharing. And we know others who slip out of the meeting room as soon as the inservice session begins or who sit off to the side conspicuously taking notes on participants' behavior, not the content of the session. The difference is not lost on the teachers.

A principal must be careful to avoid making contradictory demands and, as much as possible, protect teachers from such demands from higher up. Otherwise, teachers quickly become demoralized and avoid the new activity so as not to get caught in a bind. We observed one inner-city principal who wanted students to do more writing, but marked grammar errors herself on papers collected from each classroom, and nagged teachers more and more about drilling kids to shore up the falling test scores from the previous year. After several months, she was frustrated because teachers were assigning *less* writing and were less committed than ever to trying new writing activities.

Support collaborative effort.   Nothing breeds teacher cynicism faster than evidence that a committee task involves a predetermined outcome. "Why should I take the time for this?" the teachers ask. In an authentic curriculum study it's helpful, on the other hand, to provide constructive guidelines—clarifying the mission, choosing a reachable goal, requiring input from the rest of the staff, setting a reasonable timetable for a final report, and ensuring that the results are put to use.

And then there are a myriad of unanticipated ways in which a good administrator must help. In one study of principals promoting an innovation, Hall and Hord (1987) report that nearly two thousand separate interventions were required of each of them during one school year. One of us sat in a principal's office recently and waited while she made telephone calls around her building in immediate response to a teacher's report that the building engineer wouldn't unlock the room containing the laminating machine. It was frustrating for the visitor to wait as each stage of the drama played itself out, but she had her priorities right—and teachers were very committed to her and to the school as a result.

We've seen a few promising school change projects come unglued because districts didn't make consistent changes in each of the interlocking elements that combine to create the school experience for kids. For example, if you want a true literature-based reading program, you *must* have lots of books in each classroom—period. If the budget for books isn't there, then the program won't be there fully either, no matter what other ingredients may be in place.

So we've started using the following checklist in working with school districts, and it seems to help. The point is simple: if you really want deep, lasting change to occur across classrooms, it has to be supported by parallel, congruent changes in each factor listed:

- curriculum
- instruction
- materials
- space
- scheduling
- grouping
- special education
- staff development
- faculty hiring
- evaluation/grading/report cards
- standardized testing—state assessment
- administrative leadership
- parent and community participation
- board support
- budget

This may be a good place to also acknowledge some realities. It's fine to outline rational and revolutionary approaches to school improvement, but we are working in the real world, and we must start with what exists. Not every school system, administrator, or teacher is ready to face real issues or seek change. Therefore, some valuable efforts are initiated under the noses of unsupportive, autocratic—but fortunately often unwitting—people. It is important to help caring teachers do a more meaningful job *especially* when circumstances are difficult. More than once, grassroots efforts have ultimately led to wider acceptance. We simply need to be honest about the scope of change likely under such conditions, and not burn out in the process.

4. Teachers' Attitudes—Professionalism and the Desire to Grow

Teachers' attitudes are crucial to whether or not in-depth curricular innovation succeeds. This is just one reason why change mandated from above is likely to bog down in the long run. In surveying many studies of school change, Michael Fullan (1985) concludes that narrowly defined innovations can be made to work with a top-down approach, but complex school-wide changes need deeper commitment. What are some practical ways to promote this commitment?

Provide incentives.   Among teachers in the city of Chicago, continuing professional development was stunted until the Board of Education finally adopted pay incentives in line with those in suburban school districts. Curiously, even though the program was later terminated and pay increases no longer awarded, Chicago teachers now take graduate courses and board-credit courses in record numbers. In a society where valued actions are materially rewarded, the lack of reward sends a negative signal. On the other hand, one particular district offered such unusually high pay for a summer program that some teachers showed up just for the money and sat in the back of the room reading the newspaper (supporting Alfie Kohn's argument, in *Punished by Rewards* [1993], that behaviorist strategies don't really work to change people).

Look for the best in teachers.   The lockstep curricula and standardized test scores that tend to be popular in the news media reflect a distrust in the efficacy of individual teachers, an unwillingness to recognize that, finally, learning means teachers in classrooms understanding, supporting, and challenging each student. School systems, with their detailed curriculum guides, objectives, and standardized tests in each subject area, seem to expect very little initiative from teachers. Administrators or consultants who regard teachers as less than responsible can easily, unconsciously, signal this, even when they're trying a more participatory approach—and so defensive responses continue. Truly changing the relationship means asking the teachers to set their own agenda at the beginning of a meeting or inservice session, asking for their analyses of problems in the school or in children's learning, and respecting the realities within their answers, even when we sometimes disagree with them.

When we visit schools, we begin by asking teachers to talk about their successes and their problems, instead of starting right in to lecture about the best new way to approach teaching. We see faces change from glazed blankness to surprise, to engagement and pleasure. When asked, they have plenty to say about what is working and what the obstacles are. Again and again, we observe that when workshops and inservice activities respect teachers—by offering them ownership and control, immersing them in new perspectives on their own teaching and learning abilities, and providing opportunities to express themselves honestly—many respond with great energy. Often, the moment this begins, teachers start thinking and acting more for themselves. Self-fulfilling prophesy was never more in evidence than here.

5. Concrete Experience of New Possibilities

The workshop leaders are meeting in a branch library with seventy-five teachers to introduce a writing/reading inservice program. After introductions, the teachers are asked to jot on a 4-x-6 notecard their own goals and concerns about teaching writing and connecting it with the reading program. In pairs they discuss what they've written, and only after that do the leaders begin to hear people's thoughts and record them on a master list on the overhead.

With the list fresh in mind, the group embarks on a reading-writing activity. One leader reads aloud the book *Wednesday Surprise,* by Eve Bunting. It's a moving story about a child and her grandmother and learning to read. The other leader then guides the group through several rounds of "dialogue journal" writing. In a dialogue journal, partners each jot down thoughts about a topic and then trade notebooks, responding to the ideas and reactions of the other—a legitimized kind of note passing. With this particular book, the teachers invariably write about their own experiences with literacy—and illiteracy—in their families. People are involved and moved as volunteers read some of these aloud. Grudgingly, the teachers conclude their sharing, and then go on to discuss implications of the activity for their initial concerns and uses of the strategy with their own students.

Build inservice around experiential activity.   Of course, it's important to talk about beliefs and educational theories, for even when unconsciously held, these guide teachers' actions. But direct talk is not always the most effective way. If schools are immensely complex places with innumerable factors influencing change, so are individual classrooms. Because they know this, teachers need in-depth experiential enactments to help them visualize how a new approach works.

These activities are far more than just the "demonstrations" talked about in some training or coaching programs. We are not just training teachers to use a new tool. Rather, the best activities provide a mirror in which teachers see themselves in new ways. They draw on teachers' prior knowledge and abilities, instead of implying deficiency, and help them construct a new approach of their own, rather than just imitating an instructor. They help people renew and enjoy their own learning, something that teachers desperately need. They provide space for teachers to reconceptualize what learning and teaching can be. Only then are people well equipped—enriched, heartened, drawn into a supportive group—and ready to reflect on the activities, to bring to the surface implicitly challenged beliefs about instruction and children's learning, and to reconsider and reconstruct these beliefs and revise their practices accordingly.

Use classroom consulting and other follow-up to help teachers translate new ideas into realities.   It's not easy to bring real change to school districts. Judith Little (1988) points out that schools are not really structured to influence actual teaching. Not only do teachers work out of sight of one another, but the observations carried out by principals or department chairs are infrequent and the depth of their conceptual exploration is usually severely limited. But with focused effort, experiential inquiry can be extended throughout the cycle of staff development and classroom application. Schools can be more demanding consumers of inservice education, inquiring whether the consultants who advocate more active learning for children use such strategies with teachers. Then, because we know that inquiry and even guided practice do not lead all teachers to use a new approach, schools can schedule ongoing classroom visits by facilitators, to observe, co-teach lessons, and meet with teachers who ask for help. Once-a-week visits by a consultant for a period of eight to ten weeks can powerfully launch a willing teacher on a new trajectory with integrated learning projects or small-group literature circles to study and report on books or topics of the students' choosing. Team teaching, peer coaching, inquiry groups that study a new approach together and then try it out are all valuable ways to bring teachers into one another's classrooms and help them support each other as they engage new ideas in practice.

6. New Knowledge

Approach theory authentically.   Some academics consider teachers anti-intellectual, unresponsive to theory. But teachers remember their first year teaching, when all that theory seemed to evaporate under the pressures of the moment, since there was virtually no apprenticeship system to help make the connections. We've observed in many settings as teachers do or do not embrace new ideas, and we've tried to understand the causes. We've seen whole districts where few teachers pursue ideas any farther than the talk in immediate workshop sessions. They come, let us entertain them, and go back to their classrooms to do what they've always done. We can only say these are often places where the administrations send out extremely mixed signals—for example, paying teachers handsomely to attend a summer work-shop, but then discouraging individuals from organizing teacher-led groups that could keep the new program developing.

But we've also watched as a workshop leader unobtrusively leaves stacks of articles on a table at the end of an inservice session and then initiates discussion with individuals as they enter the room the following week. At first, a few teachers read the pieces, then others grow curious, and ulti-mately the class organizes small-group "literature circles" to compare ideas about the articles they chose to read.

There are schools where administrators encourage interested teacher groups to explore on their own, read about a new approach, meet informally to discuss it, and try it out, critiquing and adjusting both the ideas and their practice. In some schools, one can find a rack with new literature on educa-tion, set up by the principal in the teacher's lounge—even better when the principal leaves Post-it notes with short comments on some of the articles, if for no other reason than to show that someone is really reading the stuff. Some schools spend money to buy copies of a key book for everyone who participated in a recent workshop on the subject.

As with Delois Strickland, the process is contagious. At first, a teacher tries one or two new strategies, perhaps inspired more by a workshop activity than by any revolution in her thinking. But then, when it shows promise, she wants to know more, to extend the practice, and to troubleshoot the parts that aren't working as well. Just as with children: when teachers rediscover their need for new thinking and see a likelihood of results, their hunger for learning bursts forth, even if long-suppressed. But the best way to see how all the Delois Stricklands can be encouraged in a staff development program is to see a strong one at work. The story of one such district-wide program is told on the following pages.

EXEMPLARY PROGRAM
A Seven-year District-wide Staff Development Effort

School District U-46
Elgin, Illinois

Elgin has the second largest school district in Illinois, with thirty-six elementary schools, seven middle schools, three high schools, and a fourth high school under construction. Elgin is located on the far western edge of the Chicago metropolitan area, and neighborhoods range from older, poverty-stricken areas to subdivisions filled with upwardly mobile families moving into large, newly constructed homes. When Sue Bernardi began as the Reading/Language Arts Coordinator in 1990, she sent a letter to all the elementary principals asking them to identify two teachers per building to be trained on release time as teacher-leaders in current approaches to teaching writing through the Illinois Writing Project. This first group proved reluctant to serve as trainers themselves, for the workshops led them to realize how much they still had to learn. Their enthusiasm for the workshops and their new classroom strategies, however, were contagious, and four sections of thirty-hour introductory summer workshops on teaching writing were filled with participants, taught by two outstanding Illinois Writing Project teachers from Elgin, Mary Hausner and Jan Booth.

Following these first steps, Sue explains, "The sign-ups came in waves." First were the high-energy risk takers. Then came the teachers who declared, "I'm really tired of hearing my colleagues talk about how great those workshops are." The third wave had the attitude, "All right, I've heard you're so smart. Let's see what you're made of." Mary and Jan understood it was crucial that the groups, not the leaders, do most of the teaching for the third-wave people. Third-wavers are different, they explained. They even bring different sorts of treats to share.

Teachers quickly grew partisan and hungry, each demanding further courses from their favorite leader—invariably whichever one they started with. A fascinating aspect of staff development is that as teachers begin learning in a new area, they realize there's much they don't yet know and ask for more. Sue Bernardi attended the course herself, even though she knew the content, to signal the administration's involvement and to make clear that "this isn't just a remedial course for dummies." To respond to the desire for more, Sue and her team gradually offered more and more advanced workshops—on teaching writing, writing across the curriculum, reading-writing connections, literature circles, running a classrooom writing workshop, reading recovery, teaching multiage classrooms, teaching the at-risk kindergartener, plus the Early Literacy Inservice Course and the "Frameworks" course developed by Brian Cambourne, Jan Turbill, and Andrea Butler. Following each of these, Mary Hausner has made regular "house calls" to help teachers troubleshoot strategies in their classrooms. Workshops run for either fifteen or thirty contact hours. More than five hundred teachers, out of a district staff of nineteen hundred, have attended one or more programs.

Sue, Mary, and Jan have gone on to focus on reading, with the help of an outside consultant, Tony Stead, from Australia. Workshops explore emergent reading, guided reading in small groups, and keeping running records. To increase the impact, they urge attendance by all teachers in two adjacent grade levels in a building, plus bilingual and special-education teachers, and the principal. Increasingly, the district has recognized that principals must learn to become knowledgeable instructional leaders. In the first round of training, the planners advertised for twelve teams, but agreed to accept seventeen, for a total of 110 participants.

The reading workshop program very successfully highlighted the need for teamwork and better classroom management. Some principals (though not all) visited classrooms in their building to try out the strategies themselves. Some have brought Mary in for follow-up sessions. In several schools where teachers were more hesitant, Mary provided substitutes to help keep order in the room while the teachers tried out new strategies with small groups, to one side.

The staff development team continues adding pieces to the puzzle and filling in gaps. A video from the Children's Literacy Foundation, accompanied by short articles, has provided opportunities for self-run inservice and has gone well in two schools. Middle schools are developing a model in which the reading teachers work with the rest of the staff, rather than just groups of kids, to design approaches for reading in the content areas. This was planned because the content teachers agree on the need for work on reading but need help figuring out how to integrate the teaching of reading with their subjects. A one-day workshop on coaching students for success on state writing tests without distorting the whole year's curriculum has been very popular. And a committee has redesigned the report card for primary children, using a continuum of observable items for reading and writing. This has had a noticeable effect on teachers who were previously hesitant to try new approaches.

The high schools have been the most resistant to change, although an Illinois Writing Project consultant provided a series of well-received, whole-day sessions and in-classroom coaching visits for teachers of freshmen in one building. A next step being planned is to provide new strategies for class-room management that utilize individual activities and self-control, so that teachers at all levels can more successfully employ classroom workshops and small-group collaborative work.

What results emerge from this energized and extensive effort? Sixteen elementary schools, nearly half the district, have scored above the state aver-age on the Illinois Goal Assessment Program state writing test over the past four years. Ten of thirty-three of the schools showed substantial and consis-tent gains in state writing scores at third grade from 1990 to 1996, and eleven schools showed gains at sixth grade. Another seven schools showed substan-tial gains at third grade for several of the years but not all, and six showed such gains at sixth grade. Such inconsistency often reflects changes in teach-ing staff or variations in prior achievement level of the differing group of students tested each year. With a third of the district's schools serving stu-dent populations of 45 percent or more low-income, these are promising improvements, particularly because they show up in lower-income as well as middle-class sites.

The new reading efforts have thus far only been instituted in the primary grades, and are too recent to show an effect yet. However, teachers are enthusiastic, observe much more reading taking place in their classrooms, and have discovered that even classroom applications of the writing program result in students reading more—particularly the struggling readers—because they must read their own and others' products in order to work on revision.

It is important to keep reminding ourselves, too, that while accountabil-ity is important, large-scale standardized tests provide a very limited picture of what children are learning. Teachers' direct observations of children's day-to-day achievement remains the most meaningful measure of children's growth, as parents recognize all the time, when inquiring about their own children's success. As an example in Elgin, a third-grade teacher tells the story of Megan, who asked in September, "Are we going to use those read-ing books [i.e., the basals] this year?" She'd been a low-achieving reader and, when she began to thrive on choosing her own library books, her mother couldn't believe the teacher's reports. The teacher, to satisfy all doubts, had Megan read a book aloud without rehearsal into a tape recorder and then retell the story afterward. When the mother heard the tape, she admitted that her doubt stemmed from the fact that she had never been a strong reader herself. As stories like this multiply, parents in Elgin come to value the hard-won advancements their schools are making.

Works Cited

Comer, James P. 1980. *School Power.* New York: Free Press.

Darling-Hammond, Linda. 1996. "The Quiet Revolution: Rethinking Teacher Development." *Educational Leadership.* (March).

Fullan, Michael. 1985. "Change Processes and Strategies at the Local Level." *Elementary School Journal.* (January).

Goodlad, John L. 1994. *Educational Renewal: Better Teachers, Better Schools.* San Francisco: Jossey-Bass.

Hall, Gene, and Shirley Hord. 1987. *Change in Schools: Facilitating the Process.* Albany, NY: State University of New York Press.

Kidder, Tracy. 1990. *Among Schoolchildren.* Unity, ME: Thorndike Press.

Kohn, Alfie. 1993. *Punished by Rewards: The Trouble with Gold Stars, Incentive Plans, A's, Praise, and Other Bribes.* New York: Houghton Mifflin.

Levin, Henry M. 1988. *Accelerated Schools for At-Risk Students.* New Brunswick: Center for Policy Research in Education.

———. 1990. "Accelerated Schools After Three Years." *Educational Leadership.* (April).

Lieberman, Ann, and Lynne Miller. 1991. *Staff Development for Education in the '90's: New Demands, New Realities, New Perspectives* (Second Edition). New York: Teachers College Press.

Little, Judith Warren. 1988. "Assessing the Prospects for Teacher Leadership." In *Building a Professional Culture in Schools.* Edited by Ann Lieberman. New York: Teachers College Press.

Lortie, Dan. 1972. *Schoolteacher.* Chicago, IL: University of Chicago Press.

Marshall, Kim. 1996. "No One Ever Said It Would Be Easy." *Phi Delta Kappan.* (December).

Ohanian, Susan. 1985. "Huffing and Puffing and Blowing Schools Excellent." *Phi Delta Kappan.* (January).

O'Neil, John. 1995. "On Lasting School Reform: A Conversation with Ted Sizer." *Educational Leadership.* (February).

Pfeifer, R. Scott. 1986. *Enabling Teacher Effectiveness.* Washington, DC: American Educational Research Association.

Ramirez-Smith, Christina. 1995. "Stopping the Cycle of Failure: The Comer Model." *Educational Leadership.* (February).

Reitzug, Ulrich, and Leonard C. Burrello. 1995. "How Principals Can Build Self-Renewing Schools." *Educational Leadership.* (April).

Wasley, Patricia, Robert Hampel, and Richard Clark. 1997. "The Puzzle of Whole School Change." *Phi Delta Kappan.* (May).

Zemelman, Steven, and Harvey Daniels. 1986. "Authorship and Authority: Helping Writing Teachers Grow." *English Education.* (December).

Suggested Further Readings

Billings, Gloria Ladson. 1994. *The Dream Keepers: Successful Teachers of African American Children.* San Francisco: Jossey-Bass.

Darling-Hammond, Linda. 1997. *The Right to Learn: A Blueprint for Creating Schools That Work.* San Francisco: Jossey-Bass.

Fullan, Michael, and Andy Hargreaves. 1996. *What's Worth Fighting For in Your School.* New York: Teachers College Press.

Joyce, Bruce, and Beverly Showers. 1997. *Student Achievement Through Staff Development: Fundamentals of School Renewal.* New York: Longman.

Sizer, Theodore. 1993. *Horace's Hope: What Works for the American High School.* Boston: Houghton Mifflin.

Wasley, Patricia A. 1991. *Teachers Who Lead: The Rhetoric of Reform and the Realities of Practice.* New York: Teachers College Press.

————. 1993. *Stirring the Chalk Dust: Tales of Teachers Changing Classroom Practice.* New York: Teachers College Press.

10

But What About Evaluation, Test Scores, Tracking, Special Students, Classroom Management, Parents, and Other Concerns?

What About Evaluation and Grading?

In Chapter 8 and in the earlier subject-area chapters, we outlined some promising practices in what is now called "authentic assessment." Today, knowledgeable teachers are not satisfied to assess students' growth solely on the basis of classroom quizzes and standardized achievement tests. They know that these tend to treat the curriculum as a pyramid of atomized sub-skills, missing many of the essentials in each subject, and failing to reflect what kids can really do with coordinated, higher-order activities like writing, researching, experimenting, and problem solving. Instead, effective teachers are increasingly using kid-watching, observational notes, interviews, questionnaires, checklists, student artifacts and work samples, performance assessment, student self-evaluation, evaluation conferences, portfolios, and other tools to get a better understanding of kids' learning and more clearly explain their progress to the parents, the community, and the kids themselves.

A fund of helpful literature on well-designed forms of evaluation provides several books' worth of guidance on ways to better gauge, guide, and report students' learning. We won't reiterate here the ideas so carefully crafted in the many recent books we list in the suggested readings at the end of this section. We might also direct the interested reader to Chapter 16 of our own previous book, *A Community of Writers* (Zemelman and Daniels 1988), entitled "The English Teacher's Red Pen: History of an Obsession."

Still, we want to say a few words about the general problem of evalua-tion in education and its relation to the movement we've called Best Prac-tice. Very plainly, we think teachers and schools evaluate students badly, unfairly, and far too much. As we argued in *Community of Writers*, Ameri-can schoolchildren, teachers, parents, taxpayers, politicians, and policymak-ers are downright obsessed with grades and tests. Everyone involved spends far more time worrying about test scores than thinking up ways to increase student learning, which might actually raise achievement scores. Instead, we tinker with our measuring devices, planning and conducting more and more evaluations, tests, and exams. We are a country full of measurement-obsessed people who seem to believe that you can raise the temperature by improving your thermometer.

What's so bad about the way we evaluate kids in school? To begin with, the socioeconomic function of evaluation in American education has always been problematic and unsavory. Grading and testing historically have been harnessed to the screening, sorting, and classifying of children into categories of "merit" or "intelligence." These certified categories of students are then allocated certain current or future rewards, such as school prizes, invitations to honors classes, admission to good colleges, or entry to high-paying careers. As scholars like Michael Katz (1968), Joel Spring (1972), Alan Chase (1977), Stephen Jay Gould (1981), and Alfie Kohn (1993) have convincingly shown for thirty years, this vaunted American meritocracy is largely a sham. School tests and grades are part of a system that camouflages the replication of the existing social hierarchy: kids from wealthy, culturally mainstream homes are certified by schools as "deserving" rewards, while students from poor, cul-turally different homes are proven by tests and grades to "need" a vocational education or to be "unable to benefit" from a college preparatory program.

Although this historical interpretation is uncomfortable to many teachers, its reality is undeniable. The school grading system has been abused, co-opted, and enlisted in the service of some shamefully undemocratic arrangements in our culture. Even today, after the wide distribution of work by social historians and the many exposés of standardized test bias, our two most famous educa-tional exams—the Scholastic Aptitude Test and the American College Test—brazenly continue to show a near-perfect correlation between family income and score levels, and still deliver a huge score penalty for being African American or Hispanic. As a recent article in the *New York Times* (November 8, 1997, p. A8) points out, Martin Luther King, "a man who is now viewed as among the nation's greatest orators ever, was in the third quartile or below average [in verbal aptitude on the Graduate Records Exam]. His quantitative score was in the bottom 10 percent, and he was in the bottom quarter for tests in physics, chemistry, biology, social studies, and the fine arts." Understanding this distasteful history, Best Practice teachers must avoid, through every means available to them, complicity in such undemocratic and retrograde uses of educational evaluation.

But even if we admit that educational assessment has been often misused by the society at large, don't we use it more responsibly within the institution of school? Sadly, most teachers are still wedded to evaluation procedures that are ineffective, time-consuming, and hurtful to students. One example from the field of writing is particularly illustrative. Everyone is familiar with the deep-rooted school tradition called "intensive correction," where the teacher marks every error in every paper that every student ever writes. Indeed, in American schools this practice is often considered to be *the* basic, standard treatment for responding to student writing. But George Hillocks' (1986) meta-analysis of research showed that such intensive correction is *completely useless*. Marking all the errors in a student paper is no more effective, in terms of future growth or improvement, than marking none of them. The only difference is the huge expenditure of teacher time and the student demoralization that accompany this practice.

This kind of inefficient and discouraging evaluation is all too prevalent across the curriculum. Under pressure to "justify" grades with copious scores and marks in their gradebooks, teachers expend enormous energy feeding the grading machine—finding ways to quantify, measure, score, compute, and record assorted aspects of kids' behaviors. Coauthor Harvey Daniels recently worked to popularize the classroom structure called "Literature Circles" (1994) and reports that in workshops, the number-one question raised by teachers is: "How can I get a grade out of this activity?" This futile expenditure of time should remind us that the main legitimate purpose of evaluation in education is to guide instruction. Anything we do to gather and interpret information about kids' learning should provide accurate, helpful input for nurturing children's further growth. If we are generating data merely to prop up a rigged meritocracy, cater to political demands for "accountability," or simply out of habit and tradition, we aren't doing Best Practice educational evaluation.

Back in their preservice educational psychology courses, every teacher learned the distinction between summative and formative evaluation. Formative evaluation is the basic, everyday kind of assessment that teachers continually do to understand students' growth and help "form" their further learning. Summative evaluation doesn't aim to nurture learning at all, but merely quantifies what has been learned up to a given point, translating it into a score or symbol that allows students to be ranked against each other. Summative evaluation isn't actually educational; it is just a way of reporting periodically to outsiders about what has been studied or learned.

It's problem enough when tests are valid but overused or misused, but it's much worse when they don't reflect Best Practice teaching or skills that the kids are, in fact, learning. Yet over and over, even when communities and news reporters are confronted with studies showing that standardized tests are inaccurate, discriminate against minorities, and reward memorization instead of thinking, they opt to retain them anyway. Better, more complex tests are too expensive, they conclude, and besides, how can we compare ourselves to other communities if we don't use the same tests?

Meanwhile, one side effect of our overemphasis on summative evaluation and standardized testing is that we simply evaluate kids' work too much. We have a norm of grading every piece of work that students ever attempt in any school subject, duly placing a carefully computed grade in the gradebook after each attempt. We don't even laugh at the absurdity of high school course-grading systems with point totals ballooning into the thousands, pseudoscientific schemes that leave the teacher who invented them poring over computer spreadsheets for days just to generate "accurate" grades at the end of each marking period. Indeed, in many classrooms the compulsion to evaluate every piece of student work actually becomes an instructional bottleneck, limiting the amount of student practice to a level that the teacher has time to grade. The sad irony here, of course, is that practice—unmonitored practice—is the main way in which humans learn almost every valuable activity in life, from piano playing to roof shingling. But in school, kids aren't allowed to practice anything without being evaluated (we can't let their errors take root!) and so we adjust, counterproductively, by having kids just read less, write less, and think less.

We grade and test and score kids far more than is needed to effectively guide instruction. In classrooms where teachers are constantly watching, talking, and working with kids, elaborate grading systems are unnecessary, redundant, and sometimes contradictory. As far as the demand for official grades and records is concerned, teachers can produce a perfectly adequate documentation of students' growth through the occasional sampling of their work, periodic observations, and once-in-a-while examination of their products. Especially when records are backed up by a portfolio of students' actual work—the raw material upon which any grade ought to be based—there should be no problem in explaining a given grade. When teachers make this change, substituting descriptive evaluation for grading, they are essentially making a trade: they are swapping time previously spent on scoring, computing, recording, averaging, and justifying grades, and exchanging it for time to collect, save, discuss, and reflect on kids' real work.

But for teachers to change evaluation procedures can be one of the trickiest elements of moving toward Best Practice. We have been concerned to see many well-meaning teachers and aspiring Best Practice districts reinventing evaluation systems that are numbingly complex, that pit kids against each other, that devour teachers' time and goodwill, that cater to the public's hunger for official ranking of children, that promise little formative feedback, and that ultimately threaten to undermine progressive innovation. As we've said, the evaluation obsession runs deep in all of us, and there is always a terrible tendency to bring it back in some new form.

Particularly in the current climate of preoccupation with test scores and mistrust of teachers and schools, teachers are understandably susceptible to the evaluation obsession themselves. When we lead a workshop with teachers, we always begin by asking what concerns or topics they would like to discuss during the course. Evaluation is usually the first topic to be mentioned, and it *always* ends up being listed as a top priority of every group. Indeed, we've worked with more than one group of teachers who, given a completely free choice, would spend every single minute of any workshop or course on evaluation alone. To be fair, part of this obsession simply reflects the pressure that teachers feel from the public, taxpayers, the media, state assessments, and so forth. But it also reveals that teachers are, finally, just another group of Americans—and they have acquired the evaluation fixation just as deeply, and in much the same way, as any other citizens.

But let's return to the bright side. As teachers and schools move toward Best Practice, there is a clear mandate for new forms of assessment, evaluation, grading, and reporting student progress. Across subject fields, Best Practice in evaluation means:

- focus on the knowledge and abilities that are key to Best Practice learning, and on complex whole outcomes and performances of writing, reading, researching, and problem solving, rather than only on isolated subskills
- most of the time, use assessment that is formative, not summative
- employ evaluation that is descriptive or narrative, not scored and numerical
- involve students in record keeping and in judging their own work
- triangulate assessments, looking at each child from several angles, by drawing on observation, conversation, artifacts, and performances
- make evaluation activities a part of instruction (as in teacher-student conferences), rather than separate from it
- spend a moderate amount of time on evaluation and assessment, not allowing it to rule one's professional life or consume lots of instruction time
- where possible, abolish or de-emphasize competitive grading systems
- create parent-education programs to help community members understand the value of new approaches—why, for example, a portfolio of work samples is actually a far better indicator of student growth than an "83" or a "B-"

But How Will Kids Do on Standardized Tests While We Make the Transition to New Forms of Teaching? What Evidence Supports All These New Standards?

As new Best Practice teaching approaches are adopted in a school district, everyone wants to know if test scores will go up. Of course, after all we said above about evaluation, it's obvious that we think the current measures are exceedingly poor and that the redesign of educational testing is an urgent priority. But in the meantime, until new and better tests are in place, the questions remain: Will following Best Practice standards improve student learning? And will results on the existing, customary measures show progress as teachers implement Best Practice ideas? The quick answer is an emphatic *yes*. Sixty years of research, recently collected by Connie Weaver (1997), shows strong results for holistic, progressive teaching across the curriculum and up through the grades.

Nevertheless, highly politicized arguments continue to be put forth that "scientific" research on Whole Language and other student-centered approaches doesn't exist or isn't valid. Once these assertions are tossed about, the always skeptical news reporters begin to call and ask, flatfootedly, "What do you think about Whole Language, since there's no scientific proof that it works?" Those of us who work with the research understand that all of it is limited because so many variables are beyond control in any classrooms studied, and we don't have much faith in many of the measures for studying them. However, in spite of the more politically motivated statements sometimes heard, the dozens of research studies done and repeated over many years have confirmed over and over the positive outcomes of a wide range of progressive teaching strategies compared to more traditional ones.

For years, for example, cooperative education researchers have published studies confirming significant achievement gains in a wide range of content areas when classrooms were redesigned to include ample cooperative activity—one of the fundamental components of the Best Practice paradigm (Johnson and Johnson 1991). In the teaching of writing, a meta-analysis of numerous statistical studies by George Hillocks (1986) showed that while activities for engaging students with material and ideas for writing have a strong effect on writing quality, lecture presentations and grammar drills are of little use, or even bring down writing scores.

Similarly, a sixty-year body of research on Whole Language and related literature-based reading programs shows standardized achievement score gains for students in progressive, Whole Language–style programs, not just in regular education but among students with ESL, special education, or disadvantaged backgrounds. Michael Tunnell and James Jacobs, surveying studies up to 1989, listed one after another that reached the same conclusion. Since the efficacy of Whole Language has become a controversial matter, it may help for us to summarize some of the data and its interpretation.

One of the earliest inquiries, a 1968 study by Dorothy Cohen of 285 students in low socioeconomic areas of New York, compared a literature component to the use of basal readers and showed statistically significant higher test scores for the students in the literature-focused group. Another group of researchers, Bernice Cullinan, Angela Jaggar, and Dorothy Strickland, replicated the study six years later, in 1974, with the same results. Tunnell and Jacobs describe no less than eight additional studies supporting similar conclusions for a wide range of student populations.

A review of more recent studies of teaching beginning reading in primary classrooms from 1991 through 1996 reveals the following tally (the specific studies are listed by category in the bibliography at the end of this section; for summaries, see Sam Weintraub, *Summary of Investigations Related to Reading*, volumes for 1992 through 1997):

- fifteen studies that validate the comparative effectiveness, at a statistically significant level, of one or another particular element used in progressive and Whole Language classrooms
- five studies showing statistically significant higher test scores in broader Whole Language classrooms than in traditional classrooms using basal texts and worksheets
- two smaller case studies showing effectiveness of Whole Language strategies
- one study showing no difference between a Whole Language and a traditional classroom, and two showing no difference in effectiveness of a particular Whole Language element

It's important to recognize that in just about every one of these studies, skills are also taught through direct teaching, along with and integrated into the more student-centered and whole-book activities. It is the most effective *balance* of strategies that we and these researchers are talking about.

"Scientific" study of human behavior, however, is never simple. Studies of the effectiveness of phonics, phonemic awareness, or the highly structured approach called "direct instruction" also showed positive results—five large-scale studies in all, in our tally over the five-year period. One case study comparing Whole Language, Direct Instruction, and use of a basal series found all three engendered the growth of normal first-grade children (McIntyre 1993).

One reason for these seemingly contradictory results is that teachers and researchers have differing definitions of "reading," and consequently test differing aspects of it. Studies of progressive strategies usually test children's reading *comprehension*. Researchers who believe separate decoding skills are more important understandably use tests that check those skills. In fact, we found nine studies that seemed to show how children in classrooms using differing approaches simply tended to improve most in the approach stressed in their particular classroom. Often, the phonics programs showed better performance in tests of phonics skills but no difference in reading comprehension. There was crossover, however, in several cases in which children in progressive classrooms were found to do just as well or better on phonics even when the teaching did not stress it (Carlburg et al. 1992; Griffith et al. 1992).

Further, research looks not only at what "works" in classrooms, but also attempts to analytically describe what reading and other forms of learning *are*, what mental activities they consist of. It is these understandings that are supposedly used to construct standardized tests, as well as to guide instruction in the first place. Here, the philosophical and ideological controversy is intense between those who argue that reading is primarily an act of accurately decoding sounds and those who emphasize and investigate the many other cognitive acts involved, including recognizing grammatical and syntactical relationships and understanding words and sentences by means of various contexts—previous parts of the written piece, other texts the reader has read or heard, and the reader's experience. Again, decades of thorough research, including Ken Goodman's (et al. 1989) landmark studies of miscue analysis, have explored and confirmed the complex nature of reading, and have shown that even very beginning readers seek meaning as they read, rather than simply decoding sounds (Martens 1997; Bloome and Dail 1997).

At the same time, once again, researchers with other points of view design experiments that appear to confirm their beliefs. We're not saying it's all just "relative"; but it's not a simple picture either. Part of the controversy is about what people *believe is most important* in educating children. Part of it is about the nature of the balance and relationship between skills and broader comprehension of reading. And part of the issue is about *how* skills or ideas are taught—through isolated drills and worksheets or in the context of active involvement with real reading. Meanwhile, many teachers work to strike a balance, addressing as many of the aspects of reading as they can. Some versions of this balance appear to us to work very harmoniously, efficiently helping children with whatever elements of the process they need support in; other versions, when not well thought out or responsive to the needs children present, may seem chaotic and confusing. A well-organized, detailed, and judicious review of much of the research on all aspects of this controversy is provided in Jane Braunger and Jan Lewis' *Building a Knowledge Base in Reading* (1997).

Some of the most interesting and inspiring research comes from teacher-researchers, who are simultaneously bringing Best Practice to their students and carefully tracking its impact. One of our favorite examples of this data comes from Carol Carlson, a junior high teacher in a Chicago suburb who monitored her team's implementation of a workshop-style classroom as the kids started the program in seventh grade and continued through eighth. Because much of the controversy centers at the beginning stages of literacy, it's important for us to look at the effect of progressive strategies at the upper grades as well. Following are Carol's descriptions of the kids and the program, just as she reported it, including standardized test scores for her students over the phase-in of the workshop.

The Starblazers, Mannheim Junior High

105 middle school students
Heterogeneously grouped
Lower-middle-income community
Twenty percent Hispanic
Mainstreamed LD students included

Writing program = writing workshop, forty-five minutes daily
Reading program = mixed workshop and guided, forty-five minutes daily
Grades = once per term on portfolios, via conference + 10 percent for
"Daily Oral Language" exercises

CALIFORNIA ACHIEVEMENT TEST RESULTS

	Language Mechanics	Language Expression	Total Language
1990—6th	10.2	8.3	8.8
1991—7th	10.2	9.4	9.8
1992—8th	12.9	12.9	12.9

What we first notice in looking at this data is its "Lake Wobegon effect," the phenomenon that on most American standardized tests, all kids turn out to be "above average," even students from ordinary middle-class schools like Mannheim Junior High. But looking at these grade-level scores relatively, they show exactly the kinds of changes one might expect when teachers move toward new, student-centered classroom structures. In the first year of implementation, language expression rises as kids' fluency grows from increased writing practice time, choosing their own topics, regularly enjoying an audience, and so forth. Then, in the second year—as kids continue to write daily, constantly revising, editing, and publishing their work, and consistently meeting with their teachers in conferences—the mechanics score rises along with another sizeable jump in expression.

As another check on her findings, Carol looked back at the last year she herself taught eighth graders through the old teacher-centered model and came up with these figures:

	Language Mechanics	Language Expression	Total Language
1990B	10.7	9.9	10.3

All these findings gave Carol and her colleagues the boost of confidence they needed to stay with the workshop and move on the next level of innovation. Although it wasn't needed in Carol's district, the research also could have been used to persuade administrators, parents, or board members that teachers' instructional choices were valid and valuable. Carol's research serves as a good reminder to teachers: if you want evidence that Best Practice can work for your kids, you needn't wait for university researchers or government agencies to provide the data you seek—you can do great, powerful research yourself.

Suggested Readings on Authentic Assessment

Azwell, Tara and Elizabeth Schmar. 1995. *Report Card on Report Cards: Alternatives to Consider.* Portsmouth, NH: Heinemann.

Campbell-Hill, Bonnie, and Cynthia Ruptic. 1994. *Practical Aspects of Authentic Assessment*. Norwood, MA: Christopher-Gordon.

Graves, Donald, and Bonnie Sunstein. 1992. *Portfolio Portraits*. Portsmouth, NH: Heinemann.

Harp, Bill. 1991. *Assessment and Evaluation in Whole Language Classrooms*. Norwood, MA: Christopher-Gordon.

Hein, George, and Sabra Price. 1994. *Active Assessment for Active Science*. Portsmouth, NH: Heinemann.

Johnston, Peter. 1997. *Knowing Literacy: Constructive Literacy Assessment*. York, ME: Stenhouse.

Moon, Jean, and Linda Schulman. 1995. *Finding Connections: Linking Assessment, Instruction, and Curriculum in Elementary Mathematics*. Portsmouth, NH: Heinemann.

Nickell, Pat, ed. 1992. "Student Assessment in Social Studies." Theme issue of *Social Education*. (February).

Porter, Carol and Janell Cleland. 1995. *The Portfolio as a Learning Strategy*. Portsmouth, NH: Boynton/Cook.

Rhodes, Lynn, and Nancy Shanklin. 1993. *Windows into Literacy*. Portsmouth, NH: Heinemann.

Stenmark, Jean Kerr. 1991. *Mathematics Assessment: Myths, Models, Good Questions, and Practical Suggestions*. Reston, VA: National Council of Teachers of Mathematics.

Theme Issues on Assessment. *Educational Leadership*. December 1996, October 1994, and March 1994.

Tierney, Robert, Mark Carter, and Laura Desau, eds. 1991. *Portfolio Assessment in the Reading-Writing Classroom*. Norwood, MA: Christopher-Gordon.

Weaver, Connie. 1997. *Creating Support for Effective Literacy Education*. Portsmouth, NH: Heinemann.

Valencia, Sheila, Elfrieda Hiebert, and Peter Afflerbach, eds. 1994. *Authentic Reading Assessment*. Newark, DE: International Reading Association.

Wiggins, Grant. 1998. *Educative Assessment: Designing Assessments to Inform and Improve Student Performance*. San Francisco: Jossey-Bass.

Woodward, Helen. 1994. *Negotiated Evaluation: Involving Children and Parents in the Process*. Portsmouth, NH: Heinemann.

Research on Effectiveness of Best Practice Strategies

Statistical Studies Supporting Whole Language

Carlburg, Joanne, and William Eller. 1992. "Whole Language Learners: Are They Acquiring Word Attack Skills?" *The Keystone Reader*. 15 (Spring): 17–18.

Eldredge, Lloyd. 1991. "An Experiment with a Modified Whole Language Approach in First-Grade Classrooms." *Reading Research and Instruction* 30 (Spring): 21–38.

Griffith, Priscilla, Janell Klesius, and Jeffrey Kromrey. 1992. "The Effect of Phonemic Awareness on the Literacy Development of First-Grade Children in a Traditional or a Whole Language Classroom." *Journal of Research in Childhood Education* 6 (Spring-Summer): 85–92.

Milligan, Jerry, and Herbert Berg. 1992. "The Effect of Whole Language on the Comprehending Ability of First-Grade Children." *Reading Improvement* 29 (Fall): 146–154.

Taylor, Barbara, Ruth Short, Barbara Frye, and Brenda Shearer. 1992. "Classroom Teachers Prevent Reading Failure Among Low-Achieving First-Grade Students." *The Reading Teacher* 45 (April): 592–597.

Case Studies Supporting Whole Language

Berger, Melody. 1992. "Whole Language or Basal-Based Phonetics . . . Which Approach is Better in First Grade?" *WSRA Journal* 36 (Summer): 13–16.

Freppon, Penny A. 1991. "Children's Concepts of the Nature and Purpose of Reading in Different Instructional Settings." *Journal of Reading Behavior* 23 (June): 139–163.

Statistical Study in Which Whole Language Made No Difference

Klesius, Janell P., Priscilla Griffith, and Paula Zielonka. 1991. "A Whole Language and Traditional Instruction Comparison: Overall Effectiveness and Development of the Alphabetic Principle." *Reading Research and Instruction* 30 (Winter): 47–61.

Statistical Studies Supporting Particular Strategies Connected with Whole Language

Anderson, Richard, Ian Wilkinson, and Jana Mason. 1991. "A Microanalysis of the Small-Group, Guided Reading Lesson: Effects of an Emphasis on Global Story Meaning." *Reading Research Quarterly* 26: 417–441.

Baumann, James, and Bette Bergeron. 1993. "Story Map Instruction Using Children's Literature: Effects on First Graders' Comprehension of Central Narrative Elements." *Journal of Reading Behavior* 25: 407–437.

Bunt, Norene A. 1993-94. "An Experimental Comparison of Whole Language and Traditional Methods of Spelling Instruction in First-Grade Classrooms." *Journal of Clinical Reading* 4: 18–27.

Cunningham, Anne E. 1990. "Explicit Versus Implicit Instruction in Phonemic Awareness." *Journal of Experimental Child Psychology* 50 (December): 429–444.

Downhower, Sarah, and Karen Brown. 1992. "The Effects of Predictable Material on First-Graders' Reading Comprehension: A Teacher Action Research Study." *Ohio Reading Teacher* 26 (Winter): 3–10.

Foley, Christy, and Shelly Davidson. 1993. "Supplementing Kindergarten Basal Reading with Language Experience, Echo Reading, and Repeated Reading." *Contemporary Issues in Reading* 8 (Spring): 95–100.

Jenkins, Cynthia, and Dianne Lawler. 1990. "Questioning Strategies in Content Area Reading: One Teacher's Example." *Reading Improvement* 27 (Summer): 133–138.

McCarthy, Patricia, Robert Newby, and Donna Recht. 1995. "Results of an Early Intervention Program for First-Grade Children At Risk for Reading Disability." *Reading Research and Instruction* 34 (Summer): 273–294.

Morrow, Lesley. 1990. "Small-Group Story Readings: The Effects on Children's Comprehension and Responses to Literature." *Reading Research and Instruction* 29 (Summer): 1–17.

Neuman, Susan, and Cathleen Soundy. 1991. "The Effects of 'Storybook Partnerships' on Young Children's Conceptions of Stories." In *Learner Factors/ Teacher Factors Issues in Literacy Research and Instruction.* Edited by Jerry Zutell and Sandra McCormick. Chicago: National Reading Conference, 141–47.

Nielsen-Corcoran, Diane. 1993. "The Effects of Four Models of Group Interaction with Storybooks on the Literacy Growth of Low-Achieving Kindergarten Children." In *Examining Central Issues in Literacy Research, Theory, and Practice.* Edited by Donald Leu and Charles Kinzer. Chicago: National Reading Conference, 279–287.

Reutzel, D. Ray, and Paul Hollingsworth. 1991. "Using Literature Webbing for Books with Predictable Narrative: Improving Young Readers' Prediction, Comprehension, and Story Structure Knowledge." *Reading Psychology* 12 (October–December): 319–333.

Reutzel, D. Ray, Paul Hollingsworth, and Lloyd Eldridge. 1994. "Oral Reading Instruction: The Impact on Student Reading Development." *Reading Research Quarterly* 29: 41–62.

Soundy, Catherine. 1991. "Classroom Comparisons of Young Children Reading Collaboratively." *Reading Instruction Journal* 34 (Fall): 13–16.

Wham, Mary Ann, and Susan Davis Lenski. 1994. "Dialogue Journals As a Vehicle for Preservice Teachers to Experience the Writing Process." *Reading Horizons* 35: 62–70.

Case Studies Supporting Particular Strategies Connected with Whole Language

Dahl, Karin, and Penny Freppon. 1995. "A Comparison of Innercity Children's Interpretations of Reading and Writing Instruction in the Early Grades in Skills-Based and Whole Language Classrooms." *Reading Research Quarterly* 30: 50–74.

Dixon-Krauss, Lisbeth. 1992. "Whole Language: Bridging the Gap from Spontaneous to Scientific Concepts." *Journal of Reading Education* 18 (Fall): 16–26.

————— . 1995. "Partner Reading and Writing: Peer Social Dialogue and the Zone of Proximal Development." *Journal of Reading Behavior* 27 (March): 45–63.

Richards, Janet. 1996. "'They Don't Teach the Skills!': Promoting a University-School-Family Literacy Project." *Journal of Reading Education* 21 (Spring): 28–42.

Wollman-Bonilla, Julie, and Barbara Werchadlo. 1995. "Literature Response Journals in a First-Grade Classroom." *Language Arts* 72 (December): 562–570.

Statistical Studies in Which Strategies Made No Difference

Longino, Linda. 1994. "Get the Facts with K-W-L." *Kansas Journal of Reading* 10 (Spring): 12–16.

Ross, Steven, and Lana Smith. 1994. "Effects of the Success for All Model on Kindergarten Through Second-Grade Reading Achievement, Teachers' Adjustment, and Classroom-School Climate at an Inner-City School." *The Elementary School Journal* 95 (November): 121–138.

Statistical Studies Supporting Phonics or Direct Instruction

Bond, Carole, Steven Ross, Lana Smith, and John Nunnery. 1995–96. "The Effects of the Sing, Spell, Reading, and Write Program on Reading Achievement of Beginning Readers." *Reading Research and Instruction* 35: 122–141.

Foorman, Barbara, David Francis, Diane Novy, and Dov Liberman. 1991. "How Letter-Sound Instruction Mediates Progress in First-Grade Reading and Spelling." *Journal of Educational Psychology* 83 (December): 456–469.

Griffith, Priscilla, Janell Klesius, and Jeffrey Kromrey. 1992. "The Effect of Phonemic Awareness on the Literacy Development of First-Grade Children in a Traditional or a Whole Language Classroom." *Journal of Research in Childhood Education* 6 (Spring-Summer): 85–92.

Snider, Vicki E. 1990. "Direct Instruction Reading with Average First-Graders." *Reading Improvement* 27 (Summer): 143–148.

Uhry, Joanna, and Margaret Shepherd. 1993. "Segmentation/Spelling Instruction as Part of First-Grade Reading Program: Effects on Several Measures of Reading." *Reading Research Quarterly* 28: 219–233.

Case Study Supporting Phonics

Morgan, Kenneth. 1995. "Creative Phonics: A Meaning-Oriented Reading Program." *Intervention in School and Clinic* 30 (May): 287–291.

Studies Showing How Students Tended to Learn Whichever Approaches Were Taught

Campbell, Robin, and Gillian Stott. 1994. "Children's Experience of Learning to Read." *Reading* 28 (November): 8–13.

McIntyre, Ellen. 1992. "Young Children's Reading Behaviors in Various Classroom Contexts." *Journal of Reading Behavior* 24 (September): 339–371.

———. 1993. "Decoding Skills and Successful Beginning Reading in Different Instructional Settings." *Reading Horizons* 34: 122–136.

McIntyre, Ellen, and Penny Freppon. 1994. "A Comparison of Children's Development of Alphabetic Knowledge in a Skill-Based and a Whole Language Classroom." *Research in the Teaching of English* 28 (December): 391–417.

Torgeson, Joseph, Sharon Morgan, and Charlotte Davis. 1992. "Effects of Two Types of Phonological Awareness Training on Word Learning in Kindergarten Children." *Journal of Educational Psychology* 84 (September): 364–370.

What About Tracking and Ability Grouping?

One of the signal contributions of recent educational research has been the explicit rejection of tracking and the affirmation of heterogeneous grouping. One of the most shameful and unnecessary practices in American schools has been the routine division of children into separate classrooms or instructional groups on the basis of "ability." Indeed, one of the earliest common experiences of most American schoolchildren (which many remember clearly and painfully as adults) is being assigned to either the low, middle, or high reading group—sometimes disguised with cutesy and, to the children, entirely transparent, euphemistic names like "Bluebirds," "Robins," and "Owls." Thanks to researchers like Jeannie Oakes (1990) and Anne Wheelock (1992), we now have conclusive evidence that such ability grouping is academically *harmful* to kids labeled low and middle—their measured achievement is depressed when they are segregated by levels. The evidence of tracking's benefits for "high" kids is slight, ambiguous, and still under hot debate among achievement researchers. This set of findings is certainly no ringing mandate for the widespread grouping practices that exist in most schools. And then there are the social effects of ability grouping: interpersonally, tracking is destructive for *everyone*, and tends to undermine the American values of democracy, diversity, and pluralism.

Ability grouping is a fact of life in most American schools, and it will take some time to dismantle it. Most elementary teachers have been trained to teach reading in those three leveled groups. Even though we now understand that this arrangement will shortchange most children in the room, teachers will continue to use it until two things happen: (1) they have an alternative structure that they feel comfortable using; and (2) they receive administrative support and encouragement to make the change.

The good news is that the key ingredients of Best Practice classrooms—the six structures outlined in Chapter 8—offer specific models of how heterogeneous grouping can work. Classrooms run as workshops, using learning logs, cooperative groups, conferences, and other such activities, are *inherently individualized*. Every student doesn't need to be at the same level for the class to work together, for various temporary teams to be formed, for the teacher to teach one-on-one. In a writing workshop, for example, kids pick their own topics for writing, work at their own level in developing their drafts, conference with the teacher, join in heterogeneous peer writing groups to respond and help with writing in progress, and so forth. When the teacher observes that a number of students need instruction on a particular skill or concept, she may, for efficiency, draw this group aside for a particular lesson, while the other students continue to work—after which the subgroup rejoins the whole.

This is a rich, collaborative, active design for learning—but there is absolutely no need to track such a class and no benefit in doing so. Indeed, such communities of writers usually find that they prefer a wide range of values, experiences, responses, styles, and attitudes among their classroom audience. Teachers like the workshop classroom because all the students' writing is different—instead of grading 125 identical essays on "The Color Symbolism in *The Scarlet Letter*" (assignments that ultimately leave the teacher who made them bored and angry on Sunday afternoons), they receive a rich array of self-selected, varied writings for which they can be genuine, open readers.

When teachers say they prefer tracked classes, or claim that mixed-ability groups are harder to teach, they are being sincere. But they also are usually envisioning classes run in one, traditional way: teacher-directed, presentational, whole-class, lecture-test instruction. Indeed, the durability of ability grouping in schools has always stemmed from teachers' devotion to this single model of teaching. In this familiar kind of classroom, the teacher is the center: she or he tells, presents, explains, and gives assignments. When they are not listening to the teacher and taking notes, students work quietly and individually at their desks, writing answers to questions about what the teacher has presented. The teacher is a pitcher of knowledge; students are vessels being filled up. For students, the day is filled mostly with transforming what they have heard into short written repetitions: blanks filled in, bubbles darkened, and rarely, sentences or paragraphs composed.

In this narrow classroom model, there *is* a premium placed on silence, obedience, and "listening fast," and it feels convenient for teachers to sort kids into groups by squirminess or IQ or whatever factor will make them more amenable to this style of teaching. But once teachers become aware of the much wider repertoire of available classroom structures, ones that work to teach even heavy "content" subjects like math and science to heterogeneous groups, their feeling that tracking is "necessary" fades away.

Suggested Readings on Collaborative Grouping

Cohen, Elizabeth. 1986. *Designing Groupwork: Strategies for the Heterogeneous Classroom*. New York: Teachers College Press.

Daniels, Harvey. 1994. *Literature Circles: Voice and Choice in the Student-Centered Classroom*. York, ME: Stenhouse.

Girard, Suzanne, and Kathlene Willing. 1996. *Partnerships for Classroom Learning: From Reading Buddies to Pen Pals to the Community and the World Beyond*. Portsmouth, NH: Heinemann.

Hill, Bonnie Campbell, and Nancy Johnson. 1995. *Literature Circles and Response*. Norwood, MA: Christopher-Gordon.

Hill, Susan, and Tim Hill. 1990. *The Collaborative Classroom: A Guide to Cooperative Learning*. Portsmouth, NH: Heinemann.

Johnson, David, Roger Johnson, Edythe Holubec, and Patricia Roy. 1991. *Cooperation in the Classroom*. Edina, MN: Interaction Book Company.

Samway, Katharine Davies, and Gail Whang. 1995. *Literature Study Circles in a Multicultural Classroom*. York, ME: Stenhouse.

Samway, Katharine, Gail Whang, and Mary Pippitt. 1995. *Buddy Reading: Cross-age Tutoring in a Multicultural School*. Portsmouth, NH: Heinemann.

Sharan, Yael, and Shlomo Sharan. 1992. *Expanding Cooperative Learning Through Group Investigation*. New York: Teachers College Press.

Spear, Karen. 1987. *Sharing Writing: Peer Response Groups in the English Class*. Portsmouth, NH: Boynton/Cook.

What About Special Education Students?

Our response to the tracking question also expresses most of what needs to be said about children with special learning needs or handicaps: their traditional segregation from the mainstream has not resulted mainly from their differentness, but from the inability of educators to offer classrooms where they could learn along with other children. Again, the key classroom structures outlined in Chapter 8—the ones that lead to a decentralized, student-centered, inherently individualized classroom—invite the mainstreaming of kids with all sorts of difficulties and challenges. This becomes even more practical as special education teachers are increasingly delivering their assistance in the regular classroom, rather than pulling children out of that community.

As with tracking, once we discard the fantasy that everyone in a classroom ought to have the exact same IQ score or exhibit the exact same behaviors or study the exact same content, then a whole new range of appealing, exciting alternatives presents itself. We can follow the advice of educators like Lynn Rhodes and Curt Dudley-Marling (1996), Susan Stires (1991), Janet Allen (1995), and Mary Mercer Krogness (1995), who have shared a variety of strategies for making mainstreaming work in regular Best Practice classrooms. And then, where kids' problems genuinely impede such mainstreaming, we can provide self-contained programs that draw on principles of holistic, integrated learning. These experts have shown us that holistic approaches are not, as some teachers fear, inappropriate for special-education students—on the contrary, they are the answer. For so many such children, the problem is not to accumulate subskills—as the old, dying model of special education had it—but rather to "join the club."

As our colleague and reading teacher Marilyn Bizar says about struggling readers, the initial key is to "get the big picture," to get the gestalt of reading. The same goes for the feel of authorship, the sense of the scientific process, the approach of the problem solver. Above all, special kids need to connect with each school subject in a holistic way (as regular-education kids usually did earlier in life, without much help), to see and feel themselves as thinkers, readers, writers, investigators, scientists, mathematicians, readers, and citizens.

Suggested Readings on Special Needs Students

Allen, Janet. 1995. *It's Never Too Late: Leading Adolescents to Lifelong Literacy.* Portsmouth, NH: Heinemann.

Allen, Jo Beth, and Jana Mason. 1989. *Risk Makers, Risk Takers, Risk Breakers: Reducing the Risks for Young Literacy Learners.* Portsmouth, NH: Heinemann.

Krogness, Mary Mercer. 1995. *Just Teach Me, Mrs. K: Talking, Reading, and Writing with Resistant Adolescent Learners.* Portsmouth, NH: Heinemann.

National Coalititon of Education Activists. *Maintaining Inequality: A Background Packet on Tracking and Ability Grouping.* Rosendale, NY: National Coalition of Education Activists.

Rhodes, Lynn, and Curt Dudley-Marling. 1996. *Readers and Writers with a Difference.* Portsmouth, NH: Heinemann.

Stires, Susan. 1991. *With Promise: Redefining Reading and Writing for Special Students.* Portsmouth, NH: Heinemann.

What About Parents?

Not all contemporary parents immediately support the ideas described in this book. Either individually or in groups, they may object to collaborative learning, untracked classes, journal keeping, independent reading programs, or other structures that are part of the Best Practice paradigm. While parents of many children in progressive classrooms are deeply grateful to the teachers they know have helped their kids, conservative political groups have organized in recent years to demand more of something they prefer—such as phonics or math drills—or less of something they think they oppose, such as "Whole Language." Education sometimes seems more in the hands of politicians than teachers or other knowledgeable professionals, or even the parents themselves.

Why does this happen? To begin with, most American parents were schooled under a quite different educational paradigm, and because these grown-ups naturally feel that they turned out pretty well, they want the same kind of education for their own children. But these parents aren't accurately remembering what school was really like for them, how it felt, or what really worked. Nor are they factoring in the enormous learning they've done outside of school and since school; ironically, people tend to give schools credit for everything they know and can do as forty-year-olds. As a result, they may quite passionately request for their children what they think worked for them—leveled reading groups, Friday spelling tests, red ink spread over writing assignments, or even a few teacherly whacks on the behind.

This phenomenon has another dimension, and James Moffet described it at length in his book *A Storm in the Mountains* (1989). Moffet reminds us that parents in this culture are always deeply ambivalent about passing on the reigns of control and the tools of power to the next generation. While we grown-ups always want the next generation to succeed, we also usually feel that our youngsters are not quite ready, that they need to be protected, that **we** really should run things a bit longer. Moffet says this ambivalence is reflected in American parents' fixation on skills-oriented schooling—activities like diagramming sentences, studying spelling lists, filling out phonics worksheets, memorizing state capitals, computing sheets of decontextualized problems. If schools can keep kids busy with such atomized, essentially meaningless, drills, then their true empowerment is delayed. They are "protected" from big, dangerous ideas—from reading whole, real books or writing their own, potentially serious, ideas. Repeated waves of book censorship are obviously part of this picture; across America, even acknowledged classics are banned from classrooms and libraries by "concerned" parents. It seems that the only approaches to schooling American parents ever passionately advocate are those that take meaning out of the center of the curriculum—and the only kinds of schooling they oppose in any organized fashion are those that allow kids to hear, discuss, and grapple with the major ideas and values of our culture.

Yet when parents and community aren't involved in major district-wide reforms, public misunderstanding is even more likely to undercut the program down the line. We nevertheless have found that enlisting parent support for Best Practice teaching is actually one of the easier elements of the school change process. In schools and districts that have developed comprehensive parent education and involvement programs, parents quickly "buy in" to the new methods and curricula, becoming boosters of the program, participating in the community action and at-home support that are often keys to real curriculum change and improvement in student achievement (Murnane and Levy 1996, 4). How can teachers and principals promote this "buy-in?" Our experience has shown that there are two distinct levels of parental thinking about education. The first, more superficial level is composed of unexamined personal memories mixed with media generalities and educational one-liners. It's from this level of thinking that parents speak up for more skill-and-drill, higher test scores, more ability grouping, and so forth. But at a deeper level, most parents also have some more sophisticated and progressive ideas about education. Surfacing this deeper level of thinking requires reconnecting parents to their own real experience as students. If parent programs take the time to help adults carefully recover the details, events, and feelings of their own schooling, those grown-ups typically come to some very different conclusions about what really worked for them as learners—and what they really want for their own children.

What does a strong parent program look like? We've learned much about this from our friend Jim Vopat, director of the Writing Project and the Parent Project in Milwaukee, Wisconsin, and author of *The Parent Project: A Workshop Approach to Parent Involvement* (1994) and *More Than Bake Sales* (1998). We've conducted parent workshops to explore this deeper understanding in various content areas, but for illustration here we'll focus on writing. To begin with, we invite parents from a building or district to a voluntary evening meeting, usually titled "How to Help Your Child Become Better at Writing (Math, Science, Reading, etc.)." Now, if the leader were to begin this meeting by asking parents what they think the writing curriculum ought to contain, people would quickly offer a list of superficial received wisdom and undistilled nostalgia that would probably include just about everything that's *not* Best Practice. So instead, we start by helping audience members to think back over their lifetime as writers. We do a slow, careful topic search, just like a good writing teacher might in a classroom with kids, taking people step by step back through their writing history, starting with how they used writing earlier this week, and moving back gradually through their adult life, their jobs, their personal writing and correspondence, then moving down through the levels of formal education, and all the way back to the role of writing in their childhood homes.

Our goal is to help people rediscover some key moments or turning points in their development as writers. Although few adults think of themselves as "real" writers, everyone has had memorable experiences with writing, some positive and some negative, and this exercise helps dig up fresh, detailed memories of those moments. So we take a full ten or fifteen minutes pitching these prompts at people, inviting them to make notes as we go: What was the best paper you ever wrote in college (if this is a college-graduate group)? What was the biggest reaction a piece of your writing ever got? Can you remember some of your high school English teachers? What was the most important letter you ever wrote? Where did you do your writing when you had a school assignment? What was the role of writing in your mother's life? Your father's?

Next, we ask everyone to identify one experience that stood out from the rest—either good or bad—an event or moment that was particularly memorable or significant. We hand out 5-x-7 index cards and ask people to quickly write "the story of this experience." We stress that this is a one-shot rough draft, and even joke a bit about how it is not for a grade. After giving people ten minutes to write, we ask them to share with their neighbor, wherever they are sitting. They can read the card aloud, summarize it, or even talk about why they don't want to read it—just share something comfortable. Next we invite volunteers to read their stories to the whole group. Invariably, people start offering their experiences, slowly at first, but with increasing eagerness. Typically, people tell happy stories about writing that was praised or encouraged, about having some kind of real audience, about writing on topics of their own choosing, about writing collaboratively with someone, about writing experiences that were tied in with strong personal relationships. Usually, very few of these happy writing stories happened in school. Alternately, people will volunteer painful, negative experiences with writing, most of which *did* happen in school: they'll tell about endless grammar drills, teachers who drenched papers in red ink or belittled student writers, dry and rigid term-paper assignments, about feeling that writing was painful and they were bad writers.

About this time, we introduce a summary of Best Practice research findings—for writing, we use a handout of fifteen items based on George Hillocks' meta-analysis—and say something like: "We thought you were just an ordinary group of parents—we didn't know that you have all been studying the research on writing instruction!" And we go through the research summary point by point, tying the research findings to the stories the parents have just been telling: praise is more important than criticism in helping writers grow; isolated, rote grammar instruction does not improve writing; writers should choose their own topics; collaboration improves the quality of texts; and the rest. What the research does is validate parents' own personal experience.

At this point, we can explain the Best Practice approach to parents in an especially powerful way: "Remember all those ineffective, hurtful things that happened to you in the name of learning to write? We don't *ever* want those things to happen to your children. And the good, growthful things that happened for you, once in a while along the way? We want those things to happen to your child *every single day.*"

We've done this workshop with groups ranging in size from a half dozen to 250. Each and every time it shows that parents have Best Practice in their hearts, in their guts; they've learned from their own real lives what works and what doesn't in helping children grow. Sometimes, that deep, true knowledge gets distorted by the haze of time and replaced by the superficial educational platitudes spewed through our culture. But happily, that deep understanding can be recovered quickly, and can lead to a true commitment to supporting better ways of teaching and learning.

After this beginning, teachers and parents can build a Best Practice partnership that's strong and enduring. Of course, there are many ingredients to such successful collaboration. Parent Project workshops like Jim Vopat's and those conducted by our parent coordinator Pete Leki, in Chicago, involve a series of Saturday or evening meetings in which, after a start like that described above, parents gain knowledge and plan initiatives on a variety of issues from an agenda they themselves set, from improving kids' reading to neighborhood safety, to computer classes and literature circles for the parents themselves. Teachers contribute to the partnership by participating in the workshops themselves to build strong relationships and by keeping parents informed of the nature of the program and the progress of their kids, using frequent notes or newsletters, go-to-school nights, going over kids' portfolios during parent conferences, making sure that enough work samples go home so that parents always have a sense of what's up. Parents are also a real part of the instructional program in Best Practice classrooms. In the early grades, this might mean setting up regular systems by which parents read aloud with kids each night, or serve as audiences for kids' writing, or do "kitchen science" research together. As they become part of the instructional team in such activities, parents also become important evaluators and recordkeepers, all the way from sending daily reading reports back to the classroom to adding their own observations on the official quarterly report card.

Particularly in areas where parents may not have had positive or extensive educational experiences themselves, they need genuine invitations to participate in the classroom. In elementary grades, Moms and Dads can serve as one-time featured readers, bringing in a favorite children's book to read aloud, or as continuing volunteer editors who help kids prepare their writing for classroom publication. As students get older, parent participation may need to step back a notch, but there are plenty of helpful roles at a distance. For example, we know many schools that have a parent-run publishing center, where groups of volunteer parents regularly meet to print and bind student-written anthologies, books, and magazines. This way, parents can assist in the work of their teenage kids, without anyone having to actually be seen together!

Suggested Readings on Involving Parents

Garlington, Jocelyn A. 1991. *Helping Dreams Survive: The Story of a Project Involving African-American Families in the Education of Their Children.* Washington, DC: National Committee for Citizens in Education.

Henderson, Anne, Carl Marburger, and Theodora Ooms. 1986. *Beyond the Bake Sale: An Educators' Guide to Working with Parents.* Washington, DC: National Committee for Citizens in Education.

Hispanic Policy Development Project. *Together Is Better: Building Strong Partnerships Between Schools and Hispanic Parents.* Washington, DC: Hispanic Policy Development Project.

National School Boards Association. *First Teachers: Parental Involvement in the Public Schools.* Baltimore, MD: National School Boards Association.

Vopat, James. 1994. *The Parent Project: A Workshop Approach to Parent Involvement.* York, ME: Stenhouse.

————. 1998. *Beyond Bake Sales.* York, ME: Stenhouse.

How Does Best Practice Connect with Movements Like Whole Language, Language Across the Curriculum, and Integrated Curriculum?

All of the issues raised in this chapter revolve around the fact that curriculum change doesn't occur in a vacuum. When a teacher decides to approach biology or American history in a new way, she must also think about a whole range of related pieces in the complex culture called school—from grading to standardized test pressures, to tracking, to parents, and onward. Now, in this book we've described Best Practice strategies for each of the major school subjects separately, because we wanted to show how they're all converging on the same underlying progressive philosophy. However, some important educational movements in this country strive to embody the principles we've outlined in a more fully integrated way that transforms many of the aspects of school all together.

Before we briefly discuss each movement, we want to say a word about integration itself. The curriculum theorist and middle school leader James Beane defines two important dimensions of genuine educational integration:

> First, integration implies wholeness and unity rather than separation and fragmentation. Second, real curriculum integration occurs when young people confront personally meaningful questions and engage in experiences related to those questions—experiences they can integrate into their own system of meanings. When we seek to integrate the curriculum, we need to inquire into the questions and meanings that young people create rather than contrive connections across academically constructed subject boundaries.

Beane adds a further crucial point: that boundary-breeching thematic or interdisciplinary units are not automatically integrative, especially if teachers construct and conduct them without genuinely sharing responsibility with students.

Whole Language

Whole Language is a strong, grassroots movement of mostly elementary teachers. All around the country, teachers gather in local TAWL (Teachers Applying Whole Language) groups, attend conferences, and study the books of Ken Goodman, Regie Routman, Nancie Atwell, and others. Their fundamental theoretical orientation is psycholinguistic; that is, Whole Language teachers want to make the classroom a scaffolded language-learning environment that parallels the natural, efficient learning of home and community. In practice, strong Whole Language teachers follow virtually all the principles of the progressive model outlined in this book. Mature Whole Language classrooms are child-centered, sociable, cognitive places where students are deployed in choice-rich reading and writing workshops, conferences with peers and adults, and thematic group investigations, places where essential skills in writing, reading, math, science are effectively taught within these activities. Without question, Whole Language is the largest, strongest, and most coherent manifestation of the neo-progressive movement in American schools. Although it is now large enough to have its own set of internal frictions and factions, Whole Language has mostly retained its bottom-up politics and its steadfast philosophical orientation. The movement is also well supplied with books that we won't rewrite here, but have listed among the suggested readings at the end of this chapter.

These Whole Language pioneers have had some special advantages where change is concerned. Because most elementary teachers still have a single group of children for the whole day and are responsible for all subjects, they enjoy some latitude and time to experiment. Putting administrative constraints aside (which is not always easy), an elementary teacher who wants to change, to seek integration, to move toward Whole Language is free to do so within the six-hour day that she and her children spend together. For teachers in these self-contained classrooms, breaking down subject barriers and integrating instruction doesn't require a faculty vote or a working team of colleagues; often, it's simply an individual, professional decision.

Once schooling becomes departmentalized, typically beginning around fifth or sixth grade, experimentation gets trickier. The cellular organization, bell schedule, and specialized faculty become major barriers to innovation, and especially to multisubject integration. Still, individual secondary teachers can move toward integration in their own forty-five-minute blocks by making the class more whole, more active, more collaborative, more experiential—as some of their colleagues from the lower grades might say, "more Whole Language." If a progressive math teacher cannot enlist English, science, and other colleagues to create a wider program, then she can at least implement many of the elements of Best Practice on her own limited turf, as many of the teachers introduced in this book have done.

Of course, there is also the broader resistance to change and progressive teaching and learning that we've talked about. Attacks on Whole Language have involved considerable misinformation and caricaturization by critics, and indeed, some unfortunate dogmatism on the part of some Whole Language advocates themselves. Often, a district will announce a reform initiative involving *some* aspects of Whole Language, such as using published children's literature, and conduct a few inadequate inservice activities about it. Then only a fraction of teachers actually adopt the program, many do it poorly, and when reading scores go down or don't improve, "Whole Language" is blamed. In too many such places, it was never really tried.

Repeatedly, critics assert that Whole Language teachers don't teach reading skills, don't teach spelling, or don't attend to the learning styles of individual students or tendencies of particular cultural groups, leaving children to flounder when allowed to work independently. Whole Language theorists sometimes have fed this impression by failing to acknowledge and talk about the many ways that good Whole Language teachers *do,* in fact, very carefully observe children's needs and address them assertively, designing specific "mini-lessons" to help the children who haven't yet learned how to choose a book on their own, or to recognize some letter sounds in reading, or to use quotation marks in writing dialogue (see Patricia Cunningham's *Phonics They Use* [1995] for an excellent collection of strategies for teaching decoding integrated effectively with meaningful literacy activities).

Because this is a very political controversy—reflecting deep beliefs about how people's minds work, what school should look like, even what its function is in our society—the disagreements will continue, no matter how much research is quoted, how much explanation offered. But we invite the reader to visit some of the powerful progressive classrooms that we've seen and that we know exist in every city, many of them in the poorest and most troubled neighborhoods, and observe for yourself as children eagerly read and write and work at science centers and participate actively in well-conducted lessons. Kneel down next to a second grader and ask him or her to share what's being read or written or investigated. Watch the kids excitedly begin on their tasks, politely and cheerfully work and move about the room, and share their sense of fun and accomplishment. Watch the teacher calmly, even lovingly, get them back on track when a conflict erupts. If you have children in school yourself, compare which approaches turn them on and which don't. And decide for yourself what works.

Critical Literacy

Another steadily growing integrative trend, this one rooted mostly in secondary schools, is Critical Literacy (sometimes called "Writing and Reading Across the Curriculum"), a movement that brings the strategies of writing-to-learn and critical reading to the so-called content areas. Typically, what this means is showing science, math, shop, physical education, history, and other teachers some of the key experiential, cognitive, and collaborative strategies that have been developed mostly in literacy education and adapting them to the new subject matter. For example, students and teachers in any classroom can learn to harness the power of writing strategies such as clustering, free-writing, learning logs, and peer editing, and reading strategies such as predicting, reading aloud, literature circles, and semantic mapping. While spreading these activities through a school does not abolish the customary departments, it does have some positive effects. First of all, the staff development effort itself, the inservice program in which teachers learn these ideas, typically provides an important faculty conversation about the nature of learning, teaching, and evaluation. For students in the classroom, these new activities may help their teachers break the presentational habit and create a more active, cognitive, and collaborative classroom. Critical literacy, at its best, opens the door for teachers to a wider conception of thinking and learning processes in their own subjects, and invites cooperation among faculty.

Integrated Learning Programs

Beyond change within individual secondary classrooms, there is a diffuse and modest national trend toward interdisciplinary, thematic programs, in which groups of teachers and students identify large chunks of subject matter within or beyond the traditional curriculum, develop a new class and schedule, and go to work. The most venerable and familiar version of this is American Studies, which coauthor Harvey Daniels taught twenty years ago. In American Studies, one social studies teacher and one English teacher are assigned two groups of students and two periods a day to intertwine American history and literature.

Today, some educators, many of them working in middle schools, are showing the way to embody truly progressive principles in such interdisciplinary programs. As Jim Beane (1991) stresses, the fullest, most meaningful form doesn't just offer links between separate courses or feature teachers' highly structured designs, but rather puts the students' choice and authority at the core. At Marquette Middle School in Madison, Wisconsin, under the guidance of teacher-researcher Barbara Brodhagen, teachers and students design and undertake studies that become a grade level's or the school's entire curriculum. As reported by Beane (see also Brodhagen 1995), the program begins when students brainstorm questions about themselves and their world, identifying categories of shared curiosity within their lists, and eventually deciding on the main theme. For the particular year Beane describes, the topic was "Living in the Future." Next, students list activities that could help them answer the questions they have raised, and then organize themselves into investigating teams. Beane tells what eventually resulted for the sample year:

> One (project) involved designing a model for the city of Madison for the year 2020 and required integrating the work of committees on the environment, transportation, government, education, and health. Another activity called for investigating family health histories to determine personal risk factors in the future. A third brought an artist into the school to sketch pictures of how the kids might look in 30 years and to discuss the physical effects of aging. A fourth involved creating, distributing, tabulating, and analyzing a survey sent to several middle schools to find out what their peers predicted for the future. Still another activity found students investigating the accuracy of predictions made for this century 100 years ago.

These energizing investigations require students to use a wide variety of thinking skills: researching, reading, writing, debating, tabulating, calculating, graphing, charting, experimenting, interviewing, presenting, drawing, and so on. Key underlying features of the program include a strong student voice in planning, the constructivist assumption that students can make their own meanings, the jigsawing of a huge knowledge base, the blending of affect and cognition as students pursue personally relevant topics, and the fact that the program was not a segment of the day or a temporary treat—it was the whole curriculum. Perhaps most emblematic, "Living in the Future" will never be repeated at Marquette Middle School—not unless the next group of students who start the process authentically arrives at the exact same decision after listing their own questions about themselves and their world.

While such interdisciplinary programs can be genuinely progressive, they don't always work this way. For example, in Los Angeles, a nationally noted interdisciplinary high school program called "Humanitas" illustrates both the benefits and the difficulties of such ambitious innovations in secondary schools. "Humanitas" is basically a thematic three-period high school course in English, social studies, and art. Three teachers are given paid summer planning time to develop courses around themes such as "The Protestant Ethic and the Spirit of Capitalism" or "Women, Race, and Social Protest." Students meet in these three classes daily, and teachers have an hour of common planning time. According to a laudatory article by the project's official outside evaluator (Aschbacher 1991), "Humanitas" has many positive effects on students: they score higher on standardized tests, they write better essays, and they have a higher rate of school retention. These are significant and valuable outcomes, and the quality of time kids spend in this daily block is evidently more involving and challenging than the rest of their school day.

However, the Humanitas program has shortcomings that compromise the full embodiment of progressive practice. Teachers plan the courses by themselves, in the summer. While they undoubtedly take student interests into account, there is no official provision for any student involvement, goal setting, or decision making—or, for that matter, any mention of student collaboration within any strand of the course. Project research shows that Humanitas pupils spend more time in substantive discussions than students in regular classes—six minutes more per day, to be exact. This is a disturbingly modest achievement for any program claiming progressive ambitions. The official project report mentions that "some" Humanitas faculty team-teach upon occasion, but apparently the standard deployment of Humanitas students is still groups of thirty kids who cycle for one period each among the three teachers.

One of the highlighted aspects of the teachers' summer work is that they "develop essay questions early in the unit-planning process to clarify their objectives in teaching about the theme, to identify the significant issues to discuss, and to guide their selection of materials and lesson plans." This pre-planning of evaluation would seem to constrict digressions during the course and to exert great pressure against reorienting the program in response to students, or giving time to interests or questions discovered along the way.

The one sample essay question featured in the evaluator's report begins: "The cosmology of a traditional culture permeates every aspect of that culture. This is illustrated in the following three cultural groups: the Eskimos, the Southwest Indians, and the Meso-Americans. Specifically, discuss the spirit world that each group believed in, and explain how it influenced their culture and values . . ." If every student must write on predetermined questions like this one, then Humanitas is not an integrated program as we and James Beane define it, but rather a refined, polished, elegant delivery system for traditional teacher-centered, transmission-oriented instruction.

We have no wish to malign this generally admirable program or to overly exalt the Marquette project. We simply aim to illustrate the inherent difficulties of large-scale multidisciplinary programs. If teachers merely throw together the ingredients of existing courses and then present this material to students in the same old way, then no meaningful form of curriculum integration—or Best Practice—has been achieved. Students might well be better off following the bell schedule from one room to another if the teachers in those forty-five-minute segments are practicing progressive principles within their cells.

Suggested Readings on Whole Language and Some of Its Components

Atwell, Nancie. 1998. *In the Middle: Writing and Reading and Learning with Teenagers*. Portsmouth, NH: Boynton/Cook.

Braunger, Jane, and Jan Lewis. 1997. *Building a Knowledge Base in Reading*. Northwest Regional Educational Laboratory, National Council of Teachers of English, and International Reading Association (copublishers).

Crafton, Linda. 1991. *Whole Language: Getting Started, Moving Forward*. New York: Richard C. Owen.

Cunningham, Patricia. 1995. *Phonics They Use: Words for Reading and Writing* (Second Edition). New York: Harper Collins.

Daniels, Harvey. 1994. *Literature Circles: Voice and Choice in the Student-Centered Classroom*. York, ME: Stenhouse.

Edelsky, Carole, Bess Altwerger, and Barbara Flores. 1990. *Whole Language: What's the Difference?* Portsmouth, NH: Heinemann.

Goodman, Kenneth. 1988. *What's Whole in Whole Language*. Portsmouth, NH: Heinemann.

Goodman, Kenneth, E. Brooks Smith, Robert Meredith, and Yetta Goodman. 1987. *Language and Thinking in School: A Whole Language Curriculum*. New York: Richard C. Owen.

Graves, Donald. 1994. *A Fresh Look at Writing*. Portsmouth, NH: Heinemann.

Hansen, Jane. 1987. *When Writers Read*. Portsmouth, NH: Heinemann.

Heald-Taylor, Gail. 1989. *The Administrator's Guide to Whole Language*. New York: Richard C. Owen.

Manning, Gary, and Maryann Manning, eds. 1989. *Whole Language: Beliefs and Practices K–8*. Washington, DC: National Education Association.

Mayher, John. 1990. *Uncommon Sense: Theoretical Practice in Language Education*. Portsmouth, NH: Boynton/Cook.

Peterson, Ralph, and Maryann, Eeds. 1990. *Grand Conversations: Literature Groups in Action*. Ontario, Canada: Scholastic.

Rief, Linda. 1992. *Seeking Diversity: Language Arts with Adolescents*. Portsmouth, NH: Heinemann.

Routman, Regie. 1988. *Transitions: From Literature to Literacy*. Portsmouth, NH: Heinemann.

———. 1991. *Invitations: Changing as Teachers and Learners*. Portsmouth, NH: Heinemann.

———. 1996. *Literacy at the Crossroads: Crucial Talk About Reading, Writing, and Other Teaching Dilemmas*. Portsmouth, NH: Heinemann.

Shanahan, Timothy. 1990. *Reading and Writing Together*. Norwood, MA: Christopher-Gordon.

Short, Kathy, Jerome Harste, and Marilyn Burke. 1995. *Creating Classrooms for Authors and Inquirers* (Second Edition). Portsmouth, NH: Heinemann.

Weaver, Constance. 1990. *Understanding Whole Language*. Portsmouth, NH: Heinemann.

———, ed. 1997. *Lessons to Share on Teaching Grammar in Context*. Portsmouth, NH: Heinemann.

Suggested Readings on Critical Literacy and Integrated Curriculum

Bayer, Anne Shea. 1990. *Collaborative-Apprenticeship Learning: Language and Thinking Across the Curriculum K–12*. Mountain View, CA: Mayfield.

Boomer, Garth, Nancy Lester, Cynthia Onore, and Jon Cook. 1992. *Negotiating the Curriculum: Educating for the 21st Century*. Washington, DC: The Falmer Press.

Five, Cora Lee, and Marie Dionisio. 1995. *Bridging the Gap: Integrating Curriculum in Upper Elementary and Middle Schools*. Portsmouth, NH: Heinemann.

Fulwiler, Toby. 1987. *The Journal Book*. Portsmouth, NH: Boynton/Cook.

Manning, Maryann, Gary Manning, and Roberta Long. 1994. *Theme Immersion: Inquiry-Based Curriculum in Elementary and Middle Schools*. Portsmouth, NH: Heinemann.

Short, Kathy, et al. 1996. *Learning Together Through Inquiry: From Columbus to Integrated Curriculum*. York, ME: Stenhouse.

Theme Issue on Integrated Curriculum. 1991. *Educational Leadership.* (October).

Walmsley, Sean A. 1994. *Children Exploring Their World: Theme Teaching in Elementary School.* Portsmouth, NH: Heinemann.

How Can Traditionally Trained Teachers Manage the New, Student-centered Classroom?

If we want to decentralize the classroom, to transfer more responsibility and choice to students, to have configurations other than thirty kids listening to one teacher, then there are only a few basic alternatives: after all, there isn't an infinite number of ways to reshuffle a teacher and thirty children. Students can work alone, in pairs, in teams, or in groups. Kids need to be able to initiate, carry out, record, report on, and evaluate their work and the work of peers. Each of these alternate structures *does* ask teachers to redeploy the basic ingredients of schooling—kids, time, space, materials, themselves—in new combinations that neither they nor the children are accustomed to. Teachers need the management expertise to make these new alternatives work.

But many teachers lack, or feel they lack, the management skills to operate these varied structures, and it seems that administrators and communities often aren't willing to provide the resources to train them, or perhaps even doubt that the teachers have the capacity to learn such sophisticated approaches. When teachers hear about the research that links strong growth in students' writing to regular one-to-one teacher conferences, many worry: "I'd love to do conferences with one kid at a time, but if I do, the other twenty-nine will go crazy." Teachers need ways to organize their classrooms so that structures such as conferencing work, because these are the only powerful and proven alternatives we have. But these new configurations require a functional, orderly, trusting, productive, self-regulating classroom community—what some people call discipline. If kids can't work independently and in various smaller groups, then we're thrown right back to the teacher-controlling-the-whole-class model.

As people who spend plenty of time in classrooms ourselves, we are well aware of the luck of the draw and the year-to-year roulette of "good" and "bad" classes of students. Yet, we believe that groups are mainly made, not inherited. There are specific, reliable ways for teachers to establish a productive classroom climate, and thus open the way to many promising innovations. According to the literature on group dynamics, a field of study oddly neglected by educators, there are six ingredients that teachers can shape to create that initial climate (Schmuck and Schmuck 1988):

- positive expectations
- mutually developed norms
- shared leadership

- diffuse friendship patterns
- open channels of communication
- mechanisms for resolving conflicts

Wise teachers nurture these six factors, especially during the early life of a class, to create a widely overlapping network of positive interdependence. They consciously distribute acquaintance, power, responsibility among everyone, opening up every possible channel of communication—verbal, nonverbal, written, and artistic. Once this richly interdependent community has been created, when the time comes to institute complex structures like reading workshop or hands-on science projects, students are able to adjust and make the transition.

Unfortunately, some competing models of classroom management are currently being touted around the country, approaches that are entirely incompatible with Best Practice teaching. One we've observed in some schools is something called "Assertive Discipline," an approach founded on an adversarial relationship between teacher and students, on control rather than community. Under this system, the school year starts out not with building of friendship and distribution of responsibility, but with the teacher reciting a menu of possible infractions and an elaborate system of contingencies and punishments. The underlying message to children is: "You are not trustworthy." Obviously, the possibilities for genuine cooperative learning in such classrooms is compromised: because they've been trained to function only under direct teacher oversight, either the kids won't work independently or they'll do it superficially, just enough to avoid sanctions.

While the Assertive Discipline system sometimes does create quiet, orderly classrooms, it works by suppressing students, not by empowering them or transferring responsibility to them. Once the system is loosened or kids pass on to the next teacher, control and suppression must start again, because kids have internalized nothing about monitoring themselves. Much like ability grouping, Assertive Discipline is a system devised to legitimize the archaic and authoritarian model of the teacher-centered classroom. In such classrooms, the inevitable (and unsolvable) problem is to get children to be silent and motionless while an adult talks at them. But teachers who use Best Practice structures don't *need* Assertive Discipline—their classrooms already have order, discipline, and productivity that arise out of children's engagement in work, not their fear of humiliation and punishment.

Suggested Readings on Classroom Management

Glasser, William. 1986. *Control Theory in the Classroom.* New York: Harper & Row.

Levine, David, Robert Lowe, Bob Peterson, and Rita Tenorio. 1995. *Rethinking Schools: An Agenda for Change.* New York: New Press.

Peterson, Ralph. 1992. *Life in a Crowded Place: Making a Learning Community.* Portsmouth, NH: Heinemann.

Short, Kathy, and Carolyn Burke. 1991. *Creating Curriculum: Teachers and Students as a Community of Learners.* Portsmouth, NH: Heinemann.

Isn't Best Practice Just Another Educational Fad? And Is Any of This Stuff Really New? Sounds Like Open Classroom to Me, and That Was a Failure!

What we are calling the Best Practice movement at the turn of the millenium certainly has a very familiar ring to those of us school veterans who lived through the late sixties and early seventies. It's not surprising that this earlier period of progressive reform is scoffed at by some educators, just as newer incarnations are attacked. In fact, we think the ideas of the late 1960s and early 1970s were important precursors to today's developments, and it's worth understanding what went wrong back then, as well as what useful foundations were laid, to help us understand our own struggles now. Maybe we should look at one specific and controversial innovation from this era to help us revalue our heritage.

In the "open classroom" movement of the 1970s, we got a memorable demonstration of how an innovation can fail, especially when the barriers to change aren't dealt with. Schools plunged into the open-classroom experiment, tearing down walls, offering teachers a one-day inservice at the end of the summer, in which some administrator or outside consultant essentially announced: "Okay, next week we want you to throw away the one model of teaching and classroom organization that you were trained for and are experienced in, and instead we expect you to run your classroom in ten other ways you've never tried and we've never trained you for and, quite frankly, we haven't thought about either or tried ourselves. Have a nice year." The great open-education movement inevitably collapsed because teachers did not have in their professional repertoire the structures and strategies to run a variety of student-directed, independent, and small-group activities. Kids went bananas and many teachers who were working in huge rooms with hundreds of kids started sneaking in cardboard boxes, shelves, and other large objects with which they could gradually and surreptitiously rebuild a classroom-like space inside the trackless waste of the "pod."

But if you visited Joanne Trahanas' eighth-grade language arts class in Glenview, Illinois, in recent years (as a person who's always growing, she's now moved on to become a principal), you'd have seen something that looks very much like an open classroom. You'd see thirteen-year-olds—an age group not usually noted for self-discipline—working industriously and without overt supervision on their writing skills every day. They'd come into Joanne's room, get out their writing folders, and get ready to work. During a quick round of the class, each kid would announce what he or she was planning to work on that day, and then everyone, including the teacher, would go to work. Some were drafting new pieces, others going back to edit ongoing drafts. A few would quietly seek out a partner for a quick conference. After a while, Joanne would start to see kids one at a time on a schedule she keeps, and as she conferred with each student about his or her writing, she would jot a phrase or two in the book where she tracked progress. A couple of times a week, the group would gather for ten minutes to read passages aloud and discuss the progress of their writing.

This was an open classroom—an open classroom that worked. It worked because Joanne set up the structure, the norms, the schedule, the procedures, and the materials in such a way that kids quickly grew into responsible use of this special time and space. What's even more impressive to us is that Joanne had *six* writing workshops each day, with six different sets of kids. She made the structure work not just with one group of children that she could train for six hours every day, but with 125 kids who passed briefly through her room for three hours a week. Joanne's workshop reminds us that there are important links between contemporary Best Practice ideas and past innovations, and demonstrates that we've learned a lot about how to make things really stick this time around.

Is Anything Ever Going to Change? Doesn't the Educational Pendulum Just Swing Back and Forth from Progressivism to Conservatism?

One tendency we have pretty successfully avoided in this book is quoting ourselves. But on the subject of school change and the pendulum metaphor, we are unlikely to improve on what we wrote in 1988 in *A Community of Writers*:

> Those of us in teaching often use the image of a swinging pendulum to describe changing trends in education; indeed, the pendulum metaphor seems to be one of our favorite ways of talking about the history of our field. How impartial and content-free this image is, tempting us to believe that the fluctuations in educational practice merely result from pointless, random, eternal variation. However, shifting educational trends hardly reflect some impartial pendulum swings; instead, this is more like the battlefront in a war, a line that moves back and forth with assaults and retreats. The practice of education reflects a historical struggle of one set of ideas against another, continually being fought out in close relation to the social-political-economic issues. . . .
>
> The cyclic vacillations between authoritarian and progressive education in this culture are not random pendulum swings, but advances and

retreats along a battlefront—the playing out, over a huge span of time, of a war for the soul of schooling in this society. In the end, the student-centered, developmental approach will win out over the authoritarian model because it parallels the direction in which civilization itself progresses. If we look broadly enough, we can see evidence that this direction is already clearly marked: in matters of classroom management, teachers no longer whip their students in school or crown them with dunce caps; in enrollments, we now welcome females in equal numbers to all levels of education, though just a century ago they were effectively barred from anything above a grade-school education; in the curriculum, we no longer insist on endless copying of great authors' texts for penmanship practice or have kids stand and recite for elocution; and sentence diagramming, though far from dead, is quite evidently dying out of the schools even as we watch. As each of these unproductive practices is dropped, and as more effective, growth-producing methods prove themselves, we see gradual progress toward a better understanding of how human beings actually learn and grow. . . .

Of course there will always be regressions and short-term backslides. Change in schools never follows a straight, steady path, but is more like three steps forward and two and a half steps back. Perhaps tomorrow a movement will spring up to restore the teaching of sentence diagramming to its "rightful, central place in the English curriculum," and such a trend might even catch on for a few years. Indeed, it is just this sort of event which misleads us, as individuals living in a particular brief lifetime, into believing that there's always a pendulum swinging back and forth between two eternal, fixed points, ensuring that nothing ever really changes. But each time the progressive set of ideas comes back, it gains strength and coherence from the new research and practice that connects with it, and each time it appears, it exerts more influence on the schools before it is once again suppressed. . . .

So we must not forget the half-step gained in every cycle. The larger, overall direction is heading the right way. The slow, long trend always prevails. And each cycle of regression, though probably inevitable, can be shortened if classroom teachers feel the confidence to push back at any pendulums that swing their way. . . .

Best Practice, Whole Language, Interdisciplinary Studies—if taught in their true, genuine forms, adaptable to the needs of the students involved in them—reflect a set of deep educational ideas, ideas that are partisan, that are contrary to other ideas, and that contend with opposing models and paradigms. To refer to this continuing struggle as the vacillation of vacuous fads or the swinging of a pendulum cheapens the efforts of people who are working, often against much resistance, to put these ideas into practice and to show how they work.

Works Cited

Aschbacher, Pamela. 1991. "Humanitas: A Thematic Curriculum." *Educational Leadership.* (October).

Beane, James. 1991. "Middle School: The Natural Home of Integrated Curriculum." *Educational Leadership.* (October).

Bloome, David, and Alanna Rochelle King Dail. 1997. "Toward Redefining Miscue Analysis: Reading as a Social and Cultural Process." *Language Arts.* (December).

Braunger, Jane, and Jan Lewis. 1997. *Building a Knowledge Base in Reading.* Portland, OR: Northwest Regional Education Laboratory; co-published by National Council of Teachers of English and International Reading Association.

Brodhagen, Barbara. 1995. "The Situation Made Us Special." In *Democratic Schools*, Edited by Michael Apple and James Beane. Alexandria, VA: Association for Supervision and Curriculum Development.

Bronner, Ethan. 1997. "Colleges Look for Answers to Racial Gaps in Testing." *The New York Times.* (8, November).

Chase, Alan. 1977. *The Legacy of Malthus.* New York: Alfred A. Knopf.

Cohen, Dorothy. 1968. "The Effect of Literature on Vocabulary and Reading Achievement." *Elementary English* 45 (February): 209–213, 217.

Cullinan, Bernice, Angela Jaggar, and Dorothy Strickland. 1974. "Language Expansion for Black Children in the Primary Grades: A Research Report." *Young Children* 29 (January): 98–112.

Cunningham, Patricia. 1995. *Phonics They Use: Words for Reading and Writing* (Second Edition). New York: Harper Collins.

Gould, Steven Jay. 1981. *The Mismeasure of Man.* New York: Norton.

Hillocks, George. 1986. *Research on Written Composition.* Urbana, IL: National Council of Teachers of English.

Johnson, David W., Roger T. Johnson, and Edythe Holubec. 1991. *Cooperation in the Classroom.* Edina, MN: Interaction Book Company.

Katz, Michael B. 1968. *The Irony of Early School Reform: Educational Innovation in Mid-Nineteenth Century Massachusetts.* Cambridge, MA: Harvard University Press.

Kohn, Alfie. 1993. *Punished by Rewards: The Trouble with Gold Stars, Incentive Plans, A's, Praise, and Other Bribes.* Boston: Houghton Mifflin.

Martens, Prisca. 1997. "What Miscue Analysis Reveals about Word Recognition and Repeated Reading." *Language Arts.* (December).

Moffet, James. 1989. *A Storm in the Mountains: A Case Study of Censorship, Conflict, and Consciousness.* Carbondale, IL: Southern Illinois University Press.

Murnane, Richard, and Frank Levy. 1996. *Teaching the New Basic Skills.* New York: The Free Press.

Oakes, Jeannie. 1990. *Keeping Track: How Schools Perpetuate Inequality.* New Haven: Yale University Press.

Rhodes, Lynn, and Curt Dudley-Marling. 1996. *Readers and Writers with a Difference*. Portsmouth, NH: Heinemann.

Schmuck, Richard, and Patricia Schmuck. 1988. *Group Processes in the Classroom*. Dubuque, IA: William C. Brown.

Spring, Joel. 1972. *Education and the Rise of the Corporate State*. Boston: Beacon Press.

Stires, Susan. 1991. *With Promise: Redefining Reading and Writing for Special Students*. Portsmouth, NH: Heinemann.

Tunnell, Michael, and James Jacobs. 1989. "Using 'Real' Books: Research Findings on Literature-based Reading Instruction." *Reading Teacher*. (March).

Vopat, James. 1994. *The Parent Project: A Workshop Approach to Parent Involvement*. York, ME: Stenhouse.

Weaver, Constance, Lorraine Gillmeister-Krause, and Grace Vento-Zogby. 1997. *Creating Support for Effective Literacy Education*. Portsmouth, NH: Heinemann.

Weintraub, Sam. 1991–1997. *Summary of Investigations Related to Reading*. Newark, DE: International Reading Association.

Wheelock, Anne. 1992. *Crossing the Tracks: How "Untracking" Can Save America's Schools*. New York: The New Press.

Zemelman, Steven, and Harvey Daniels. 1988. *A Community of Writers*. Portsmouth, NH: Heinemann.

11

Yes, But . . . Will It Work in City Schools?

Throughout this book, we've described everyday teachers who teach beauti-fully and who are improving. We've pictured ordinary kids who can learn and grow. We've visited a number of inner-city, all-minority schools that are working. Yet most people conclude that, by and large, urban schools across the country are *not* working, that so-called "at risk" kids *aren't* learning as well as they might, and that too many city teachers *haven't* discovered the secrets of Best Practice. If you study national achievement scores or, better yet, visit some urban schools, you realize that the disparity is genuinely cat-astrophic. In a very real sense, America has two school systems: perhaps three-fourths of our kids attend decent public and private schools in towns and suburbs, while the other fourth attend big-city schools often weighed down with grievous problems. Only by averaging together these two separate and different systems, and ignoring reforms and improvements in many exciting city schools, can you derive the picture—the false and misleading picture—that America's main educational problem is mediocrity.

But we've also argued throughout this book—and research strongly confirms—that all kids can and do learn well under even some pretty trying circumstances. So if the children aren't really dumb, if learning is so natural to human beings, and if the teachers and their schools are not really hope-less, then what goes wrong? What makes learning and teaching so much harder in the inner city? If we are ever to achieve school reform beyond the successes of a few charismatic individual teachers and principals, we had better be clear about what is standing in the way. In this chapter, we review the factors we believe to be most damaging, and separate some of the myths from the realities of urban education. Finally, we share a description of an exemplary program that shows how the state-of-the-art instructional practices described in this book are just as powerful in inner-city schools as they are in prosperous suburban ones.

Poverty

No one questions the deadening effects of poverty, and we've witnessed its devastations all too often. One most unfortunate effect on schools is student mobility and turnover. In Chicago, for example, a study by the Center for School Improvement (CSI) revealed that only two of every five students stay in the same school from first through sixth grade (1996). Many students change schools four to six times, and 48 percent of a sample of sixth graders said they'd switched schools during the academic year rather than between grades (Consortium on Chicago School Research 1994). The CSI study identified 118 schools, of a total of 477 on which data were available, that it classified as highly unstable (1996). Thus, even if a school develops the most outstanding of programs, 40 percent of the children who might benefit from them will be gone before the year is over. A similar number will arrive in the middle of the year, forcing teachers to try to catch up each new pupil on what she's missed.

Even if the incoming kids had the same achievement levels, the turnover saps energy from the teachers, slows down the progress of the class, and requires constant readjustment of the group's dynamics each time a child comes or goes. As we've explained repeatedly throughout this book, the key structures of Best Practice teaching require a cohesive, interactive, interdependent classroom community where students assume high levels of responsibility for their own and classmates' learning. In schools where the classroom community is constantly reshuffled, teachers are, at best, driven back to the early stages of group building and, at worst, constantly preoccupied with discipline.

Outside of school, instability in families and violence in neighborhoods pressure children tragically. We are currently working in several schools where large numbers of children have witnessed shootings and deaths. In our observation, the younger kids—in grades one to four or five—nevertheless remain quite open to schooling, although some are withdrawn, overly needy of attention because of troubles at home or in the neighborhood, or untrained in self-discipline and social cooperation. One such school, Jenner Elementary, has faced threats by Chicago's mayor and the school's CEO to close it because of gang gunfire; children cling to the empathic principal and ask, "Will I get home okay today, Mrs. Satinover?" Alex Kotlowitz (1991), in his moving and detailed chronicle *There Are No Children Here*, describes how the brutality of neighborhood violence leaves a child unable to concentrate and perform in school. But it's the older students who are increasingly drawn away from school by the magnetism and danger of the streets, especially when they compare this with repeated experiences of failure in school.

Yet the culture of poverty also has been overly blamed and deeply misunderstood. The common belief among middle-class people and many city teachers is that poor children speak a defective language and have little exposure to learning outside school because their parents are either too over-worked, lazy, or illiterate to help them. Repeatedly, sociology and linguistics researchers—and even court cases—have shown how wrong this is. For example, Black English ("Black English Vernacular" or "Ebonics" to socio-linguists) differs from school dialect in its grammar in relatively minor ways (even if those ways stand out sharply to the middle-class ear), and involves just as rich and complex, if different, uses of expression as any other lan-guage. Similarly, children of Hispanic background may be limited in English, but may also be well on their way to literacy in Spanish, giving them much to build on.

Further, ethnographic studies of children's activity in poor homes show that many are quite involved in literacy activities through play, drawing, and even television, which, contrary to the standard platitudes, is actually full of print (Taylor and Dorsey-Gaines 1988). These "at-risk" children often engage more print at home than during the school day itself. And detailed research on children's literacy development during their early years reveals that at age three, children have acquired all the basic concepts for reading, such as the stability of meaning, representation of reality through symbols, and linear directionality of print. *There are no observable differences of such acquisition at this stage between* any *groups, rich or poor, urban or rural, black or white* (Harste et al. 1988).

Perhaps the most helpful explanation of this puzzle is provided by anthropologist Shirley Brice Heath, who found, by comparing different working-class communities, that some had family customs for language use that were in harmony with the usual patterns of student-teacher communica-tion, while other groups did not (1983). In other words, preschool-age chil-dren in some cultural groups get lots of practice using school-type talk, answering questions about toys and books, or giving factual information. In other groups, the kids simply acquire a different communication style. If these kids don't pick up the new talk quickly in school or get specific help learning it, they fall behind and stay behind—thus, the repeated experience with failure that drives children to reject school later on.

Class Issues

Schoolteachers are just about 100 percent middle-class people, while many of the children they work with in the inner city are poor; considerable fric-tion and misunderstanding occur as a result. This is not a matter of race, although race issues can certainly be present. Black, white, Hispanic teach-ers, all are middle-class by income, and many come from families that strug-gled hard to get there. The motives of most of these teachers working with poorer children are positive—they earnestly want to help the next generation escape from poverty, just as they or their parents did.

But it's not so simple, because class in urban America isn't just a matter of how much money you have. Class involves the way you talk, the games you play, the music you listen to, your family's attitude toward single parenthood, your beliefs about education. Sociologists help us understand that there's not just one *right* approach to these things (i.e., *my* approach); social groups simply do differ about them. However, the cultural gap between teachers and their students—which would already be present anyway because the younger generation always needs to distinguish itself—can grow to unfortunate proportions.

Teachers (*and* students) can make dysfunctional assumptions or take damaging actions as a result. One research project showed how some urban teachers grossly underestimated parents' willingness to intervene and help their kids or support the teacher's policies. In a sample study, the teacher failed to contact parents whose children were having trouble, and when contact was finally made very late in the year, the teacher was surprised at the cooperation and resulting improvement that took place (Allen and Mason 1989). Of course, *every* community has parents who don't help when children are having trouble with school. But the *assumption* that they won't, or the failure to communicate clearly or sympathetically with the parents, can mean unfortunate lost opportunities.

More heartbreaking is the amount of anger and hostility we sometimes see in urban schools. The kids can seem wild, and the teachers feel the need to yell at them frequently and to label them harshly to their faces, just to maintain basic control. In workshops, the teachers assert quite openly that these kids lack discipline and manners in their homes and therefore respond only to such tactics. Some education writers and theorists have argued that only a skills-and-worksheets approach will succeed with minority disadvantaged children, because they are culturally different from white middle-class families. What makes this phenomenon puzzling is that in the many effective urban classrooms we've observed in the poorest areas, discipline isn't a problem at all. The teachers may have to work hard on it at the start, but the kids are industrious and polite, the teachers calm and positive. We recognize that there *are* cultural differences among groups, and that it's important for teachers to understand them and respond to them, just as Heath learned. However, we've observed so many inner-city classrooms (some of which are described in this book) where kids of *all* colors and backgrounds thrive on self-directed and collaborative tasks, that we know the problem must be a deeper, more subtle one.

It appears that an unfortunate cycle of conflict perpetuates itself in the more negative classrooms. Based on past experiences and a sense of social differences, the teachers expect the worst of the kids and don't believe these kids have the internal resources to control themselves. The children come to believe this themselves because, after all, the adults dealing with them tell them so in words and actions. The children's anger and uncertainty are then acted out, providing apparent confirmation of the teachers' negative beliefs.

There's both danger and irony in this sad cycle. If schools decide that "these kids" are already accustomed to authoritarian discipline at home, and that they will respond only to rigid controls, then the schools actually reproduce stereotypical and dysfunctional elements of a poverty culture right in the classroom. Instead, it's arguable that these kids especially should experience a middle-class culture in school, being part of classroom communities that enact self-control, responsibility, self-monitoring, sharing, cooperation, and some deferral of gratification. If city kids never see these values enacted, never internalize them, how can they ever escape poverty and function in mainstream society?

Other factors can cause problems with learning, but all the difficulty gets ascribed instead to the children's social background. For example, as we observed one teacher trying unsuccessfully to help her third graders with punctuation, she turned to us in frustration, saying, "These kids just don't *want* to learn!" When we asked one child to read a sample aloud, she read in monotones, like a robot. It was clear that she had learned to decode words but not to read for meaning—a problem typical of the school's skills-oriented reading program, not a problem of attitude. She had never been trained to listen to sentences rather than just individual words, and so she couldn't find where to add punctuation. However, when we asked for volunteers from among the children who *couldn't* understand, she raised her hand again and again, bravely risking embarrassment because she wanted so badly to learn!

Thus, in spite of the best of intentions, many teachers and children become embroiled in what seem like endless skirmishes of a class war, a war that eats up all too much energy. In still another way, then, too many urban kids experience school as a succession of failures, and while they tolerate this for a few early years, they ultimately tune themselves out of what is for them an unproductive setting.

Yet—when we work with teachers who have struggled in this saddening whirlpool, it nearly always turns out that they are desperate to escape it. They are delighted to discover that meaningful classroom activities yield the side effect of improving children's behavior. Such activities almost always have this effect because they communicate respect for children's voices and allow the children to realize they are smarter than they thought. Under the battle-scarred surface of almost every angry teacher, there still lives the idealist, the believer in kids' ability to grow and learn. The class war does not have to cycle on forever.

Resources

It's standard politics these days to assert that just throwing money at a problem like education won't solve it. And it's certainly true that a considerable amount of money has been wasted over the years on programs that didn't work. On the other hand, without the funds, how will we ever retrain the twenty thousand teachers in a city like Chicago, most of whom need to learn new methods of teaching writing, reading, math, science, and social studies? Jonathan Kozol (1991) has reminded us in *Savage Inequalities* that city kids, teachers, and schools simply don't get their fair share of the money available for education in this society.

It's instructive to compare the situation in a large city with that of a working-class suburb like Elgin, Illinois, which we described just a few pages ago. By offering numerous fifteen- and thirty-hour inservice workshops each year on teaching writing and reading, Elgin has intensively trained more than a quarter of its staff during a seven-year period. Now, morale and success in this area of the curriculum are high, and the in-district teacher-leaders are offering advanced workshops on special topics and techniques.

Elgin employs 1,850 teachers. What would it take to deliver the same services for a big-city staff of twenty thousand? Our own Illinois Writing Project programs in Chicago city schools have trained more than 1,300 teachers in the past six years. That same work, if carried out in Elgin, would have involved nearly 70 percent of all the teachers. However, in a large city it's such a drop in the bucket that it can't possibly build momentum for system-wide change. The estimated cost for retraining just one-fourth of the Chicago staff in one subject area, such as reading or math (i.e., five thousand teachers, a number which, though limited, would create a significant impact and very likely influence even the nonparticipants) would require about $2 million out of a total budget of $1.1 billion. It's a small percentage, but ask anyone at the Chicago Board of Education how difficult it would be to find such funds right now! Yet, this number is based on very conservative calculations for materials, administrative costs, and pay for the time of workshop leaders and teachers.

"Why didn't the teachers get this training in college, so they wouldn't need it now?" one might ask. It's a good question, of course, but because the Best Practice processes of teaching described in this book were far less understood twenty years ago, very few teachers received the help needed then. It will be years before a significant proportion of the staffs turn over—even though teacher preservice training is gradually being brought up to date. This deficit affects small, rich suburbs just as much as it does big cities, but our example shows how much harder it is to make up for the lack in the larger setting where proportionately fewer resources are available to do the job.

Size

We've already said a lot about size by talking about resources. But there's another aspect of size that was just briefly mentioned: momentum. In any large organization or community, change depends on more than just a few individuals. There's plenty of pressure for everyone to behave alike, and even if variety is tolerated, the very different ones are isolated or labeled so their example will pose no threat: "Oh, Ms. Wilde? Yes, she sure uses some unusual methods, and they work great for **her**. But you have to be a little crazy to be able to do it that way!" Teachers aren't the only ones who operate this way. It's hard to find a group of human beings who don't.

This means that for new ideas to take hold beyond an enthusiastic few, a critical mass of adherents must be established. A "movement" needs enough people to encourage and support one another, to exert some constructive peer pressure on the others, and to demonstrate that the new approaches work not just for the far-out risk takers, but for any ordinary professional who wants to try them. However, too many big-city programs involve training for one or two "experts" per building or one or two "lighthouse" schools. These programs usually don't spread because it's easy for the "example" folks to be kept isolated, labeled, and ultimately discouraged and burned out. The process is rarely malicious or anti-anything. It's just the way people seem to operate in large systems. Ask any manager trying to initiate change in a large corporation.

Bureaucracy

Americans love to sneer at it. We have more than our share of it. To a certain extent, we need it—after all, should classroom teachers be ordering toilet paper and writing the checks to pay for repairing school buses? But bureaucracy almost inevitably creates obstacles to change, and larger urban school systems simply have more of it to deal with. In big-city bureaucracies, programs need to be approved at more levels. People can pass the buck more easily. The system comes to serve the needs of politics and entrenched groups more than the needs of teachers and children.

Here's one typical way the politics of a large bureaucracy can undermine change. As the program is being launched, an administrator worries that people in one building or area will be offended if services are offered elsewhere but not for them. Yet, there isn't enough money to do the job right in every location. So the administrator decides to give a little bit to *each* location, but not enough to run the program fully in any one place. The program limps along in its many sites, isolated planners and change agents get discouraged, the program finally fails.

One highly visible effort to address the inertia and self-serving preoccupation of a bureaucracy is the City of Chicago's system of local school governance. It has been quite successful in allowing individual schools to institute special programs and activities on their own. About one-third of Chicago's schools have established major school-improvement efforts of one kind or another. However, the central board office has gradually reasserted control in a myriad of small ways and issues a steady stream of restrictive, bureaucratic rules and requirements that wear down even the most coura-geous of principals in the city. Decisions continue to be based more on whether they will appear as bold steps in the newspapers, rather than whether children will complete school more able to lead fulfilling and productive lives. And yet, as we describe below, the improvement efforts of many local Chicago schools have been surprisingly successful.

Misguided Curriculum

People outside the educational world assume that teaching is teaching; teach-ers either have what it takes or they don't. Ordinary citizens can hardly be expected to be aware of the revolutions that have occurred over the past twenty-five years in our understanding of what and how to teach. But the fact is that we really do know more now about how learning works, and this isn't a matter of fads or philosophical pendulum swings. From detailed psycholin-guistic studies, we know that all language learning—speaking, reading, writing—is active and holistic. Children don't learn rules first and then apply them, or sounds first and then words. From the very beginning, young chil-dren engage in full, actual communication: requests, complaints, expressions of love, surprise, and hurt, questions, and answers.

And so we've found that to teach school subjects, creating real purposes and options for real communication works; assigning rote, audienceless topics like "What I Did Last Summer" doesn't. Helping kids employ the processes of prewriting and revision that actual writers use works; following arbitrary textbook outlining doesn't. Similarly with reading, practicing whole-group reading with "predictable" stories (i.e., with patterns and refrains children can repeat) works. Teachers reading good children's literature aloud works. Prac-ticing separate sound-decoding skills is of limited usefulness because it leaves many children reproducing sounds but never learning to look for meaning in the sentences. Teachers have adopted these more effective Best Practice ap-proaches to reading and writing in considerable numbers. But larger, older school districts are sometimes the slowest to change, and the most wedded to lockstep, bureaucratically controlled programs.

The isolated-skills approach to learning, however, is not the "traditional" approach. It was, in fact, an innovation that started in the 1920s. Some nineteenth-century educators actually came closer to Best Practice strategies, though we now understand the rationale and effective application of them far more completely. However, a massive bureaucratic support system, includ-ing reams of competency testing, grew up around the isolated-skills method. A tremendous amount of energy and resources was expended on all the basal readers, workbooks, and scope-and-sequence curriculum plans that were used to guide teachers' every classroom action. These systems were espe-cially embraced by large-city schools looking for ways to ensure uniform, if minimum, performance by huge teaching staffs.

One thing that strikes an observer in urban schools is just how much class time is taken with testing and preparation for testing. And, of course, the children who have trouble with reading and writing have particular trouble with the tests *because they can't read the directions*! It's a vicious circle, because more time on effective reading strategies, rather than test practice, would help especially those kids who do poorly on the tests—the very tests that are supposed to ensure that the teachers are doing their job.

The result? We've certainly not become a nation of avid readers, as any newspaper circulation manager will tell you, nor are we fluent writers or eager mathematicians or active citizens. Kids in well-off schools still have learned to read tolerably well, partly because children generally will learn what society and families expect of them, barring major disruptions in their lives. The toll on learning exacted on poorer urban children has been far more visible, however, because those children and their schools have been vulnerable in the other ways we've described. That is, the kids who have needed the most effective support have suffered the most when they didn't get it.

Resistance to Change

Another perspective on the slowness of change in urban schools is that change is actually slow *everywhere*, because that's just what human beings do—resist change. Think of some new technology you are now comfortable with and recall your feelings just before you tried it, and as you moved into learning it. For Steve, a good example was cash machines. The first time he tried one, it ate his card. He went to the main office of the bank feeling foolish, and a condescending "account representative" walked him through the process a few times. Who wants to go through that?

Even for some of the most enjoyable activities, many of us find a dozen reasons to put them off if they're new—until finally some supportive but urgent friend, or perhaps a growing inner need of our own, or the pressure of necessity (like no cash on a Sunday afternoon) brings us to take the plunge. At the opposite pole, psychologists tell us that a person who is unhappy or dissatisfied clings to unrewarding situations and behaviors—at least in part because they are predictable, familiar, part of the definition of self and world the person has depended on for a long time.

Therefore, many of us who work to help teachers and schools change their approaches to teaching have learned to be patient, to respect the educators we work with, and to listen supportively. We've found that the most effective path to change is not through arguing and accusing, but through simply immersing people in activities that are new, enjoyable, and filled with implications about their work, and then giving them a chance to talk with each other about the experience and what it means. This sort of change process takes time, but it's deep and lasting.

In Spite of All These Obstacles

In spite of all the obstacles, significant improvements can be achieved in urban schools. A 1997 study by the school-reform organization Designs for Change reports that of 420 Chicago elementary schools studied (out of 523 in the Chicago system), 49 percent had Iowa Basic Skills test scores that were either substantially increased, tending upward, or already had been initially above the national norm, from 1990 to 1997. One hundred and eleven schools, serving a total of sixty-five thousand students, located in all areas of the city and attended by children of all socioeconomic groups, showed substantial score increases in reading or mathematics or both. While the Iowa tests are not the best measure of Best Practice learning, the study showed that a wide variety of factors significantly correlated with these increases, factors such as the principal actively working as instructional leader, teachers reaching out to parents, improvements in school culture, teacher collaboration and innovation, and an improved instructional program. In sample "profile" schools,

> The use of drill and test preparation plays some role . . . but these activities are regarded as one among a number of important elements of the educational process. . . .
>
> In reading, the profile schools carry out a "balanced" instructional approach. For example, they explicitly teach phonics, but also create a variety of opportunities for students to discuss, act out dramas, write, and draw—based on what they have read. Students also have regular opportunities to read books of their own choosing.

We must not delude ourselves to think that a single institution like the public schools can, without better support from other social services and better resources, overcome all the problems facing impoverished and disadvantaged groups. And yet we also must not allow naysayers to obscure the fact that serious, intensive, well-executed efforts in urban schools do pay off. What follows is the story of how one of those "substantially improved" schools did it.

EXEMPLARY PROGRAM
Building-level Change

Washington Irving School
Chicago, Illinois

What has excited us most during the past ten years of close work with city teachers and kids is that once a good thing takes hold in a classroom or a workshop—an effective strategy for using math manipulatives, or getting writing edited, or making self-selected reading work—teachers and kids alike embrace it with great energy and real results. Principals manage to find resources, teachers flock to workshops on teaching hands-on science, children's literature, and math, and complain when we haven't scheduled more. Kids dig in, work hard, produce, and have a good time. Improving teaching and learning doesn't seem nearly as difficult as we thought. Just as the many negatives can combine to weigh a school down and discourage its teachers, so a strategic selection of positives can add up, synergistically.

We can best illustrate this with a final story about how one school has changed. School reform experts and researchers have asserted for years that the most potent locus for educational change is not individual classrooms or teachers, whole districts or states, but rather the individual school building. Here, after all, we have one complete but manageable educational community, with all of the elements and ingredients necessary to sustain itself and to grow. And while the three of us know many heroic (sometimes crafty) teachers who manage to excel and innovate in unsupportive buildings, our predominant experience in city and suburban schools generally bears out our axiom: change works best at the level of whole buildings, as long as they aren't too large (two to four hundred kids is optimal).

Washington Irving School is an elementary building on Chicago's West Side, where half the students are Black and half are Hispanic. Irving struggled under the burden of Chicago's weighty bureaucracy and the educational disconnection of its poverty-stricken attendance area until a new building replaced the crumbling structure that was torn down to make way for a medical research park. With a new building came a new principal, Madeleine Maraldi, the driving force in Irving's development. Maraldi challenged the teachers to do more, rather than just blame the kids for their low achievement. She obtained grants; organized new labs for writing, reading, math, and science; scheduled inservice workshops (on writing first because it was the teachers' chosen priority); regularly circulated articles on new teaching methods; and signaled that she would support experimental teaching efforts, even if they didn't yield immediate results.

In the fall of 1991, the PBS television affiliate in Chicago aired a one-hour documentary about Washington Irving, and we were happy to participate for several reasons. First, after years of media reports relentlessly exposing the failures and foibles of public education in Chicago, this program spent sixty minutes showing how one school was improving itself. Second, we were happy because the show focused on curriculum renewal as the engine of reform. The program showed a whole school community—teachers, parents, kids, principal, and a few outside helpers—thinking seriously, regularly, and sometimes passionately about what gets taught and how. Finally, we enjoyed the program because all three of us, in different roles, had worked with Washington Irving School, assisting in its approach to curriculum reform, teacher empowerment, and parent involvement.

The professional development work at Irving began with a thirty-hour after-school teachers' workshop on teaching writing, offered to volunteers and taught by two talented teacher-leaders from another Chicago school. Then, when other teachers grew interested, a second section of the same workshop enrolled a mix of Irving and outside teachers, as well as a few principals who had heard about things percolating at Irving. Next, teachers asked for further support with writing, so the workshop leaders, Tom and Kathy Daniels, agreed to hold an after-school writing program at Irving, half the time writing with kids and half the time talking about instruction with teachers. Meanwhile, the faculty started asking for ideas about math, and so the school brought in a thirty-hour math workshop, which used the same processes as the writing workshop: personal exploration, direct experience, professional discussion of research, trying and debriefing classroom efforts (as well as eating lots of after-school snacks). Throughout all these teacher-development activities were stranded parent-involvement efforts and many supportive interventions by the principal. When the PBS camera crew eventually came along, what they were able to document was the fertile, exciting start of an eight-year cycle of school-based, teacher-led, curriculum-driven change.

An important finding of school-change research is that the principal plays an absolutely key role. This is especially true in city schools like Irving, where the stultifying bureaucracy can crush teachers and where years of teaching in degraded conditions leave a great need for morale boosting. Madeleine

Maraldi is extraordinarily skilled at both deflecting bureaucracy and uplifting teachers. But more important than these skills, she knows curriculum, understands the research on best educational practice, and trusts teachers and kids. She sees her main role as that of facilitator, not as a boss or an expert, though she *is* both. It's deeply symbolic that at our workshops, although Madeleine participated as a regular member of the group, she always found time to check the level in the coffeepot, adjust the temperature in the room, or roll the photocopying machine from the office into the meeting room. With each of these actions, she signaled to teachers the importance of the work they were doing in studying curriculum and planning changes in instruction.

Staff development at Irving began with some very important cues from Madeleine. (In a less archaic school system, some of these ideas might have come from a teacher committee—but in Chicago, hierarchies still prevail.) The first nudge came from Madeleine's decision that the school's improvement would come best through teacher renewal in key content areas. She might have invested in one of the now-popular "effective schools" projects that focuses on generic issues like discipline, critical thinking, or cooperative learning. Instead, Madeleine committed herself to an inservice program rooted in subject fields. While arguments can certainly be made for the content-free, across-the-curriculum approach, it has been our experience that most of the useful strategies promoted in generic courses eventually come up anyway in our curriculum-based workshops. For example, teachers in a writing workshop must learn how to train and organize children for the collaborative structure called peer editing, just as in a math workshop teachers must learn how to prepare and supervise kids in problem-solving teams.

Tom and Kathy Daniels, the teacher-consultants who led the first wave of inservice programs along with Emily Garland, Pam Sourelis, and Dee Wozniak, describe how the workshops unfolded. In their words, we think, are eloquently woven the themes already well established in this book about how anyone, adult or child, learns best.

When we first approached the Washington Irving School, we had no idea how special this experience was going to be. We thought we were just going to begin another thirty-hour writing-across-the-curriculum workshop for some fellow teachers. We had been conducting similar workshops in a wide variety of Chicago schools for about five years. As we drove through this near West Side neighborhood, we noticed a large abandoned and vandalized factory, lots of old, smallish houses, empty lots, and evidence of some new housing construction. We were totally unprepared for the school building itself, which was brand new and graffiti-free.

As we walked through the clean, cheery halls, full of familiar prints, beautifully presented, and lots of student work arranged with pride, it affirmed our hunch that something good was already going on here. Even the name of the school, taken from the old American storyteller, seemed to fit with the writing workshop we were about to start. In fact, the group of teachers we met that night would soon name themselves after one of Washington Irving's legends: we called our Wednesday night writing workshop "The Sleepy Hollow Gang."

We plugged in the coffeepot and set out the snacks, and participants began to arrive for the first session. Although there were a few teachers from nearby Brown and Jefferson schools, the majority were from Irving itself. We noticed several men and even a couple of young teachers, rare commodities in our prior workshops. The smiling Irving principal, Madeleine Maraldi, took her place with the other participants.

We always start our sessions by inviting pairs of teachers to interview each other, to seek out unusual stories and experiences, and then to write a paragraph introducing—or reintroducing—their colleagues to the group. The Irving teachers took their time listening carefully to each other, and struggled with their paragraphs to get the words just right. From the beginning, everyone wanted to read his or her paper aloud. People told about their experiences and attitudes toward writing, teaching, and life. The principal wrote every assignment, read hers aloud, and shared her personal struggles fearlessly. The eagerness to share and listen built a strong sense of community.

We began each weekly meeting by sharing and troubleshooting experiences with particular writing strategies: brainstorming, clustering, journals, guided imagery, and the rest. There are always a few reluctant "show-me" personalities in any workshop, but when our group's skeptics announced their doubts, lots of practical and encouraging advice was offered by those with similar problems. Several teachers began to emerge as cheerleaders, and by the time we got to the middle of the third session, almost everybody felt we were riding a tidal wave moving toward conversion of the whole group.

Watching the Group Grow

Some veteran teachers came into the first session pessimistic and discouraged about the state of their teaching and the attitude of their students. They had been trying hard for a long time, and seemed likely candidates for "burnout." But by the third session, they were trying out variations of the classroom strategies we discussed. Enthusiasm crept into their descriptions and experiences. At first, the younger teachers were rather quiet. As more and more teachers shared their personal and classroom struggles and reported trying new strategies with their students, these younger teachers began to experiment and share their results. Veteran teachers reached out to the new teachers, and the new teachers responded with their enthusiasm and idealism. Everyone seemed eager to contribute something to the group. People started to bring in their favorite classroom literature; each week, we began with an oral reading from at least one beloved book, and so we built a considerable list of favorite titles for classroom libraries.

It had also become obvious that having the principal there every session, writing every time, carefully listening to every teacher, was an enormous advantage for the teachers and students of Washington Irving. She supported a strong writing program. She modeled by writing to students and having them write to her. She recognized the powerful connection between reading and writing, and supported classroom libraries and a literature-based approach. Toward the end of the workshop, she purchased a number of professional books on teaching and literacy for her teachers, and over the summer both she and they read voraciously.

By September 1990, each classroom had a set of portfolios for student writing, the basals were set aside in favor of real books, and a literature lab had been established. In addition, a follow-up writing workshop was planned, this time including both kids and teachers, as part of an after-school program. Twelve teachers and thirty-five students would meet twice a week to work on writing, using the computer labs. Before the program started, we held a few planning sessions with the teachers to brainstorm possibilities and work out details. Half were familiar faces from the workshop, but there were newcomers without the writing process background, including a few doubters who didn't think kids would come after school to do more school stuff.

The teachers decided to work in pairs and a sort of buddy system developed between the workshop "graduates" and the non-workshoppers. Teachers who had never team-taught before worked together, sharing ideas and encouraging each other. By the time the kids' after-school writing program got underway, it was just a couple of weeks before Halloween, a natural time for spooky stories filled with terror and screaming. Older kids made up raps, put them to music, and performed them on videotape. Others wrote and illustrated their stories, made books and banners, and performed their tales of horror and thrills. They composed their pieces both individually and collectively, using the word processors. Most of them acted, sang, danced, mugged, and rapped their words for the videocamera. At the end of each session, teachers got together with us to share, ask for suggestions, read works in progress, and encourage each other to continue.

Involving Parents

Our culminating activity was the "Washington Irving Family Album Night," which took place in December. We carefully selected this name, feeling that our initial label, "Family Writing Night," might scare away parents for whom writing is a challenge. More than a hundred parents, students, and relatives showed up for a simple meal, a night of reading and writing, and rich fellowship. Families had been encouraged to bring photographs that held special memories, and Madeleine had purchased a photo album for each family to take home as a souvenir. After a dinner of hot dogs, chips, and punch, and a short welcoming speech in English and Spanish, students in the after-school writing program stood up and introduced their families. The introductions were carefully videotaped one by one. Then all of the students and teachers got up and performed a rap they had written about Washington Irving School.

Next, we wanted to create a generation-spanning, cafeteria-wide writing workshop, so we set the mood by reading aloud a wonderful children's book about memory, *Wilfred Gordon McDonald Partridge*, by Mem Fox. We introduced the idea of everyone's writing a personal memoir: children writing a memory of their parents and parents of their children. We passed paper to everyone, young and old. Instructions were given in English and Spanish, and writing was invited in either language. To our delight, everyone started writing. Occasionally, kids or parents would stop writing to read to each other, to check a fact, or to get help finding the right word or the right spelling. Kids who were too young or too tired to write found a corner we had set up with books and pillows and read to themselves or to each other. As everyone wrote, we took Polaroid pictures of each family. Someone helped glue their pictures on the memoirs, and we photocopied everything on the machine that Madeleine had wheeled into the lunchroom. Families kept their original memoirs, and the school kept copies, which were later published in a special album. As families lined up at the copy machine, Joe Perlstein, one of the teachers, played the videotape of the family introductions and the kids' Halloween stories on the big-screen television. Families who previously seemed ready to leave stayed to watch themselves and their children on TV. As they left, many asked if Family Album Night would become an annual event, since they enjoyed themselves so much. As we cleaned up that night, we were exhausted and elated.

Staff development at Irving continued in a number of other forms. A thirty-hour inservice workshop on teaching math was conducted by Arthur Hyde and teachers Eva Belisle-Chatte, Kathy Schaller, and Donna Nowatski. A third inservice series on writing was attended not only by Irving staff, but also by teachers and principals from other nearby schools. The Daniels provided help designing curriculum plans to institutionalize the Irving teachers' long-term change, and the teachers requested a further workshop series on helping students revise their writing. Faculty now stress fluency in writing through grade five, and revision is emphacized in grades six through eight.

Maraldi and her teachers, meanwhile, introduced more and more initiatives to complement the inservice training and regular classroom activity. Collaborative working groups replaced ability groups in reading instruction. A school-wide reading program has students discuss their self-selected books with any adult in the school in order to have their reading "verified" for report-card tallies. Phonics is taught as the teacher observes a need for it, but not in a lockstep program that would waste time for those who don't need it. Every classroom has fifty minutes per day of sustained silent reading. Teachers read aloud to students daily. And twenty to forty minutes of reading is assigned for home each night. Parents verify this with signatures on homework.

In the reading lab, seventh-eighth–grade teacher Joe Perlstein gives out buttons to new members of the "thousand club" when they've completed a thousand pages of reading. A grant funds monthly trips to a bookstore, where children pick out books for their own classroom libraries. The children don't own the books, but inside each is a stamp that reads:

> THIS BOOK WAS SELECTED
> FOR THE IRVING SCHOOL LIBRARY
> BY _____
> ON _____

The children eagerly start reading "their" books on the bus ride back and then add them to the permanent classroom collection with their name as selector forever inscribed inside. At holiday time, another grant allows each child to choose a book he or she can keep and take home—for many, the first book they have ever owned. Classes regularly visit the local library. A Reading Recovery program serves primary students who are having difficulties. Two computer labs staffed with full-time certified teachers, plus numerous computers in each classroom, facilitate kids' copious writing and revising work. Maraldi was able to purchase lots of computers by focusing discretionary Chapter One funds on equipment before committing it to extra staff lines.

Twice-weekly visits to the math and science labs help classroom teachers and kids strengthen their use of hands-on learning. Students in many grades have art classes several times per week. By sending half-classes to some of the labs, teachers are able to work with the remaining students, who divide further into their Literature Circle discussion groups and receive plenty of individual attention.

A radically redesigned report card for fourth through eighth grades provides for teacher check-off of significant reading behaviors, student self-evaluation, and parents' evaluation of their children's progress. A weekly newsletter goes home to keep parents abreast of school programs. Persistent pursuit of parents is part of the school culture and, as a result, more than fifty parent volunteers come to the school regularly.

Perhaps no one of these strategies alone would have kick-started improvement in the school. But taken together they've made a tremendous difference. Parents are involved and active. Kids come to school with enthusiasm, plunging into activities in the math lab and science lab, reading and writing with pride and fascination. The children sometimes surprise themselves. As one eighth-grade girl put it:

When I came to Irving, I told my friends, "I ain't readin' no books, I ain't readin' no books." And then I saw this book by Judy Blume. It was called *Superfudge*, and I read it and it was *good*. And then I read another one. And I found myself reading *another* one of her books. I got to the point where I had read almost all her books. I've got about two more to read.

Scores on standardized tests, though they don't really measure the true import of the changes, are up dramatically. The percent of students scoring at or above national norms on reading in grades four through eight has gone from 18.8 percent in 1990 to 35.4 percent in 1997. Interestingly, there were several years of dips as teachers and kids adjusted to the new approaches before steady growth took over. Math started at 14.4 percent of scores at or above national norms, then dipped, and began to rise to a 1997 level of 27.9 percent. Writing scores on the Illinois Goal Assessment Program state tests went from 18.7 in 1990 to 21.2 (actual score points, not percents) in 1996, for sixth graders. For eighth grade, the jump was from 22.9 to 24.7.

When a camera crew videotaped one teacher inservice session at Irving as part of the documentary on the school's improvements, the surprised grins on the faces of the camera crew offered an unexpected validation for our work. As these strangers eavesdropped on the workshop, listened to the teachers writing, sharing, and debating, they were drawn into the spirit of the occasion. The crew exclaimed about the passion and professionalism of the teachers they had taped. All the teachers who were interviewed in the documentary spoke honestly and eloquently about the anxieties, pleasures, and rewards of change in their own classrooms. Second-grade teacher Norma Barron-High admitted feeling pressured by the principal's enthusiasm and the sheer volume of ideas:

> I sometimes feel like I'm still in school at the university level, because she [Maraldi] gives us so much material that I feel a little bit overwhelmed by everything in there. . . . It's not familiar territory. It means letting go of what I've been trained to use. . . . One thing that relaxes me a little bit about this is that she has stated over and over that she is evaluating us and the program according to whether or not our children are reading more and writing more. They may not be writing perfect English papers, but they are *definitely* writing more.

Pat Mark, the computer-lab teacher who taught at Irving for thirty years, explained:

> When people asked me, "What do you do for a living?" I would never say, "Teacher." . . . I wasn't proud to be named a Chicago teacher. But now I boast about it. . . . If we would walk into a suburban school, we would not see the kind of work that's coming out of Irving School today. . . . I'm rejuvenated. I can't wait to get here in the morning. And when I go home,

I hurry up with dinner because I'm [always] down at the computer trying to think of what I should do tomorrow.

And as Joe Perlstein, the energetic, prematurely gray-haired twenty-year veteran says at the end of the documentary:

It's very difficult to change. It takes a lot out of a person. However, you don't mind if there's a payback, if you feel that the children are growing, that they appreciate what is going on. If you see a light at the end of the tunnel, then you say to yourself, "Don't stop now. Keep pushing, keep pressing." Because it will all be worth it in the end.

Works Cited

Allen, Jo Beth, and Jana Mason. 1989. *Risk Makers, Risk Takers, Risk Breakers: Reducing the Risks for Young Literacy Learners.* Portsmouth, NH: Heinemann.

Center for School Improvement and the Chicago Panel on School Policy. 1996. *Pervasive Student Mobility: A Moving Target for School Improvement.* Chicago, IL: Center for School Improvement and the Chicago Panel on School Policy.

Consortium on Chicago School Research. 1994. *Charting Reform: The Students Speak.* Chicago, IL: Consortium on Chicago School Research.

Harste, Jerome, Virginia A. Woodward, and Carolyn L. Burke. 1984. *Language Stories and Literacy Lessons.* Portsmouth, NH: Heinemann.

Heath, Shirley Brice. 1983. *Ways with Words: Language, Life, and Work in Communities and Classrooms.* New York: Cambridge University Press.

Kotlowitz, Alex. 1991. *There Are No Children Here: The Story of Two Boys Growing Up in the Other America.* New York: Doubleday.

Kozol, Jonathan. 1991. *Savage Inequalities.* New York: Crown Publishers.

Taylor, Denny, and Catherine Dorsey-Gaines. 1988. *Growing Up Literate: Learning from Inner-City Families.* Portsmouth, NH: Heinemann.

Index

Stires, Susan, 260
Stop-N-Write, 64
Storm in the Mountains, A (Moffet), 262
Strickland, Delois, 221–25, 226–27
Strickland, Dorothy, 250
struggling readers, 261
student-centered learning
  defined, 8, 9
  making transition to, 217–39
  in reading, 44
  research on, 250
student-directed learning
  support for, 211
student portfolios, 207
student-teacher conferences. *See* conferences
student/teacher dialogue, in social studies, 147
study teams, 190
summative evaluation, 208, 247, 248
supplies and materials
  for arts activities, 170, 172
  for mathematics, 98
  for reading, 42
  in science, 123
  for writing, 66–67

Tafel, Linda, xvi
Tangrams table, 99–100
TAWL (Teachers Applying Whole Language), 266
teacher certification, literacy education and, 28
teacher-directed activities, 209–12, 212
teachers
  ability grouping and, 259
  as artists, 167–68, 171
  autonomy of, 233
  change and, 220–25, 225–28, 285–86
  classroom management, 273–74
  classroom structure and, 208–12
  classroom workshops and, 259
  cohesion among, 232–33
  collaboration by, 226, 230–32, 234–35
  dependency on, 16
  empowerment of, 220–21
  evaluation of, 248–49
  incentives for, 236
  isolation of, 218, 226, 230
  mutual respect among, 231–32
  parent communication, 42
  parent workshop participation, 265
  peer leadership, 43, 230–32
  principals and, 42–43
  professionalism of, 227, 228, 235–36
  reading modeled by, 32
  reflection by, 228
  respect for, 236
  role of, 208–12
  socioeconomic class issues and, 283–84
  support of, 226
  time for, 229–30
  time together, 226
  writing instruction role, 59–61
  writing workshops, 57, 291–98
"Team Games Tournament," 190
technology, 119
television, 169
terminology of writing, in the home, 66

testing. *See also* evaluation; standardized tests
  obsession with, 246
  status quo and, 218–19
textbooks
  mathematics, 93–94
  status quo and, 219
text sets, 190
themes, 185. *See also* integrative units
There Are No Children Here (Kotlowitz), 281
thinking skills
  arts and, 165
  integrated learning programs and, 269–70
time
  for the arts, 164
  for reading, 36
  for teachers, 229–30
Tooley, Mary, 176
topic choice
  in social studies, 140
  in writing, 59, 60
toys, mathematics and, 96
tracking, 258–59
  in social studies, 144–45
Trahanas, Joanne, 275–76
Tunnell, Michael, 250
Turbill, Jan, 241
turning points, in social studies, 133
"twelve-inch voice," 190

urban schools, 280–98
  bureaucracy in, 286–87
  class issues, 282–84
  exemplary programs, 290–98
  improvements in, 289
  misguided curriculum in, 287–88
  poverty and, 281–82
  resistance to change in, 288
  resources for, 284–85
  size of, 285–86

Venn diagrams, 100
video documentaries, student production of, 205
violence, urban schools and, 281–82
Vopat, Jim, 41, 263, 264, xvi
Voss, Linda, 156

Walloon Institute, xvii
Washington Irving School (Chicago), 156–58, 290–98, xvi–xvii
Wasson High School (Colorado), 186
Weaver, Connie, 250
Wednesday Surprise (Bunting), 237
Weiss, Cynthia, 156–57
What Real Authors Do (Christelow), 76
"What Your First (Second, Third, or Fourth) Grader Needs to Know," 188
Wheelock, Anne, 258
Whirlwind Performance Company, 162
White, Jan, 84–85
whole-class activities
  meetings, 192–93
  role of, 209–11
Whole Language, 7, 186, 266–68. *See also* Best Practice

For more than twenty years, Steve Zemelman, Harvey Daniels, and Arthur Hyde have worked on school renewal projects in Chicago and around the country. Their most recent collaboration, the Best Practice network, has brought models of state-of-the-art instruction to thousands of teachers, across the curriculum and up through the grades.

Steve Zemelman is director of the Center for City Schools at National-Louis University. The center provides instructional improvement programs for a network of fifteen Chicago schools and supports the broad school reform effort in Chicago. Zemelman is also a founder and codirector of the Illinois Writing Project. His other books include *A Writing Project* (Heinemann 1985) and *A Community of Writers* (Heinemann 1988), both coauthored with Harvey Daniels.

Harvey Daniels is a professor of Interdisciplinary Studies at National-Louis University, where his students are veteran teachers earning graduate degrees in nontraditional, school-based programs. He founded and directs Walloon Institute, a national summer seminar for teacher and parent leaders. Daniels is the author of seven other books on education, the most recent of which are *Literature Circles: Voice and Choice in the Student-Centered Classroom* (Stenhouse 1994) and *Methods that Matter: Six Structures for Best Practice Classrooms* (Stenhouse 1998).

Arthur Hyde teachers Mathematics Education at National-Louis University and conducts staff development on mathematics, problem solving, and curriculum integration. His previous books include *Mathwise* (Heinemann 1991), *Thinking in Context: Teaching Cognitive Processes Across the Elementary School Curriculum* (Longman 1989) and *Effective Staff Development for School Change* (Ablex 1992).